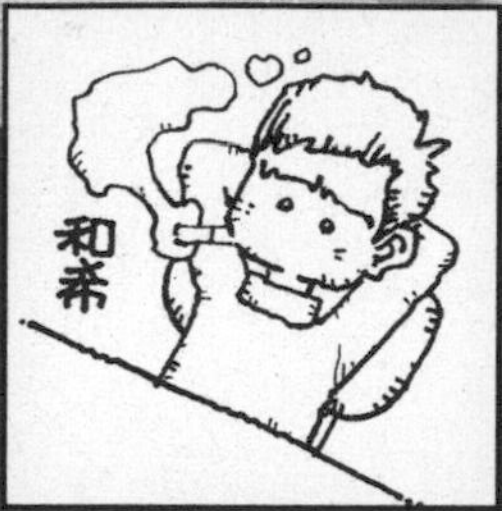
和希

KAZUKI TAKAHASHI

I'm going to driving school! It'd be great if I had my license by the time this volume comes out. Last time, it felt like too much work, so I quit partway through—but this time I'm serious!

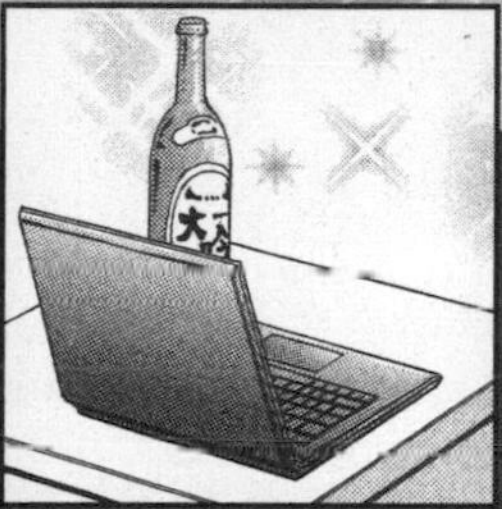

SHIN YOSHIDA

We're coming up on the climax of the *ZEXAL* manga! We're at the very peak of the action, but when I think about how soon I'll have to say goodbye to Yuma, Astral and the rest, my loneliness peaks too!

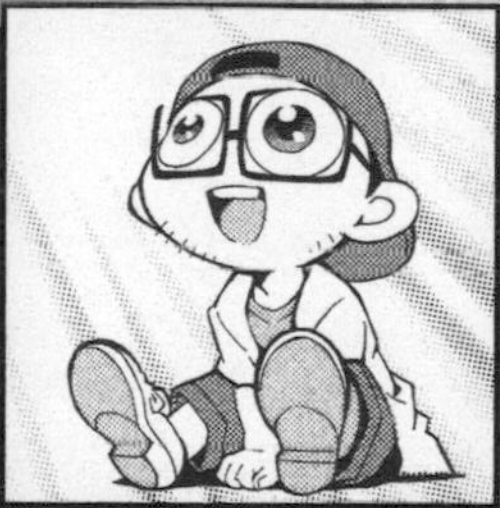

NAOHITO MIYOSHI

A long time ago, some people more experienced in the industry said that when a manga gets serialized, the artist gains weight... Now I'm experiencing that firsthand! I never go outside anymore... (LOL) But health is important for drawing good pictures!

Volume 8
SHONEN JUMP Manga Edition

Original Concept by **KAZUKI TAKAHASHI**
Production Support: STUDIO DICE
Story by **SHIN YOSHIDA**
Art by **NAOHITO MIYOSHI**

Translation & English Adaptation **TAYLOR ENGEL AND IAN REID, HC LANGUAGE SOLUTIONS**
Touch-up Art & Lettering **JOHN HUNT**
Designer **STACIE YAMAKI**
Editor **MIKE MONTESA**

Published by VIZ Media, LLC
P.O. Box 77010
San Francisco, CA 94107

10 9 8 7 6 5 4 3 2 1
First printing, March 2016

www.viz.com

www.shonenjump.com

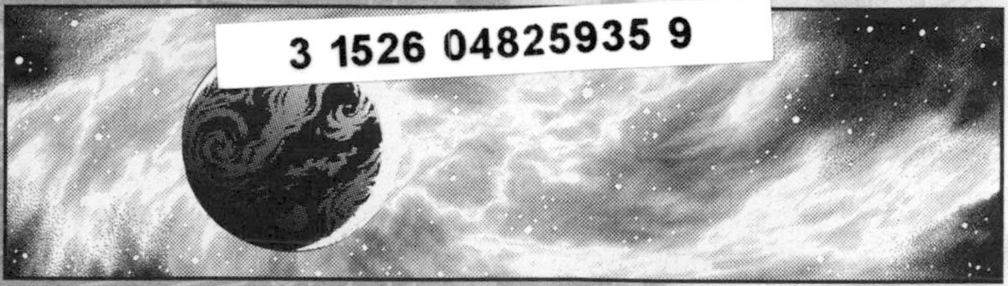

YU-GI-OH! ZEXAL

VOLUME 8:
A Bond Between Us!!

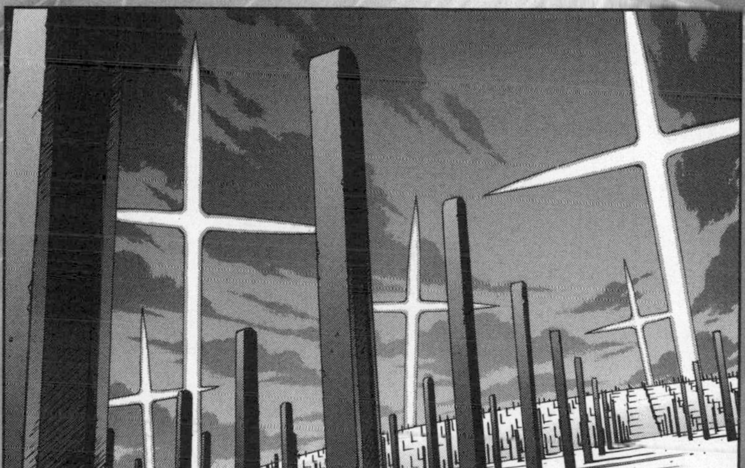

Original Concept by KAZUKI TAKAHASHI
Production Support: STUDIO DICE
Story by SHIN YOSHIDA
Art by NAOHITO MIYOSHI

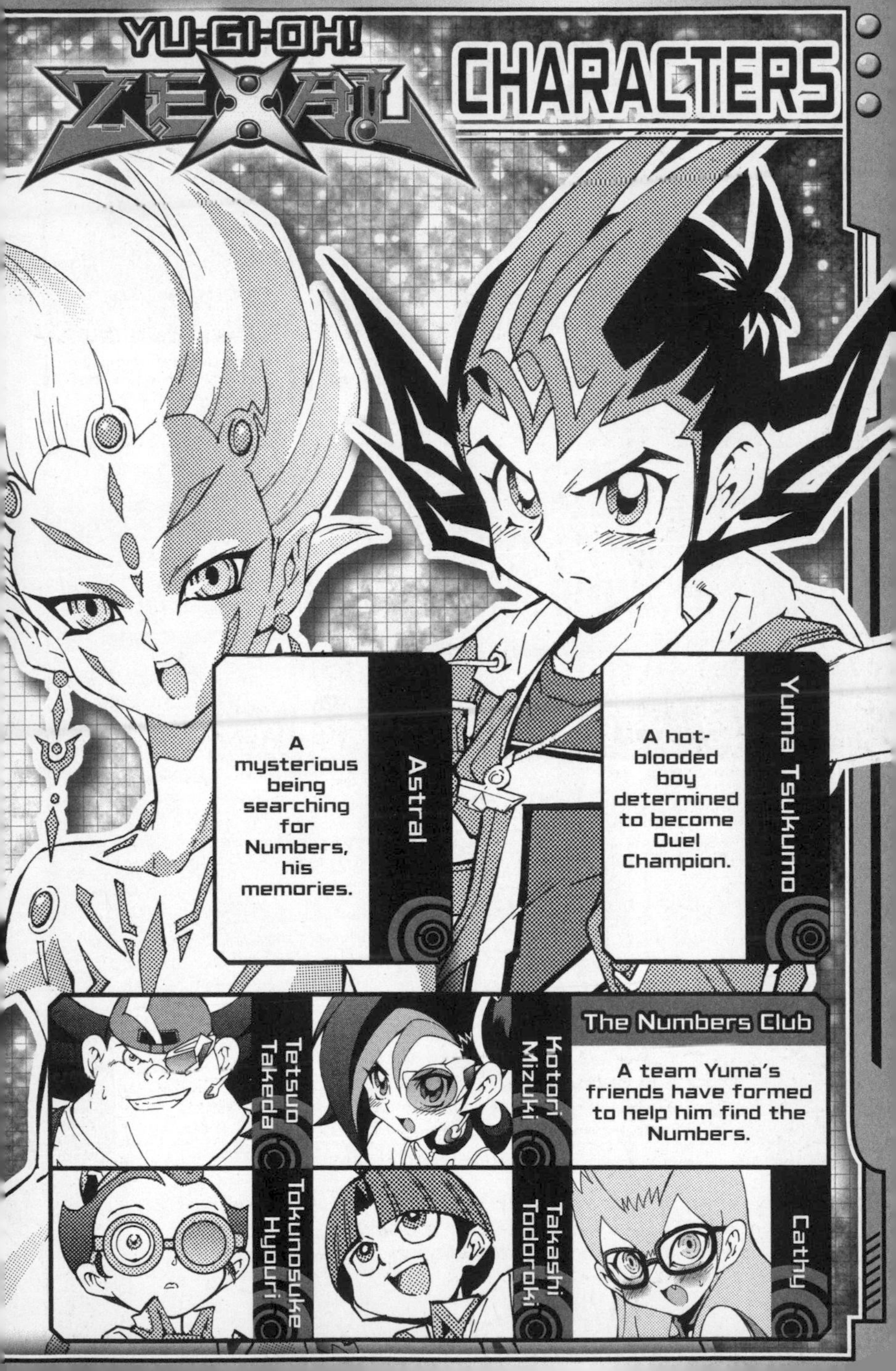
YU-GI-OH!
ZEXAL
CHARACTERS
Yuma Tsukumo
A hot-blooded boy determined to become Duel Champion.
Astral
A mysterious being searching for Numbers, his memories.
The Numbers Club
A team Yuma's friends have formed to help him find the Numbers.
Kotori Mizuki
Tetsuo Takeda
Cathy
Takashi Todoroki
Tokunosuke Hyouri

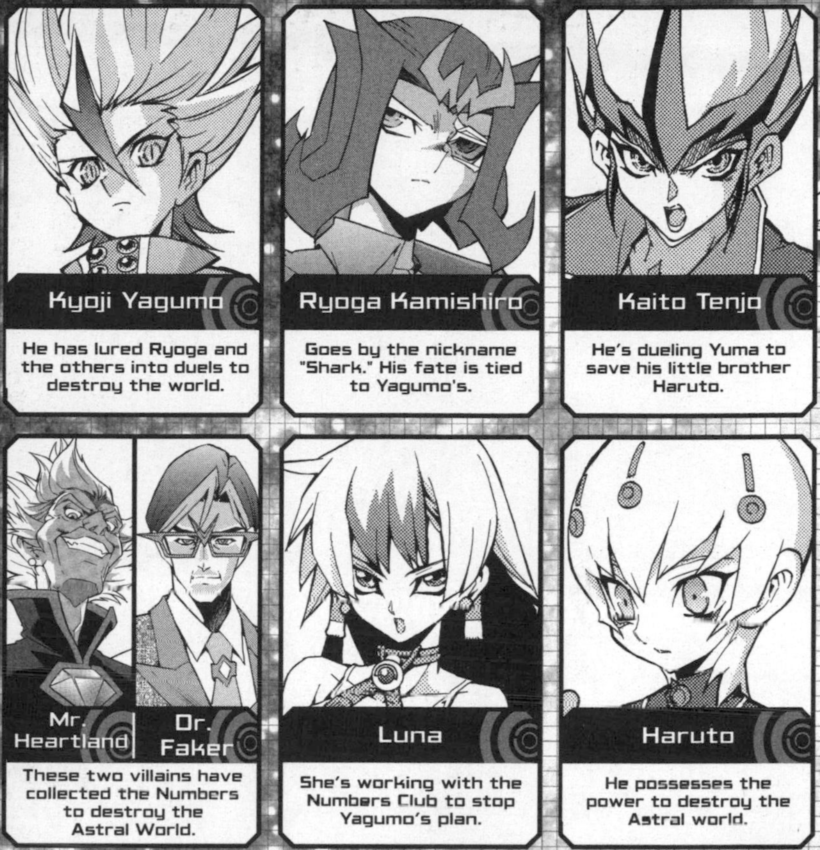
Kyoji Yagumo
He has lured Ryoga and the others into duels to destroy the world.
Ryoga Kamishiro
Goes by the nickname "Shark." His fate is tied to Yagumo's.
Kaito Tenjo
He's dueling Yuma to save his little brother Haruto.
Mr. Heartland
Dr. Faker
These two villains have collected the Numbers to destroy the Astral World.
Luna
She's working with the Numbers Club to stop Yagumo's plan.
Haruto
He possesses the power to destroy the Astral world.

Previously...

Yuma Tsukumo is crazy about dueling. One day during a duel, the charm his parents left him—"the Emperor's Key"—triggers an encounter with a strange being who calls himself Astral. Astral is a genius duelist, but his memories have been turned into special cards called "Numbers" and have been lost. Yuma begins working with Astral to find them!

Standing in their way are Dr. Faker, who's trying to use the power of the Numbers cards to destroy the Astral World, and Kaito, who's hunting the Numbers to help his little brother! Ryoga and Luna are also working to wipe out the Numbers. Meanwhile, Yagumo joins forces with Dr. Faker and declares war on Yuma and friends! The Numbers War begins.

Yuma's power of believing in people saves Kaito and Ryoga, and a bond begins to form between them. But then Yagumo takes Haruto hostage, forcing Yuma and Kaito into a duel. Meanwhile, Ryoga also faces off against Yagumo. How will these two duels end?

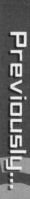

VOLUME 8
A Bond Between Us!!

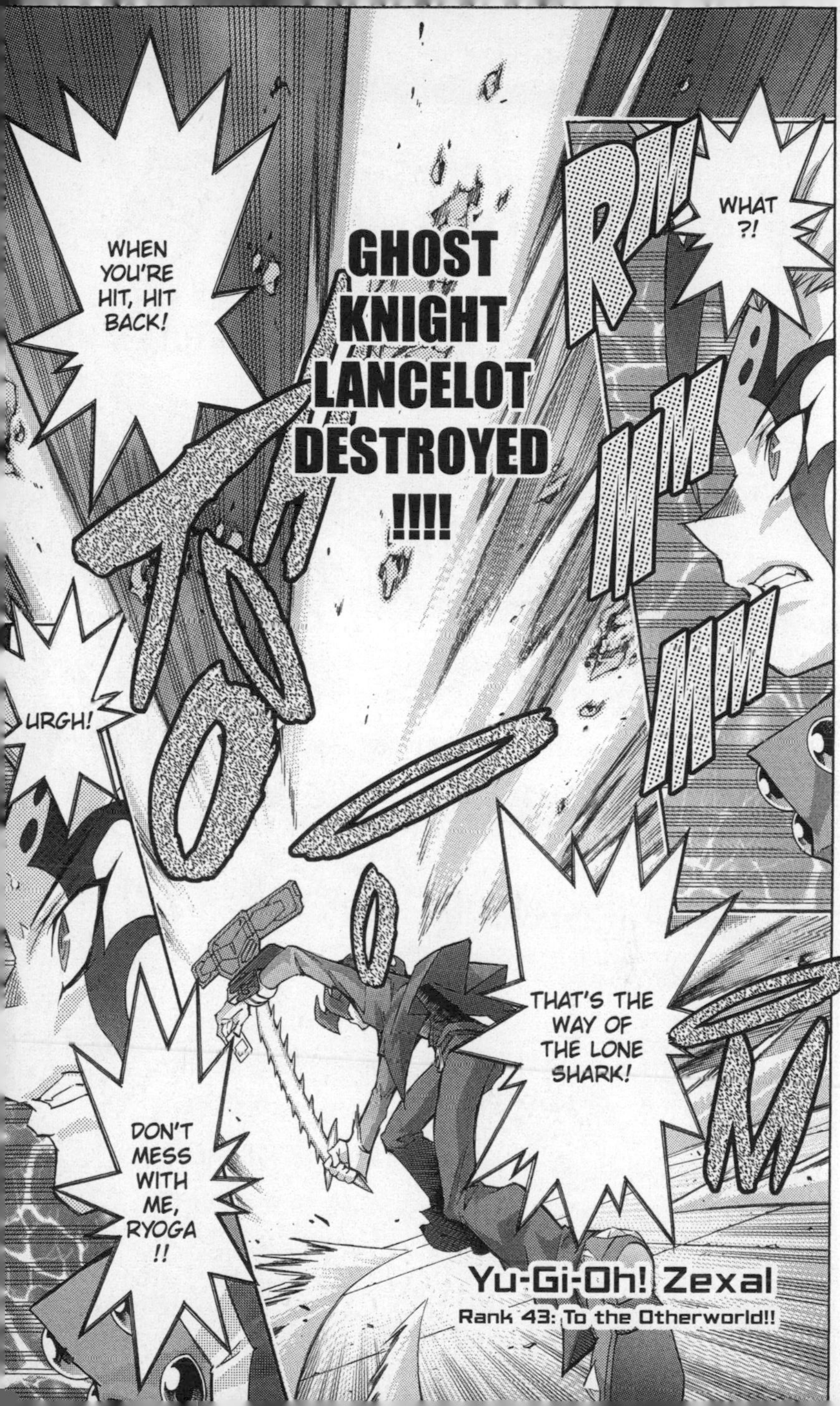
WHAT?!
RMMMM
GHOST KNIGHT LANCELOT DESTROYED!!!!
WHEN YOU'RE HIT, HIT BACK!
TOOOOM
URGH!
THAT'S THE WAY OF THE LONE SHARK!
DON'T MESS WITH ME, RYOGA!!
Yu-Gi-Oh! Zexal
Rank 43: To the Otherworld!!

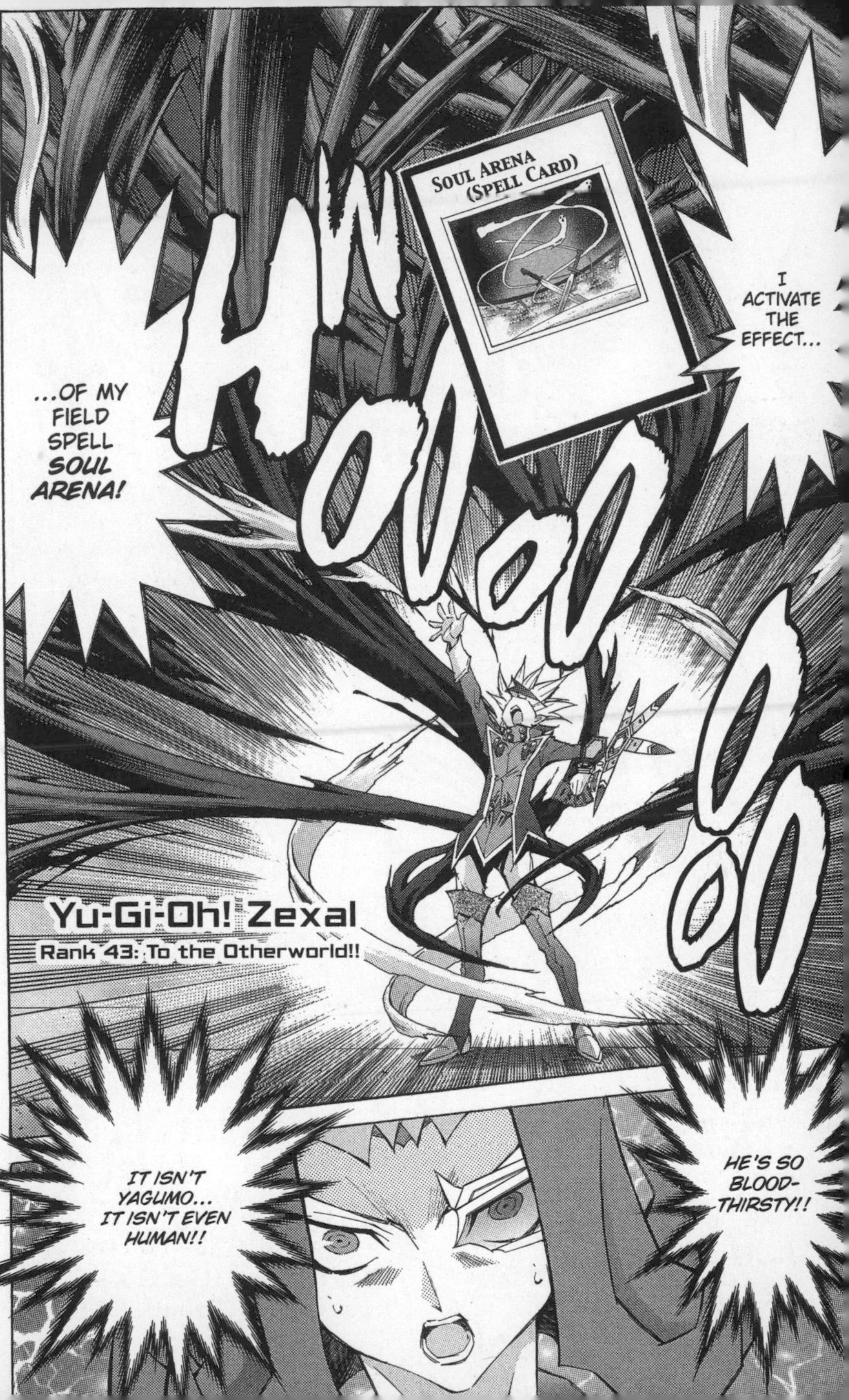
SOUL ARENA (SPELL CARD)
I ACTIVATE THE EFFECT...
...OF MY FIELD SPELL SOUL ARENA!
Yu-Gi-Oh! Zexal
Rank 43: To the Otherworld!!
HE'S SO BLOOD-THIRSTY!!
IT ISN'T YAGUMO... IT ISN'T EVEN HUMAN!!

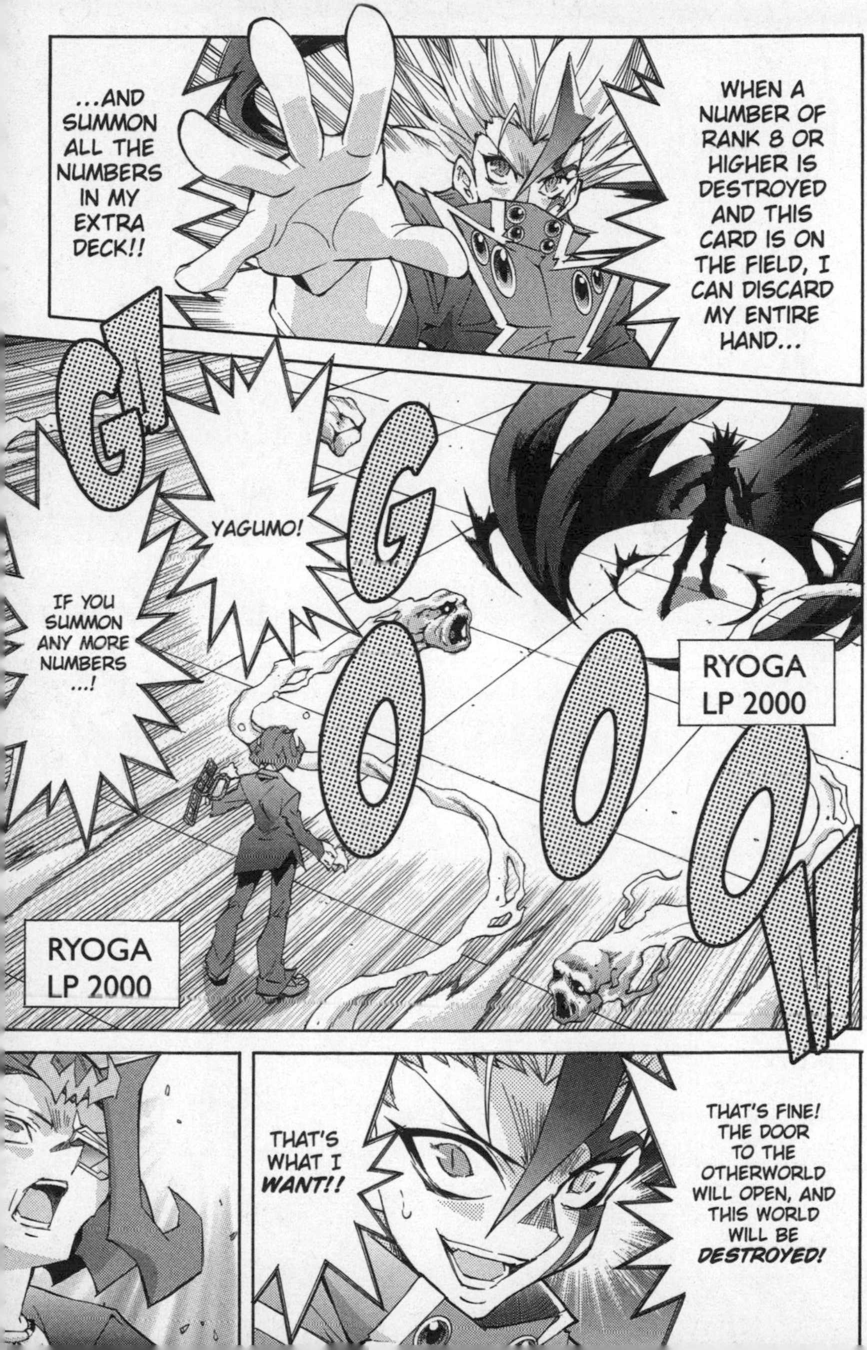
WHEN A NUMBER OF RANK 8 OR HIGHER IS DESTROYED AND THIS CARD IS ON THE FIELD, I CAN DISCARD MY ENTIRE HAND...
...AND SUMMON ALL THE NUMBERS IN MY EXTRA DECK!!
RYOGA LP 2000
G! GOOOM
YAGUMO!
IF YOU SUMMON ANY MORE NUMBERS ...!
RYOGA LP 2000
THAT'S FINE! THE DOOR TO THE OTHERWORLD WILL OPEN, AND THIS WORLD WILL BE *DESTROYED!*
THAT'S WHAT I *WANT!!*

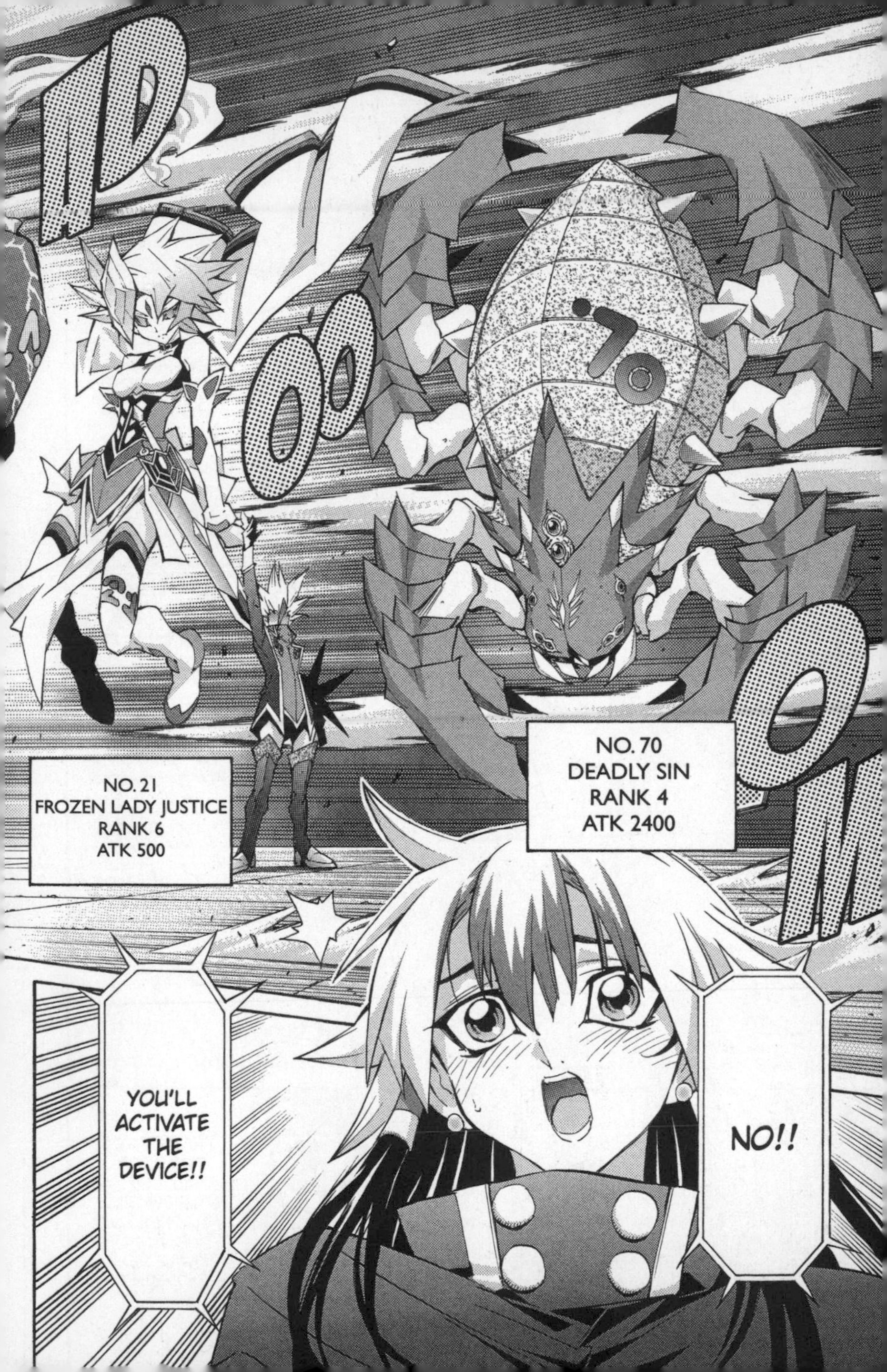
NO. 70
DEADLY SIN
RANK 4
ATK 2400
NO. 21
FROZEN LADY JUSTICE
RANK 6
ATK 500
NO!!
YOU'LL ACTIVATE THE DEVICE!!

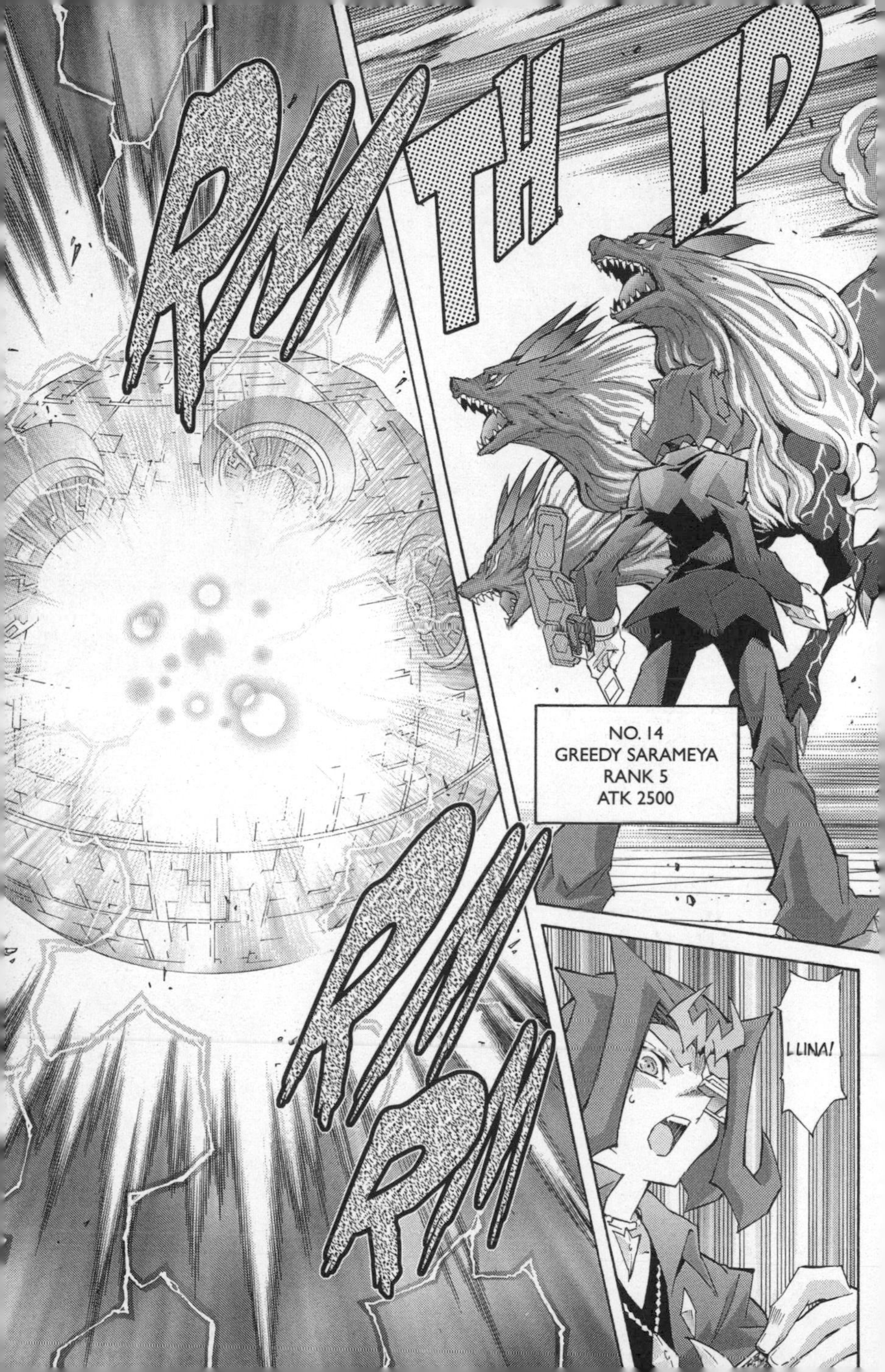
NO. 14
GREEDY SARAMEYA
RANK 5
ATK 2500
L LINA!

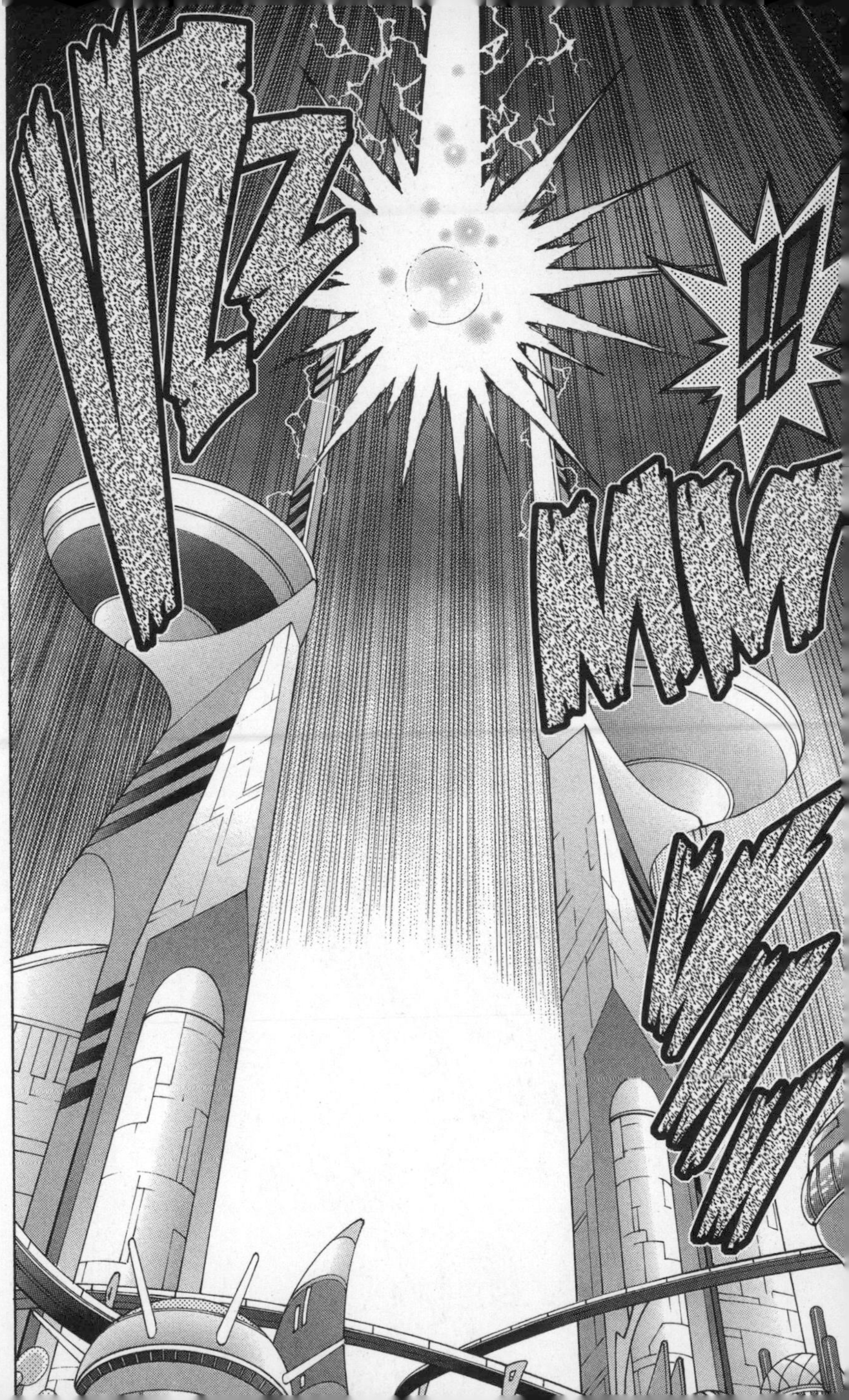
!!

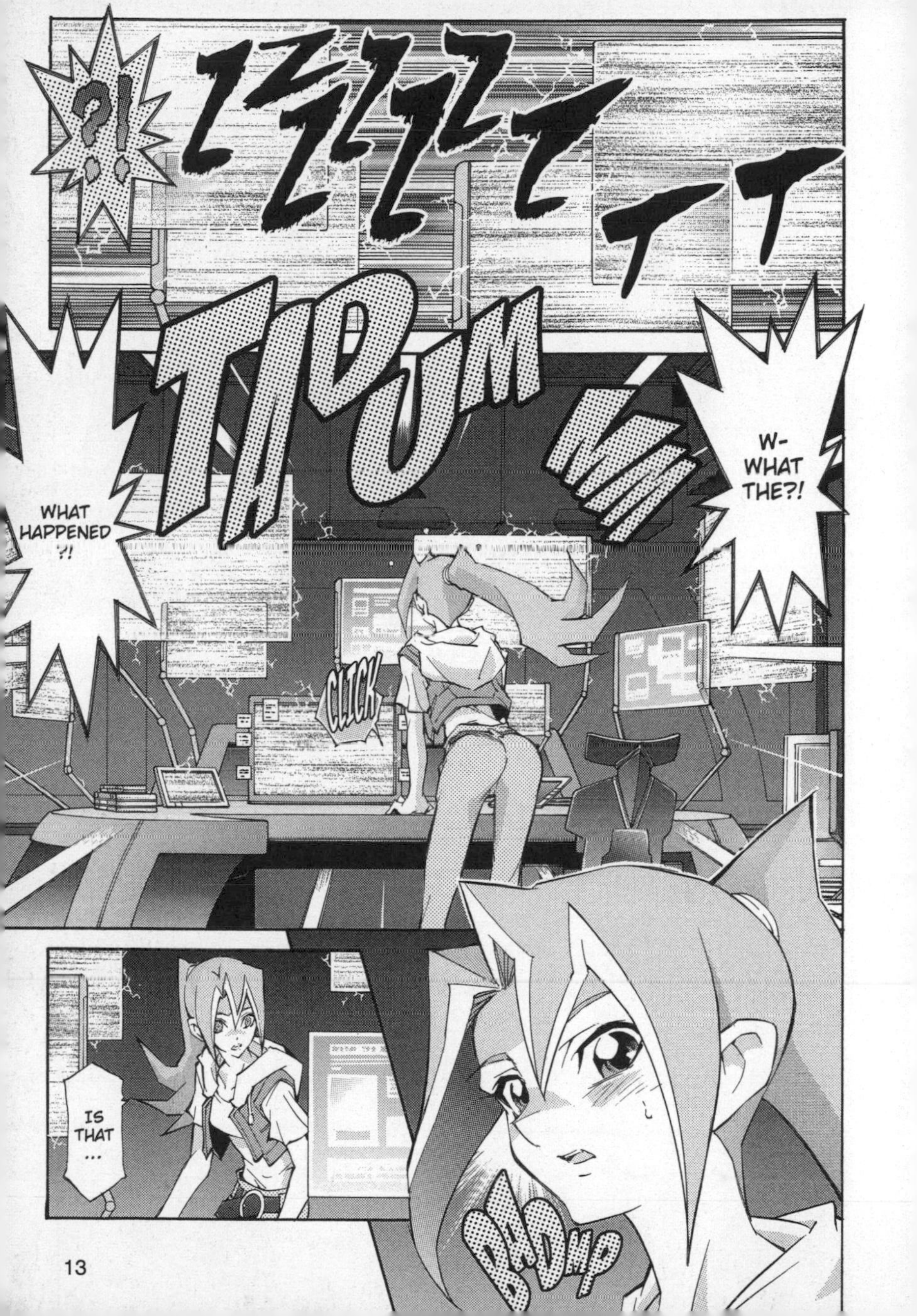
ZZZZZTT
?!
THOOM
W- WHAT THE?!
WHAT HAPPENED ?!
CLICK
BADUMP
IS THAT ...

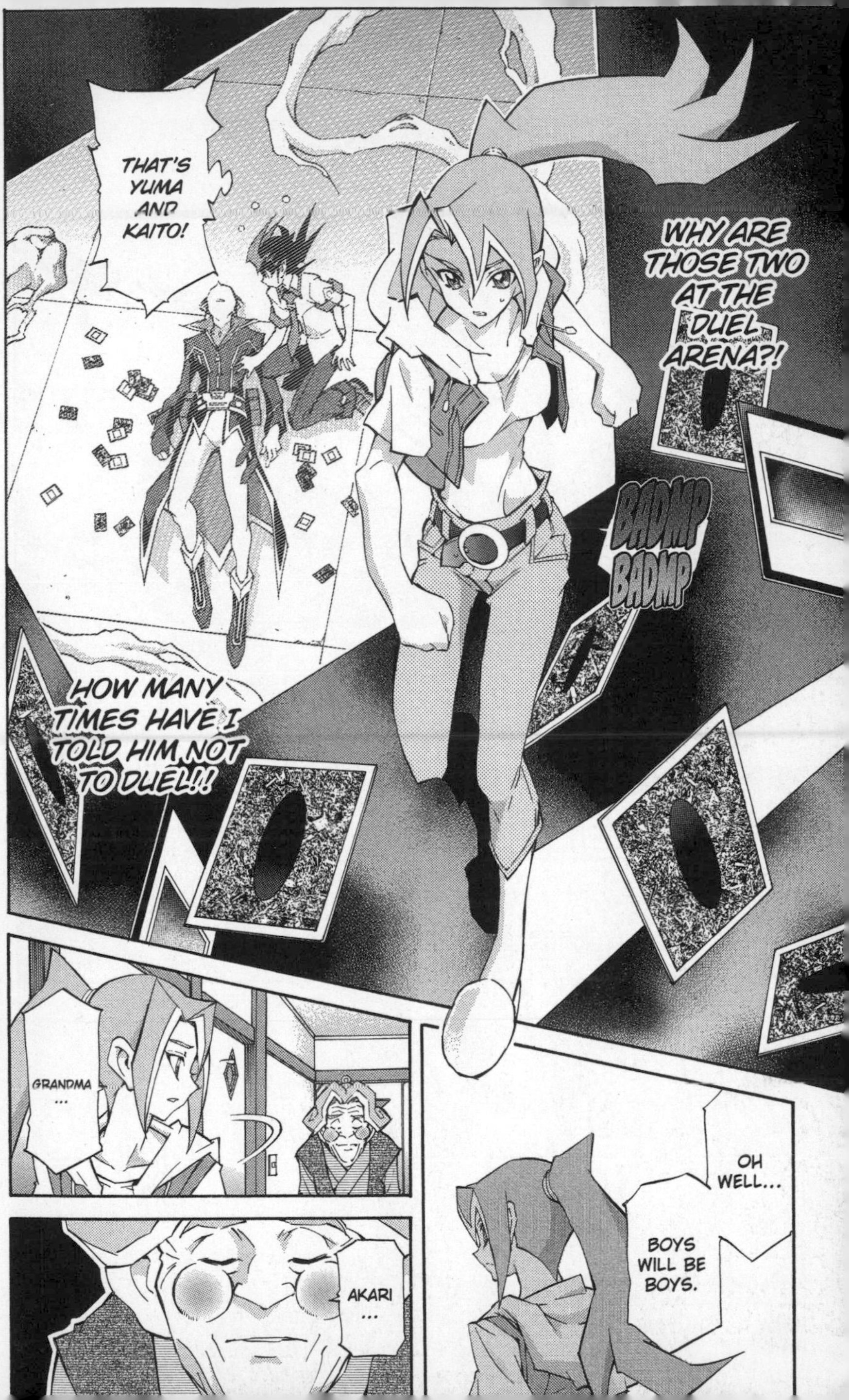
THAT'S YUMA AND KAITO!
WHY ARE THOSE TWO AT THE DUEL ARENA?!
BADMP BADMP
HOW MANY TIMES HAVE I TOLD HIM NOT TO DUEL!!
OH WELL...
BOYS WILL BE BOYS.
GRANDMA ...
AKARI ...

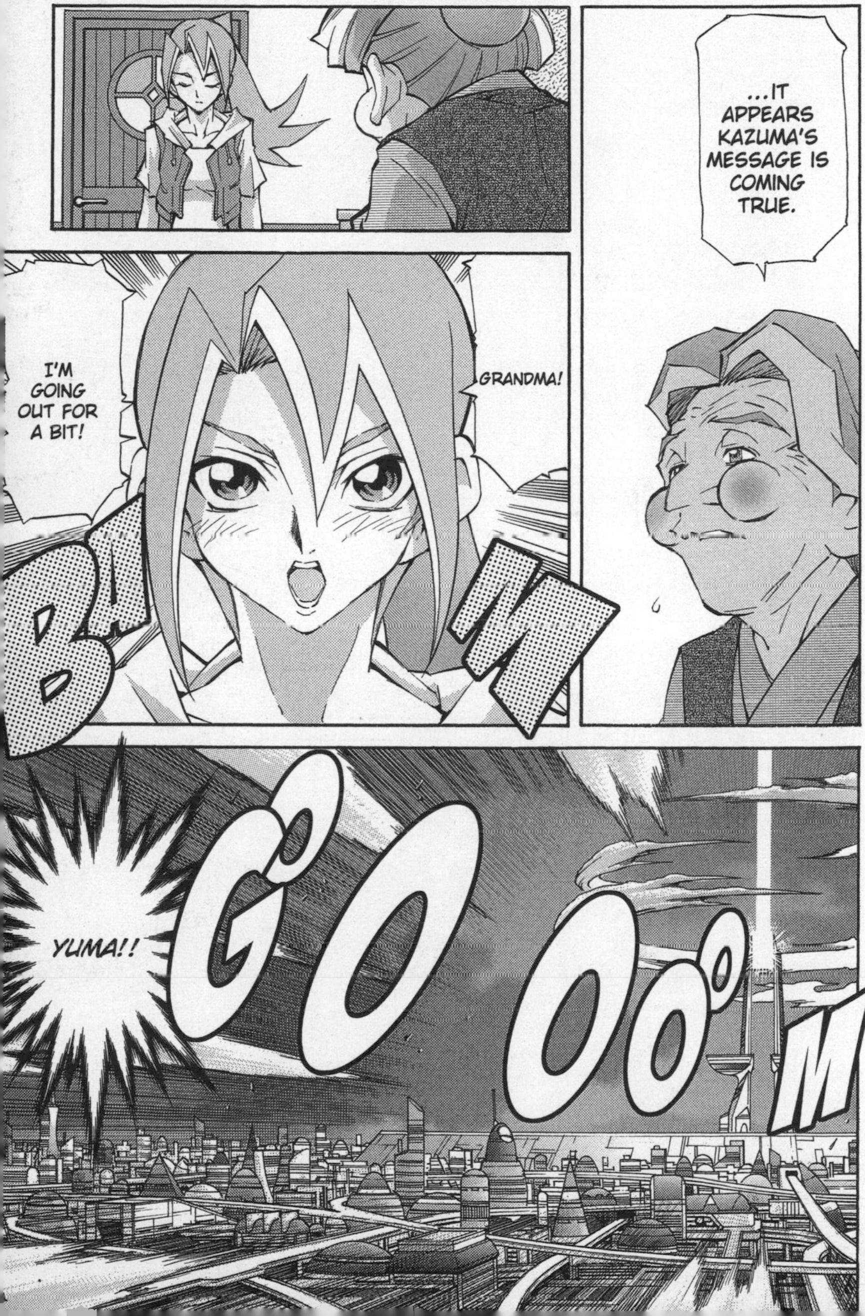
...IT APPEARS KAZUMA'S MESSAGE IS COMING TRUE.
GRANDMA!
I'M GOING OUT FOR A BIT!
BAM
GOOOOM
YUMA!!

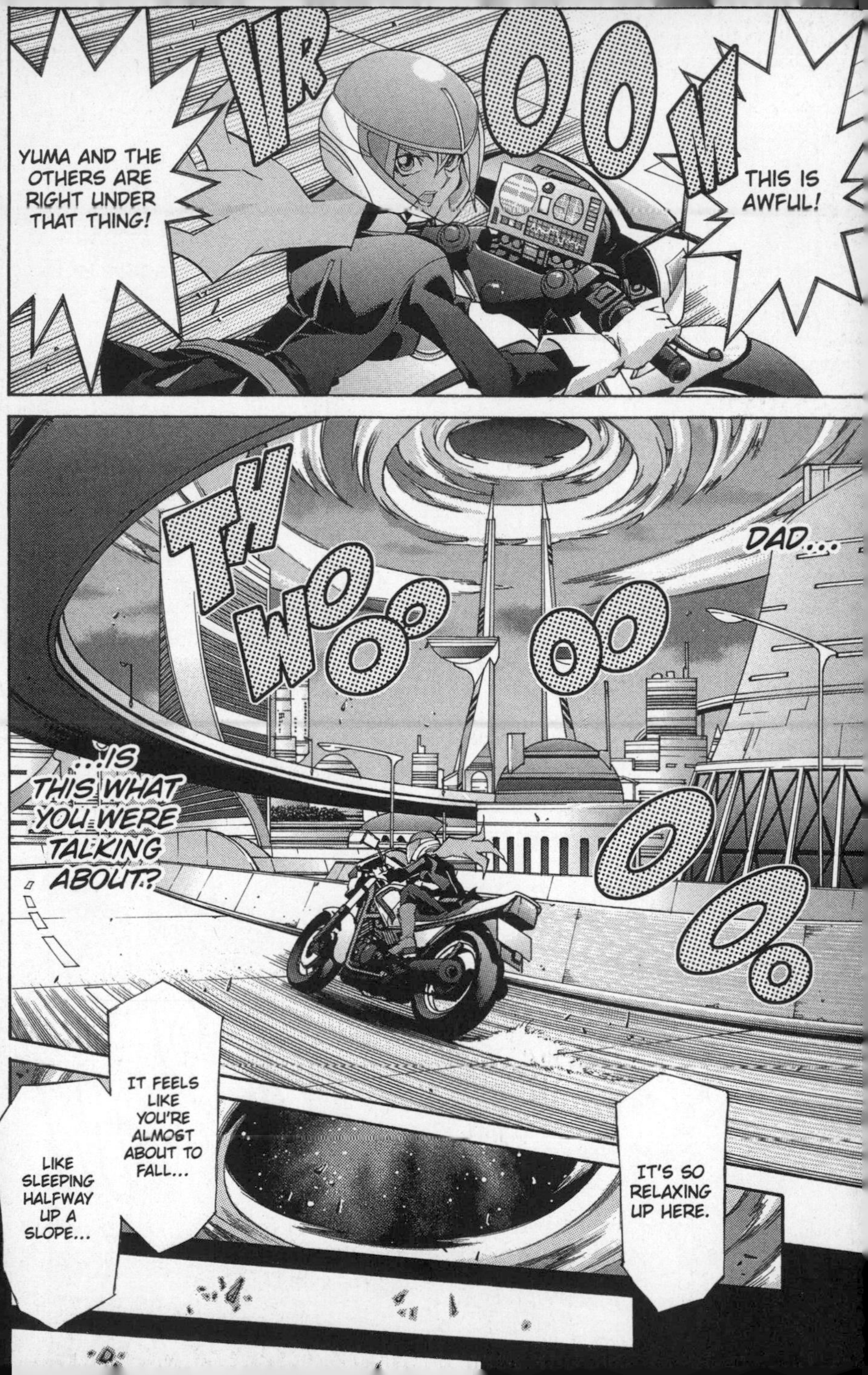
VROOOM
THIS IS AWFUL!
YUMA AND THE OTHERS ARE RIGHT UNDER THAT THING!
DAD...
...IS THIS WHAT YOU WERE TALKING ABOUT?
THWOOOOOOOO
IT'S SO RELAXING UP HERE.
IT FEELS LIKE YOU'RE ALMOST ABOUT TO FALL...
LIKE SLEEPING HALFWAY UP A SLOPE...

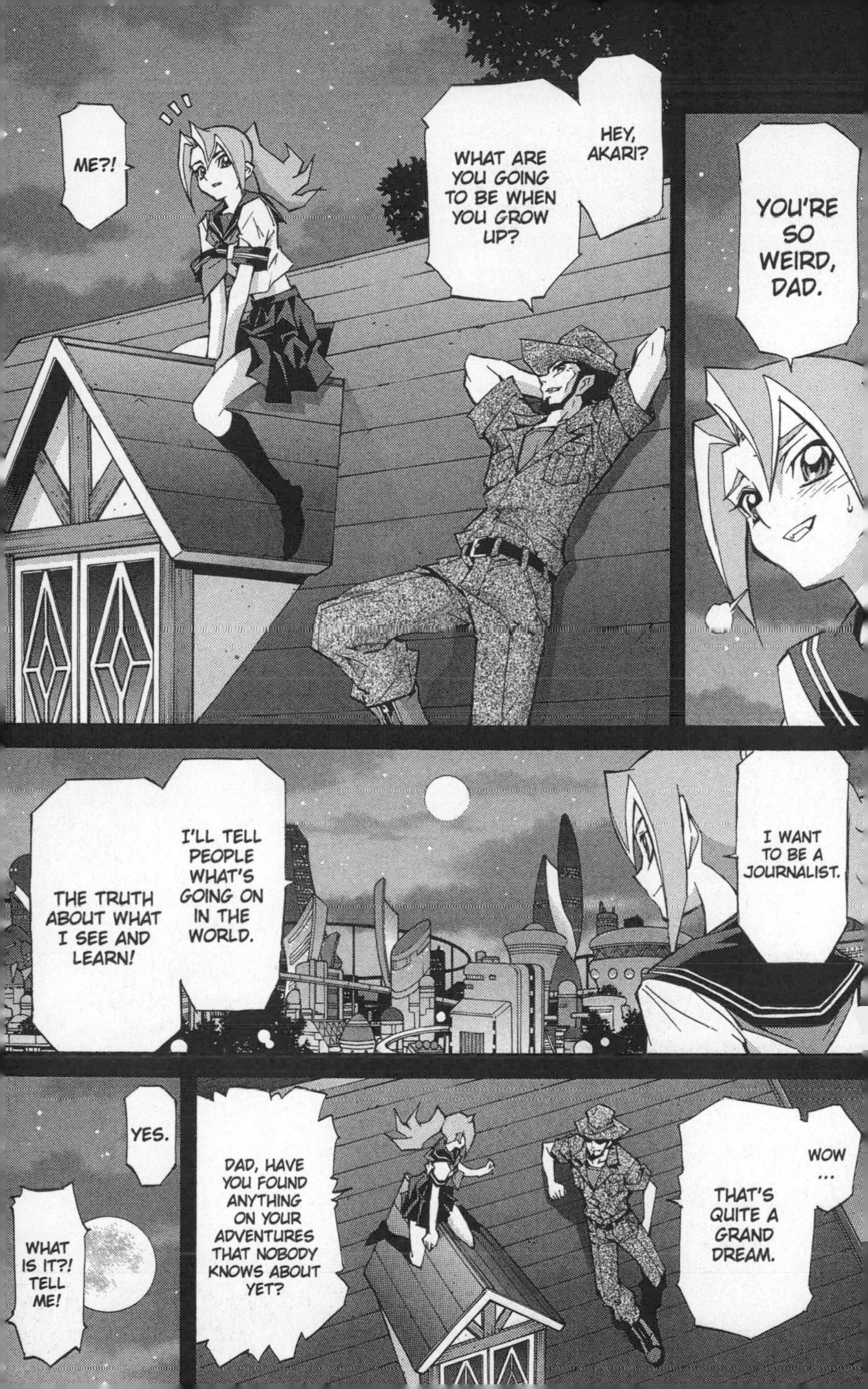
YOU'RE SO WEIRD, DAD.
HEY, AKARI?
WHAT ARE YOU GOING TO BE WHEN YOU GROW UP?
ME?!
I WANT TO BE A JOURNALIST.
I'LL TELL PEOPLE WHAT'S GOING ON IN THE WORLD.
THE TRUTH ABOUT WHAT I SEE AND LEARN!
WOW ...
THAT'S QUITE A GRAND DREAM.
DAD, HAVE YOU FOUND ANYTHING ON YOUR ADVENTURES THAT NOBODY KNOWS ABOUT YET?
YES.
WHAT IS IT?! TELL ME!

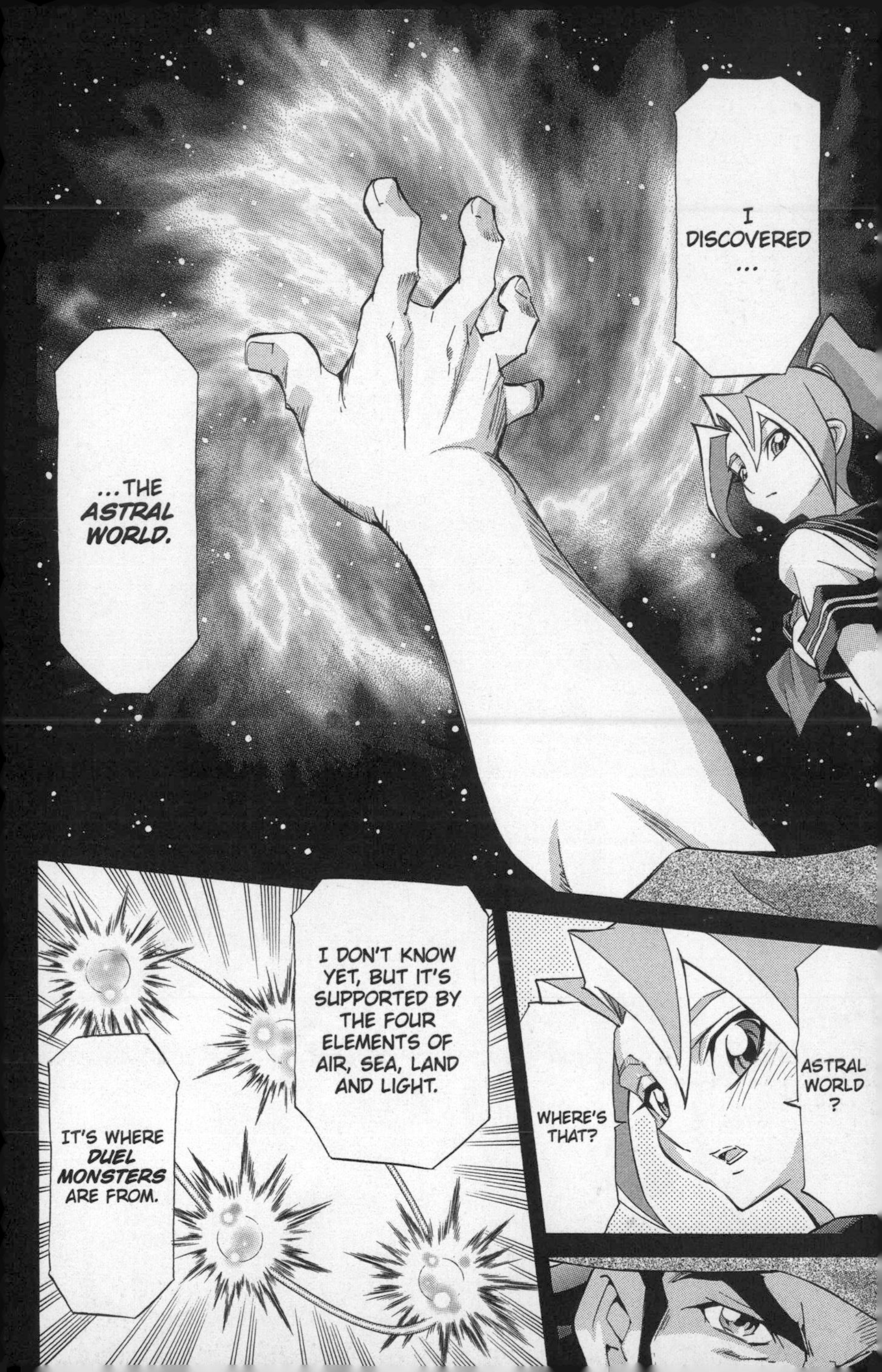
I DISCOVERED ...
...THE *ASTRAL WORLD.*
ASTRAL WORLD?
WHERE'S THAT?
I DON'T KNOW YET, BUT IT'S SUPPORTED BY THE FOUR ELEMENTS OF AIR, SEA, LAND AND LIGHT.
IT'S WHERE *DUEL MONSTERS* ARE FROM.

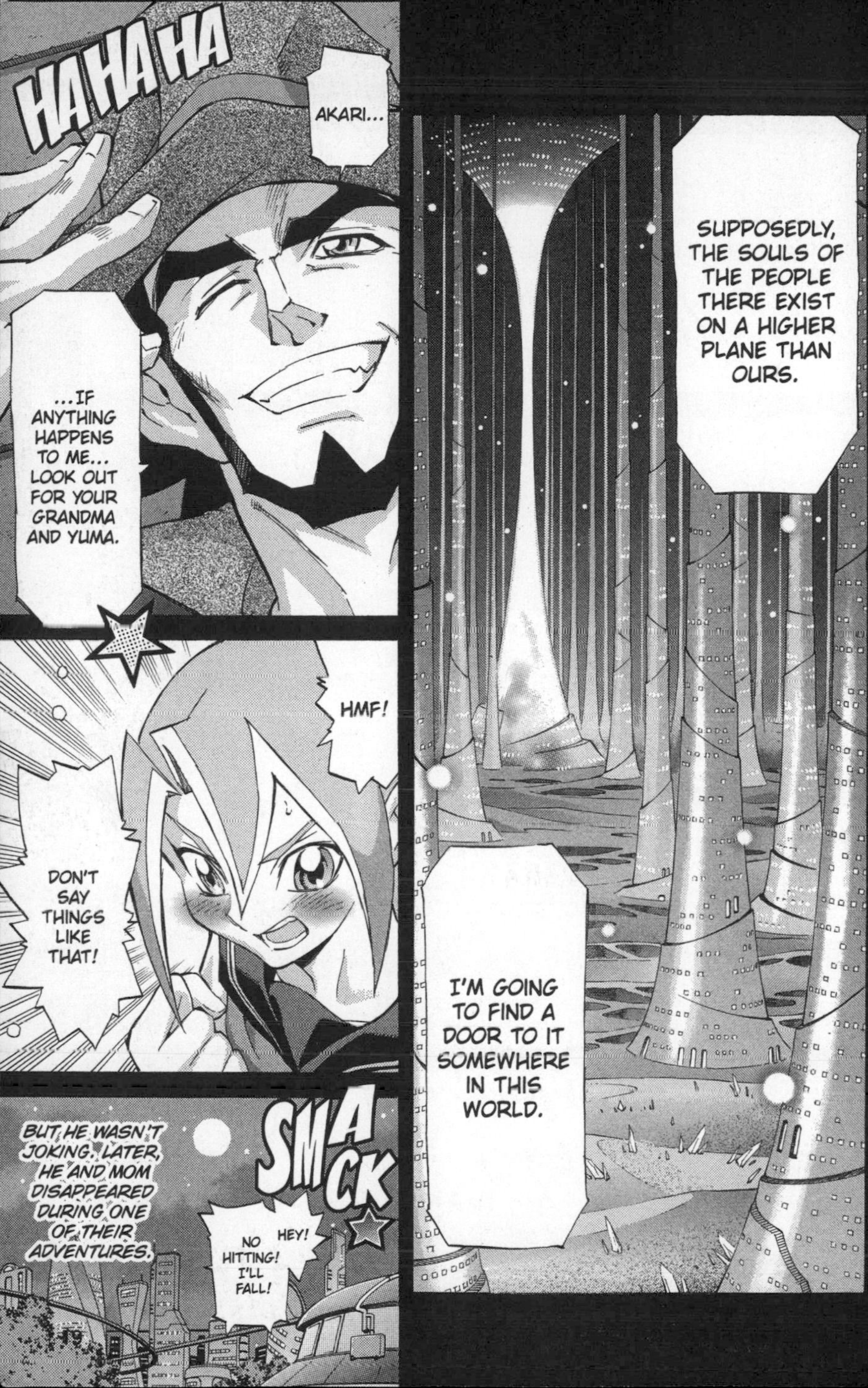
SUPPOSEDLY, THE SOULS OF THE PEOPLE THERE EXIST ON A HIGHER PLANE THAN OURS.
I'M GOING TO FIND A DOOR TO IT SOMEWHERE IN THIS WORLD.
AKARI...
HAHAHA
...IF ANYTHING HAPPENS TO ME... LOOK OUT FOR YOUR GRANDMA AND YUMA.
HMF!
DON'T SAY THINGS LIKE THAT!
SMACK
HEY!
NO HITTING! I'LL FALL!
BUT HE WASN'T JOKING. LATER, HE AND MOM DISAPPEARED DURING ONE OF THEIR ADVENTURES.

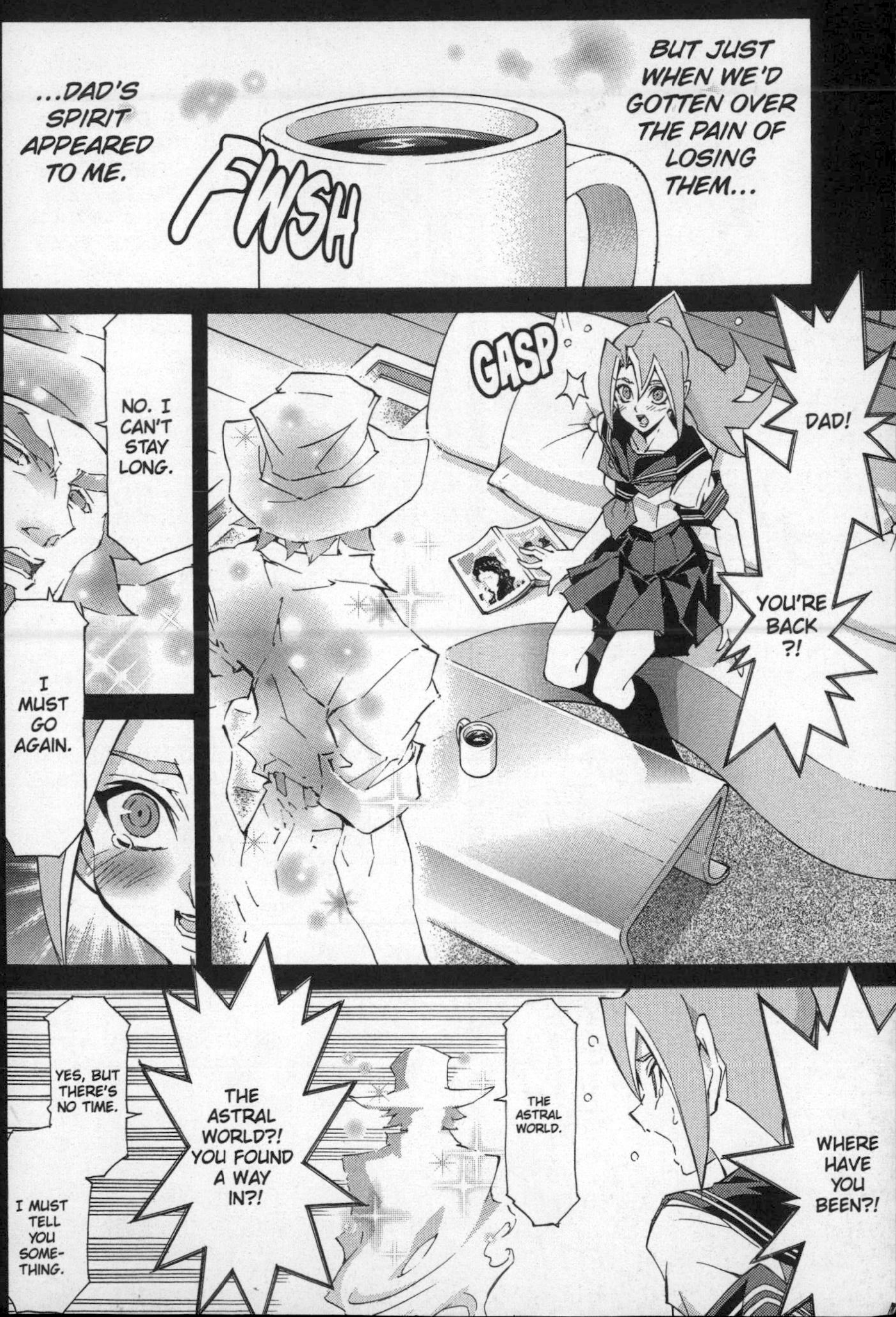
BUT JUST WHEN WE'D GOTTEN OVER THE PAIN OF LOSING THEM...
...DAD'S SPIRIT APPEARED TO ME.
FWSH
DAD!
YOU'RE BACK?!
GASP
NO. I CAN'T STAY LONG.
I MUST GO AGAIN.
WHERE HAVE YOU BEEN?!
THE ASTRAL WORLD.
THE ASTRAL WORLD?! YOU FOUND A WAY IN?!
YES, BUT THERE'S NO TIME.
I MUST TELL YOU SOMETHING.

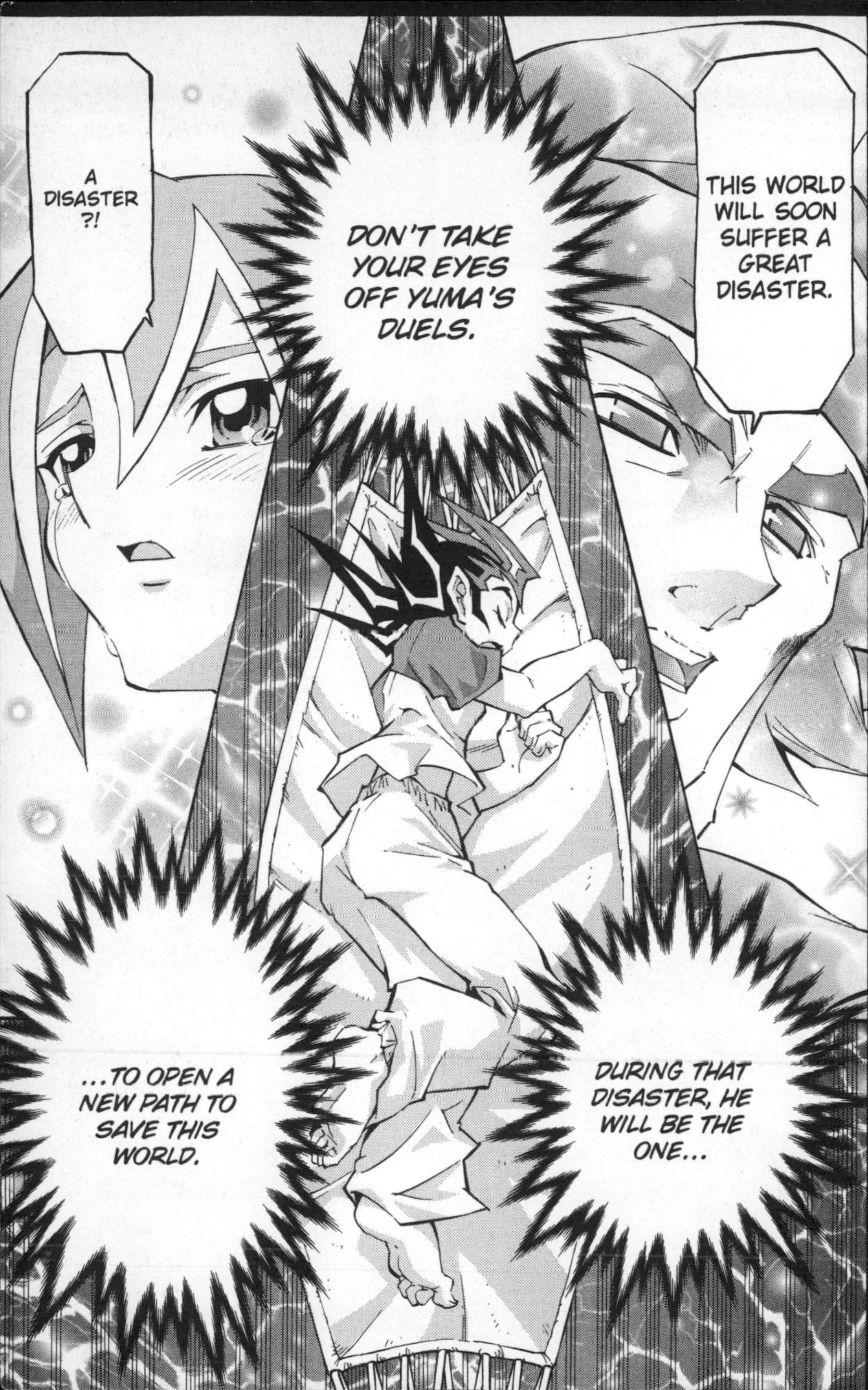
THIS WORLD WILL SOON SUFFER A GREAT DISASTER.
A DISASTER?!
DON'T TAKE YOUR EYES OFF YUMA'S DUELS.
DURING THAT DISASTER, HE WILL BE THE ONE...
...TO OPEN A NEW PATH TO SAVE THIS WORLD.

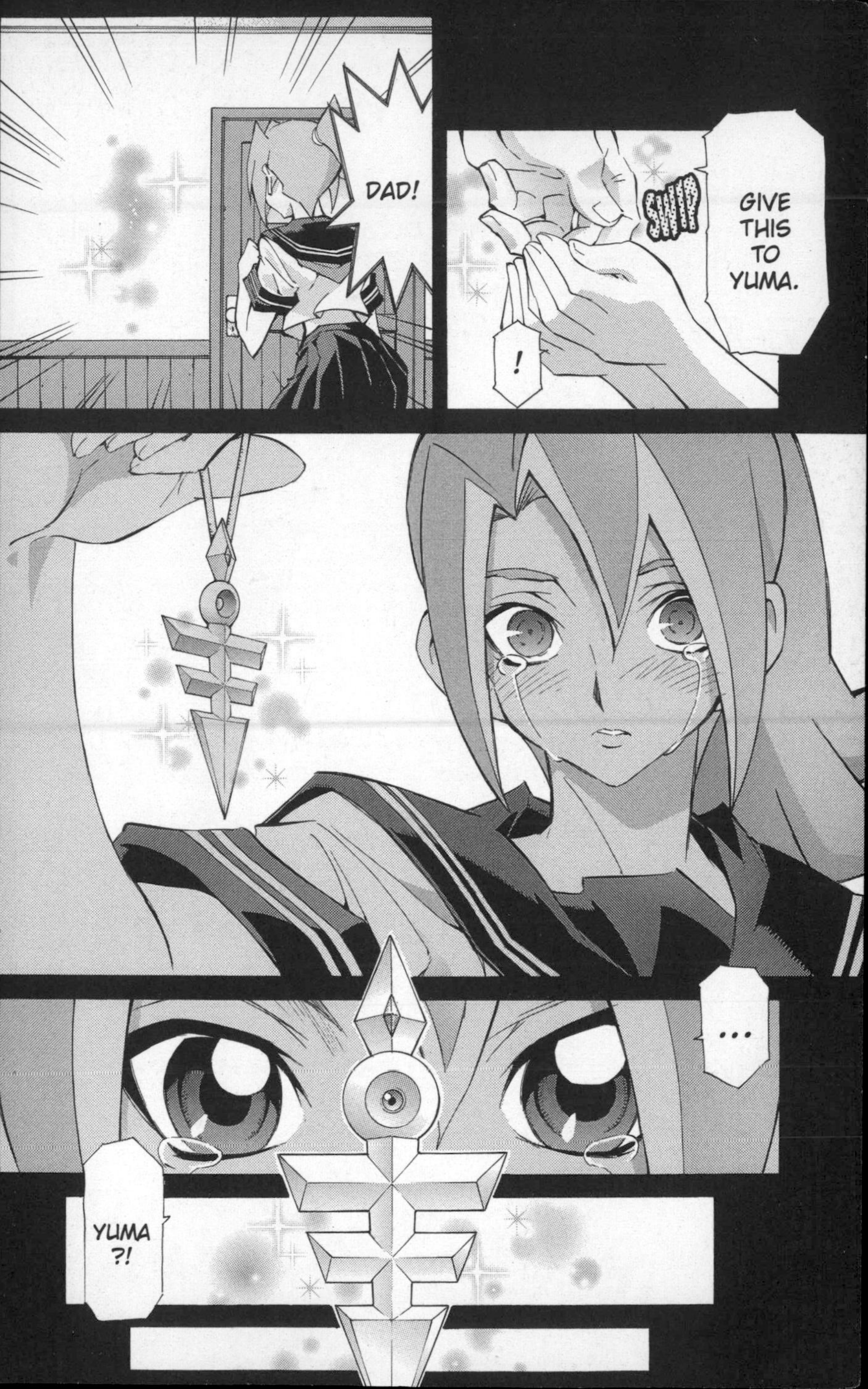
GIVE THIS TO YUMA.
SWIP
!
DAD!
...
YUMA ?!

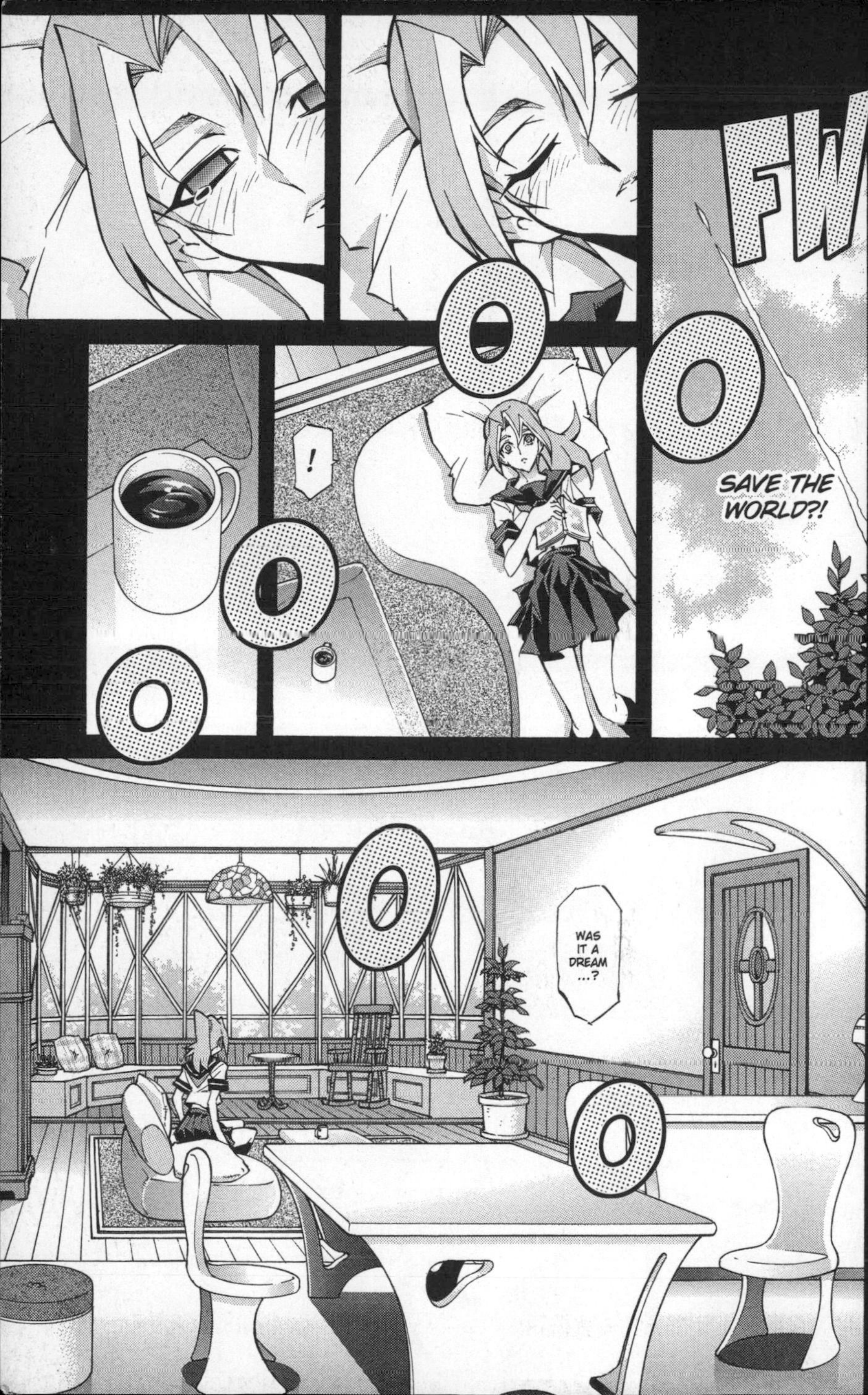

FWOOOOOO
SAVE THE WORLD?!
!
WAS IT A DREAM ...?

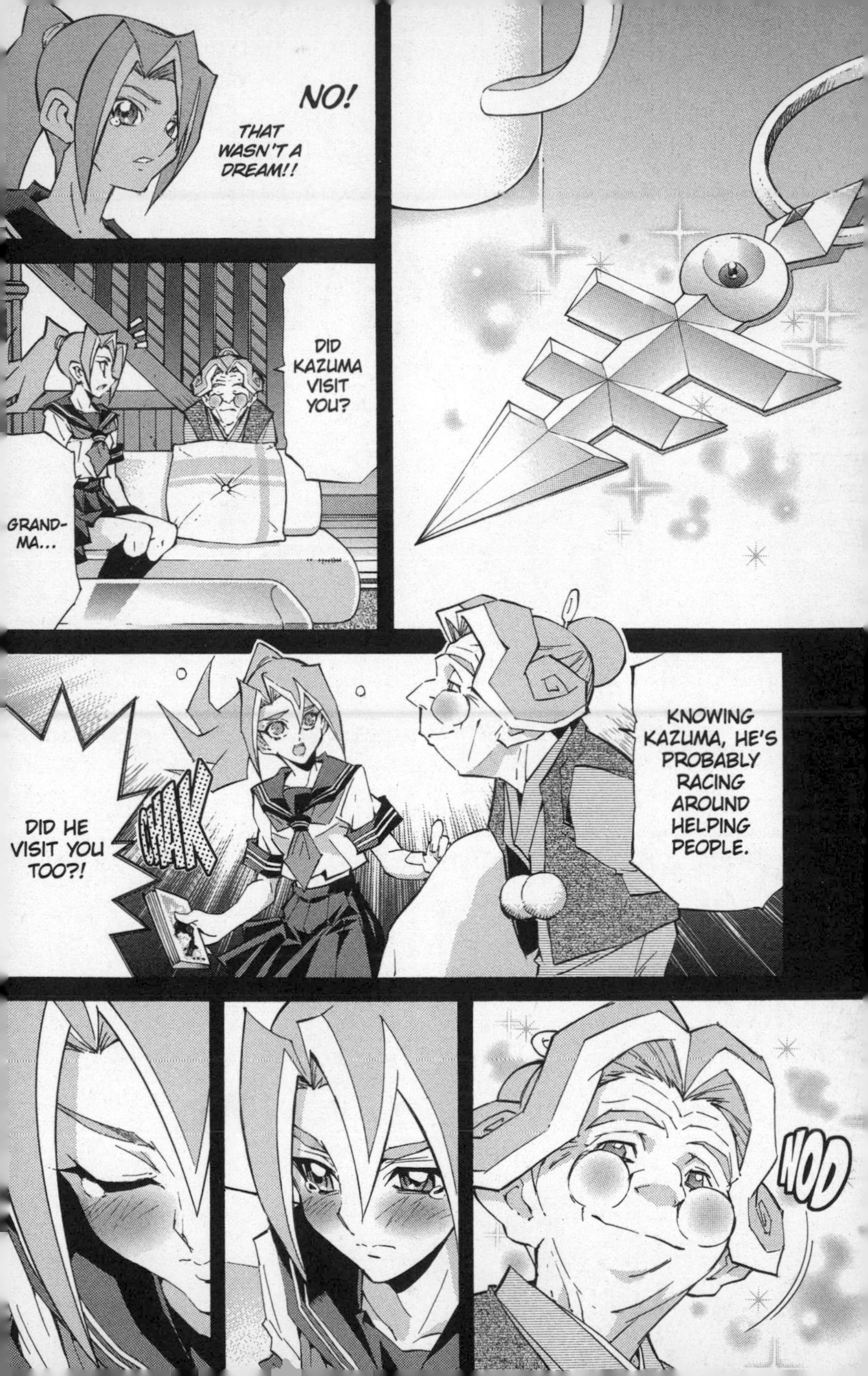
NO!
THAT WASN'T A DREAM!!
DID KAZUMA VISIT YOU?
GRAND-MA...
KNOWING KAZUMA, HE'S PROBABLY RACING AROUND HELPING PEOPLE.
CHAK
DID HE VISIT YOU TOO?!
NOD

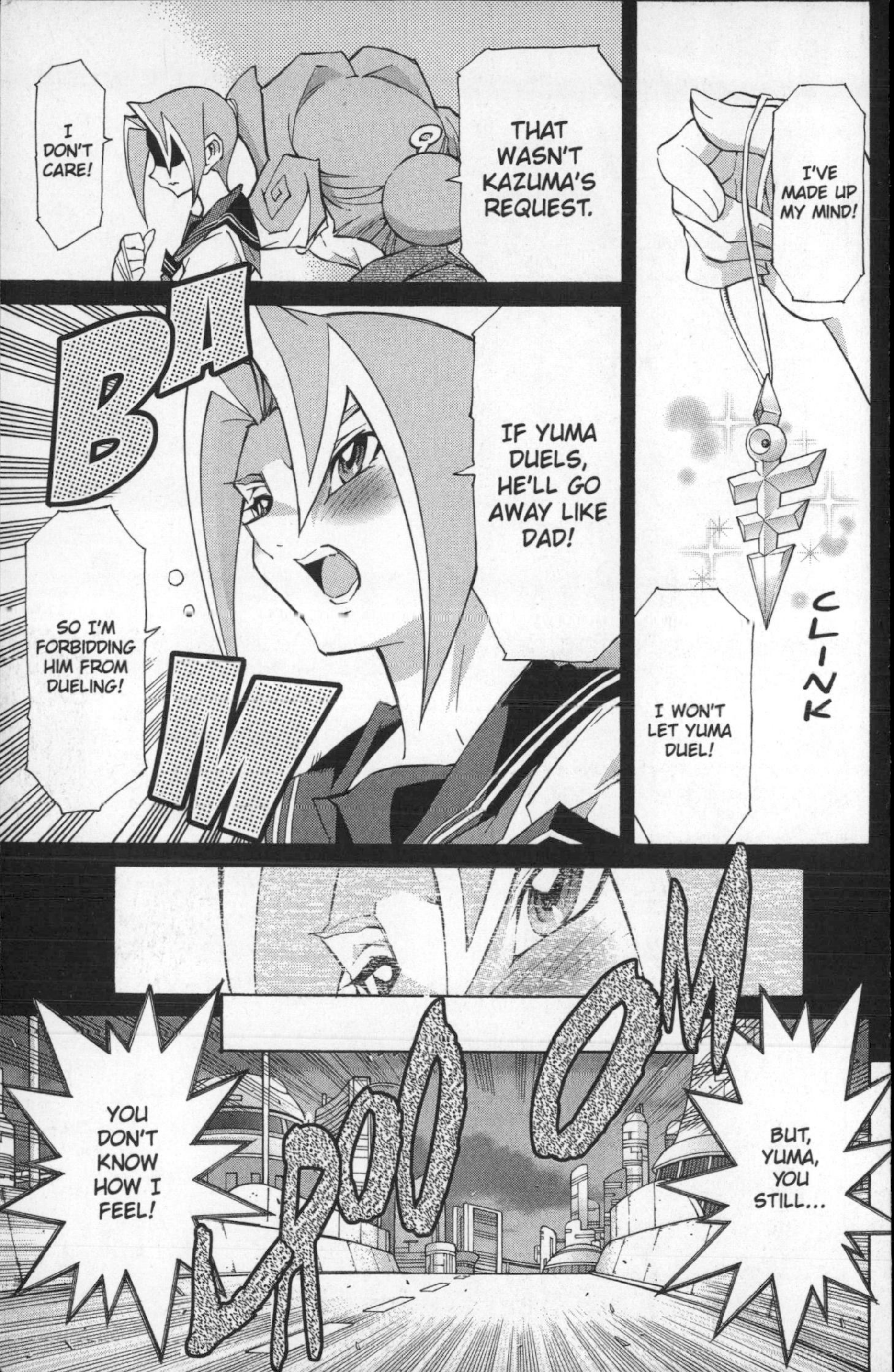

I'VE MADE UP MY MIND!
CLINK
I WON'T LET YUMA DUEL!
THAT WASN'T KAZUMA'S REQUEST.
I DON'T CARE!
BAM
IF YUMA DUELS, HE'LL GO AWAY LIKE DAD!
SO I'M FORBIDDING HIM FROM DUELING!
BUT, YUMA, YOU STILL...
VROOOM
YOU DON'T KNOW HOW I FEEL!

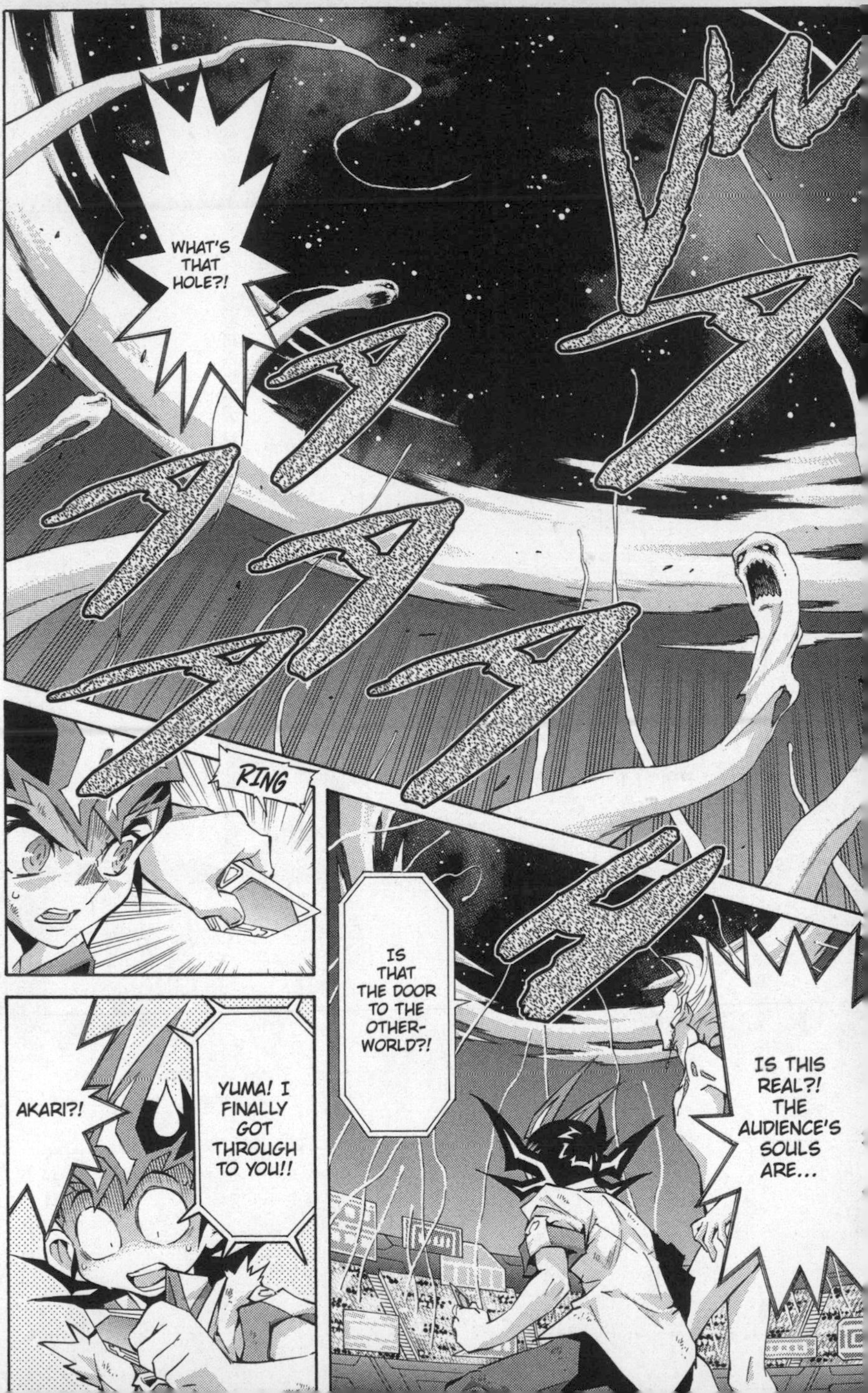
WHAT'S THAT HOLE?!
IS THIS REAL?! THE AUDIENCE'S SOULS ARE...
IS THAT THE DOOR TO THE OTHER-WORLD?!
RING
YUMA! I FINALLY GOT THROUGH TO YOU!!
AKARI?!

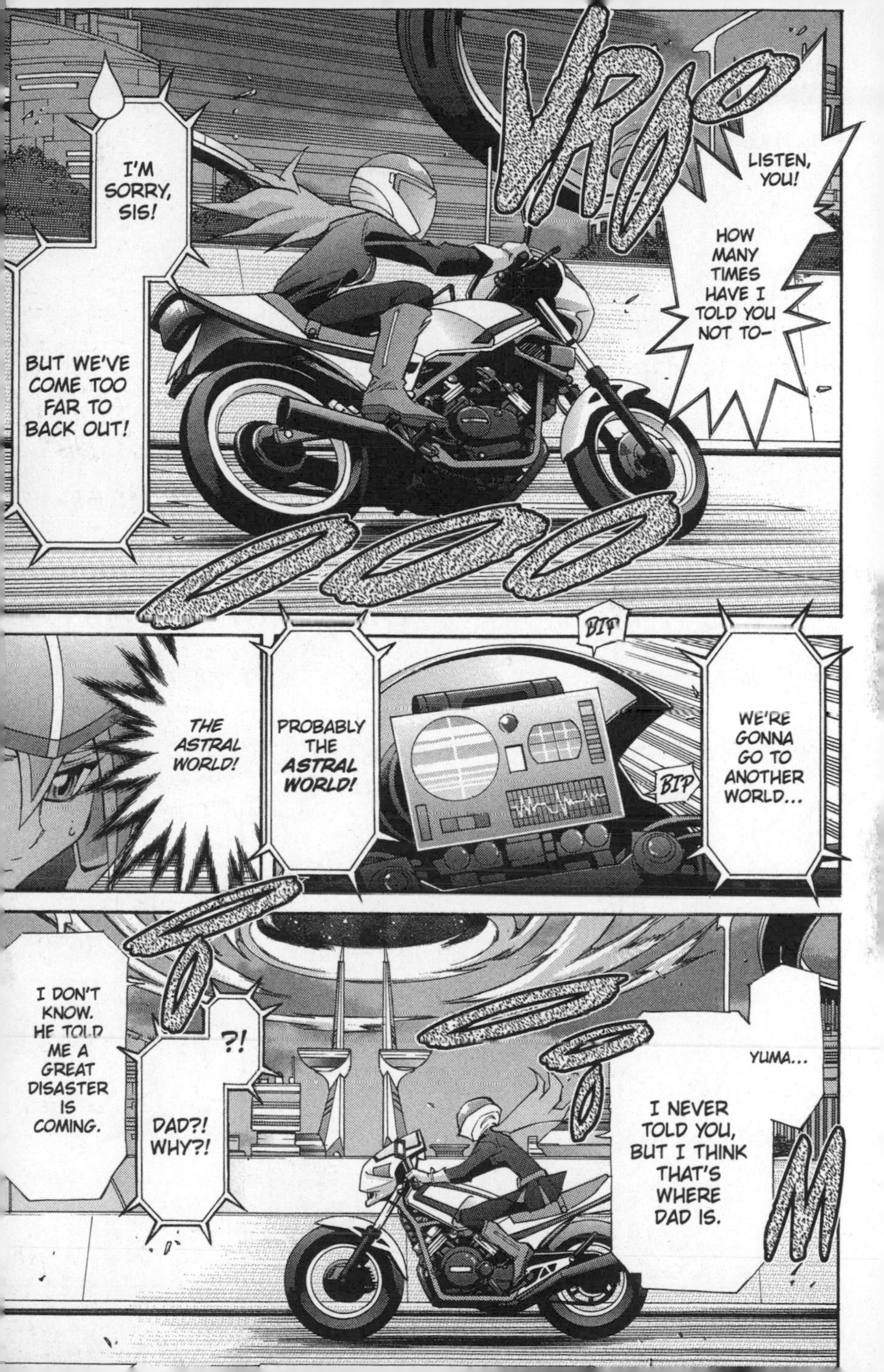
LISTEN, YOU!
HOW MANY TIMES HAVE I TOLD YOU NOT TO–
I'M SORRY, SIS!
BUT WE'VE COME TOO FAR TO BACK OUT!
BIP
WE'RE GONNA GO TO ANOTHER WORLD...
BIP
PROBABLY THE ASTRAL WORLD!
THE ASTRAL WORLD!
YUMA...
I NEVER TOLD YOU, BUT I THINK THAT'S WHERE DAD IS.
?!
DAD?! WHY?!
I DON'T KNOW. HE TOLD ME A GREAT DISASTER IS COMING.

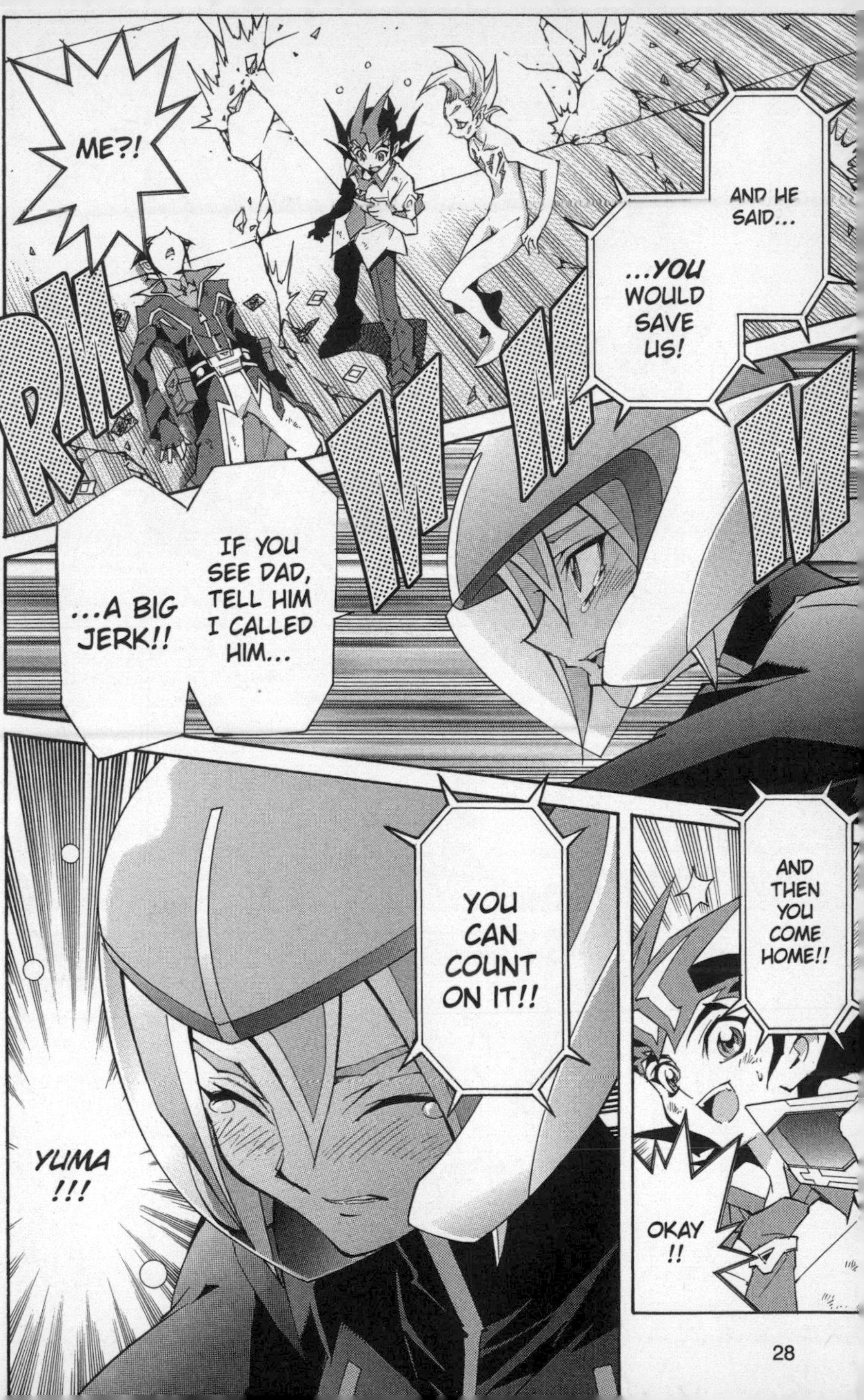
AND HE SAID...
...YOU WOULD SAVE US!
ME?!
IF YOU SEE DAD, TELL HIM I CALLED HIM...
...A BIG JERK!!
AND THEN YOU COME HOME!!
OKAY!!
YOU CAN COUNT ON IT!!
YUMA!!!

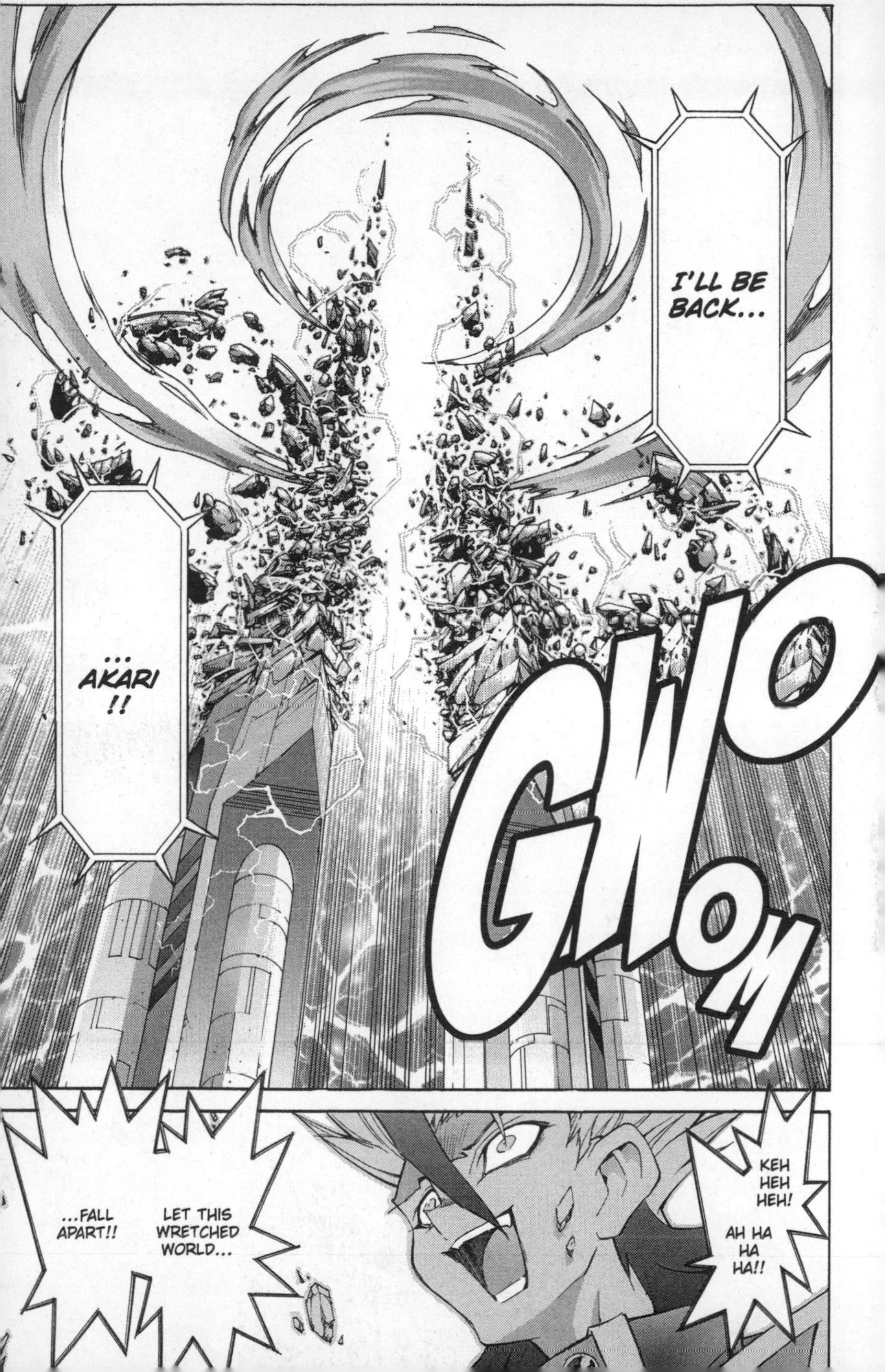
I'LL BE BACK...
...AKARI!!
GWOOM
KEH HEH HEH!
AH HA HA HA!!
LET THIS WRETCHED WORLD...
...FALL APART!!

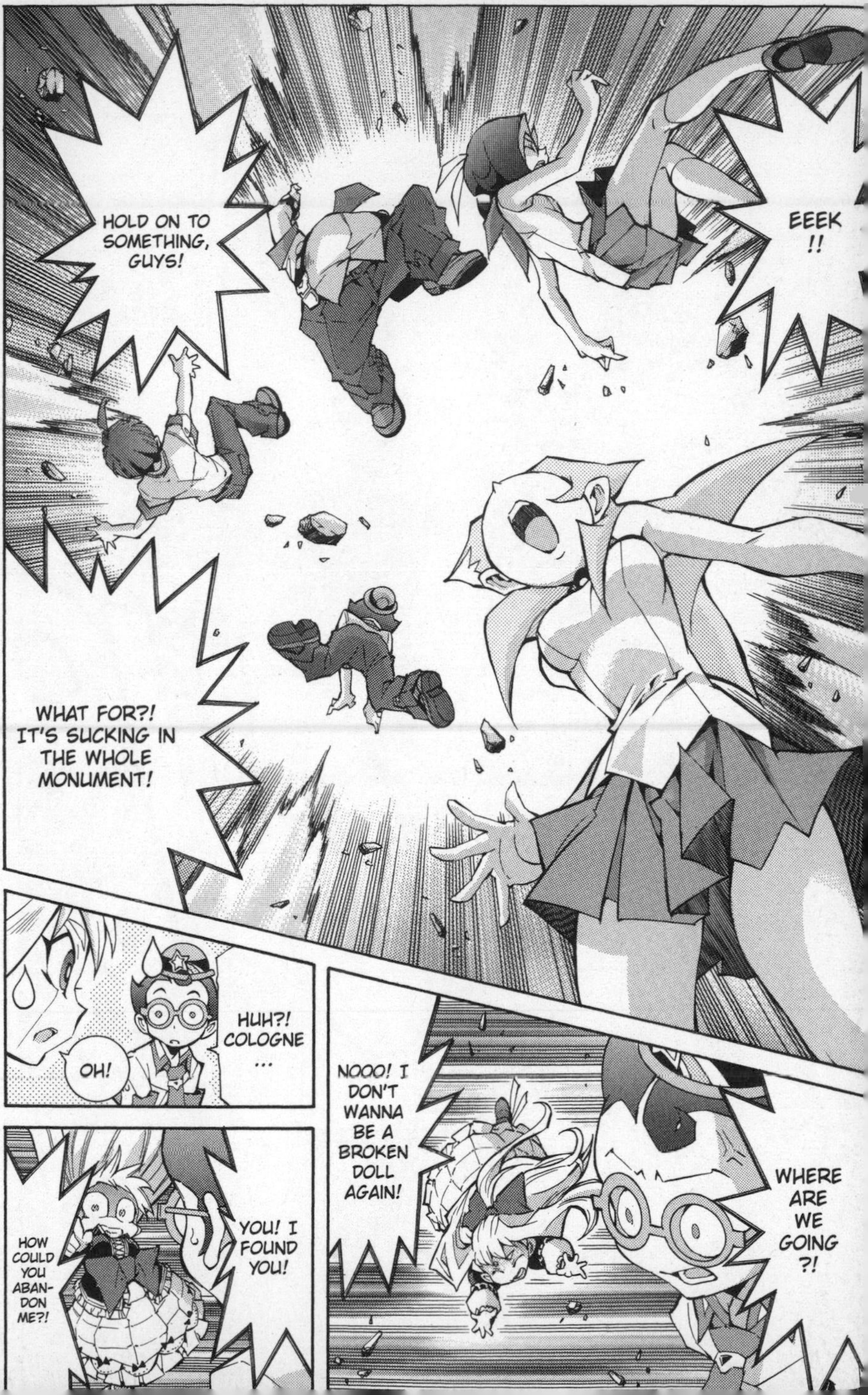
EEEK!!
HOLD ON TO SOMETHING, GUYS!
WHAT FOR?! IT'S SUCKING IN THE WHOLE MONUMENT!
WHERE ARE WE GOING?!
NOOO! I DON'T WANNA BE A BROKEN DOLL AGAIN!
HUH?! COLOGNE ...
OH!
YOU! I FOUND YOU!
HOW COULD YOU ABAN-DON ME?!

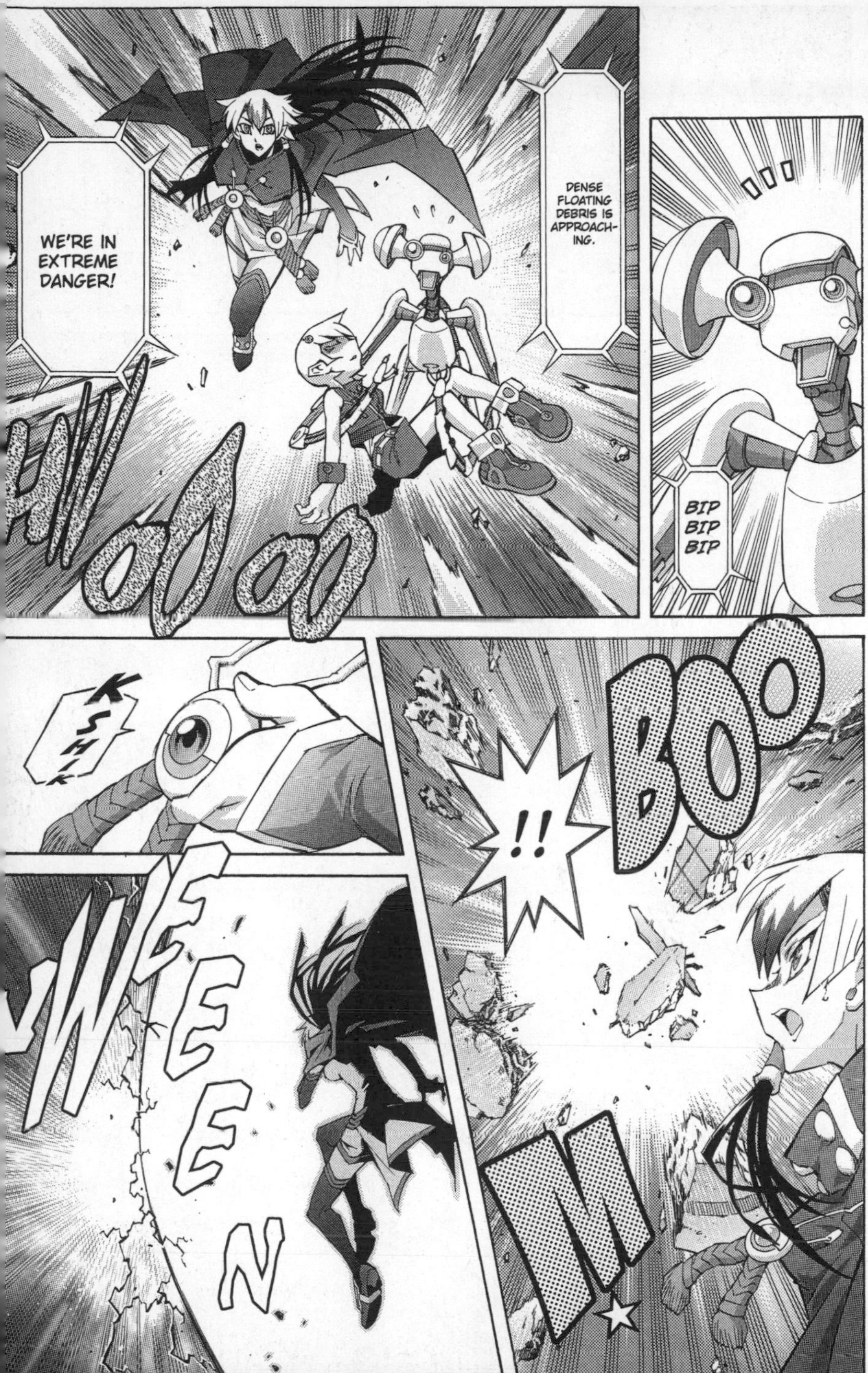
BIP
BIP
BIP
DENSE FLOATING DEBRIS IS APPROACH-ING.
WE'RE IN EXTREME DANGER!
!!
KSHIK

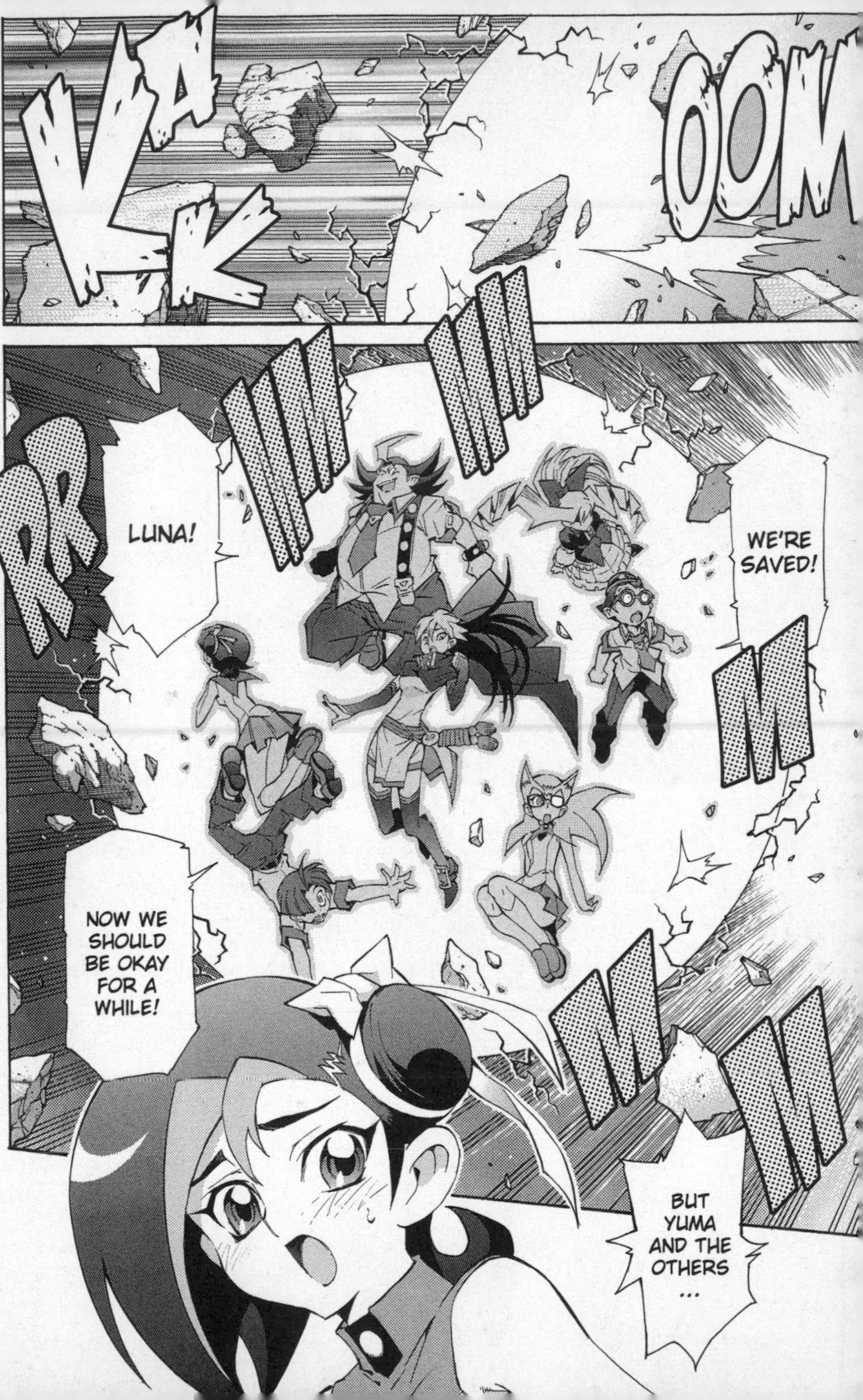
OOM
WE'RE SAVED!
LUNA!
NOW WE SHOULD BE OKAY FOR A WHILE!
BUT YUMA AND THE OTHERS ...

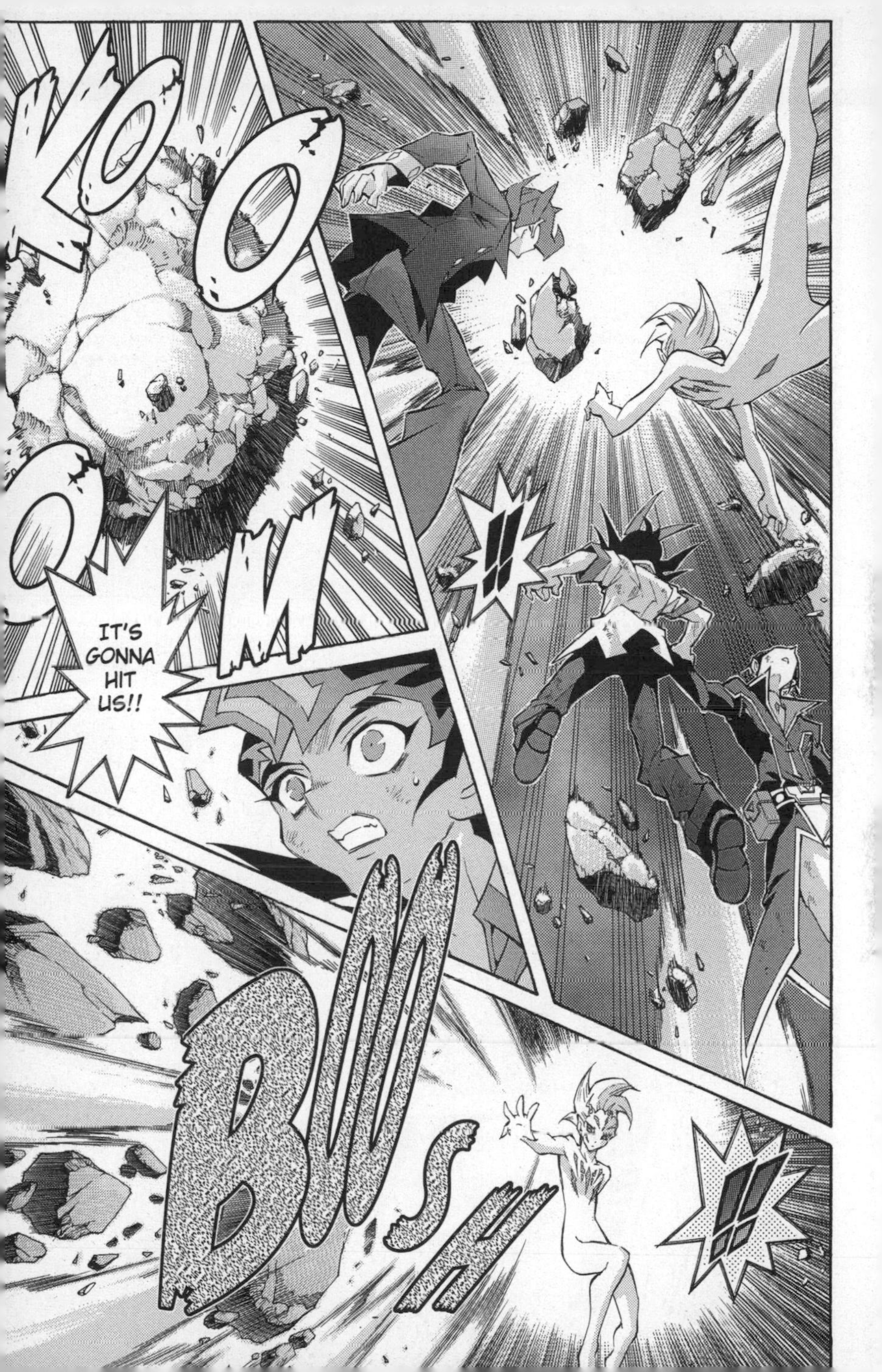
!!
IT'S GONNA HIT US!!
!!

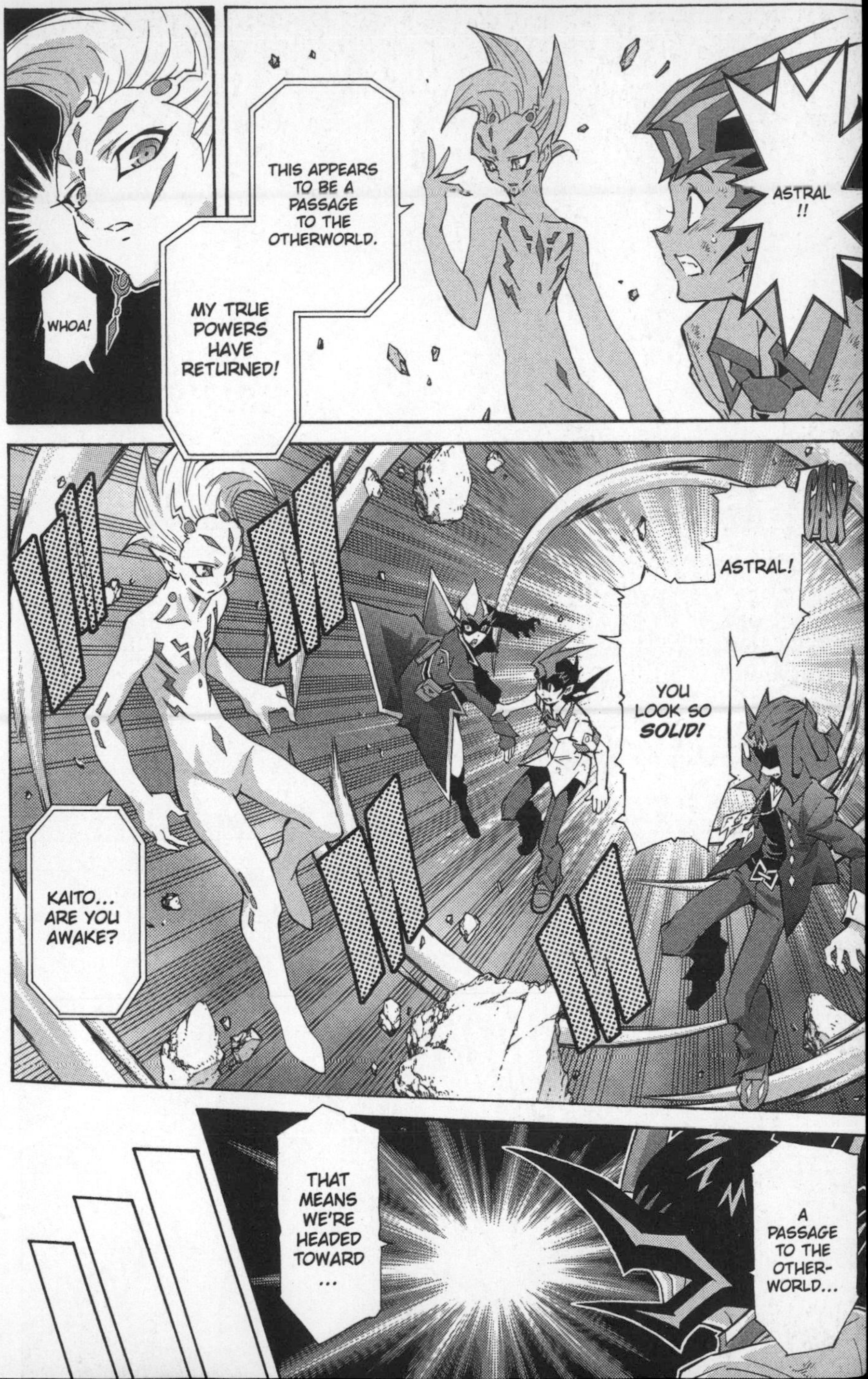
ASTRAL !!
THIS APPEARS TO BE A PASSAGE TO THE OTHERWORLD.
MY TRUE POWERS HAVE RETURNED!
WHOA!
GASP
ASTRAL!
YOU LOOK SO SOLID!
KAITO... ARE YOU AWAKE?
A PASSAGE TO THE OTHER-WORLD...
THAT MEANS WE'RE HEADED TOWARD ...

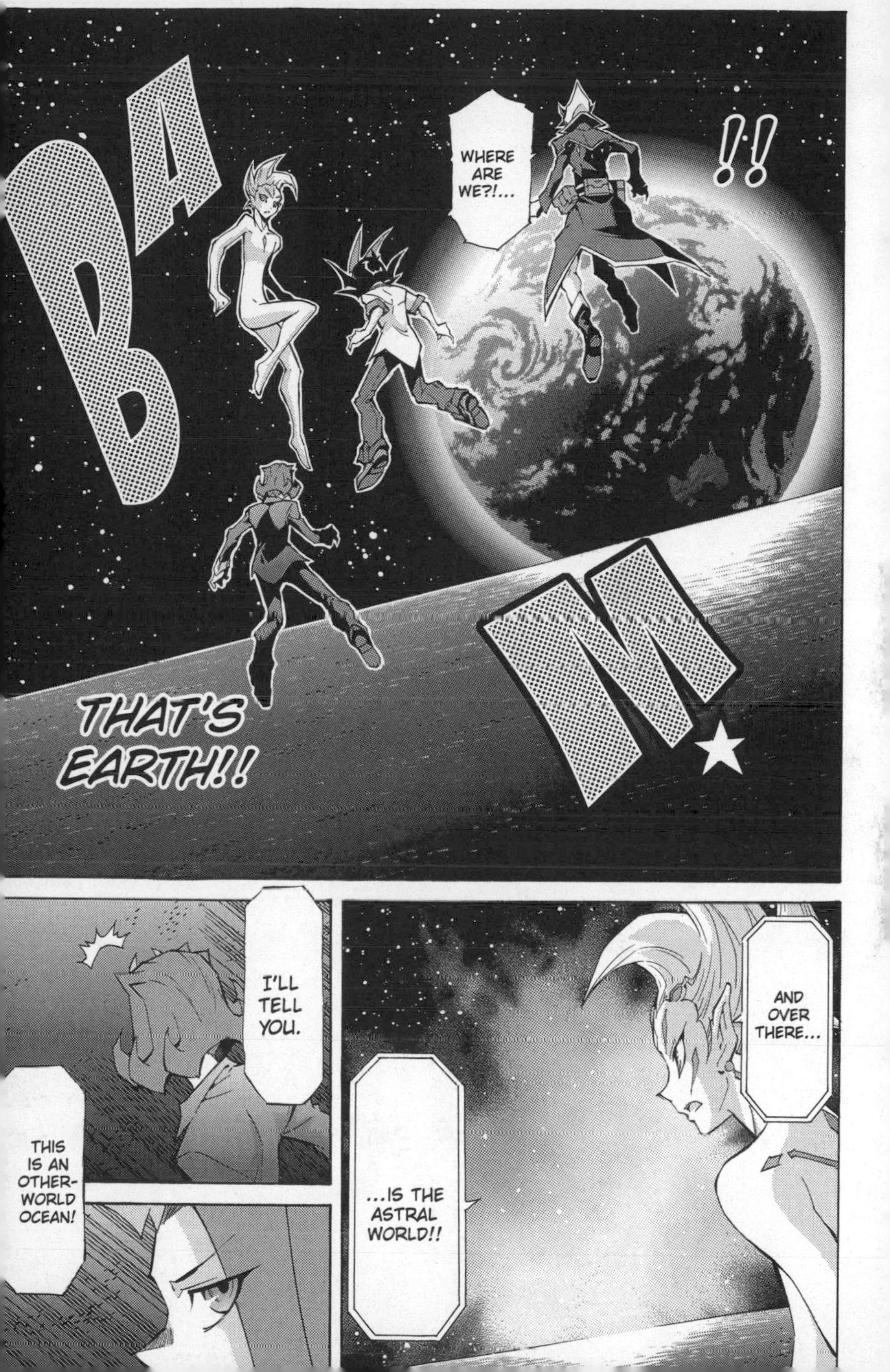
WHERE ARE WE?!...
!!
BA
THAT'S EARTH!!
M★
I'LL TELL YOU.
THIS IS AN OTHER-WORLD OCEAN!
AND OVER THERE...
...IS THE ASTRAL WORLD!!

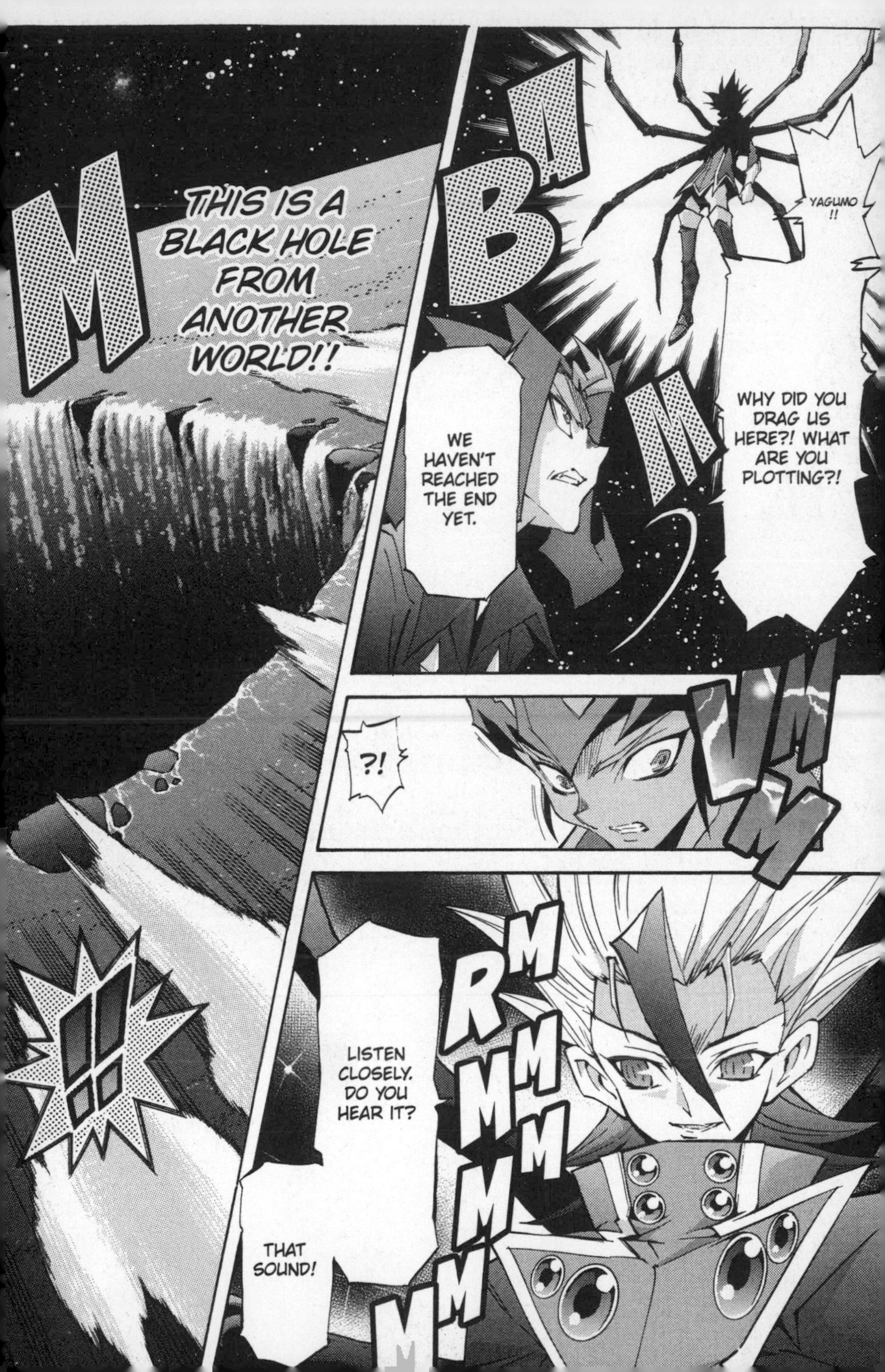

YAGUMO!!
WHY DID YOU DRAG US HERE?! WHAT ARE YOU PLOTTING?!
WE HAVEN'T REACHED THE END YET.
?!
LISTEN CLOSELY. DO YOU HEAR IT?
THAT SOUND!
THIS IS A BLACK HOLE FROM ANOTHER WORLD!!
!!

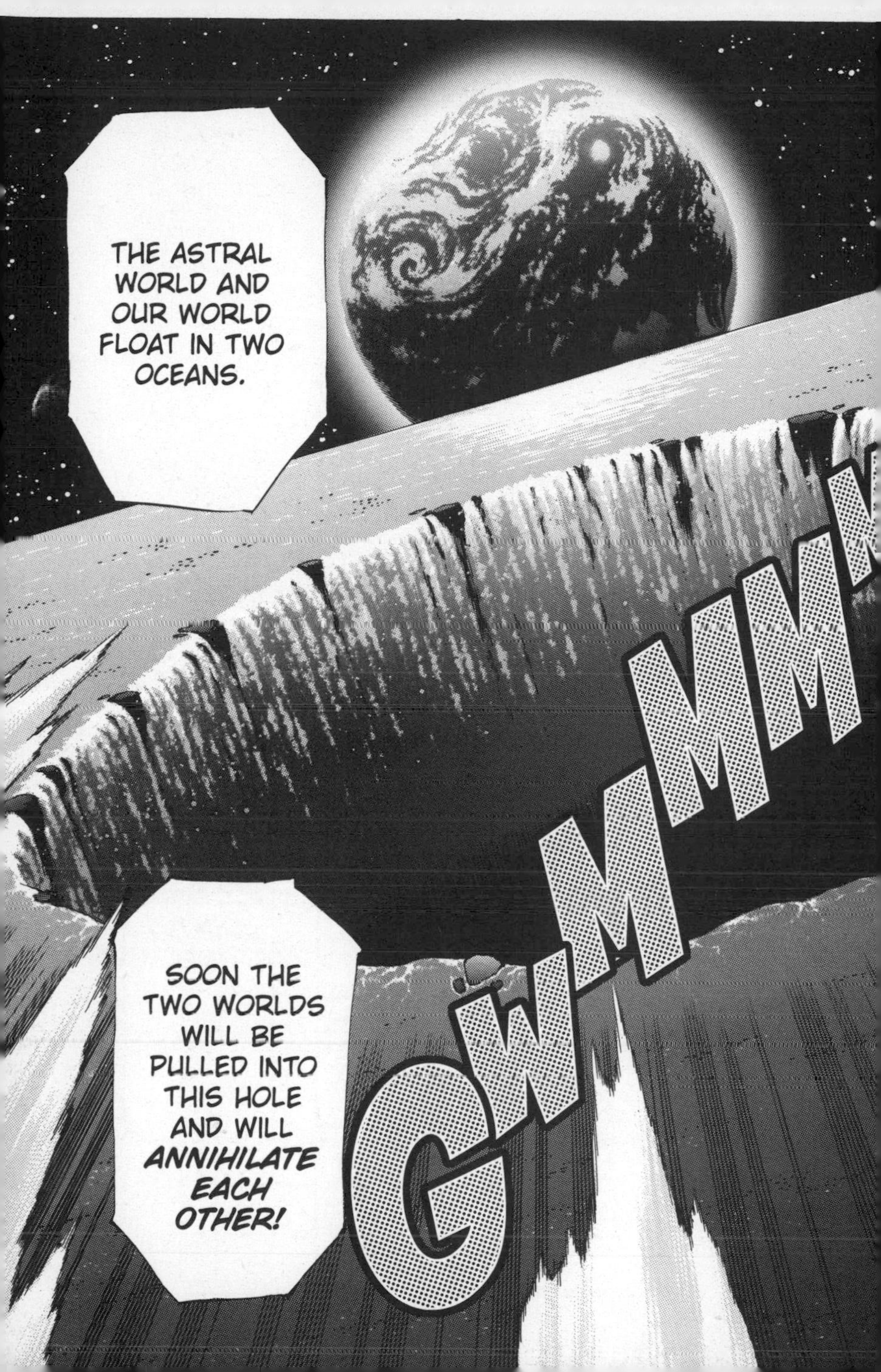
THE ASTRAL WORLD AND OUR WORLD FLOAT IN TWO OCEANS.
GWMMMM
SOON THE TWO WORLDS WILL BE PULLED INTO THIS HOLE AND WILL *ANNIHILATE EACH OTHER!*

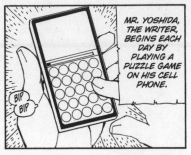

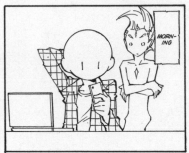

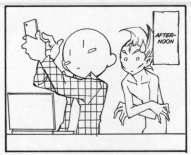

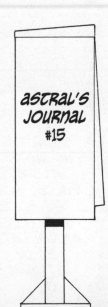

ASTRAL'S JOURNAL #15

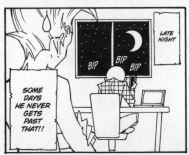

MR. YOSHIDA, THE WRITER, BEGINS EACH DAY BY PLAYING A PUZZLE GAME ON HIS CELL PHONE.
BIP BIP
MORN-ING
AFTER-NOON
LATE NIGHT
BIP
BIP
BIP
SOME DAYS HE NEVER GETS PAST THAT!!

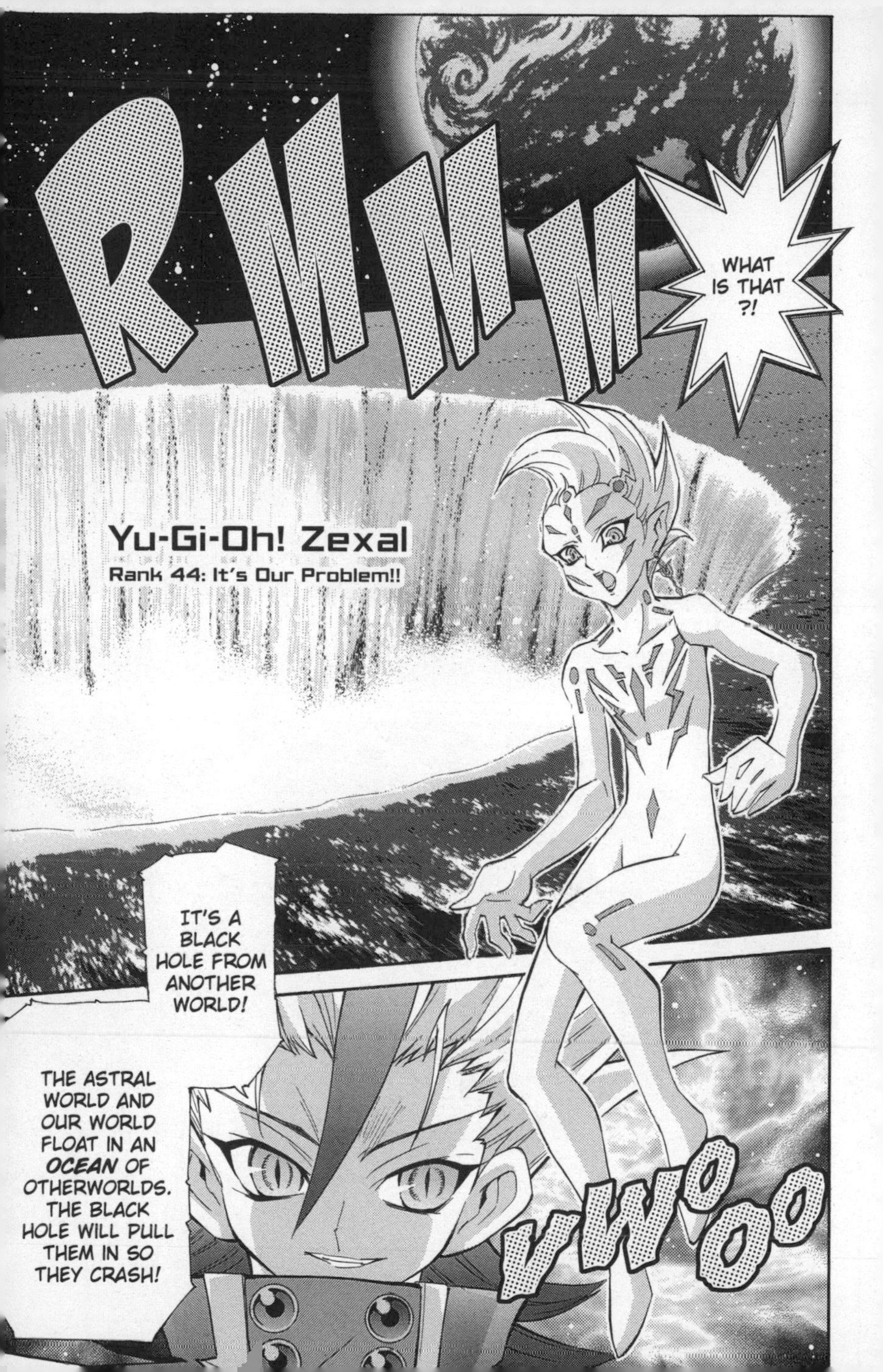
RMMM
WHAT IS THAT?!
Yu-Gi-Oh! Zexal
Rank 44: It's Our Problem!!
IT'S A BLACK HOLE FROM ANOTHER WORLD!
THE ASTRAL WORLD AND OUR WORLD FLOAT IN AN *OCEAN* OF OTHERWORLDS. THE BLACK HOLE WILL PULL THEM IN SO THEY CRASH!
VWOOOO

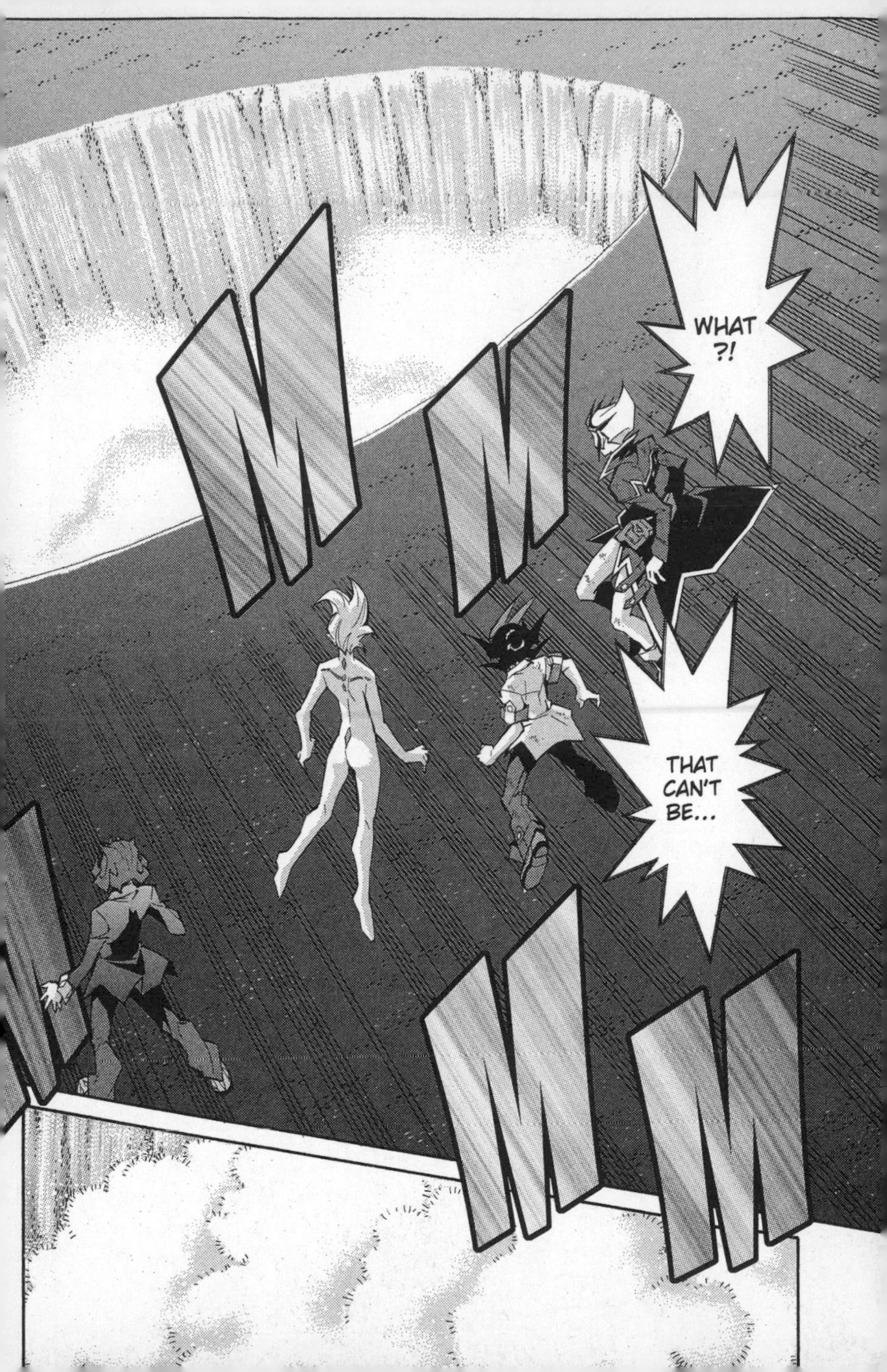
WHAT ?!
MM
THAT CAN'T BE...
MM

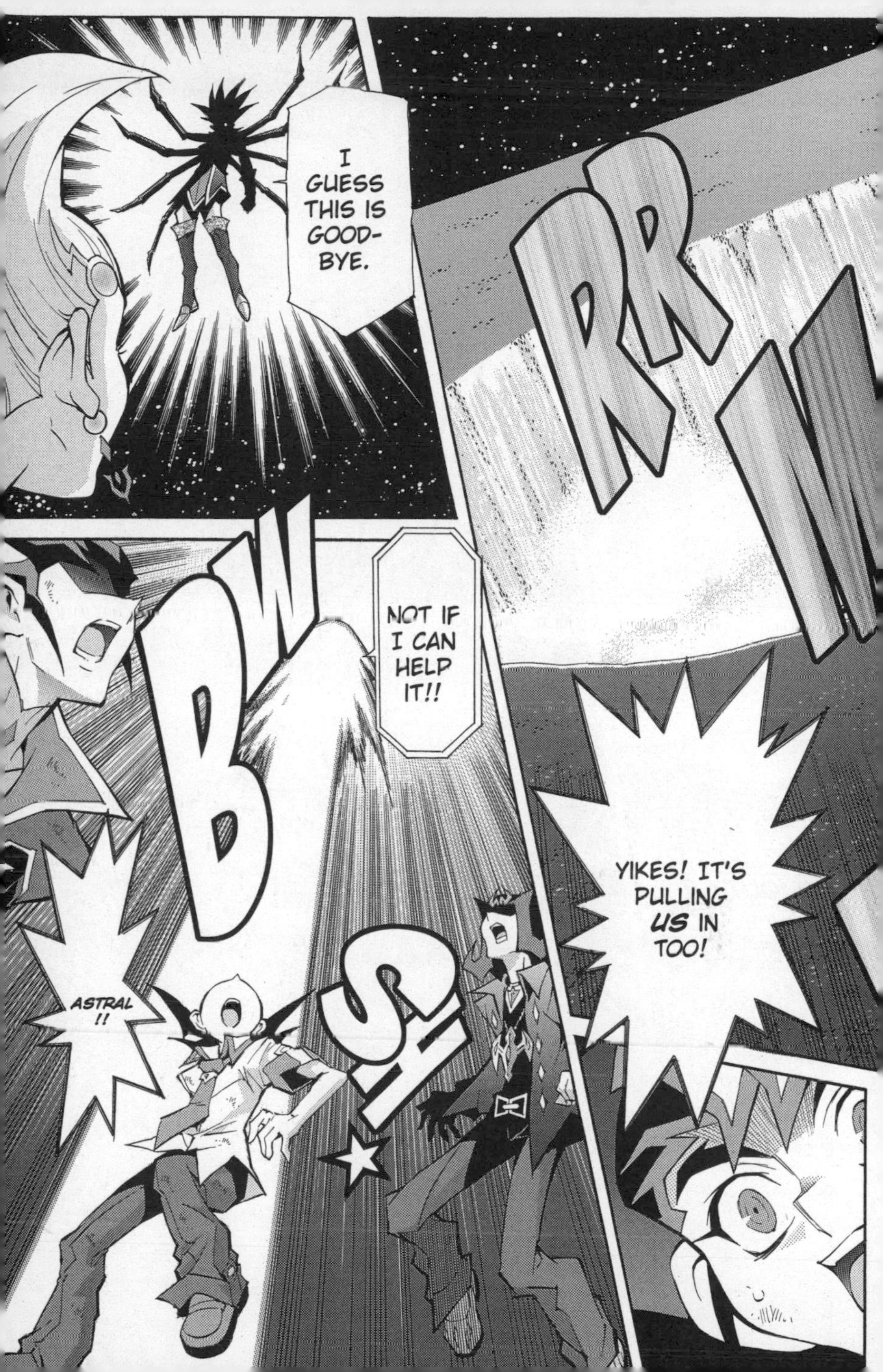
RRW
I GUESS THIS IS GOOD-BYE.
YIKES! IT'S PULLING US IN TOO!
NOT IF I CAN HELP IT!!
BWSH
ASTRAL !!

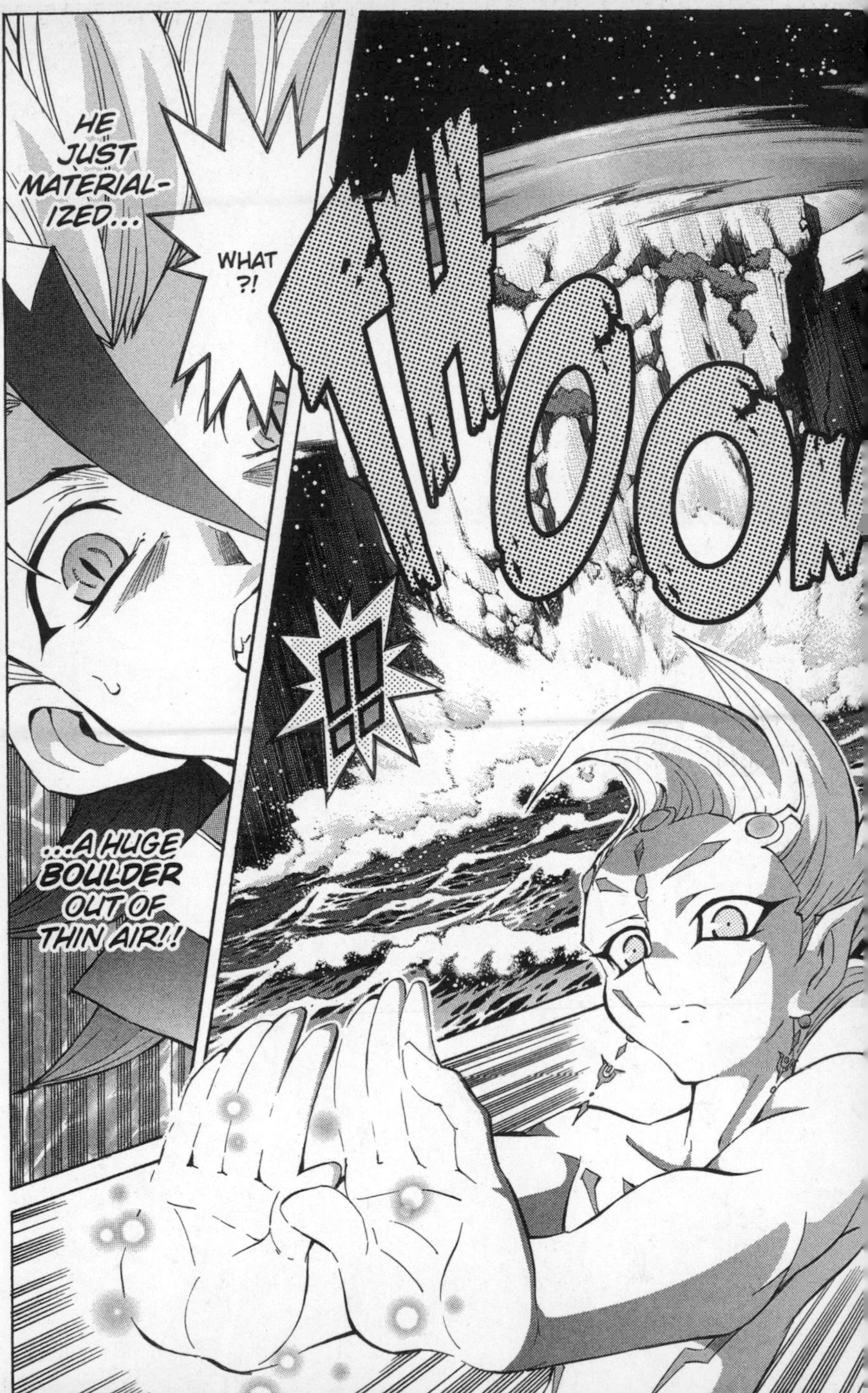
THOOM
!!
WHAT ?!
HE JUST MATERIAL-IZED...
...A HUGE BOULDER OUT OF THIN AIR!!

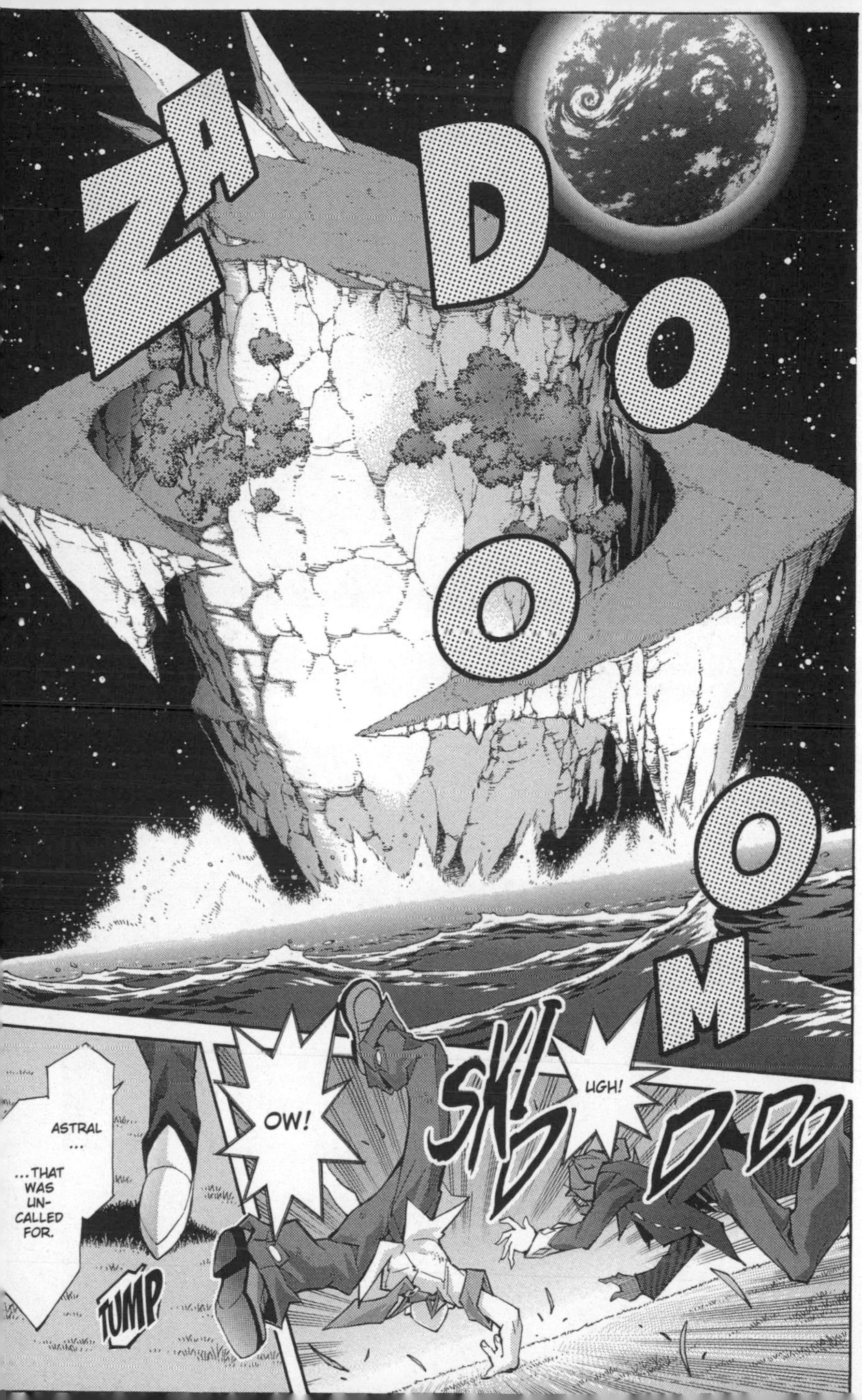
ZADOOOOM
UGH!
SKIDDDO
OW!
ASTRAL...
...THAT WAS UNCALLED FOR.
TUMP

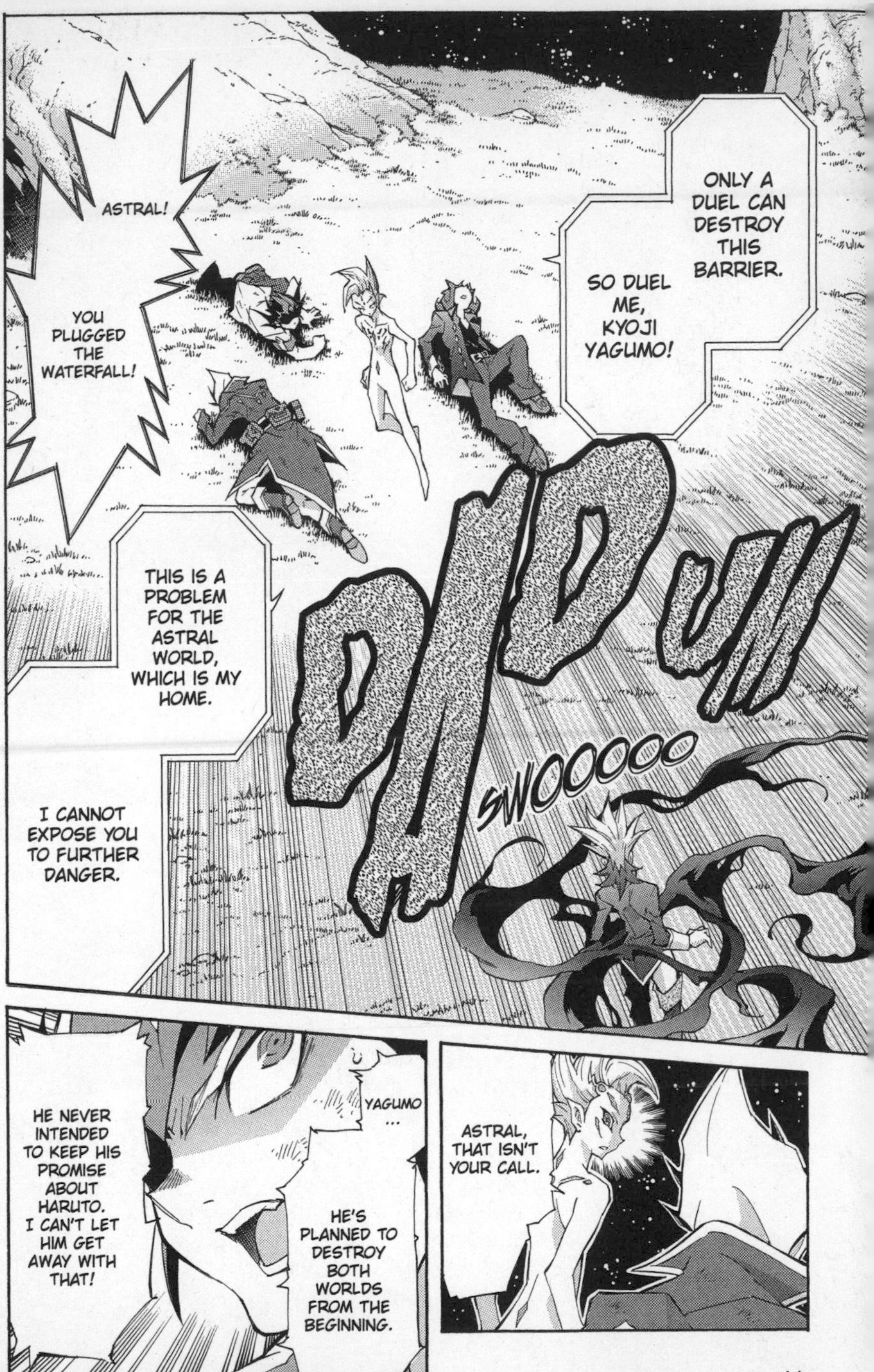
ONLY A DUEL CAN DESTROY THIS BARRIER.
SO DUEL ME, KYOJI YAGUMO!
ASTRAL!
YOU PLUGGED THE WATERFALL!
THIS IS A PROBLEM FOR THE ASTRAL WORLD, WHICH IS MY HOME.
SWOOOOOO
I CANNOT EXPOSE YOU TO FURTHER DANGER.
ASTRAL, THAT ISN'T YOUR CALL.
YAGUMO...
HE'S PLANNED TO DESTROY BOTH WORLDS FROM THE BEGINNING.
HE NEVER INTENDED TO KEEP HIS PROMISE ABOUT HARUTO. I CAN'T LET HIM GET AWAY WITH THAT!

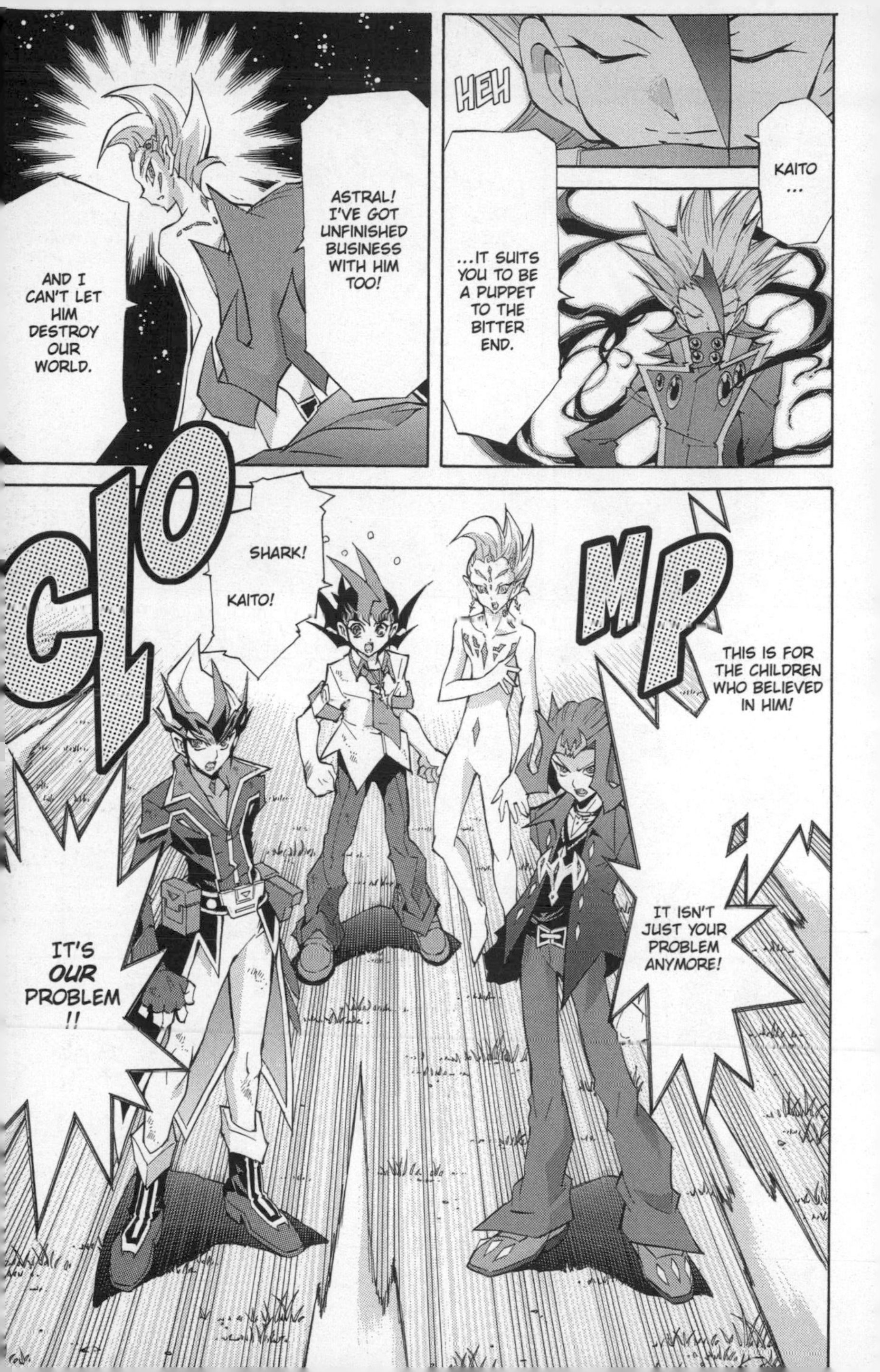
HEH
KAITO ...
...IT SUITS YOU TO BE A PUPPET TO THE BITTER END.
ASTRAL! I'VE GOT UNFINISHED BUSINESS WITH HIM TOO!
AND I CAN'T LET HIM DESTROY OUR WORLD.
CLOMP
SHARK!
KAITO!
THIS IS FOR THE CHILDREN WHO BELIEVED IN HIM!
IT ISN'T JUST YOUR PROBLEM ANYMORE!
IT'S *OUR* PROBLEM !!

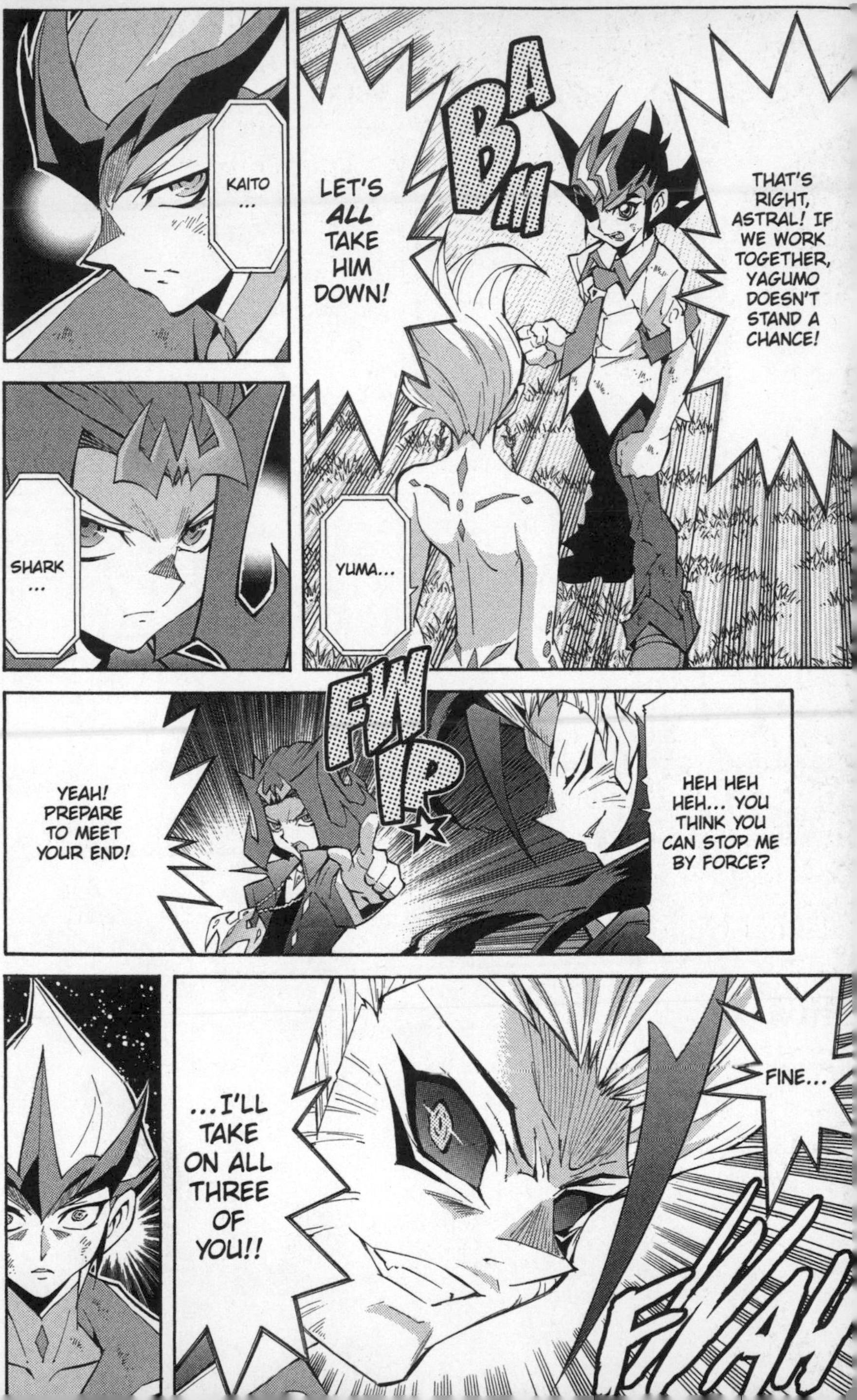
THAT'S RIGHT, ASTRAL! IF WE WORK TOGETHER, YAGUMO DOESN'T STAND A CHANCE!
BAM
LET'S ALL TAKE HIM DOWN!
YUMA...
KAITO ...
SHARK ...
HEH HEH HEH... YOU THINK YOU CAN STOP ME BY FORCE?
FWIP
YEAH! PREPARE TO MEET YOUR END!
FINE...
...I'LL TAKE ON ALL THREE OF YOU!!
FLAH

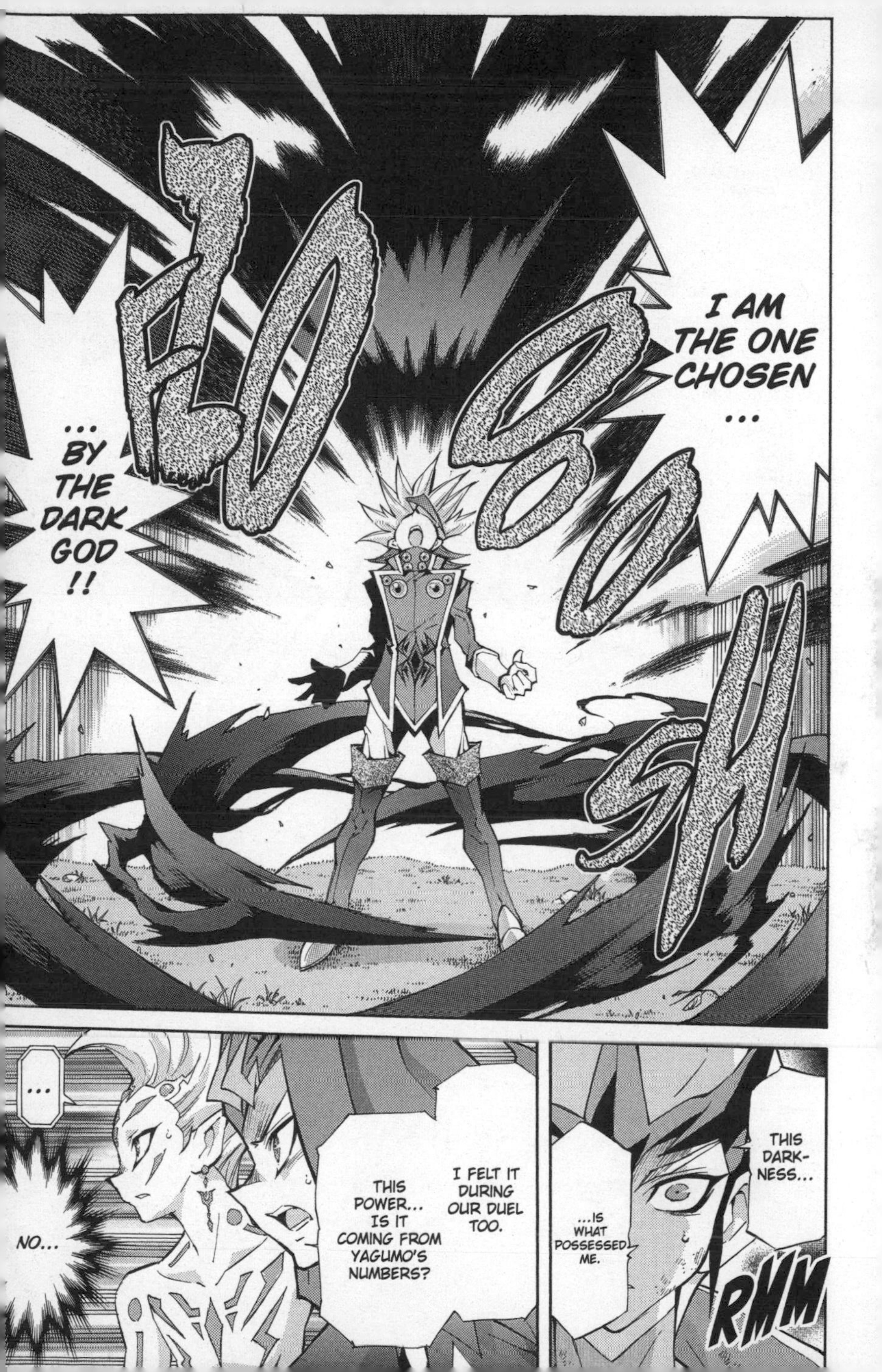
I AM THE ONE CHOSEN ...
FLOOOOSH
... BY THE DARK GOD !!
THIS DARK-NESS...
...IS WHAT POSSESSED ME.
RMM
I FELT IT DURING OUR DUEL TOO.
THIS POWER... IS IT COMING FROM YAGUMO'S NUMBERS?
...
NO...

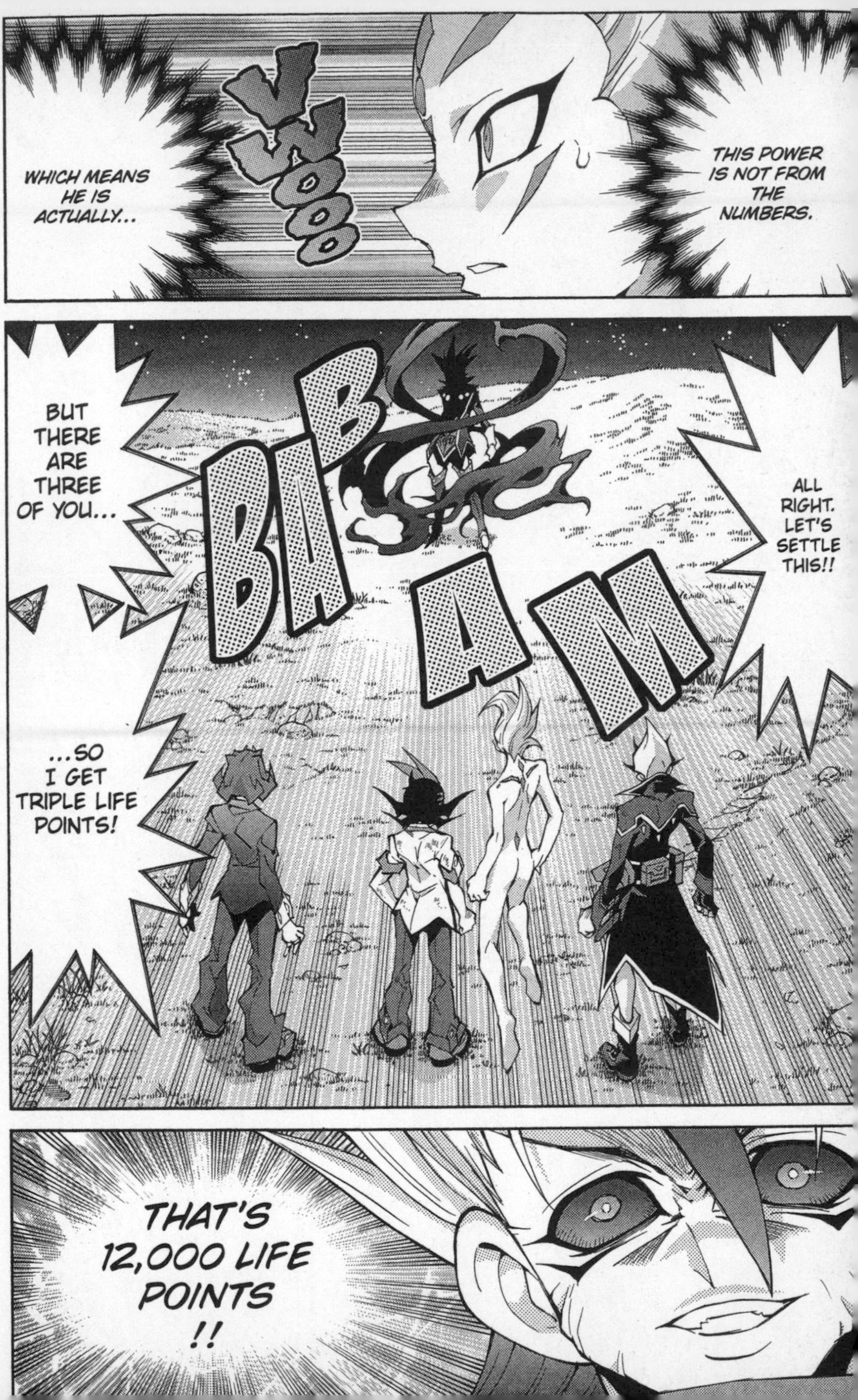
THIS POWER IS NOT FROM THE NUMBERS.
VWOOO
WHICH MEANS HE IS ACTUALLY...
ALL RIGHT. LET'S SETTLE THIS!!
BABAM
BUT THERE ARE THREE OF YOU...
...SO I GET TRIPLE LIFE POINTS!
THAT'S 12,000 LIFE POINTS !!

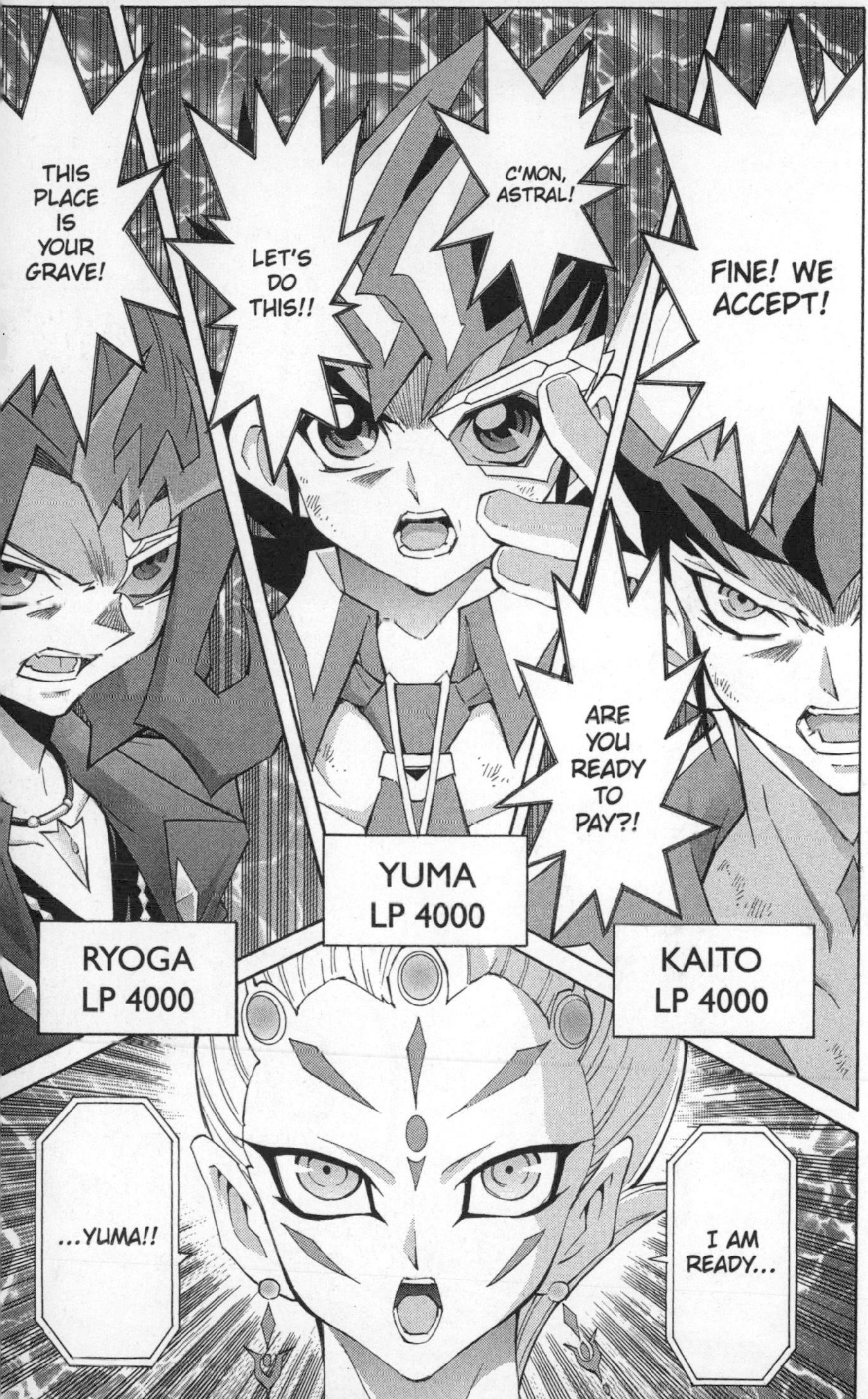

FINE! WE ACCEPT!
C'MON, ASTRAL!
LET'S DO THIS!!
THIS PLACE IS YOUR GRAVE!
ARE YOU READY TO PAY?!
KAITO LP 4000
YUMA LP 4000
RYOGA LP 4000
I AM READY...
...YUMA!!

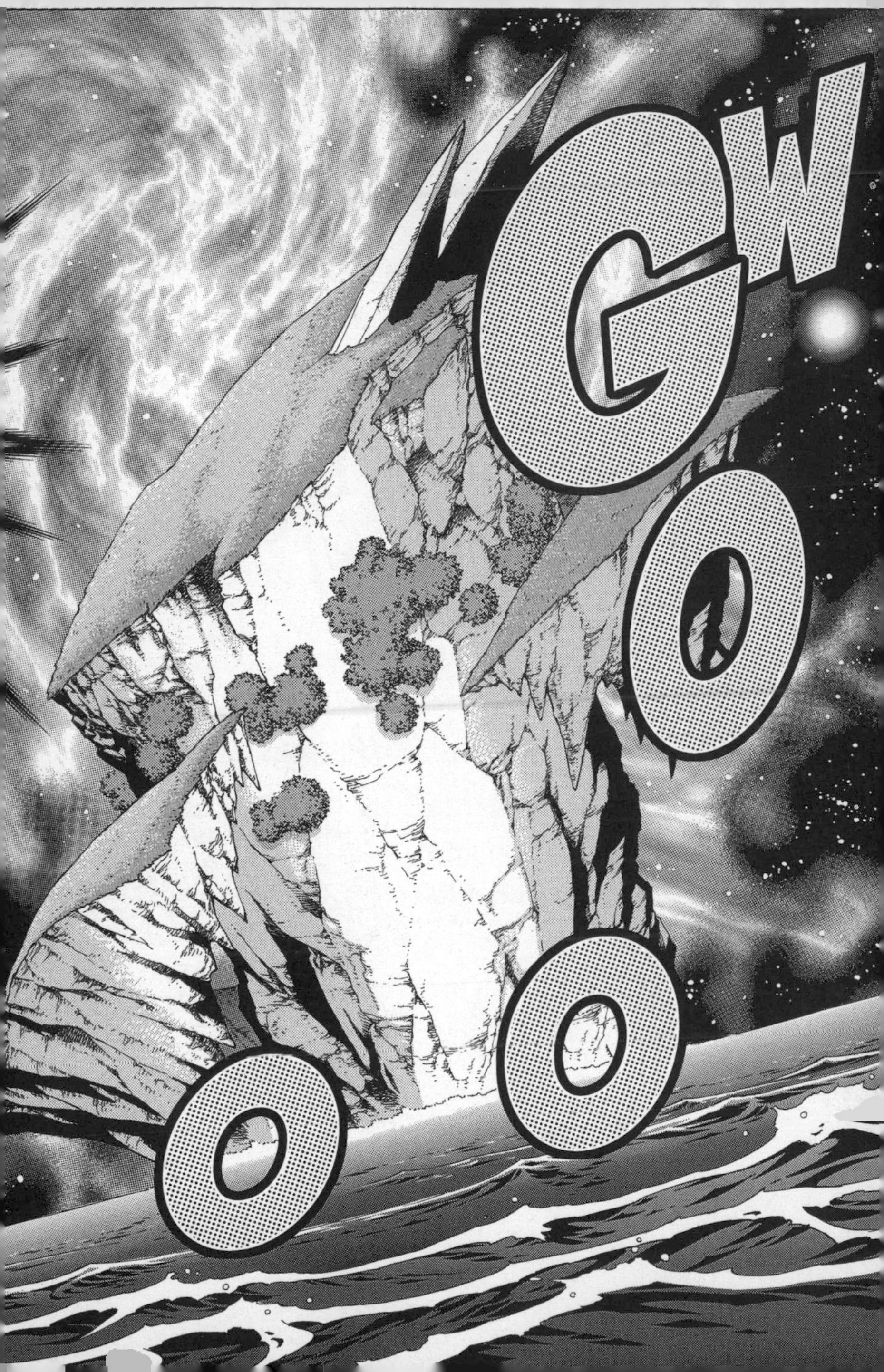
GWOOOO

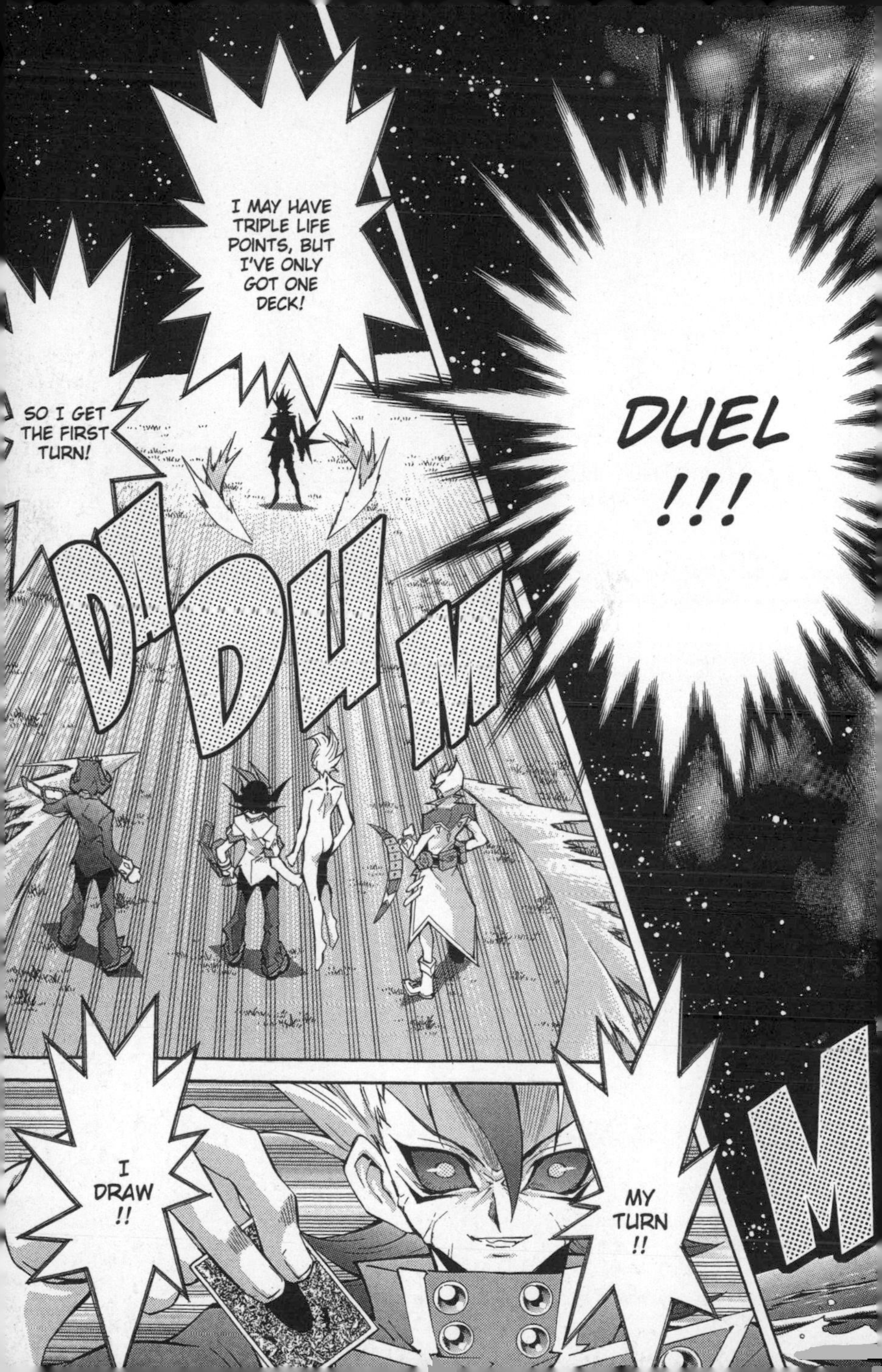
DUEL !!!
I MAY HAVE TRIPLE LIFE POINTS, BUT I'VE ONLY GOT ONE DECK!
SO I GET THE FIRST TURN!
DADUMM
MY TURN !!
I DRAW !!

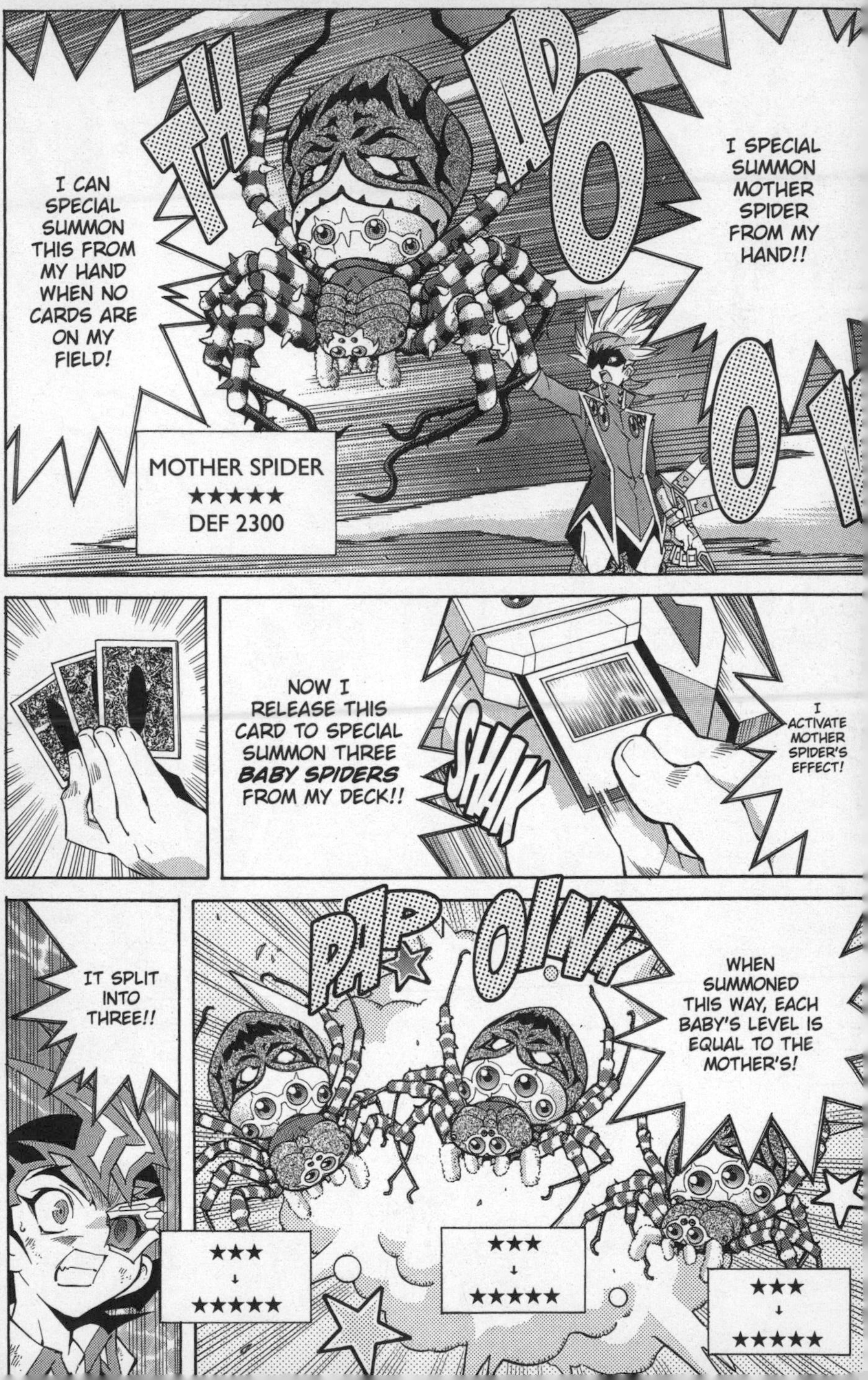
I SPECIAL SUMMON MOTHER SPIDER FROM MY HAND!!
I CAN SPECIAL SUMMON THIS FROM MY HAND WHEN NO CARDS ARE ON MY FIELD!
MOTHER SPIDER
★★★★★
DEF 2300
I ACTIVATE MOTHER SPIDER'S EFFECT!
SHAK
NOW I RELEASE THIS CARD TO SPECIAL SUMMON THREE *BABY SPIDERS* FROM MY DECK!!
WHEN SUMMONED THIS WAY, EACH BABY'S LEVEL IS EQUAL TO THE MOTHER'S!
★★★
↓
★★★★★
★★★
↓
★★★★★
★★★
↓
★★★★★
IT SPLIT INTO THREE!!

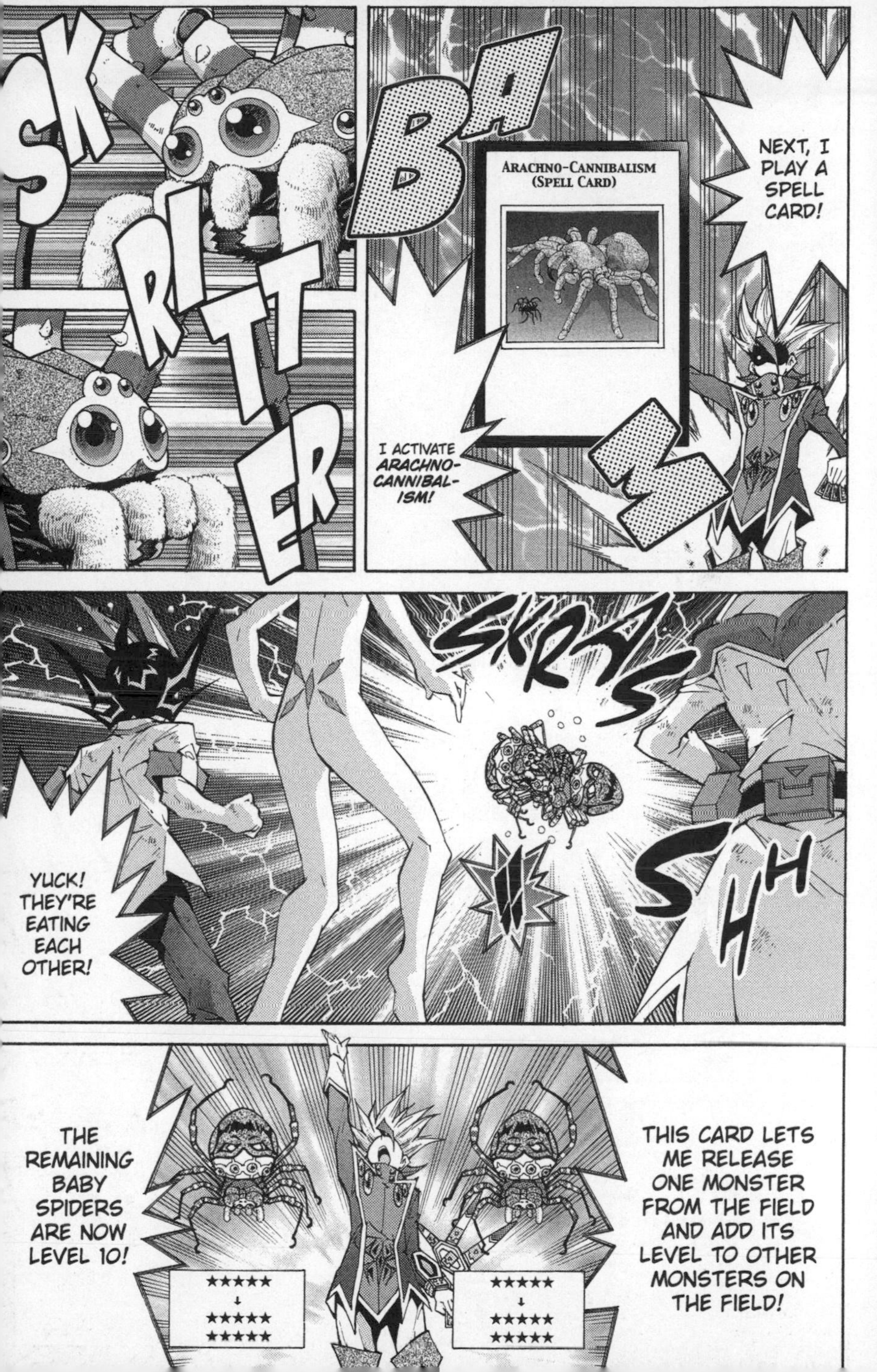
NEXT, I PLAY A SPELL CARD!
BAM
ARACHNO-CANNIBALISM
(SPELL CARD)
I ACTIVATE ARACHNO-CANNIBALISM!
SKRITTER
SKRASH
SHH
!!
YUCK! THEY'RE EATING EACH OTHER!
THIS CARD LETS ME RELEASE ONE MONSTER FROM THE FIELD AND ADD ITS LEVEL TO OTHER MONSTERS ON THE FIELD!
THE REMAINING BABY SPIDERS ARE NOW LEVEL 10!
★★★★★
↓
★★★★★
★★★★★
★★★★★
↓
★★★★★
★★★★★

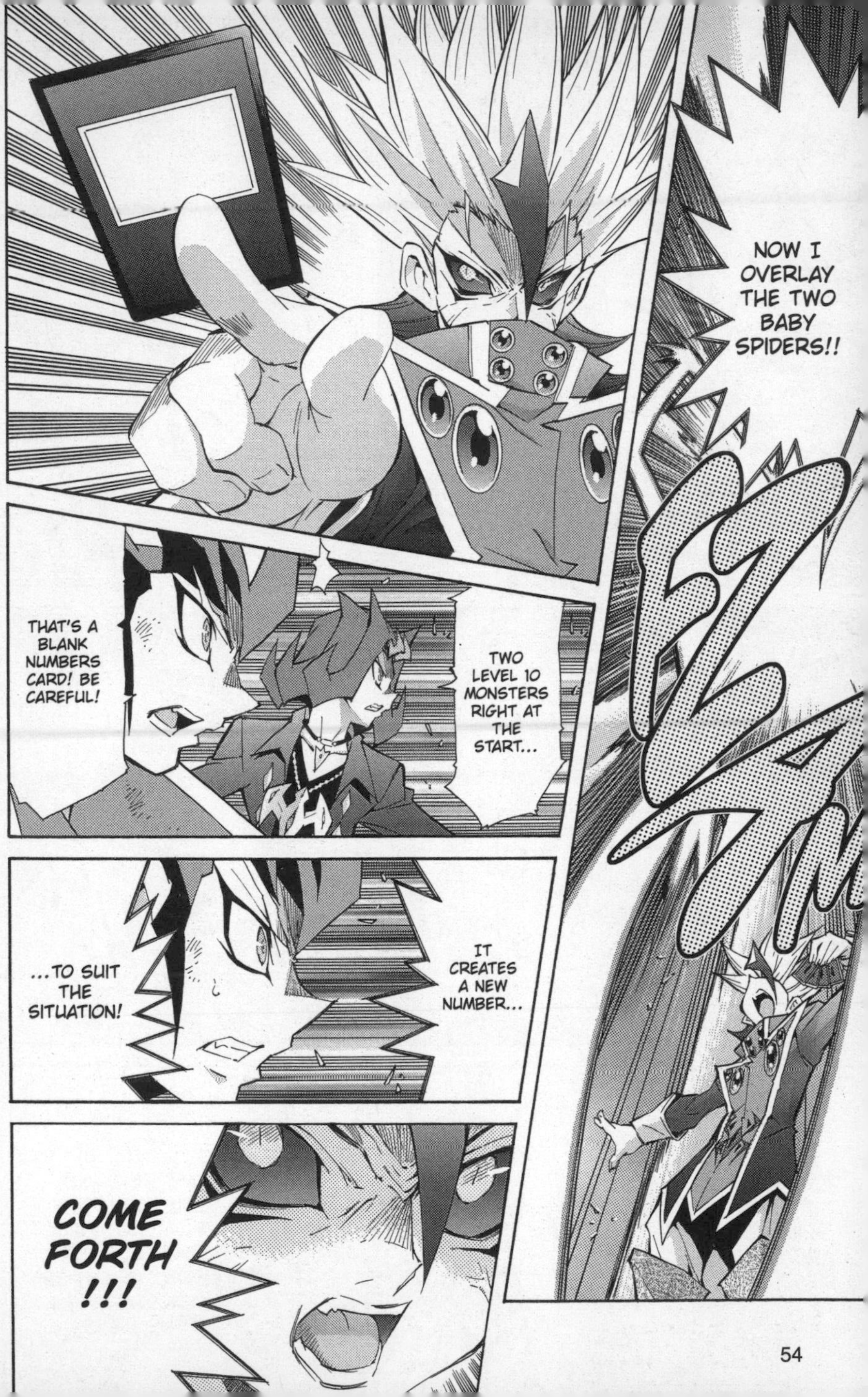
NOW I OVERLAY THE TWO BABY SPIDERS!!
TWO LEVEL 10 MONSTERS RIGHT AT THE START...
THAT'S A BLANK NUMBERS CARD! BE CAREFUL!
IT CREATES A NEW NUMBER...
...TO SUIT THE SITUATION!
COME FORTH !!!

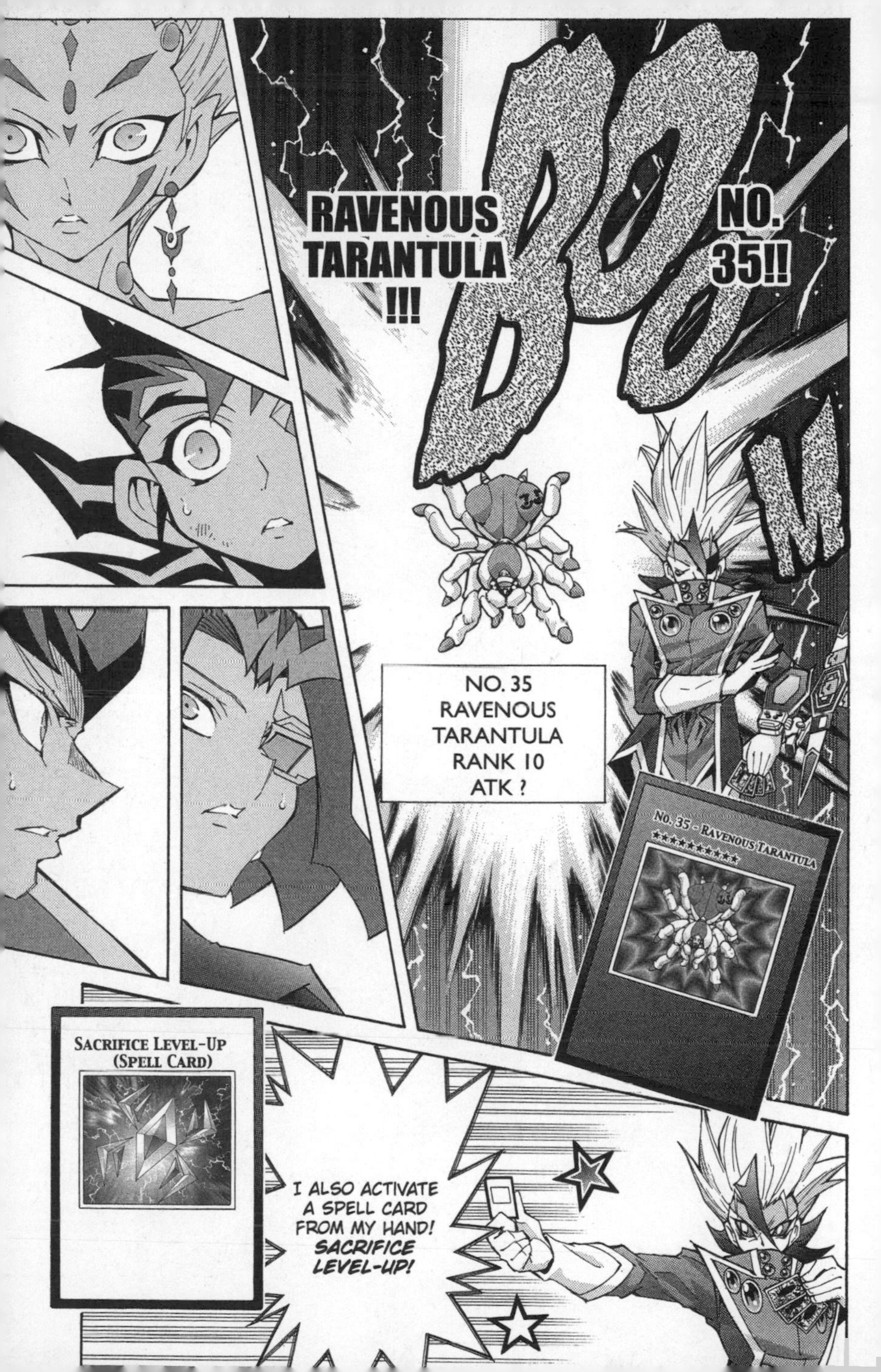
NO. 35!!
BOOM
RAVENOUS TARANTULA !!!
NO. 35 RAVENOUS TARANTULA RANK 10 ATK ?
No. 35 - Ravenous Tarantula
I ALSO ACTIVATE A SPELL CARD FROM MY HAND! SACRIFICE LEVEL-UP!
Sacrifice Level-Up (Spell Card)

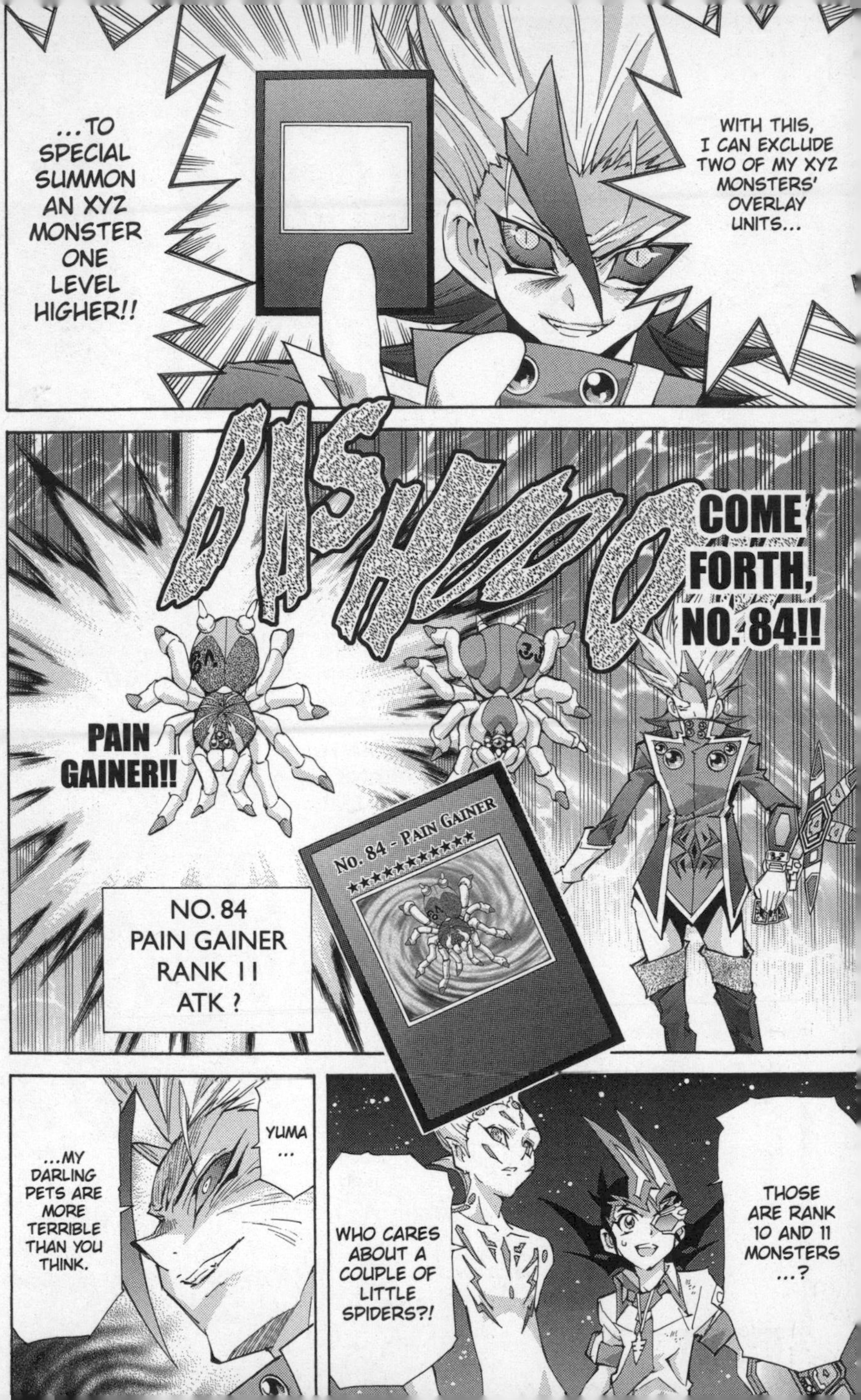
WITH THIS, I CAN EXCLUDE TWO OF MY XYZ MONSTERS' OVERLAY UNITS...
...TO SPECIAL SUMMON AN XYZ MONSTER ONE LEVEL HIGHER!!
BASHOOO
COME FORTH, NO. 84!!
PAIN GAINER!!
NO. 84 - PAIN GAINER
NO. 84
PAIN GAINER
RANK 11
ATK ?
THOSE ARE RANK 10 AND 11 MONSTERS ...?
WHO CARES ABOUT A COUPLE OF LITTLE SPIDERS?!
YUMA ...
...MY DARLING PETS ARE MORE TERRIBLE THAN YOU THINK.

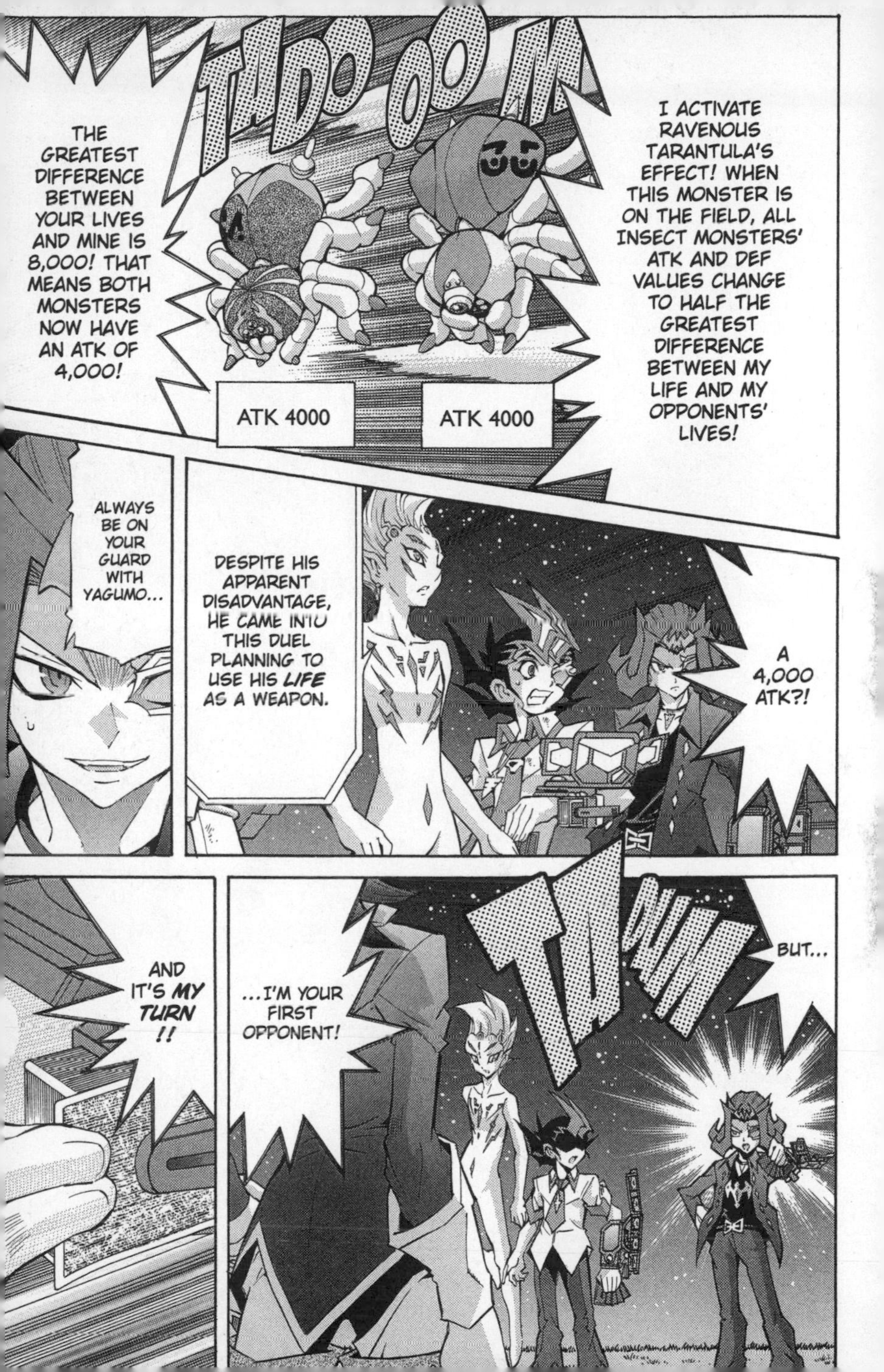
TADOOOOM!
I ACTIVATE RAVENOUS TARANTULA'S EFFECT! WHEN THIS MONSTER IS ON THE FIELD, ALL INSECT MONSTERS' ATK AND DEF VALUES CHANGE TO HALF THE GREATEST DIFFERENCE BETWEEN MY LIFE AND MY OPPONENTS' LIVES!
THE GREATEST DIFFERENCE BETWEEN YOUR LIVES AND MINE IS 8,000! THAT MEANS BOTH MONSTERS NOW HAVE AN ATK OF 4,000!
ATK 4000
ATK 4000
A 4,000 ATK?!
DESPITE HIS APPARENT DISADVANTAGE, HE CAME INTO THIS DUEL PLANNING TO USE HIS *LIFE* AS A WEAPON.
ALWAYS BE ON YOUR GUARD WITH YAGUMO...
BUT...
...I'M YOUR FIRST OPPONENT!
AND IT'S ***MY TURN*** !!

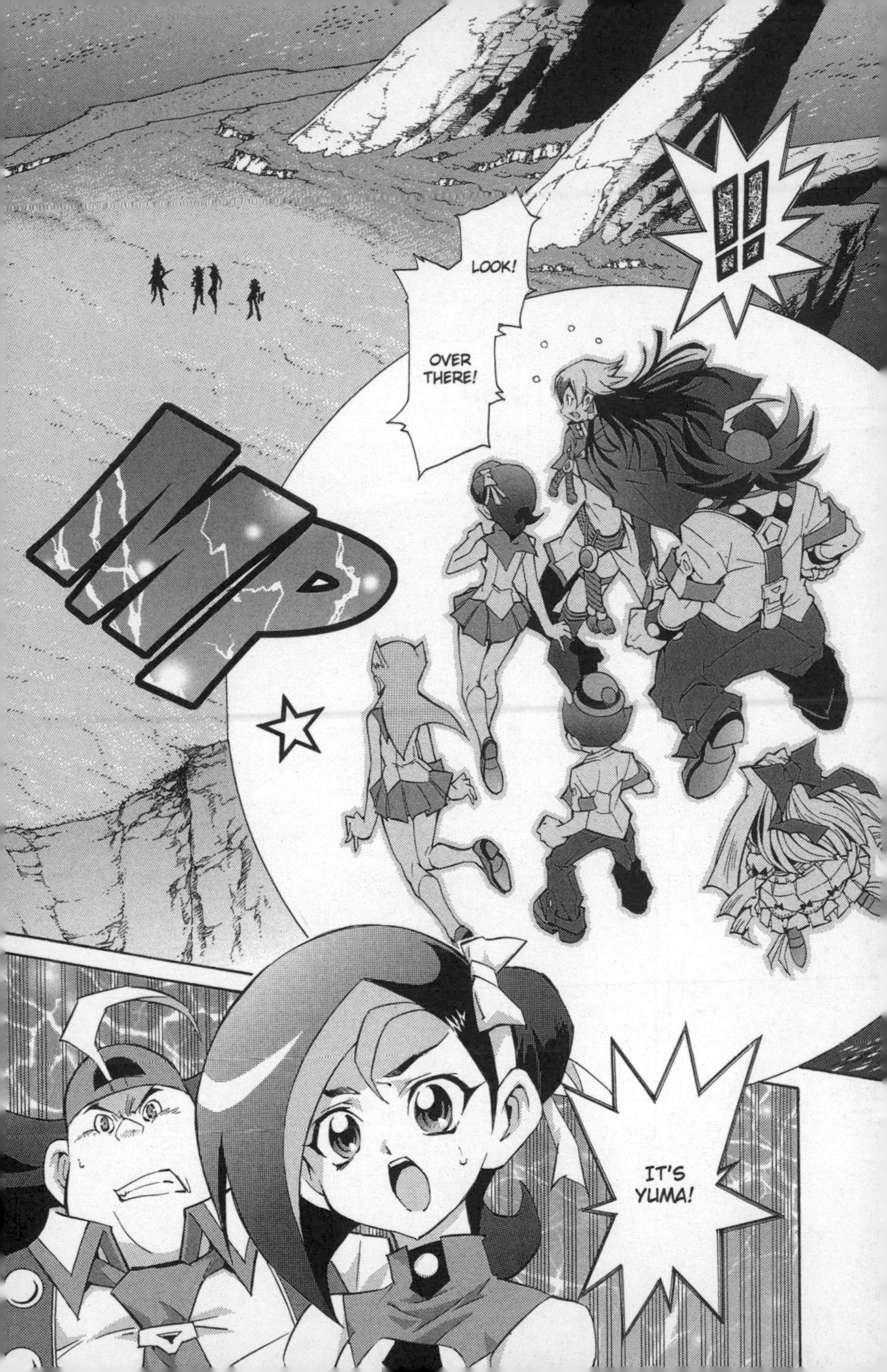
!!
LOOK! OVER THERE!
IT'S YUMA!

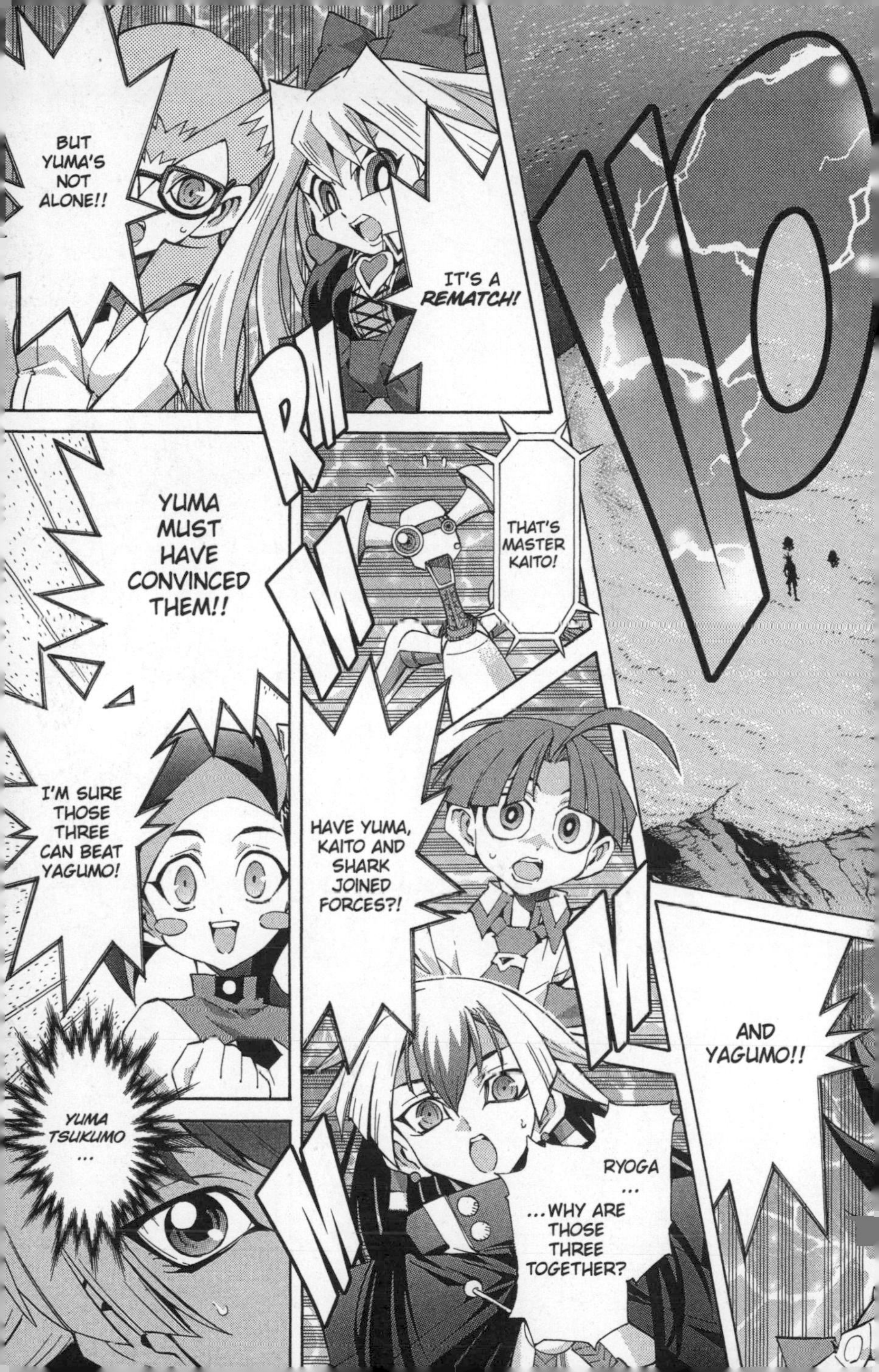
IT'S A *REMATCH!*
BUT YUMA'S NOT ALONE!!
THAT'S MASTER KAITO!
YUMA MUST HAVE CONVINCED THEM!!
HAVE YUMA, KAITO AND SHARK JOINED FORCES?!
I'M SURE THOSE THREE CAN BEAT YAGUMO!
AND YAGUMO!!
RYOGA ...
...WHY ARE THOSE THREE TOGETHER?
YUMA TSUKUMO ...

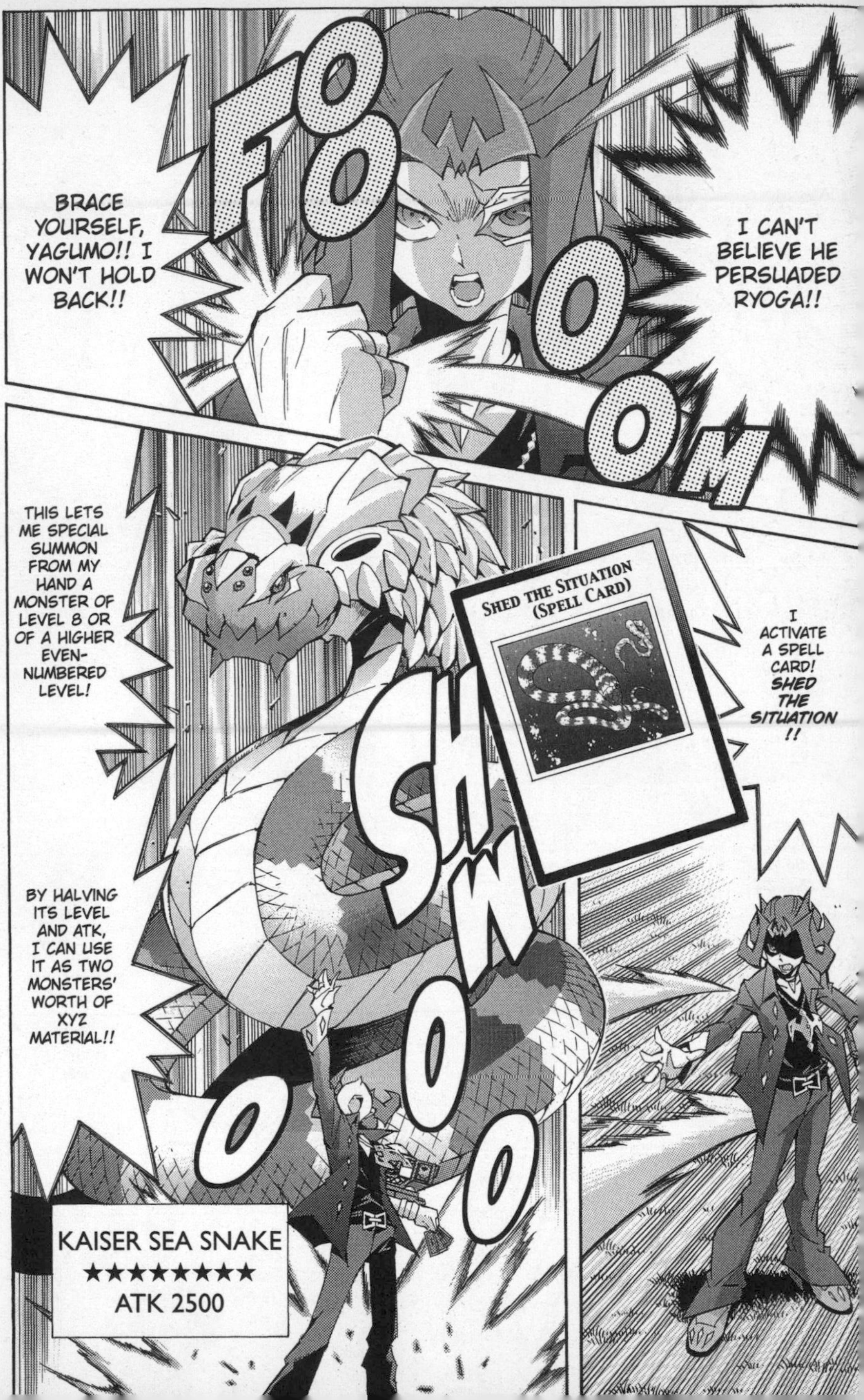

I CAN'T BELIEVE HE PERSUADED RYOGA!!
FOOOOOOM
BRACE YOURSELF, YAGUMO!! I WON'T HOLD BACK!!
I ACTIVATE A SPELL CARD! SHED THE SITUATION!!
SHED THE SITUATION (SPELL CARD)
SHWOOOOO
THIS LETS ME SPECIAL SUMMON FROM MY HAND A MONSTER OF LEVEL 8 OR OF A HIGHER EVEN-NUMBERED LEVEL!
BY HALVING ITS LEVEL AND ATK, I CAN USE IT AS TWO MONSTERS' WORTH OF XYZ MATERIAL!!
KAISER SEA SNAKE
★★★★★★★★
ATK 2500

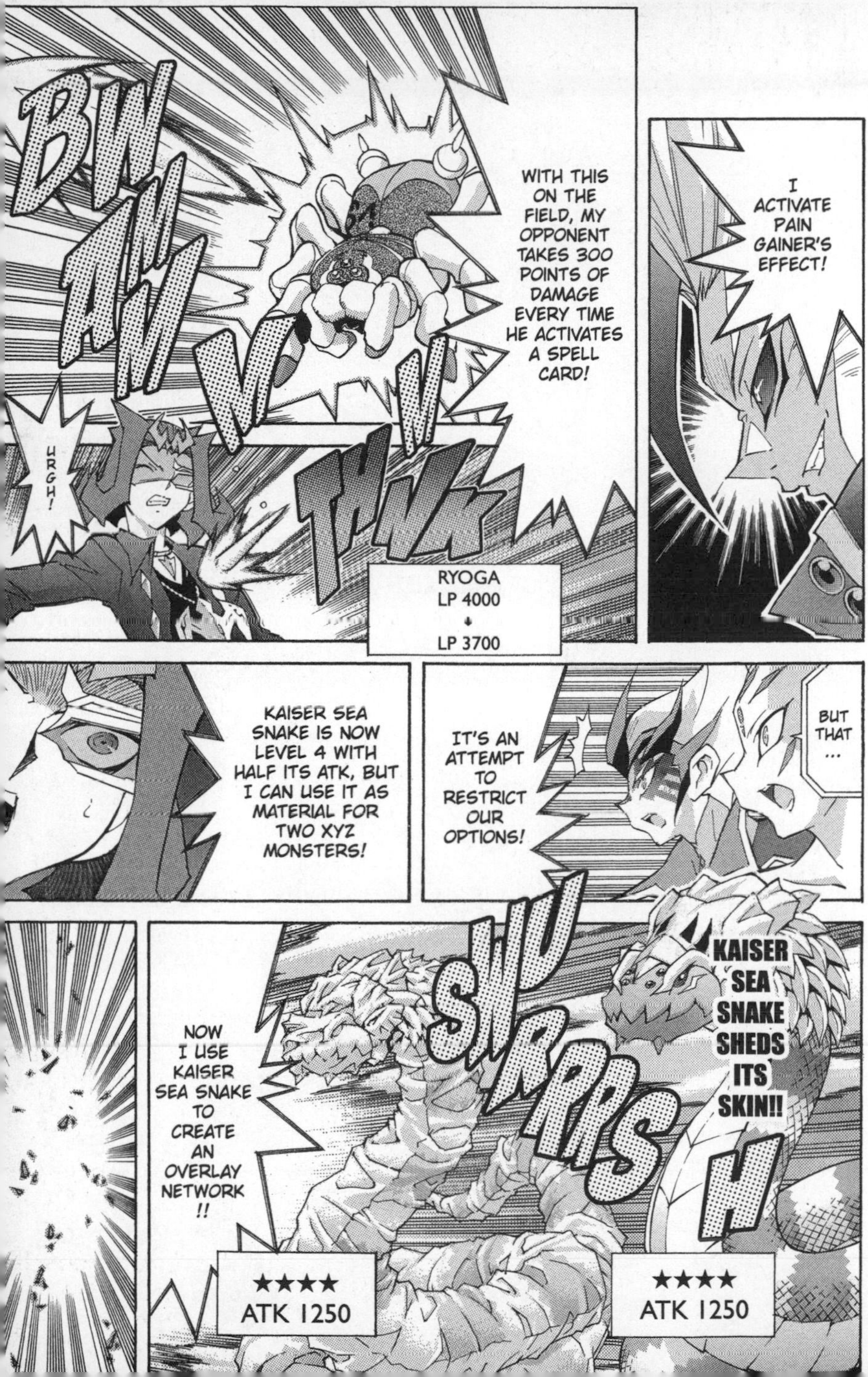
I ACTIVATE PAIN GAINER'S EFFECT!
WITH THIS ON THE FIELD, MY OPPONENT TAKES 300 POINTS OF DAMAGE EVERY TIME HE ACTIVATES A SPELL CARD!
URGH!
RYOGA LP 4000 ↓ LP 3700
BUT THAT ...
IT'S AN ATTEMPT TO RESTRICT OUR OPTIONS!
KAISER SEA SNAKE IS NOW LEVEL 4 WITH HALF ITS ATK, BUT I CAN USE IT AS MATERIAL FOR TWO XYZ MONSTERS!
KAISER SEA SNAKE SHEDS ITS SKIN!!
★★★★ ATK 1250
NOW I USE KAISER SEA SNAKE TO CREATE AN OVERLAY NETWORK !!
★★★★ ATK 1250

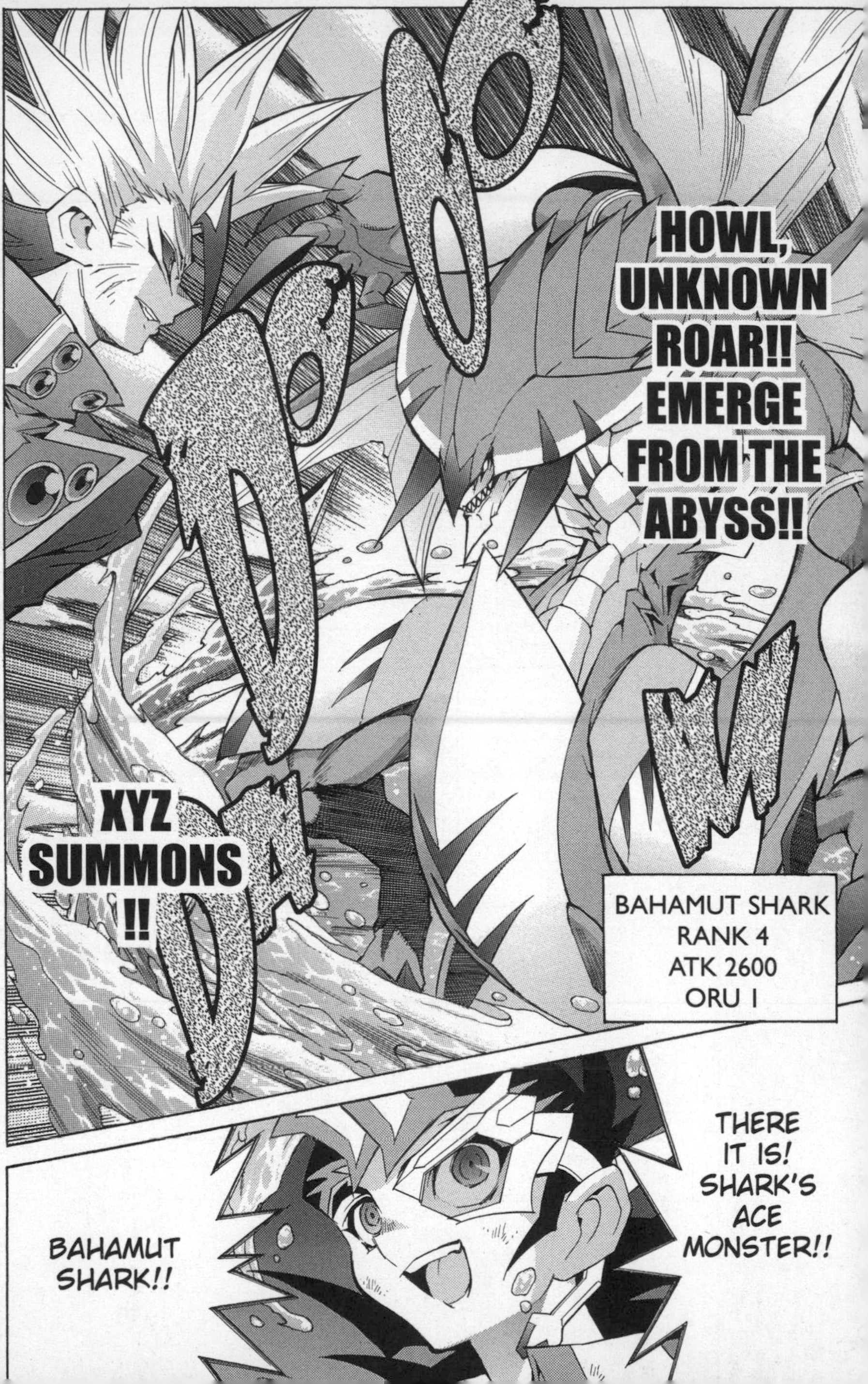
HOWL, UNKNOWN ROAR!! EMERGE FROM THE ABYSS!!
XYZ SUMMONS!!
BAHAMUT SHARK
RANK 4
ATK 2600
ORU 1
THERE IT IS! SHARK'S ACE MONSTER!!
BAHAMUT SHARK!!

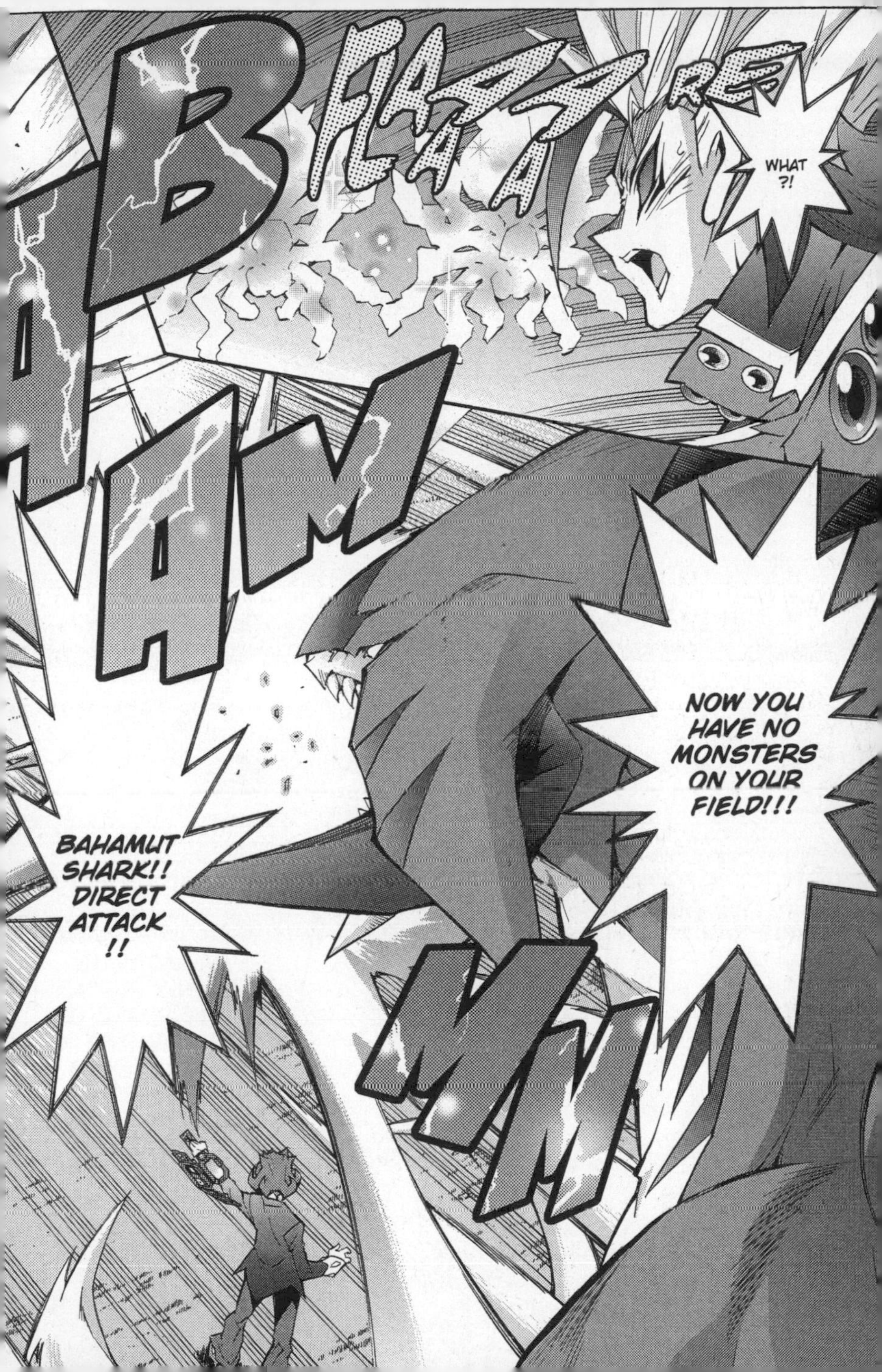
WHAT ?!
NOW YOU HAVE NO MONSTERS ON YOUR FIELD!!!
BAHAMUT SHARK!! DIRECT ATTACK !!

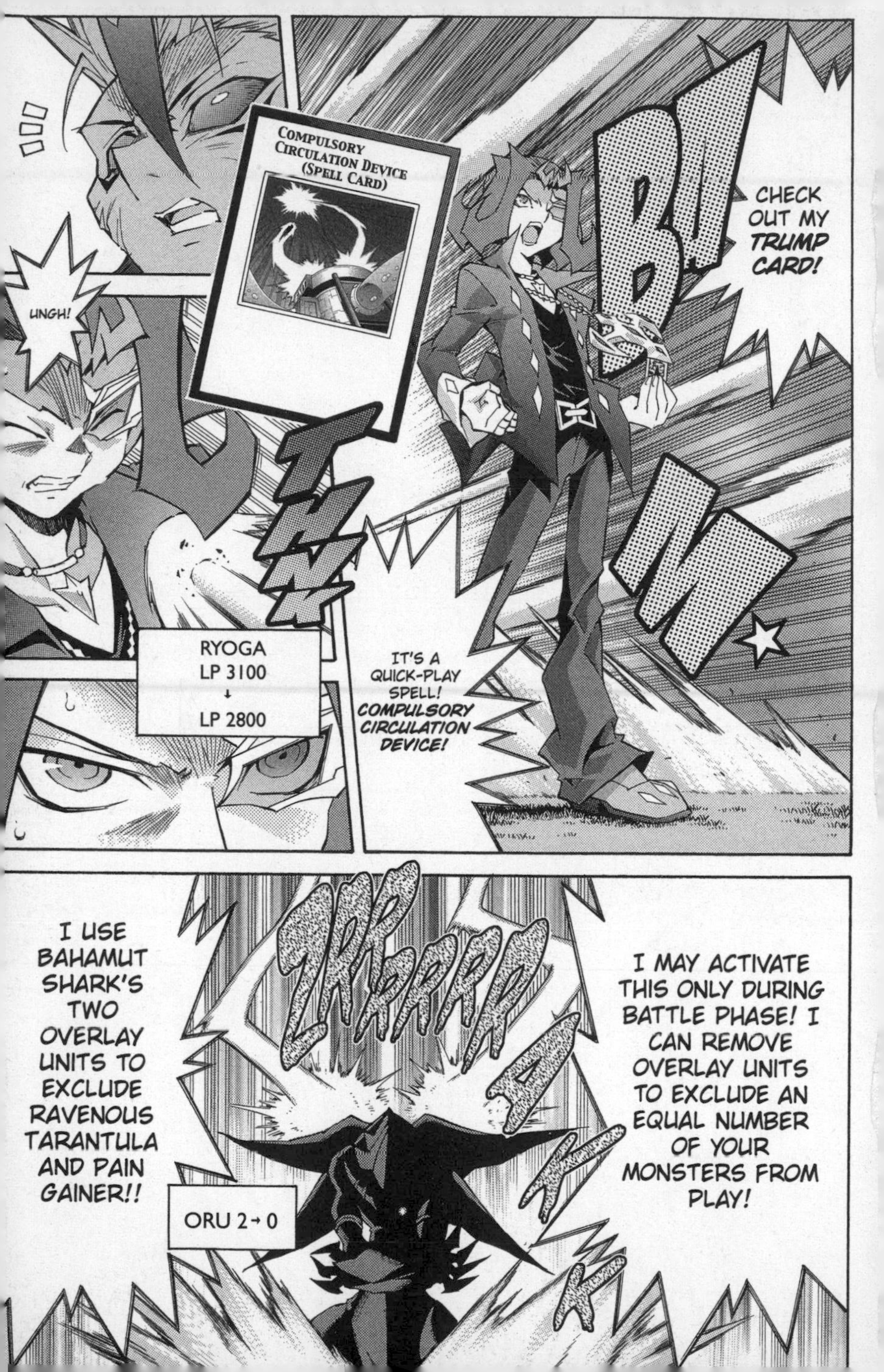
CHECK OUT MY TRUMP CARD!
COMPULSORY CIRCULATION DEVICE (SPELL CARD)
IT'S A QUICK-PLAY SPELL! COMPULSORY CIRCULATION DEVICE!
UNGH!
RYOGA LP 3100 ↓ LP 2800
I MAY ACTIVATE THIS ONLY DURING BATTLE PHASE! I CAN REMOVE OVERLAY UNITS TO EXCLUDE AN EQUAL NUMBER OF YOUR MONSTERS FROM PLAY!
I USE BAHAMUT SHARK'S TWO OVERLAY UNITS TO EXCLUDE RAVENOUS TARANTULA AND PAIN GAINER!!
ORU 2→0

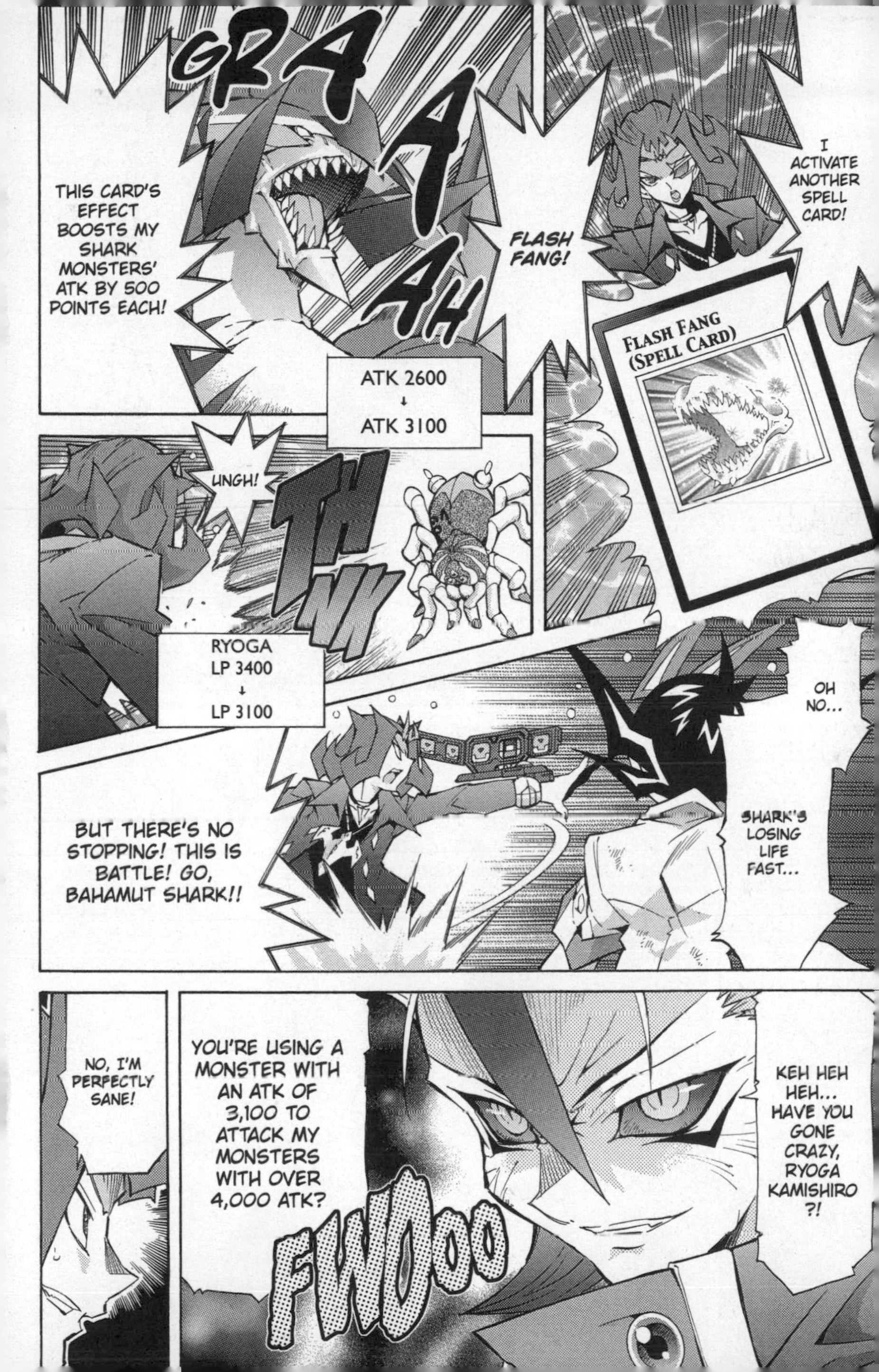
I ACTIVATE ANOTHER SPELL CARD!
FLASH FANG!
FLASH FANG (SPELL CARD)
GRAAAAH
THIS CARD'S EFFECT BOOSTS MY SHARK MONSTERS' ATK BY 500 POINTS EACH!
ATK 2600 ↓ ATK 3100
UNGH!
RYOGA LP 3400 ↓ LP 3100
OH NO...
SHARK'S LOSING LIFE FAST...
BUT THERE'S NO STOPPING! THIS IS BATTLE! GO, BAHAMUT SHARK!!
KEH HEH HEH... HAVE YOU GONE CRAZY, RYOGA KAMISHIRO?!
YOU'RE USING A MONSTER WITH AN ATK OF 3,100 TO ATTACK MY MONSTERS WITH OVER 4,000 ATK?
FWOOO
NO, I'M PERFECTLY SANE!

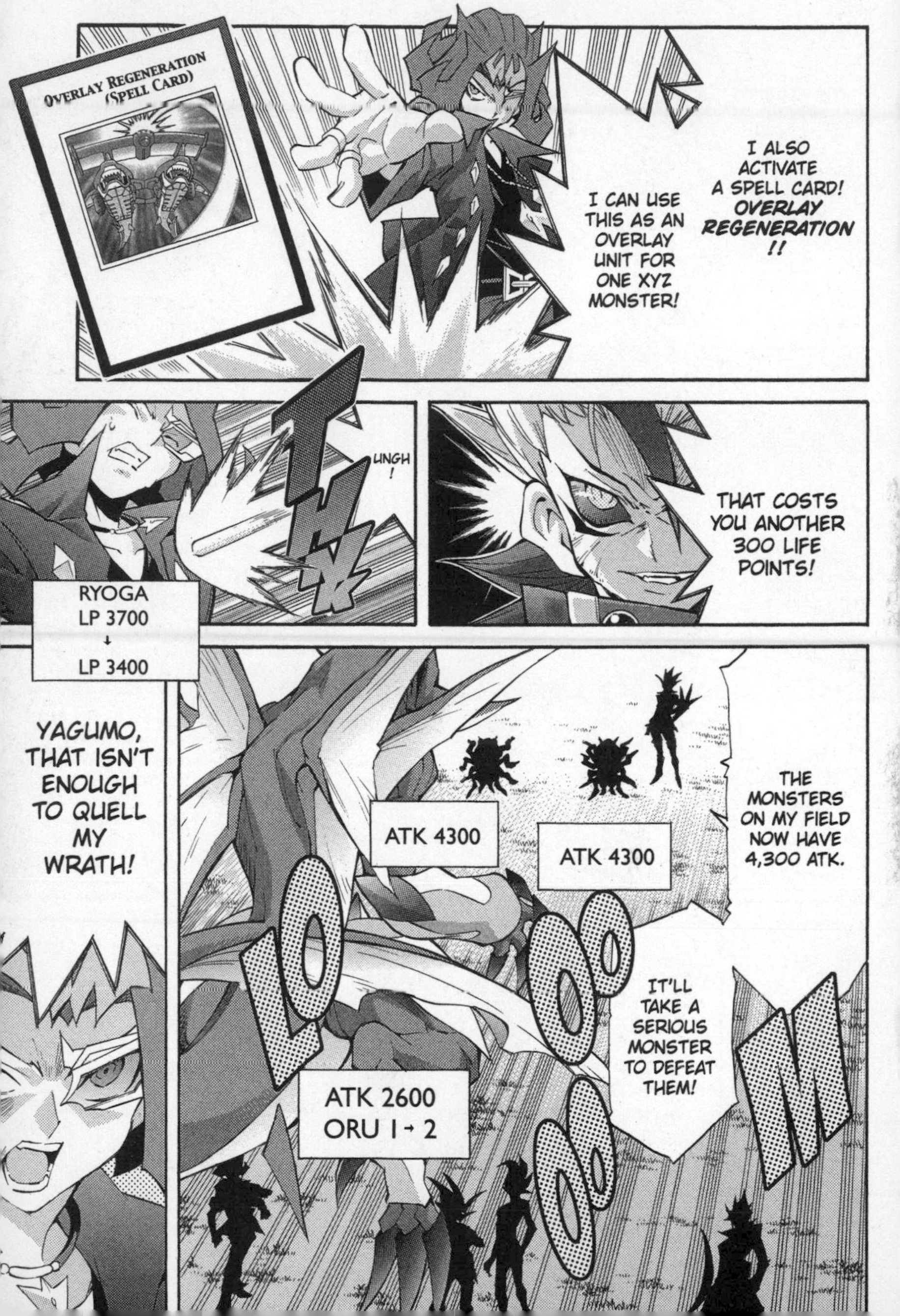
I ALSO ACTIVATE A SPELL CARD! OVERLAY REGENERATION!!
I CAN USE THIS AS AN OVERLAY UNIT FOR ONE XYZ MONSTER!
OVERLAY REGENERATION (SPELL CARD)
THAT COSTS YOU ANOTHER 300 LIFE POINTS!
UNGH!
THNK
RYOGA LP 3700 → LP 3400
THE MONSTERS ON MY FIELD NOW HAVE 4,300 ATK.
ATK 4300
ATK 4300
LOOOOOOM
IT'LL TAKE A SERIOUS MONSTER TO DEFEAT THEM!
ATK 2600 ORU 1 → 2
YAGUMO, THAT ISN'T ENOUGH TO QUELL MY WRATH!

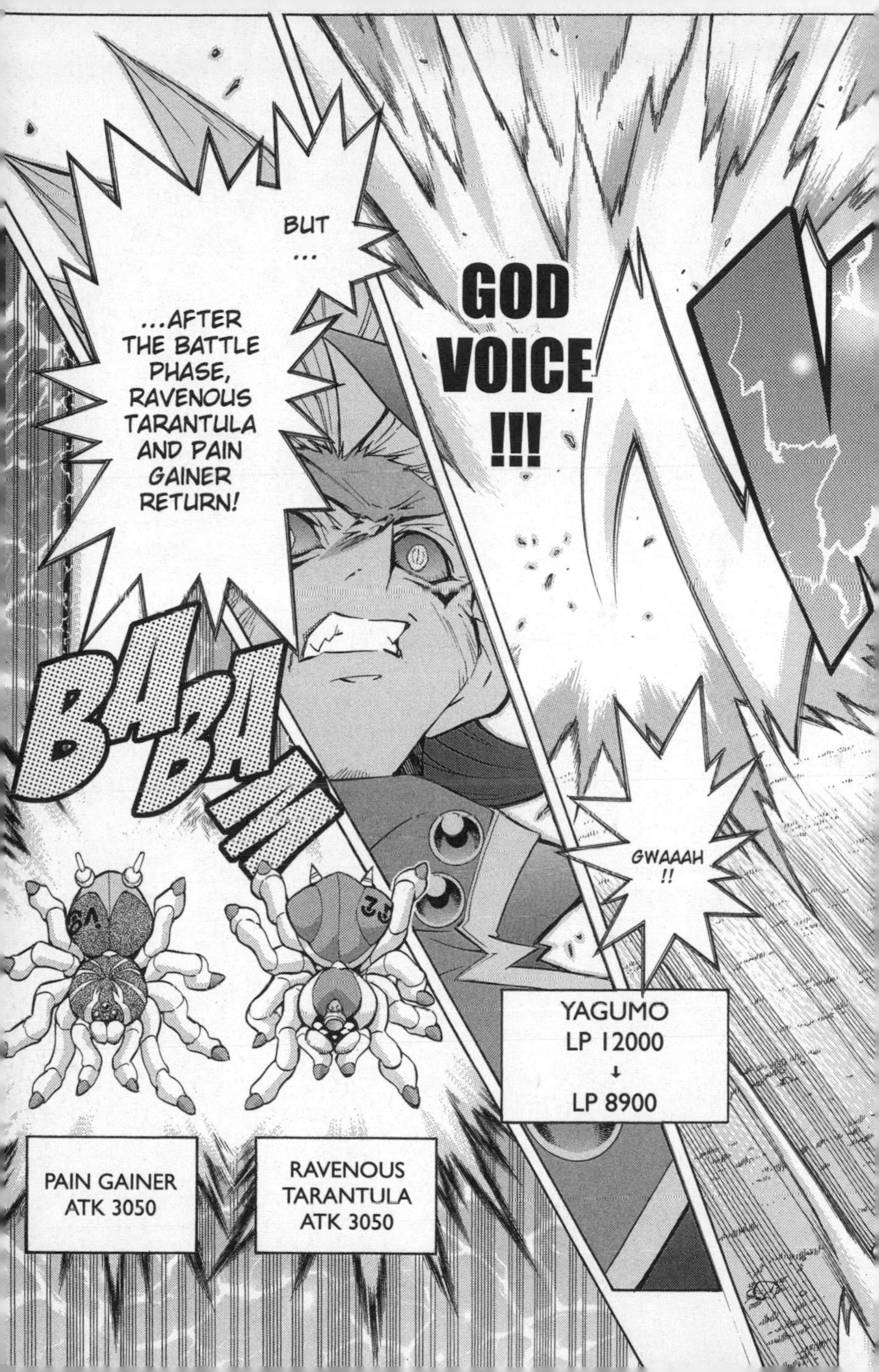
GOD VOICE !!!
BUT ...
...AFTER THE BATTLE PHASE, RAVENOUS TARANTULA AND PAIN GAINER RETURN!
BABAM
GWAAAH !!
YAGUMO LP 12000 ↓ LP 8900
RAVENOUS TARANTULA ATK 3050
PAIN GAINER ATK 3050

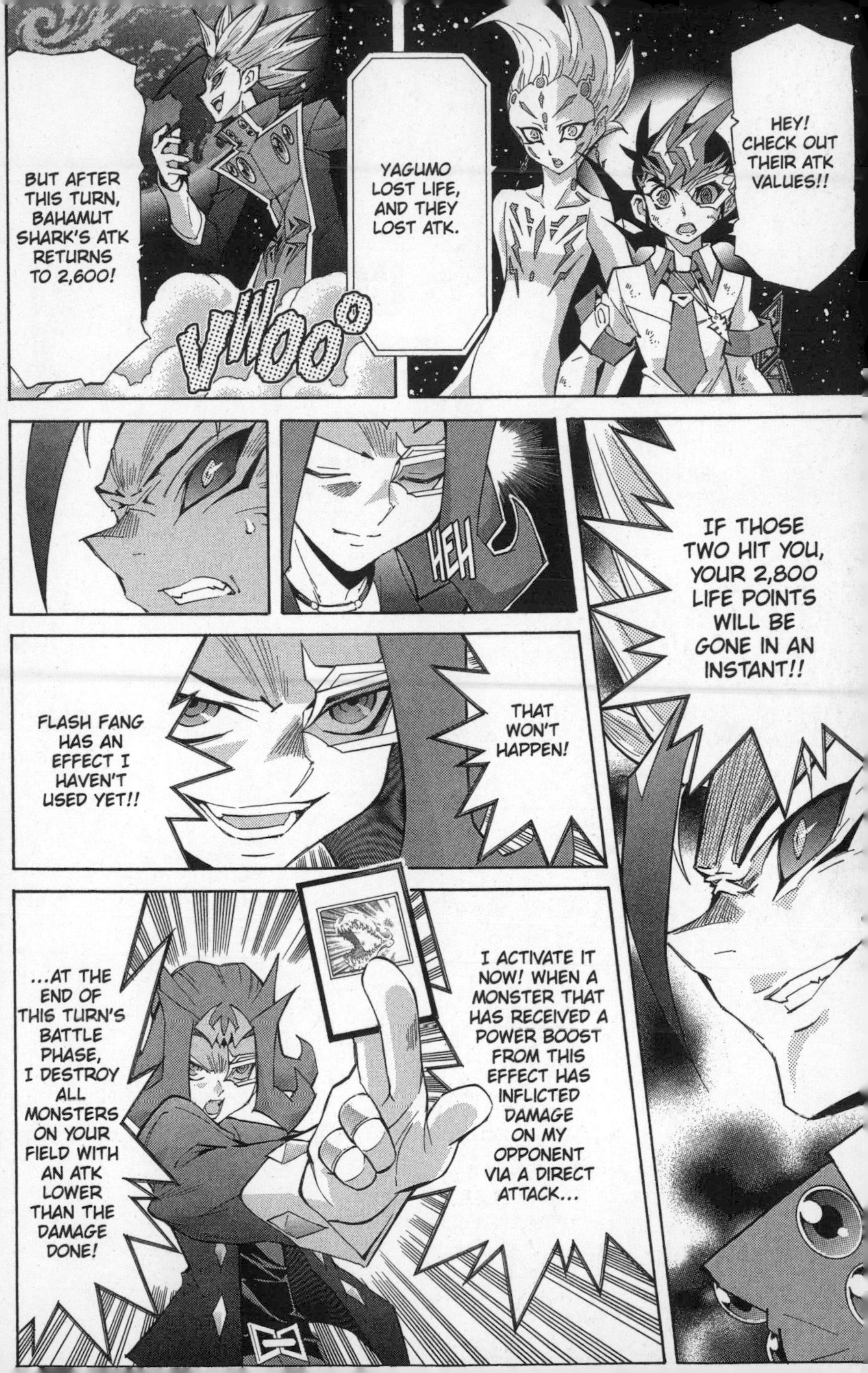
HEY! CHECK OUT THEIR ATK VALUES!!
YAGUMO LOST LIFE, AND THEY LOST ATK.
BUT AFTER THIS TURN, BAHAMUT SHARK'S ATK RETURNS TO 2,600!
VWOOO
IF THOSE TWO HIT YOU, YOUR 2,800 LIFE POINTS WILL BE GONE IN AN INSTANT!!
HEH
THAT WON'T HAPPEN!
FLASH FANG HAS AN EFFECT I HAVEN'T USED YET!!
I ACTIVATE IT NOW! WHEN A MONSTER THAT HAS RECEIVED A POWER BOOST FROM THIS EFFECT HAS INFLICTED DAMAGE ON MY OPPONENT VIA A DIRECT ATTACK...
...AT THE END OF THIS TURN'S BATTLE PHASE, I DESTROY ALL MONSTERS ON YOUR FIELD WITH AN ATK LOWER THAN THE DAMAGE DONE!

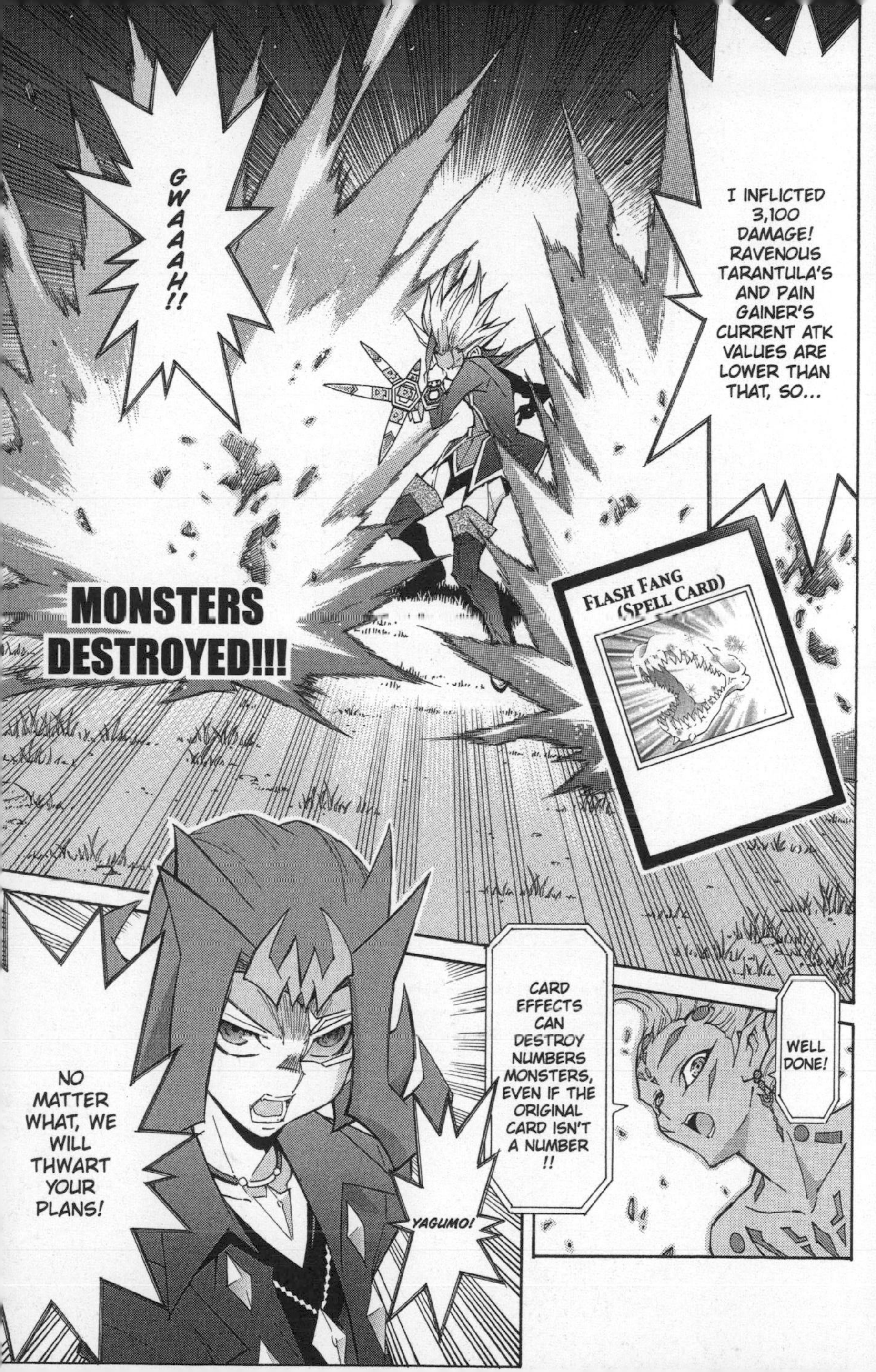

I INFLICTED 3,100 DAMAGE! RAVENOUS TARANTULA'S AND PAIN GAINER'S CURRENT ATK VALUES ARE LOWER THAN THAT, SO...
GWAAAAH!!
MONSTERS DESTROYED!!!
FLASH FANG (SPELL CARD)
WELL DONE!
CARD EFFECTS CAN DESTROY NUMBERS MONSTERS, EVEN IF THE ORIGINAL CARD ISN'T A NUMBER!!
YAGUMO!
NO MATTER WHAT, WE WILL THWART YOUR PLANS!

astral's
journal
#16

MR. YOSHIDA ALWAYS CHECKS THE INTERNET TOO!
SURFING
MORNING
TAK TAK
?!
SURFING...
AFTERNOON
TAK TAK
PUZZLE GAME
GAH
BIP BIP BIP
THE SCRIPT'S FINISHED?! HOW?!
BAM
NOW THAT'S A PRO!

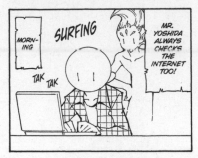

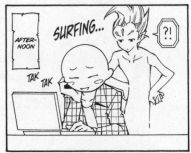

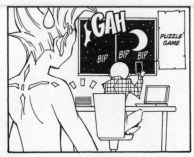

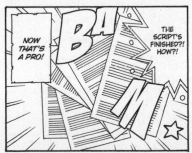

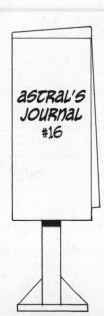

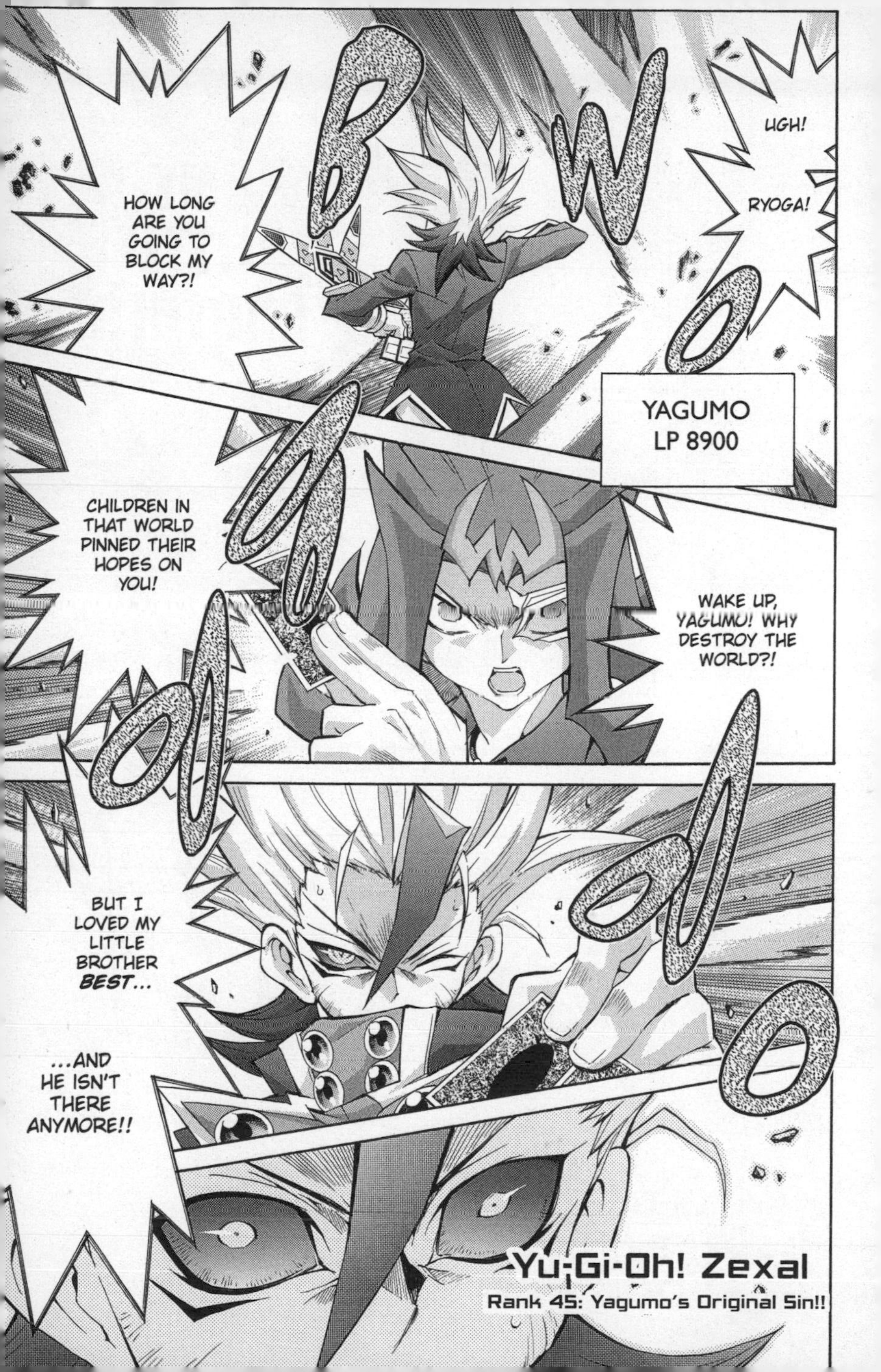
UGH!
RYOGA!
HOW LONG ARE YOU GOING TO BLOCK MY WAY?!
YAGUMO LP 8900
WAKE UP, YAGUMO! WHY DESTROY THE WORLD?!
CHILDREN IN THAT WORLD PINNED THEIR HOPES ON YOU!
BUT I LOVED MY LITTLE BROTHER ***BEST***...
...AND HE ISN'T THERE ANYMORE!!
Yu-Gi-Oh! Zexal
Rank 45: Yagumo's Original Sin!!

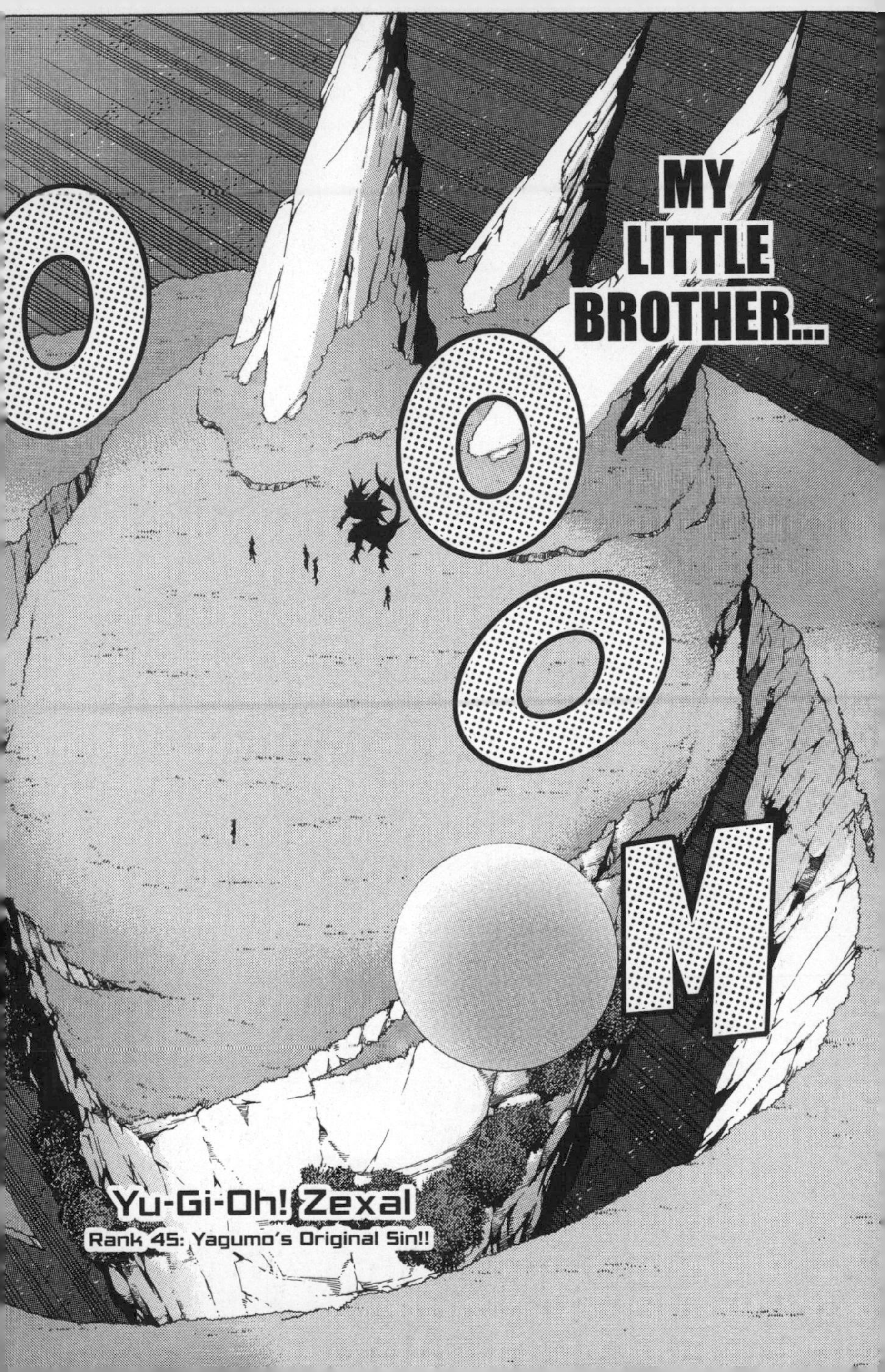
MY LITTLE BROTHER...
OOOM
Yu-Gi-Oh! Zexal
Rank 45: Yagumo's Original Sin!!

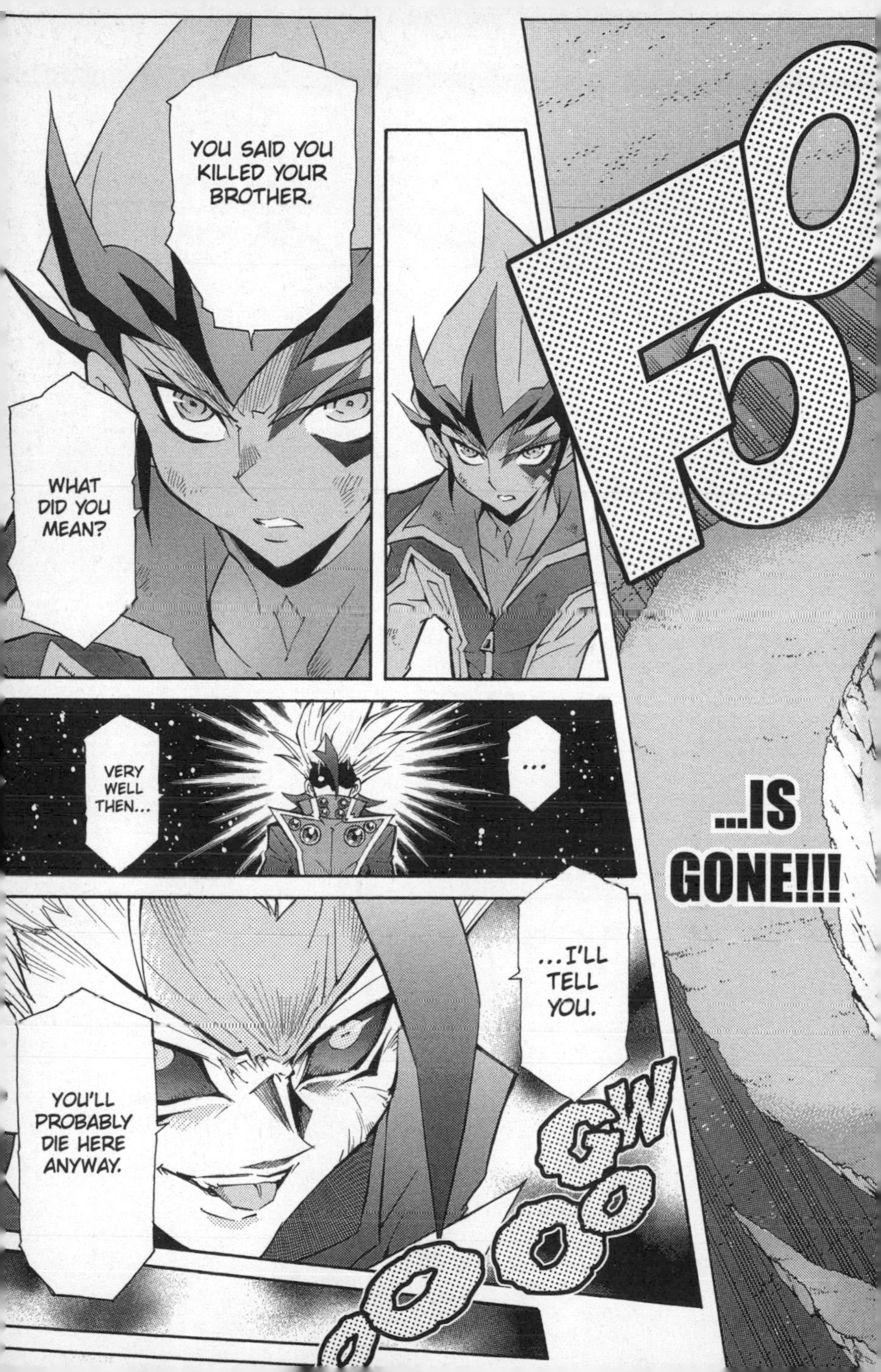
...IS GONE!!!
YOU SAID YOU KILLED YOUR BROTHER.
WHAT DID YOU MEAN?
...
VERY WELL THEN...
...I'LL TELL YOU.
YOU'LL PROBABLY DIE HERE ANYWAY.
GWOOOO

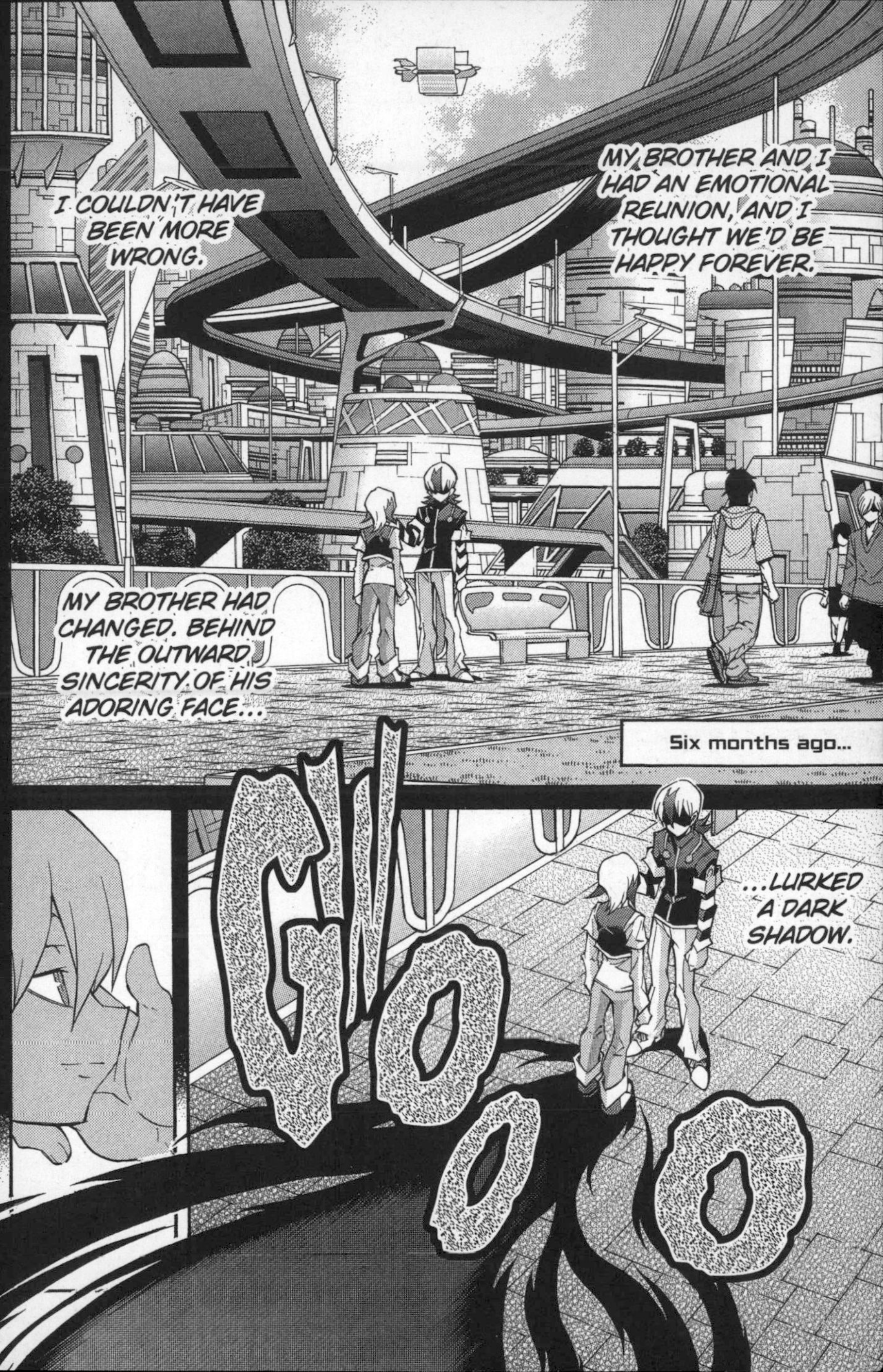
MY BROTHER AND I HAD AN EMOTIONAL REUNION, AND I THOUGHT WE'D BE HAPPY FOREVER.
I COULDN'T HAVE BEEN MORE WRONG.
MY BROTHER HAD CHANGED. BEHIND THE OUTWARD SINCERITY OF HIS ADORING FACE...
Six months ago...
...LURKED A DARK SHADOW.
GWOOO

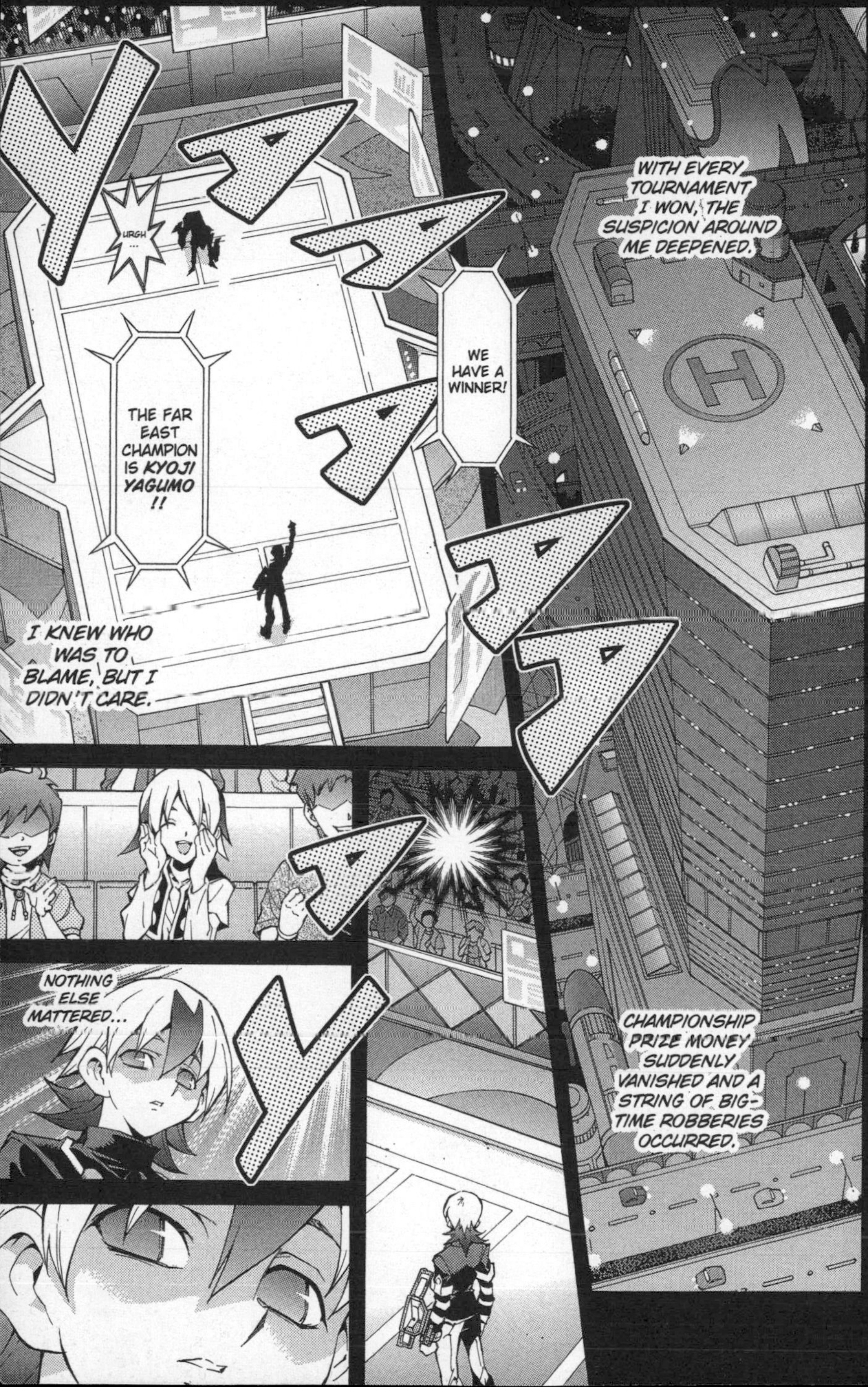
WITH EVERY TOURNAMENT I WON, THE SUSPICION AROUND ME DEEPENED.
CHAMPIONSHIP PRIZE MONEY SUDDENLY VANISHED AND A STRING OF BIG-TIME ROBBERIES OCCURRED.
URGH...
YAAAAAAY
WE HAVE A WINNER!
THE FAR EAST CHAMPION IS KYOJI YAGUMO!!
I KNEW WHO WAS TO BLAME, BUT I DIDN'T CARE.
NOTHING ELSE MATTERED...

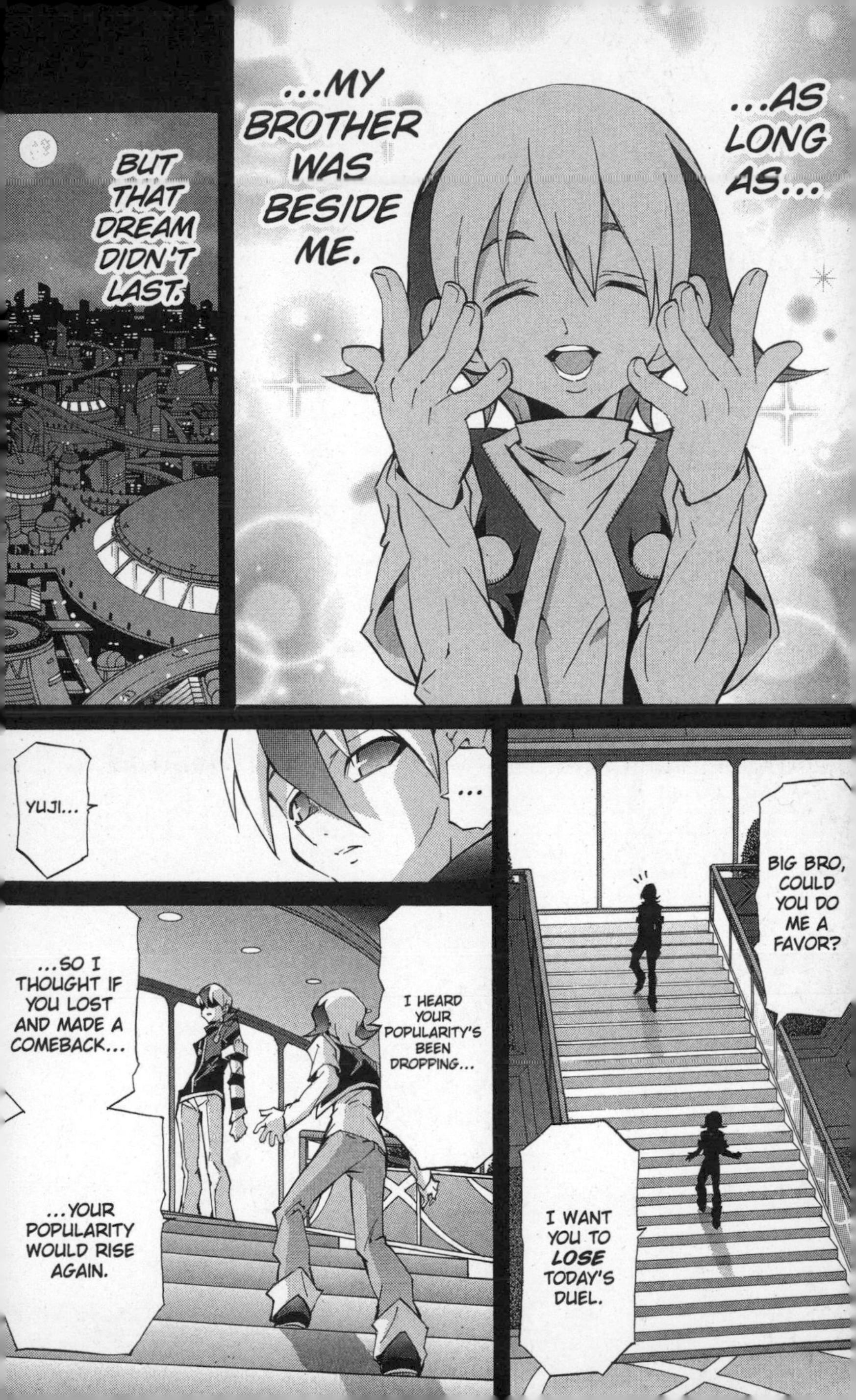
...AS LONG AS...
...MY BROTHER WAS BESIDE ME.
BUT THAT DREAM DIDN'T LAST.
BIG BRO, COULD YOU DO ME A FAVOR?
I WANT YOU TO ***LOSE*** TODAY'S DUEL.
...
YUJI...
I HEARD YOUR POPULARITY'S BEEN DROPPING...
...SO I THOUGHT IF YOU LOST AND MADE A COMEBACK...
...YOUR POPULARITY WOULD RISE AGAIN.

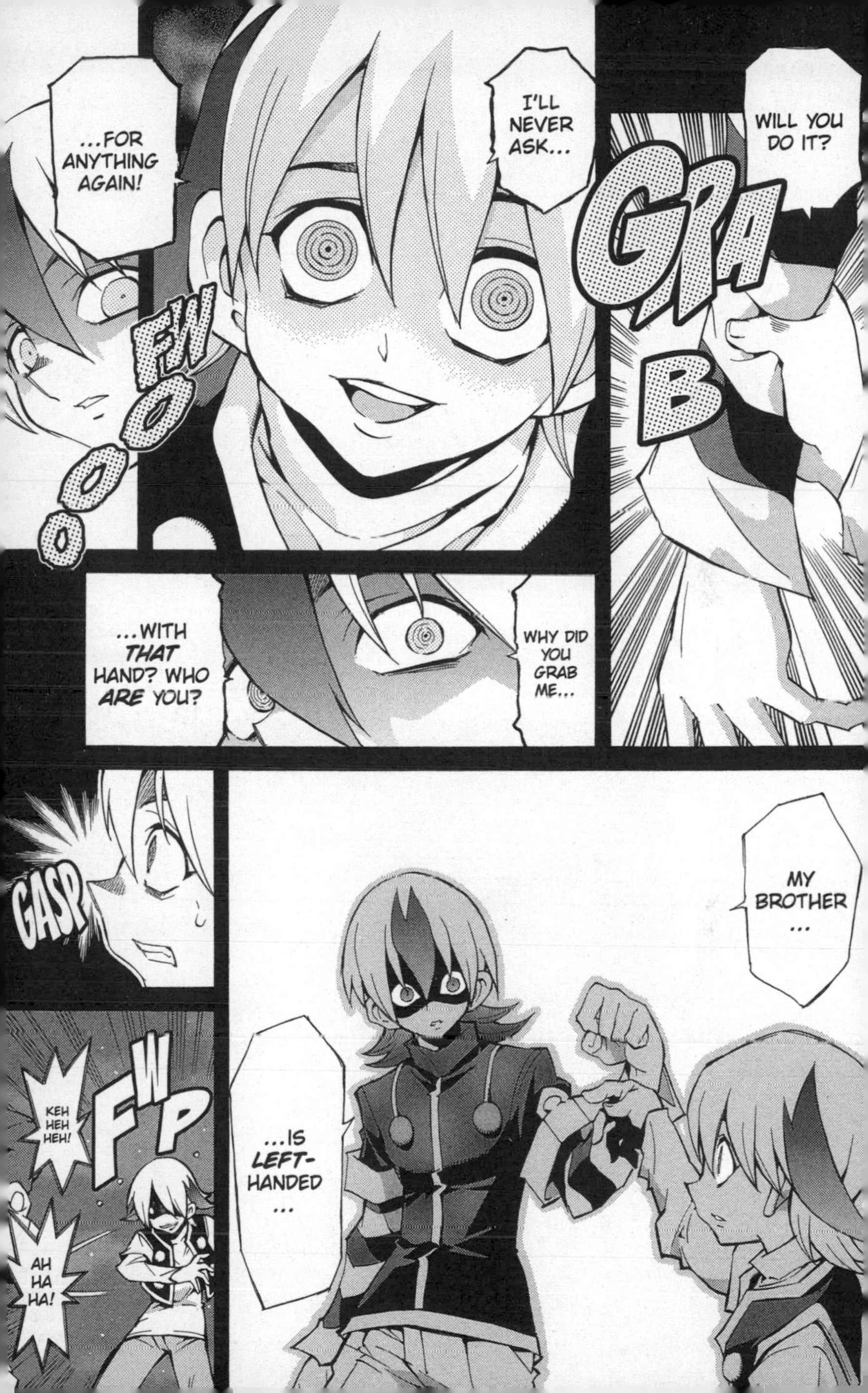

WILL YOU DO IT?
GRAB
I'LL NEVER ASK...
...FOR ANYTHING AGAIN!
FWOOOO
WHY DID YOU GRAB ME...
...WITH *THAT* HAND? WHO *ARE* YOU?
MY BROTHER ...
...IS *LEFT-HANDED* ...
GASP
FWP
KEH HEH HEH!
AH HA HA!

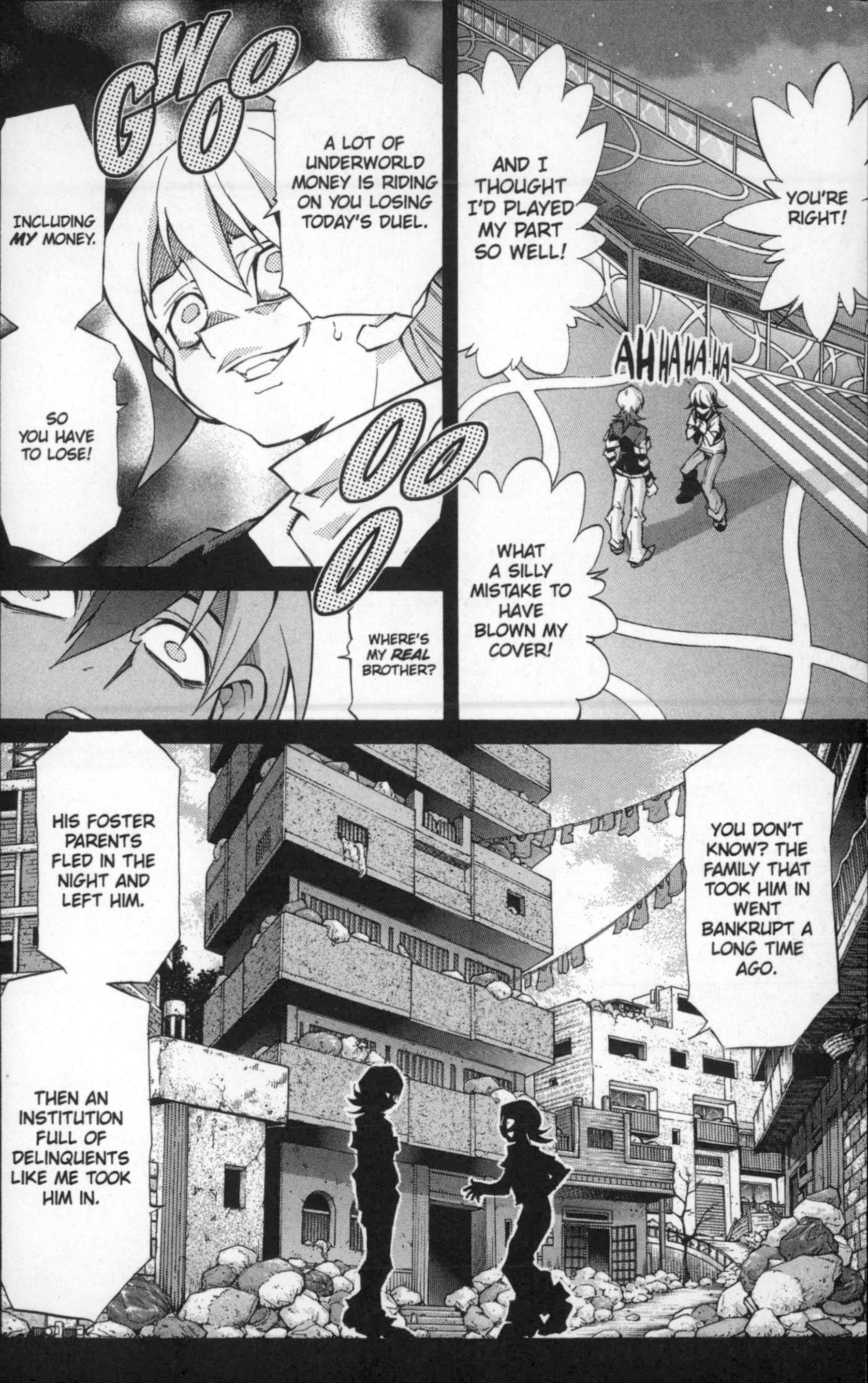
YOU'RE RIGHT!
AND I THOUGHT I'D PLAYED MY PART SO WELL!
AH HA HA HA
WHAT A SILLY MISTAKE TO HAVE BLOWN MY COVER!
GWOOO
A LOT OF UNDERWORLD MONEY IS RIDING ON YOU LOSING TODAY'S DUEL.
INCLUDING *MY* MONEY.
SO YOU HAVE TO LOSE!
OOO
WHERE'S MY *REAL* BROTHER?
YOU DON'T KNOW? THE FAMILY THAT TOOK HIM IN WENT BANKRUPT A LONG TIME AGO.
HIS FOSTER PARENTS FLED IN THE NIGHT AND LEFT HIM.
THEN AN INSTITUTION FULL OF DELINQUENTS LIKE ME TOOK HIM IN.

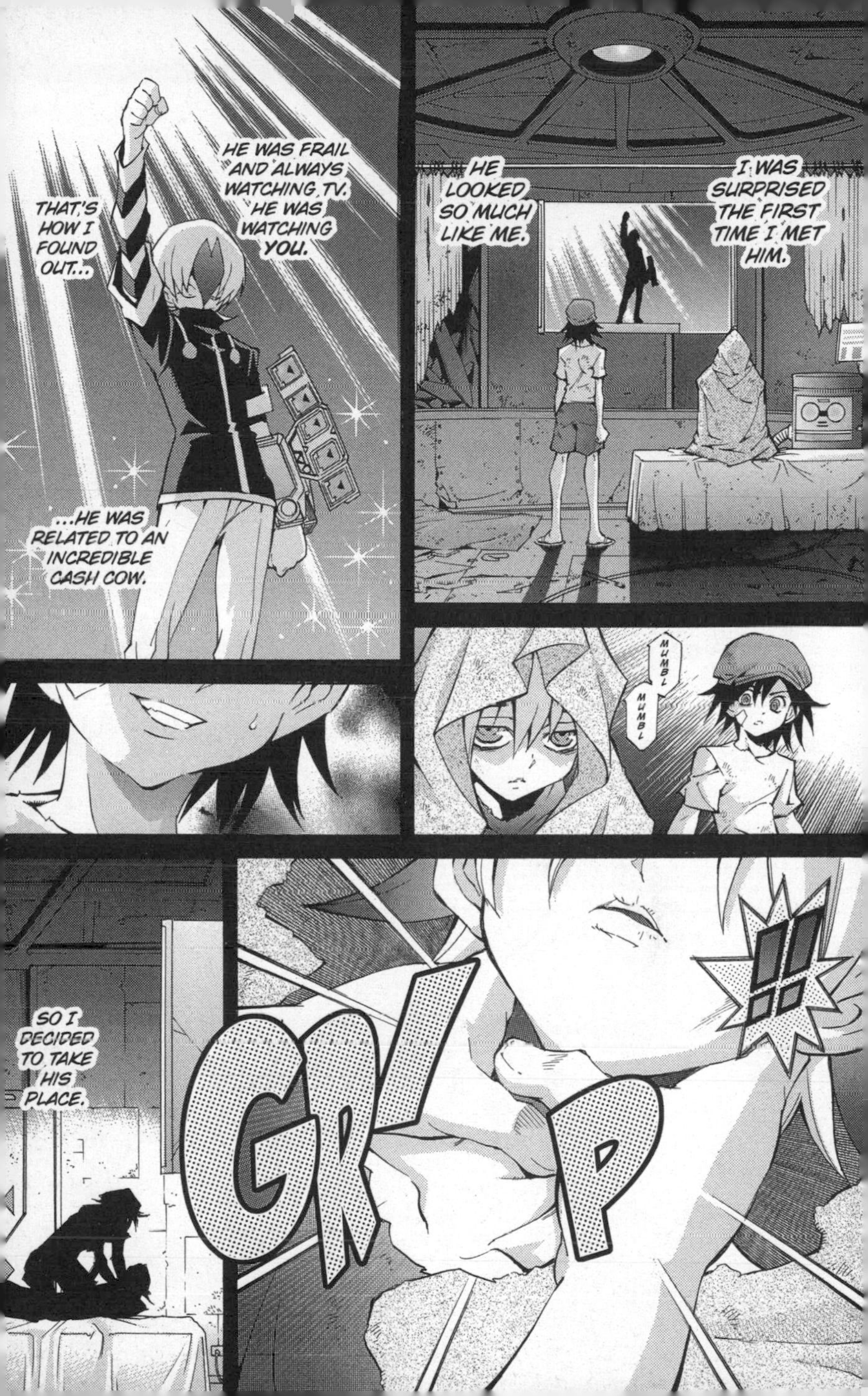
I WAS SURPRISED THE FIRST TIME I MET HIM.
HE LOOKED SO MUCH LIKE ME.
HE WAS FRAIL AND ALWAYS WATCHING TV. HE WAS WATCHING YOU.
THAT'S HOW I FOUND OUT...
...HE WAS RELATED TO AN INCREDIBLE CASH COW.
MUMBL
MUMBL
!!
GRIP
SO I DECIDED TO TAKE HIS PLACE.

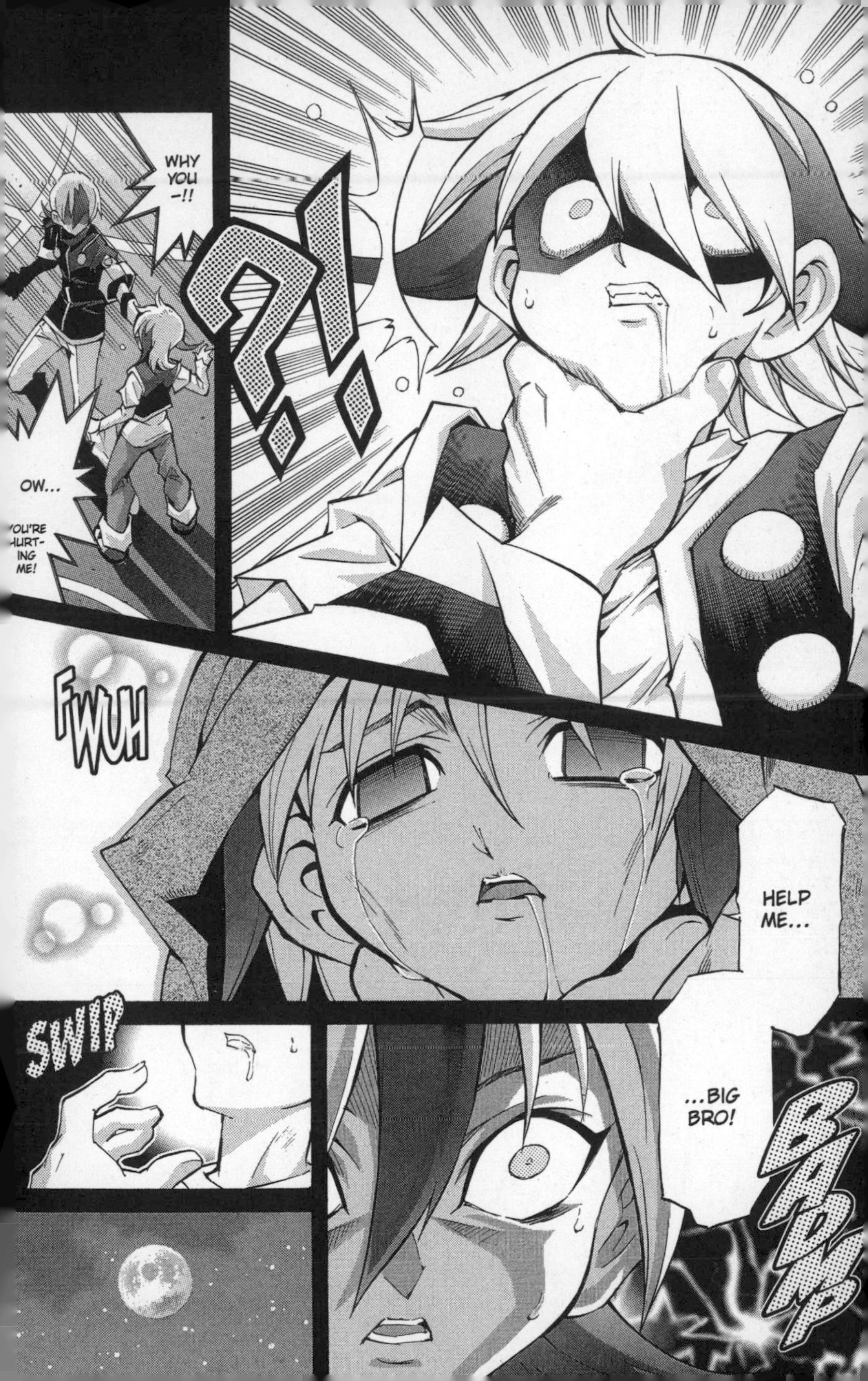
?!
WHY YOU —!!
OW...
YOU'RE HURT-ING ME!
HELP ME...
FWUH
...BIG BRO!
BADMP
SWIP

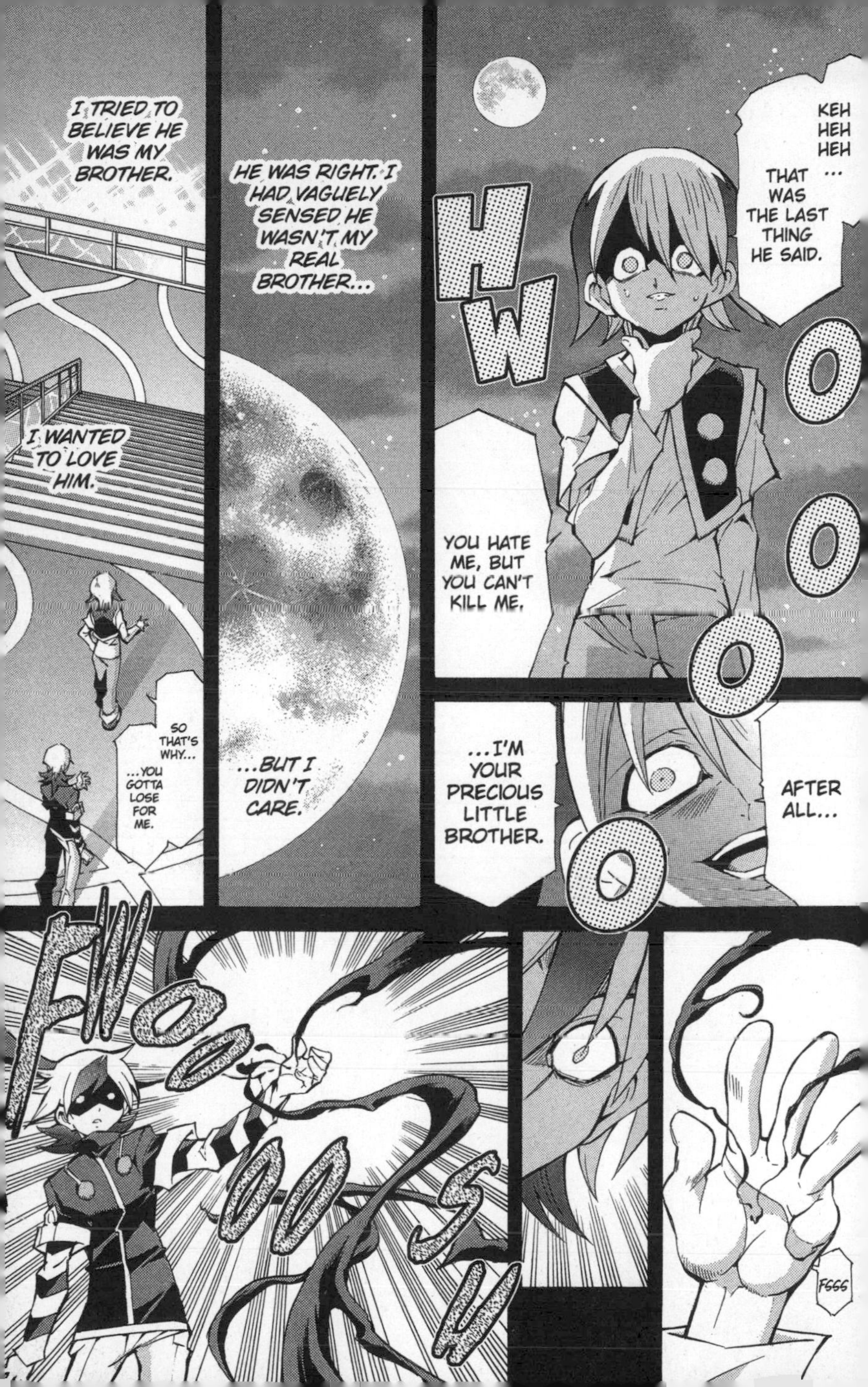
KEH HEH HEH ... THAT WAS THE LAST THING HE SAID.
HWOOOO
YOU HATE ME, BUT YOU CAN'T KILL ME.
AFTER ALL...
...I'M YOUR PRECIOUS LITTLE BROTHER.
HE WAS RIGHT. I HAD VAGUELY SENSED HE WASN'T MY REAL BROTHER...
...BUT I DIDN'T CARE.
I TRIED TO BELIEVE HE WAS MY BROTHER.
I WANTED TO LOVE HIM.
SO THAT'S WHY...
...YOU GOTTA LOSE FOR ME.
FSSS
FWOOOOSH

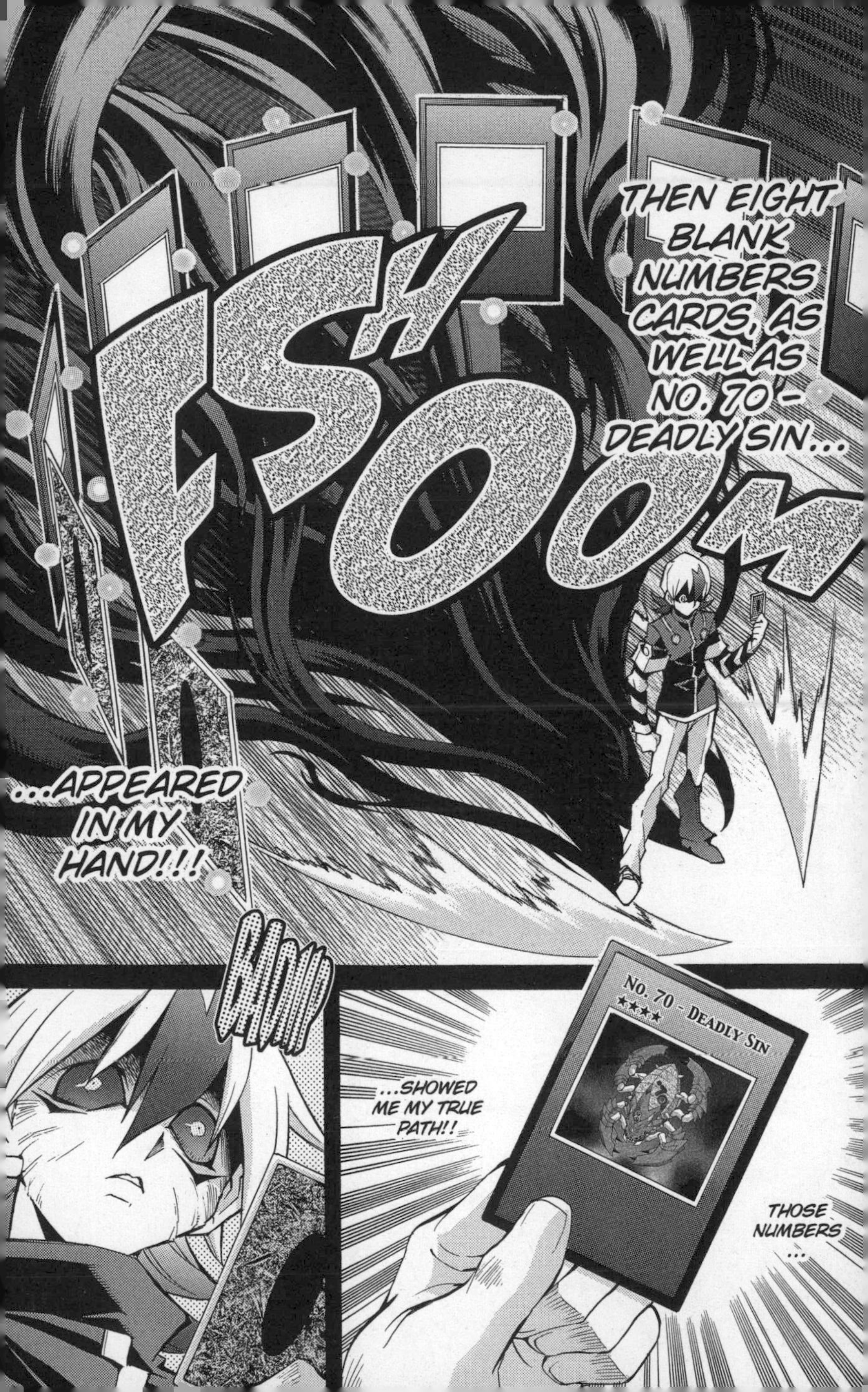
THEN EIGHT BLANK NUMBERS CARDS, AS WELL AS NO. 70 - DEADLY SIN...
FSHOOM
...APPEARED IN MY HAND!!!
No. 70 - Deadly Sin
THOSE NUMBERS ...
...SHOWED ME MY TRUE PATH!!

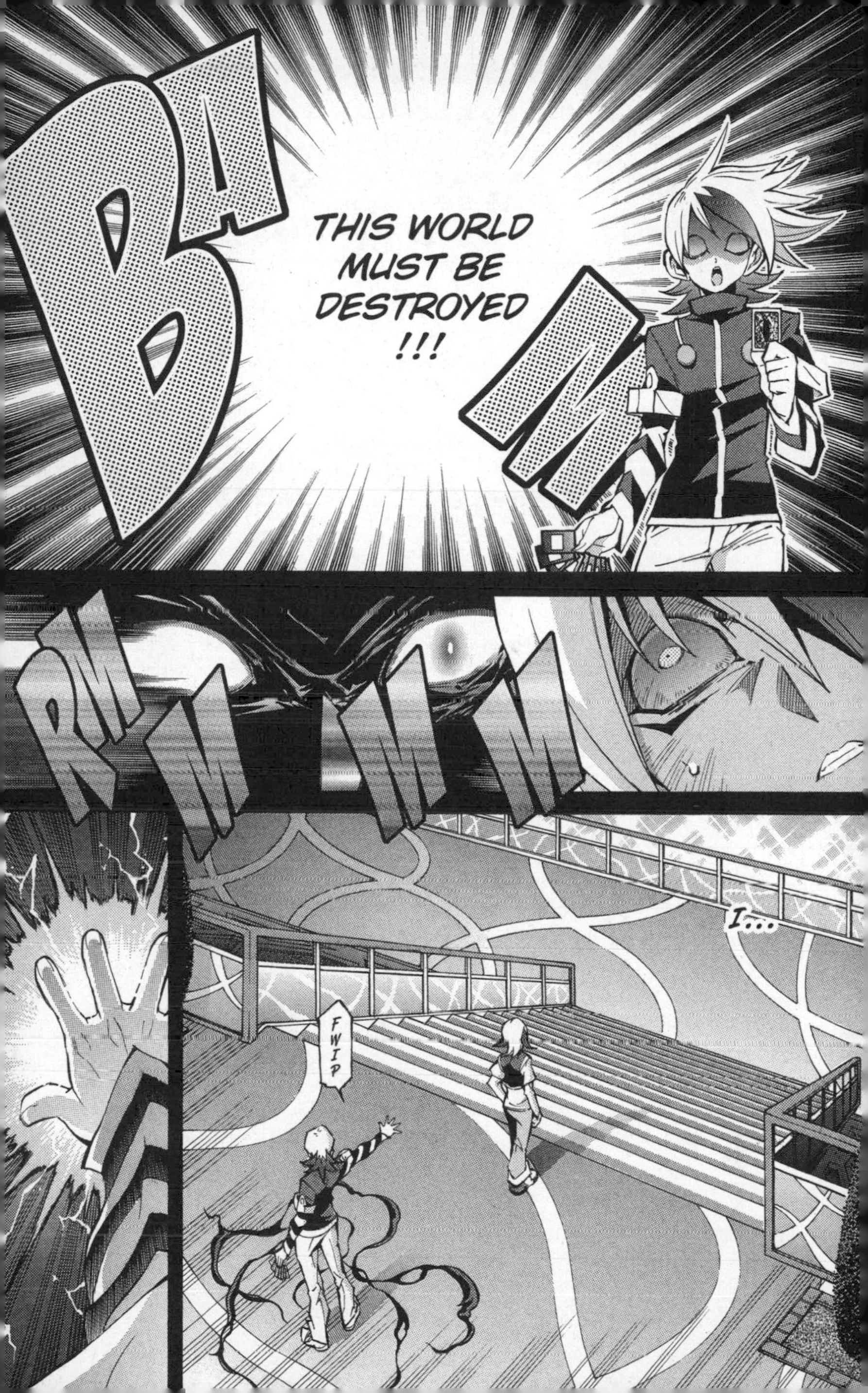
THIS WORLD MUST BE DESTROYED !!!
I...
FWIP

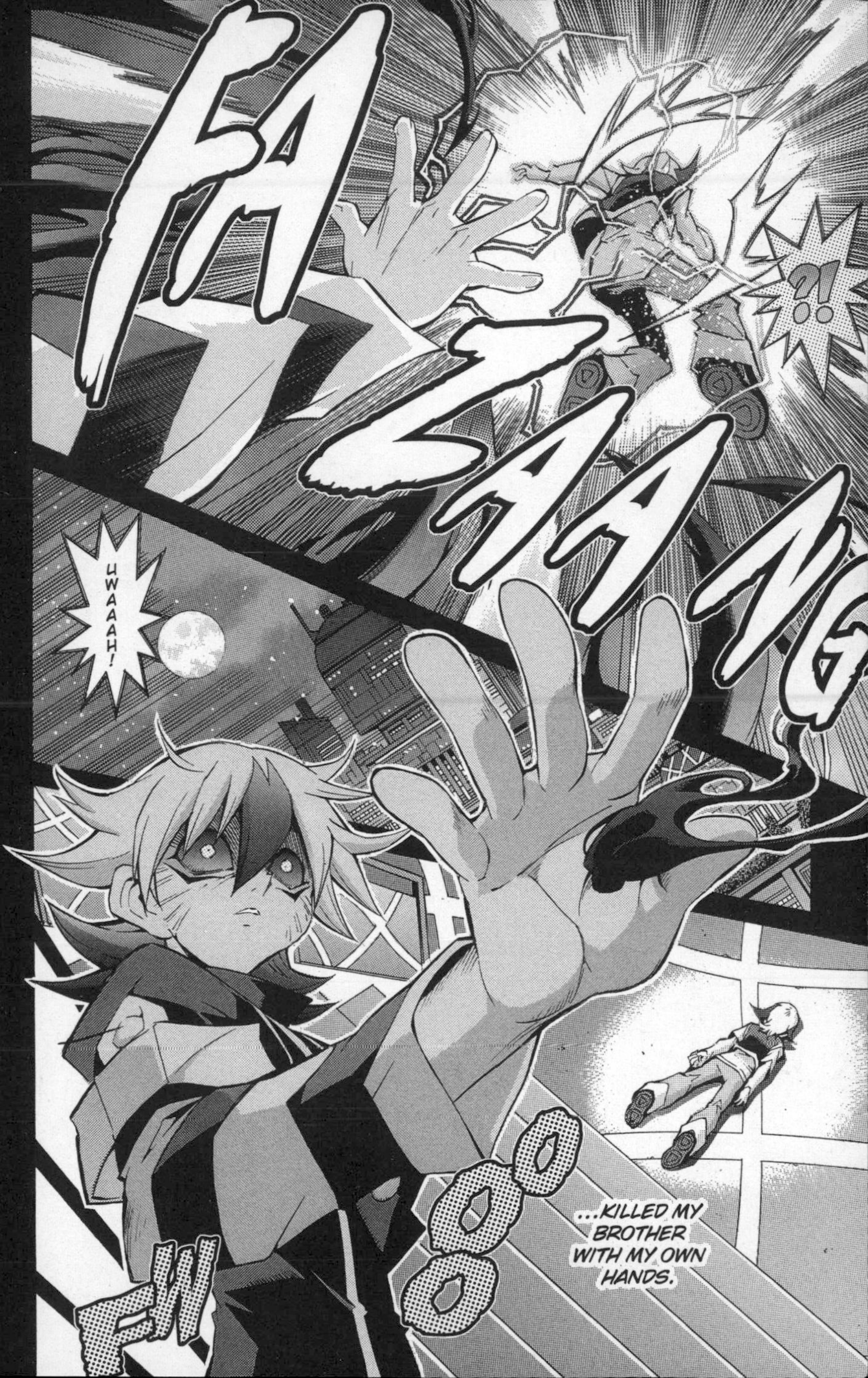
?!
FAZAANG
UWAAAAH!
FWOOOO
...KILLED MY BROTHER WITH MY OWN HANDS.

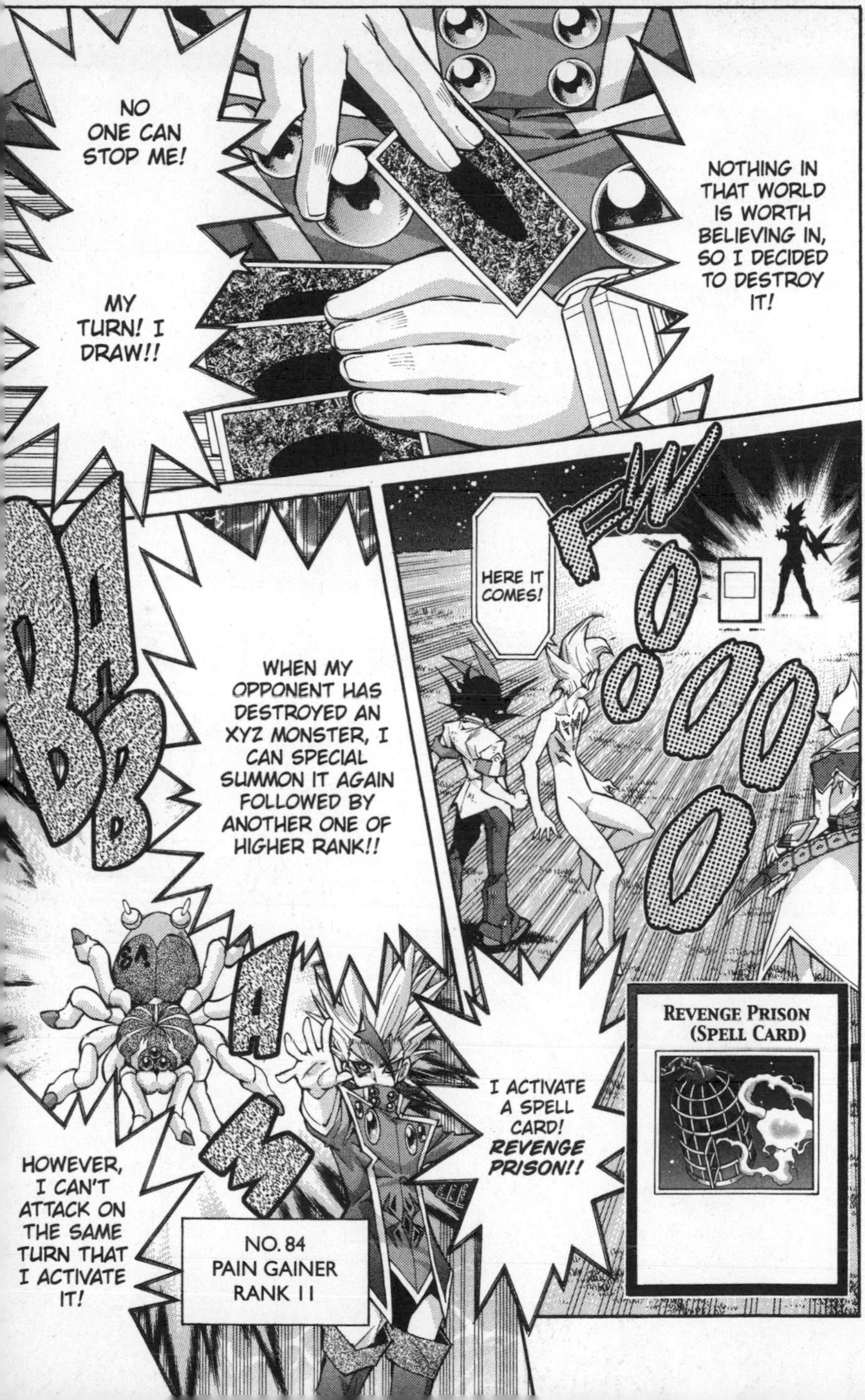
NOTHING IN THAT WORLD IS WORTH BELIEVING IN, SO I DECIDED TO DESTROY IT!
NO ONE CAN STOP ME!
MY TURN! I DRAW!!
HERE IT COMES!
WHEN MY OPPONENT HAS DESTROYED AN XYZ MONSTER, I CAN SPECIAL SUMMON IT AGAIN FOLLOWED BY ANOTHER ONE OF HIGHER RANK!!
REVENGE PRISON (SPELL CARD)
I ACTIVATE A SPELL CARD! REVENGE PRISON!!
NO. 84 PAIN GAINER RANK 11
HOWEVER, I CAN'T ATTACK ON THE SAME TURN THAT I ACTIVATE IT!

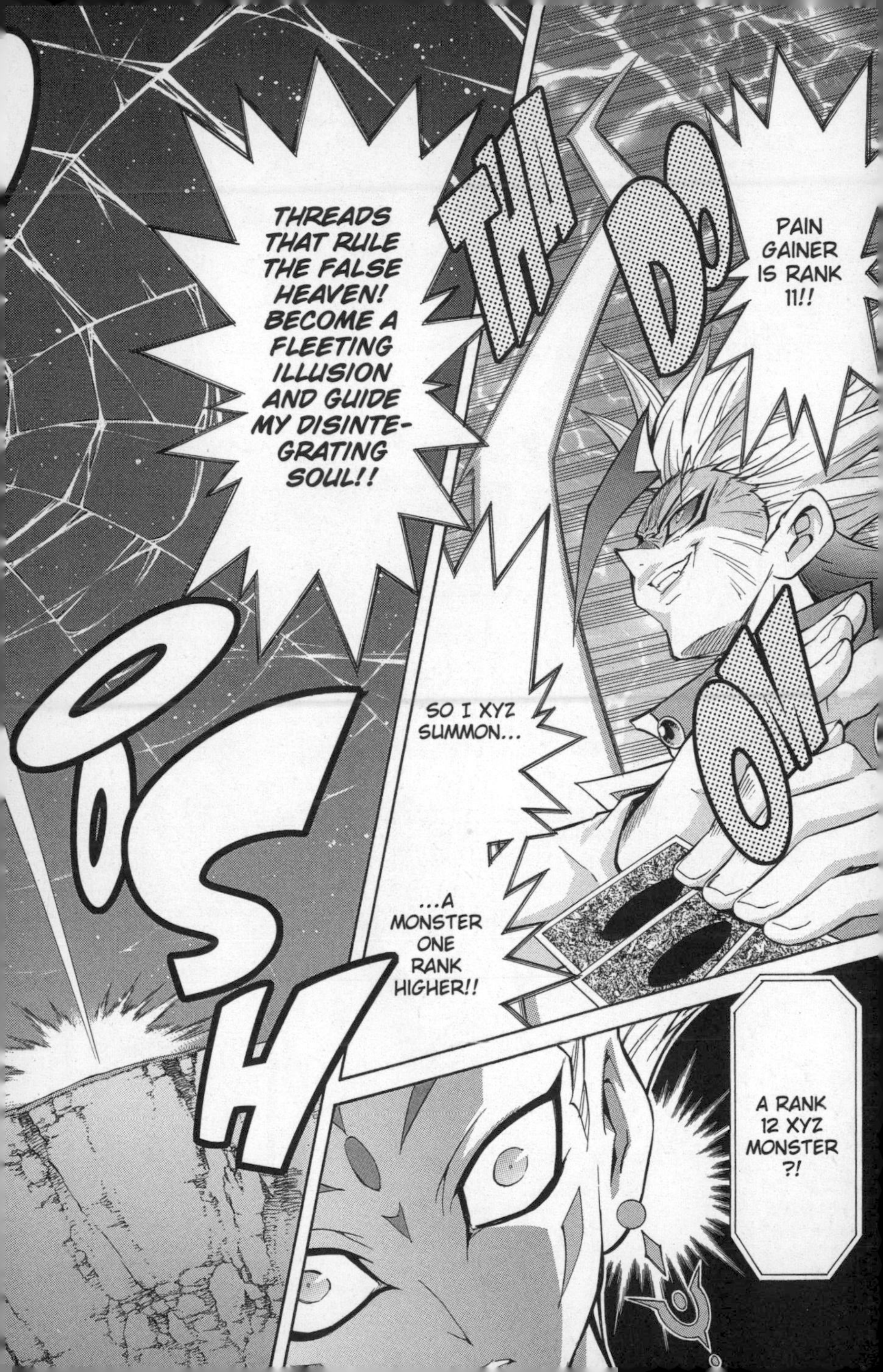
PAIN GAINER IS RANK 11!!
THADOOM!!
SO I XYZ SUMMON...
...A MONSTER ONE RANK HIGHER!!
THREADS THAT RULE THE FALSE HEAVEN! BECOME A FLEETING ILLUSION AND GUIDE MY DISINTE-GRATING SOUL!!
OOSH
A RANK 12 XYZ MONSTER ?!

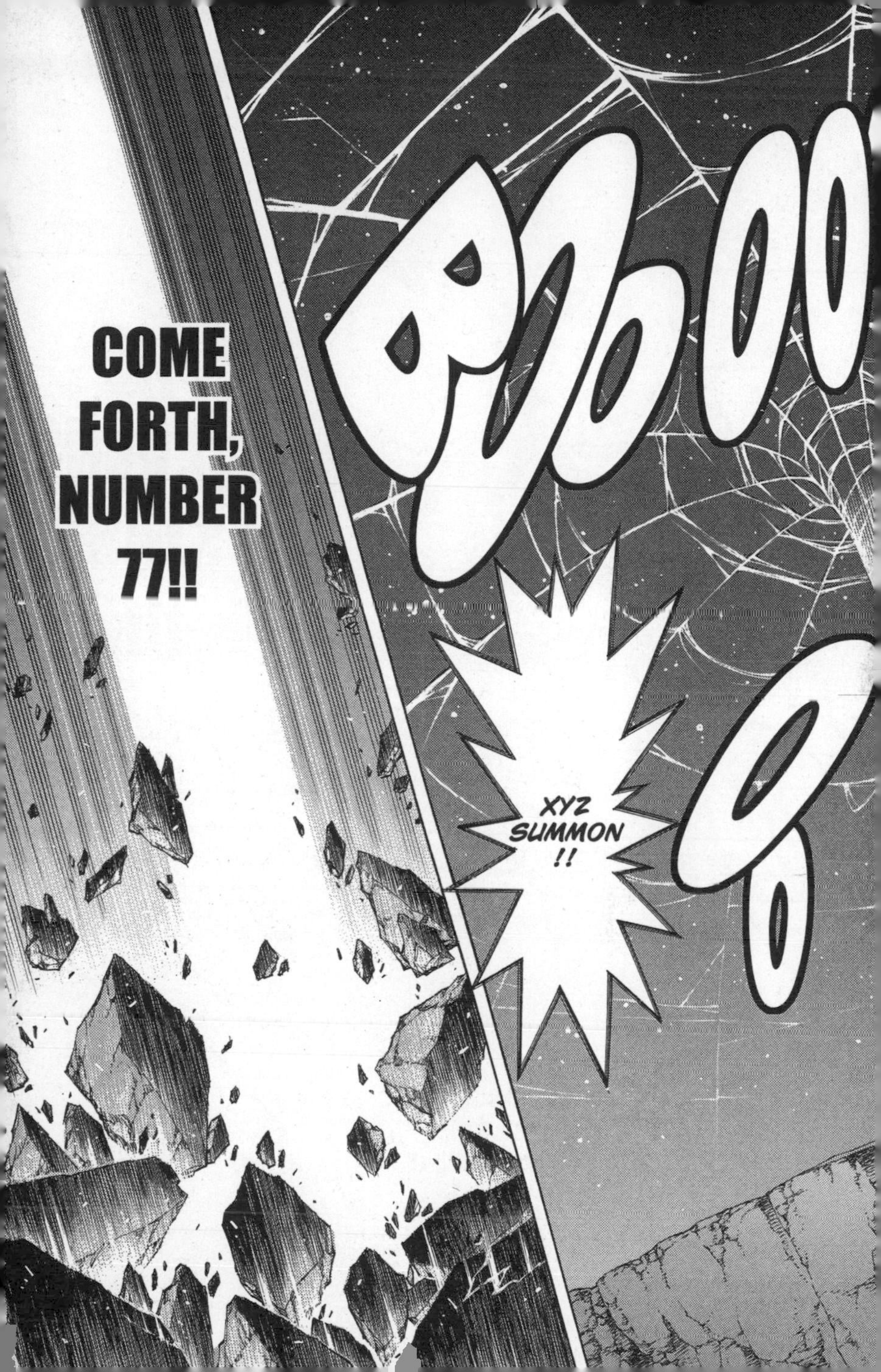
XYZ SUMMON!!
COME FORTH, NUMBER 77!!

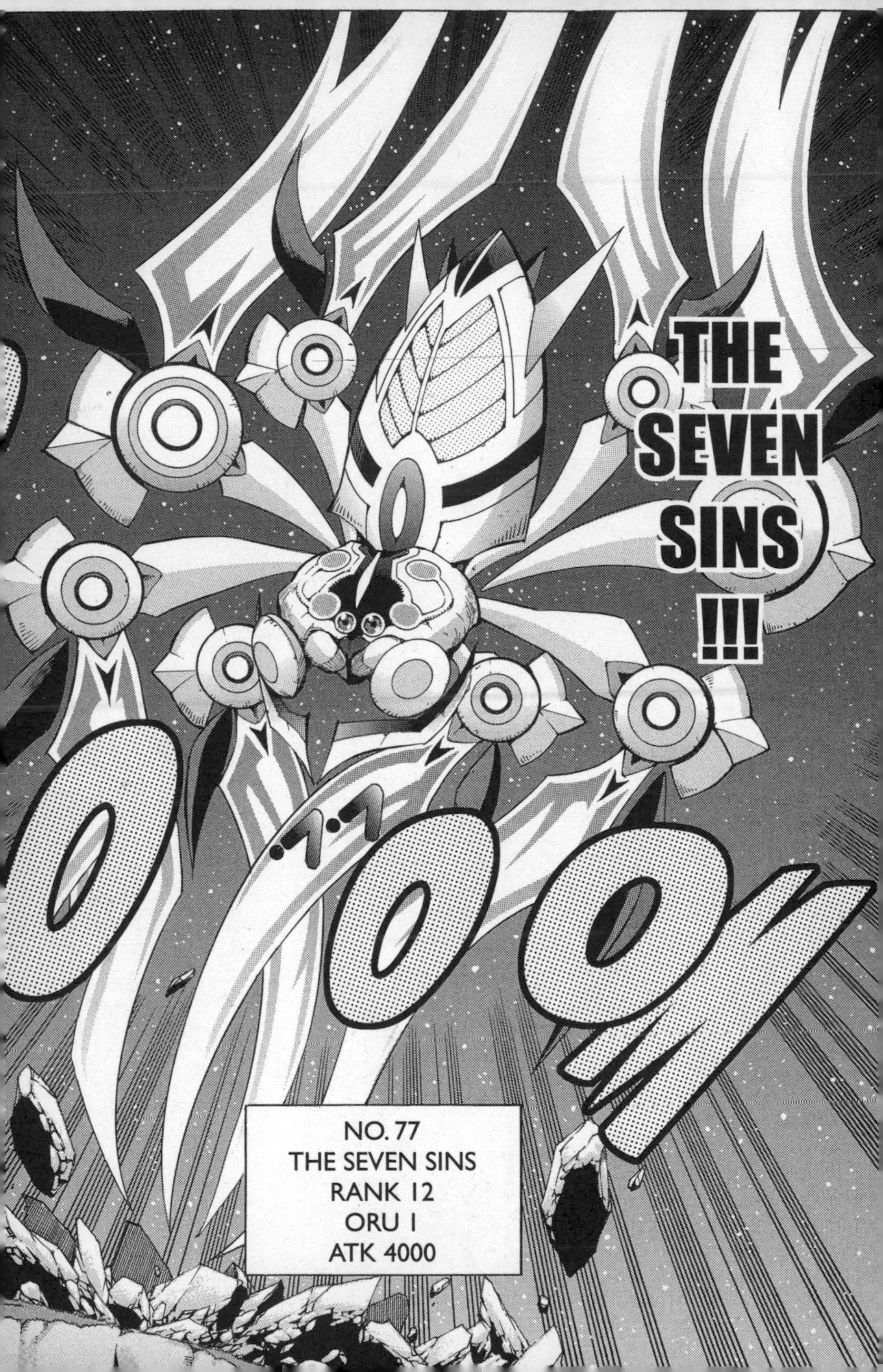
THE SEVEN SINS !!!
NO. 77
THE SEVEN SINS
RANK 12
ORU 1
ATK 4000

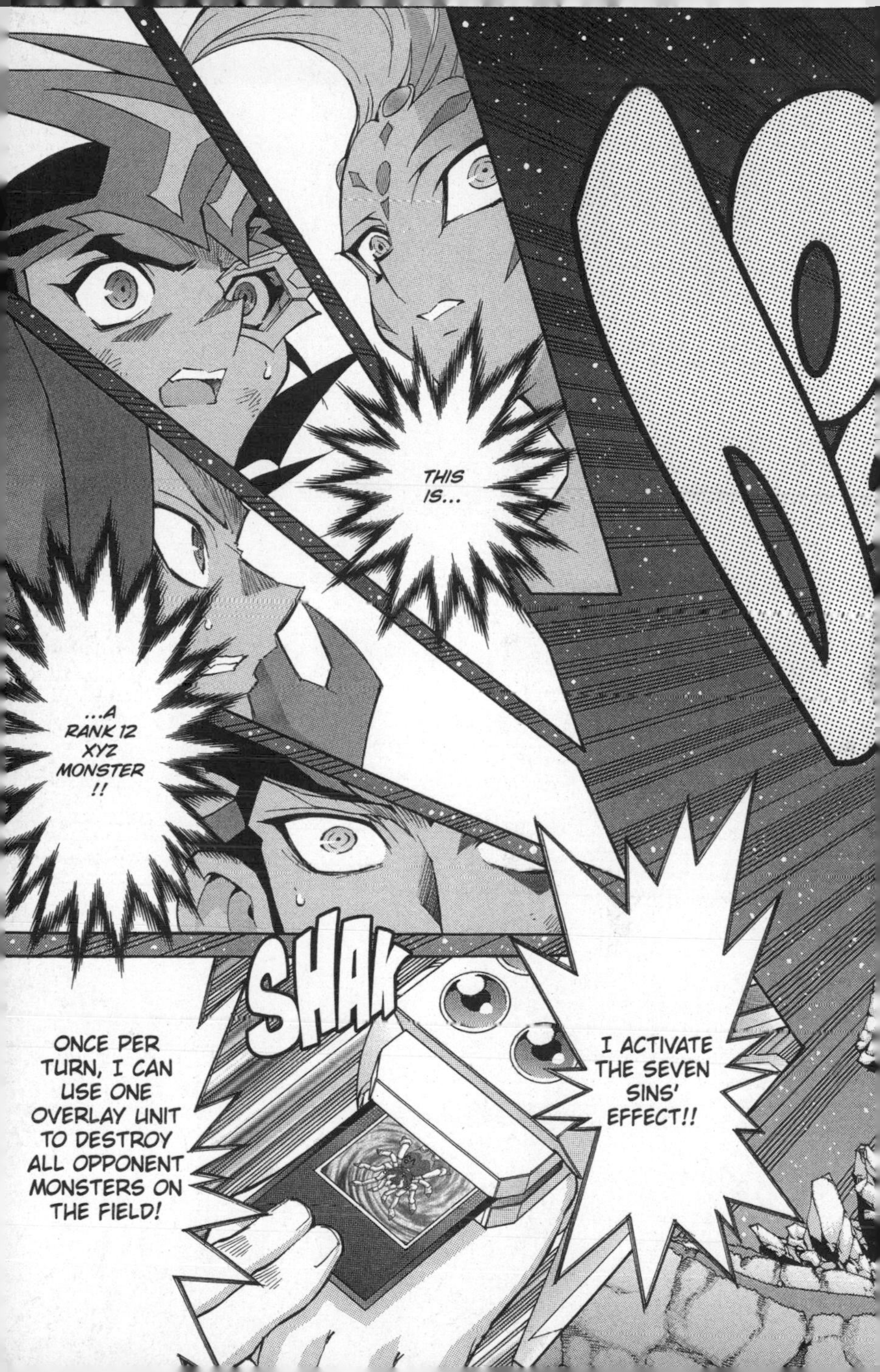
THIS IS...
...A RANK 12 XYZ MONSTER!!
I ACTIVATE THE SEVEN SINS' EFFECT!!
SHAK
ONCE PER TURN, I CAN USE ONE OVERLAY UNIT TO DESTROY ALL OPPONENT MONSTERS ON THE FIELD!

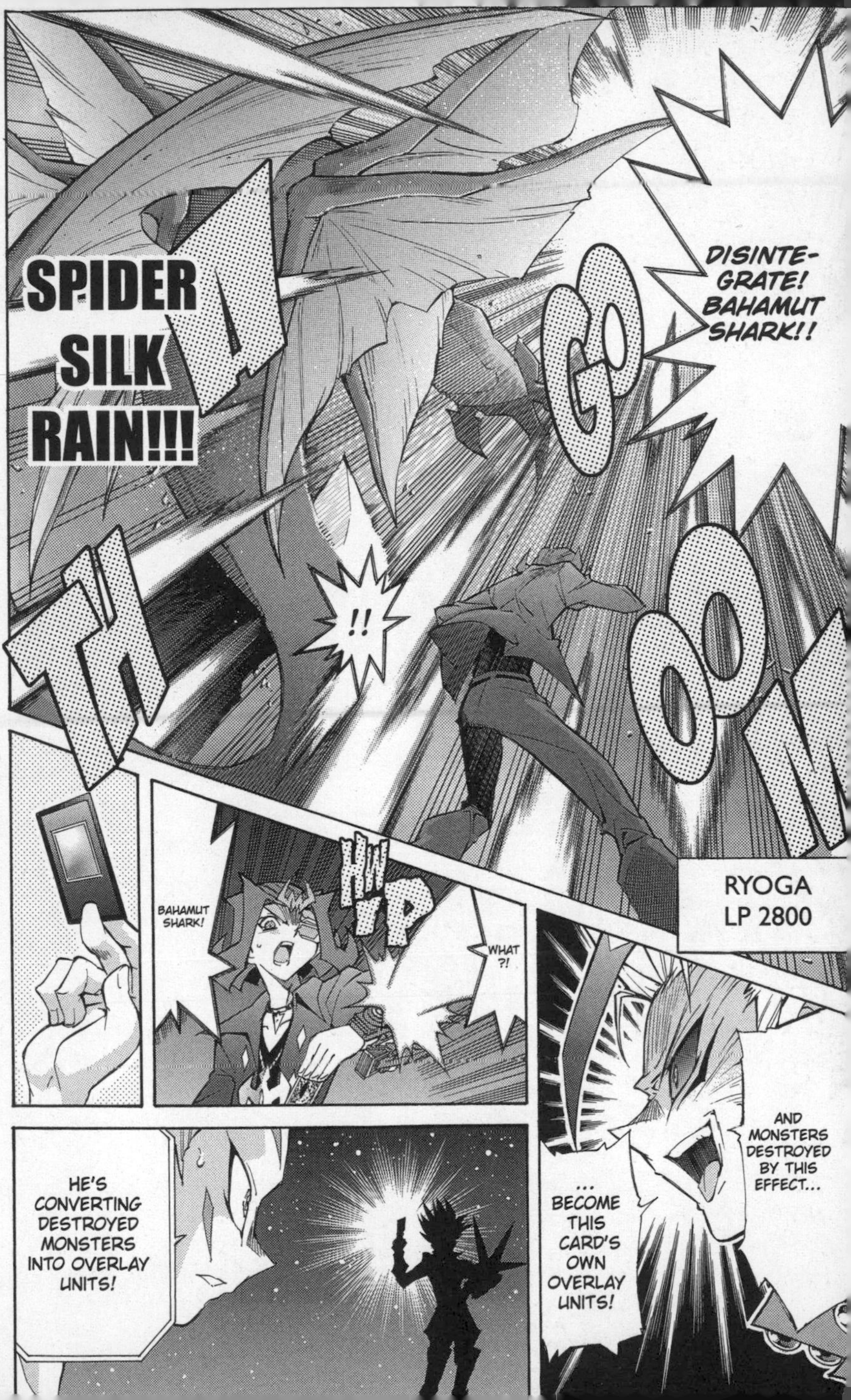
DISINTE-GRATE! BAHAMUT SHARK!!
GO
SPIDER SILK RAIN!!!
OOOM
TH
!!
RYOGA LP 2800
AND MONSTERS DESTROYED BY THIS EFFECT...
... BECOME THIS CARD'S OWN OVERLAY UNITS!
HWIP
WHAT ?!
BAHAMUT SHARK!
HE'S CONVERTING DESTROYED MONSTERS INTO OVERLAY UNITS!

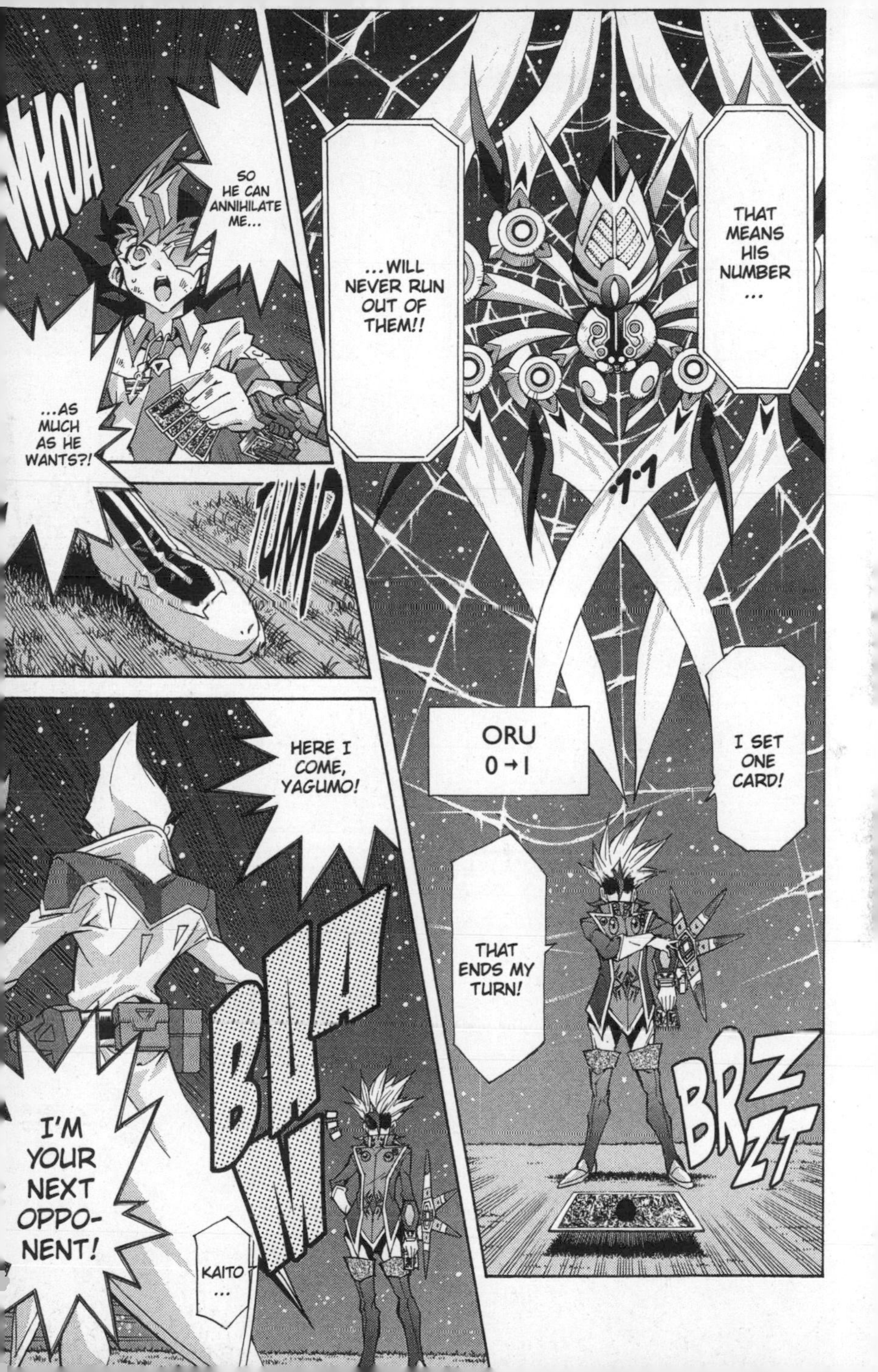
THAT MEANS HIS NUMBER ...
...WILL NEVER RUN OUT OF THEM!!
ORU
0 → 1
I SET ONE CARD!
THAT ENDS MY TURN!
BRZZT
WHOA
SO HE CAN ANNIHILATE ME...
...AS MUCH AS HE WANTS?!
TUMP
HERE I COME, YAGUMO!
I'M YOUR NEXT OPPO-NENT!
BAM
KAITO ...

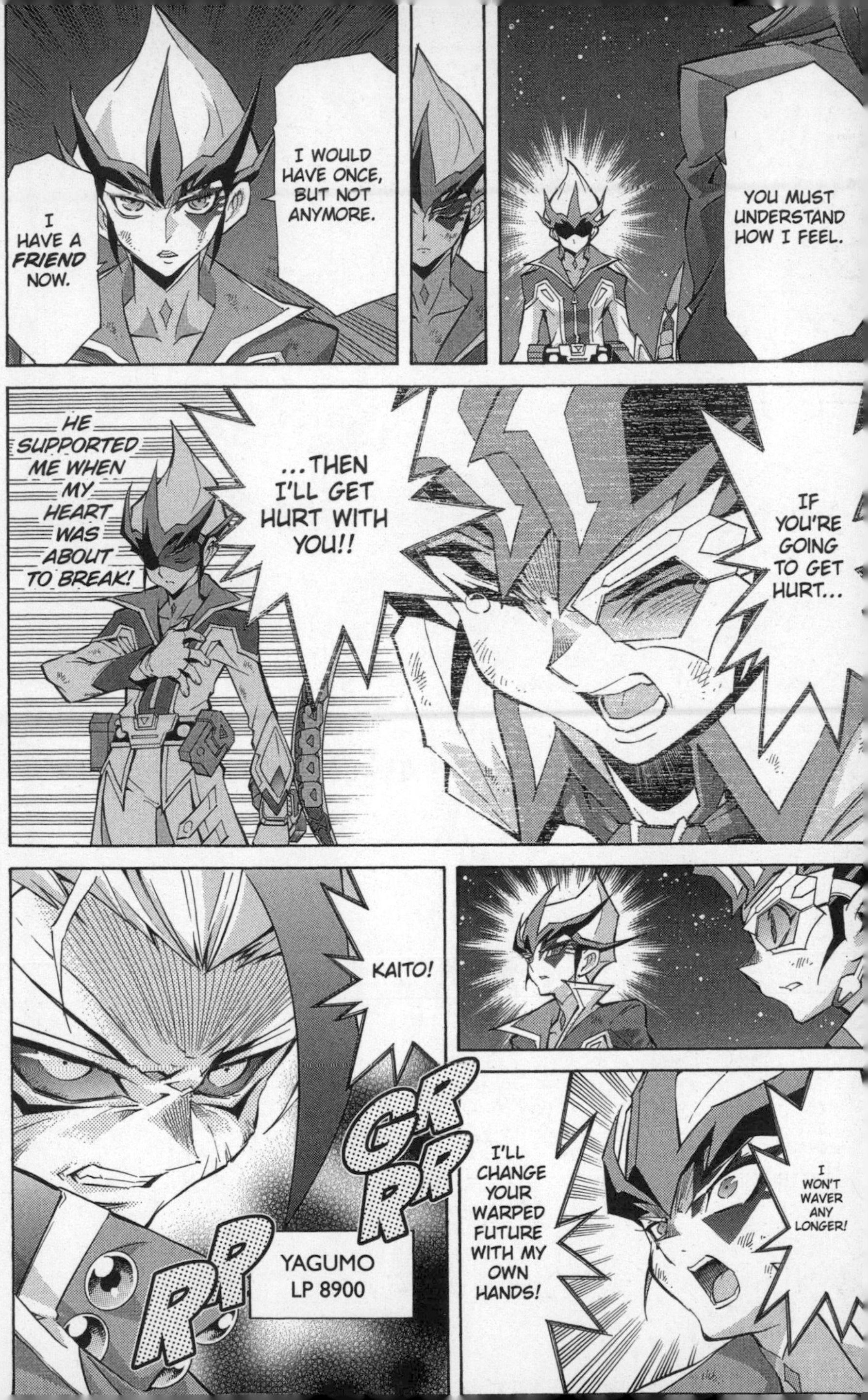
YOU MUST UNDERSTAND HOW I FEEL.
I WOULD HAVE ONCE, BUT NOT ANYMORE.
I HAVE A *FRIEND* NOW.
IF YOU'RE GOING TO GET HURT...
...THEN I'LL GET HURT WITH YOU!!
HE SUPPORTED ME WHEN MY HEART WAS ABOUT TO BREAK!
I WON'T WAVER ANY LONGER!
I'LL CHANGE YOUR WARPED FUTURE WITH MY OWN HANDS!
KAITO!
GRRRRR
YAGUMO LP 8900

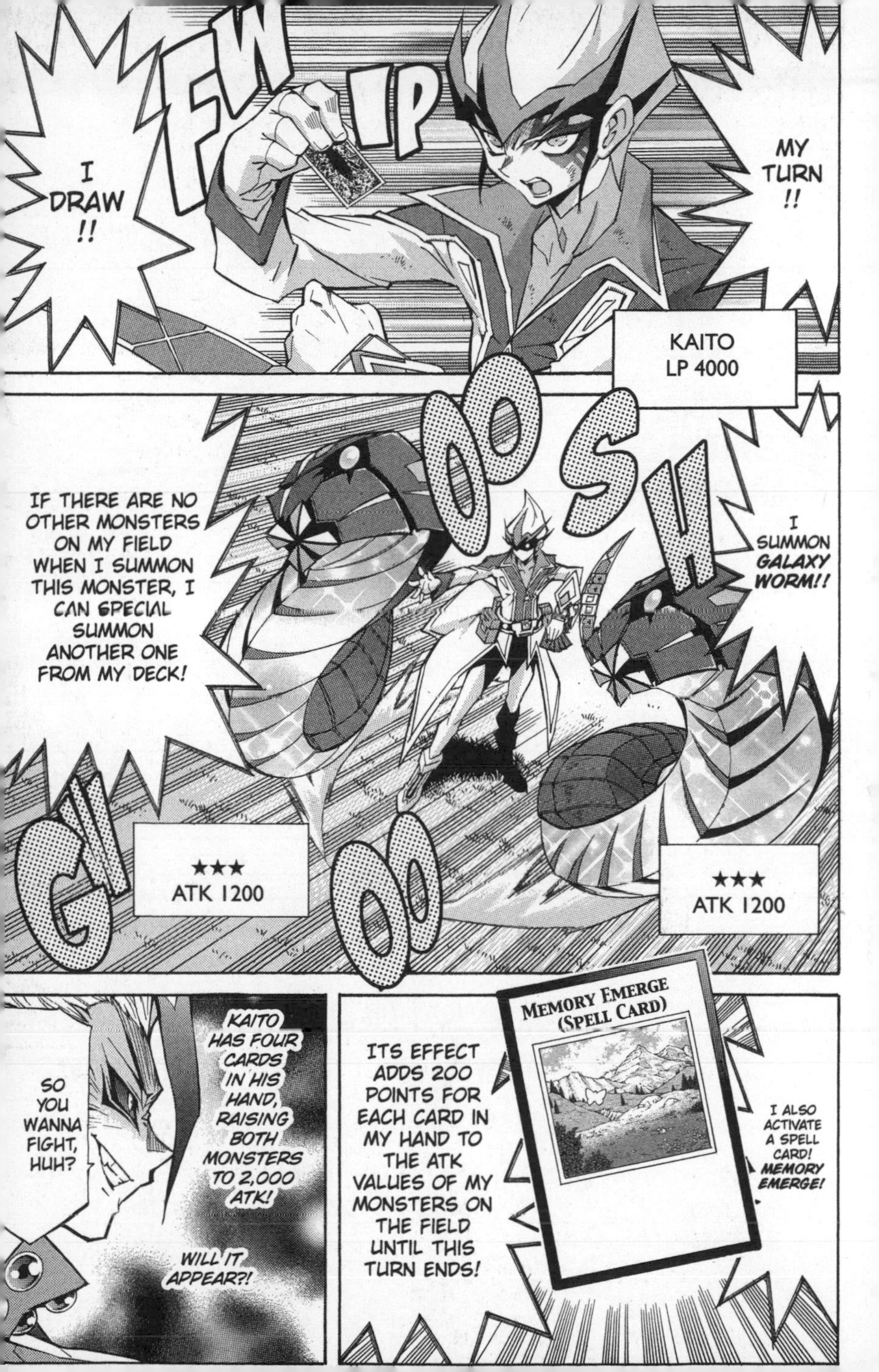
MY TURN!!
FWIP
I DRAW!!
KAITO LP 4000
I SUMMON GALAXY WORM!!
OOOSH
IF THERE ARE NO OTHER MONSTERS ON MY FIELD WHEN I SUMMON THIS MONSTER, I CAN SPECIAL SUMMON ANOTHER ONE FROM MY DECK!
★★★ ATK 1200
OOO
G!!
★★★ ATK 1200
I ALSO ACTIVATE A SPELL CARD! MEMORY EMERGE!
MEMORY EMERGE (SPELL CARD)
ITS EFFECT ADDS 200 POINTS FOR EACH CARD IN MY HAND TO THE ATK VALUES OF MY MONSTERS ON THE FIELD UNTIL THIS TURN ENDS!
KAITO HAS FOUR CARDS IN HIS HAND, RAISING BOTH MONSTERS TO 2,000 ATK!
SO YOU WANNA FIGHT, HUH?
WILL IT APPEAR?!

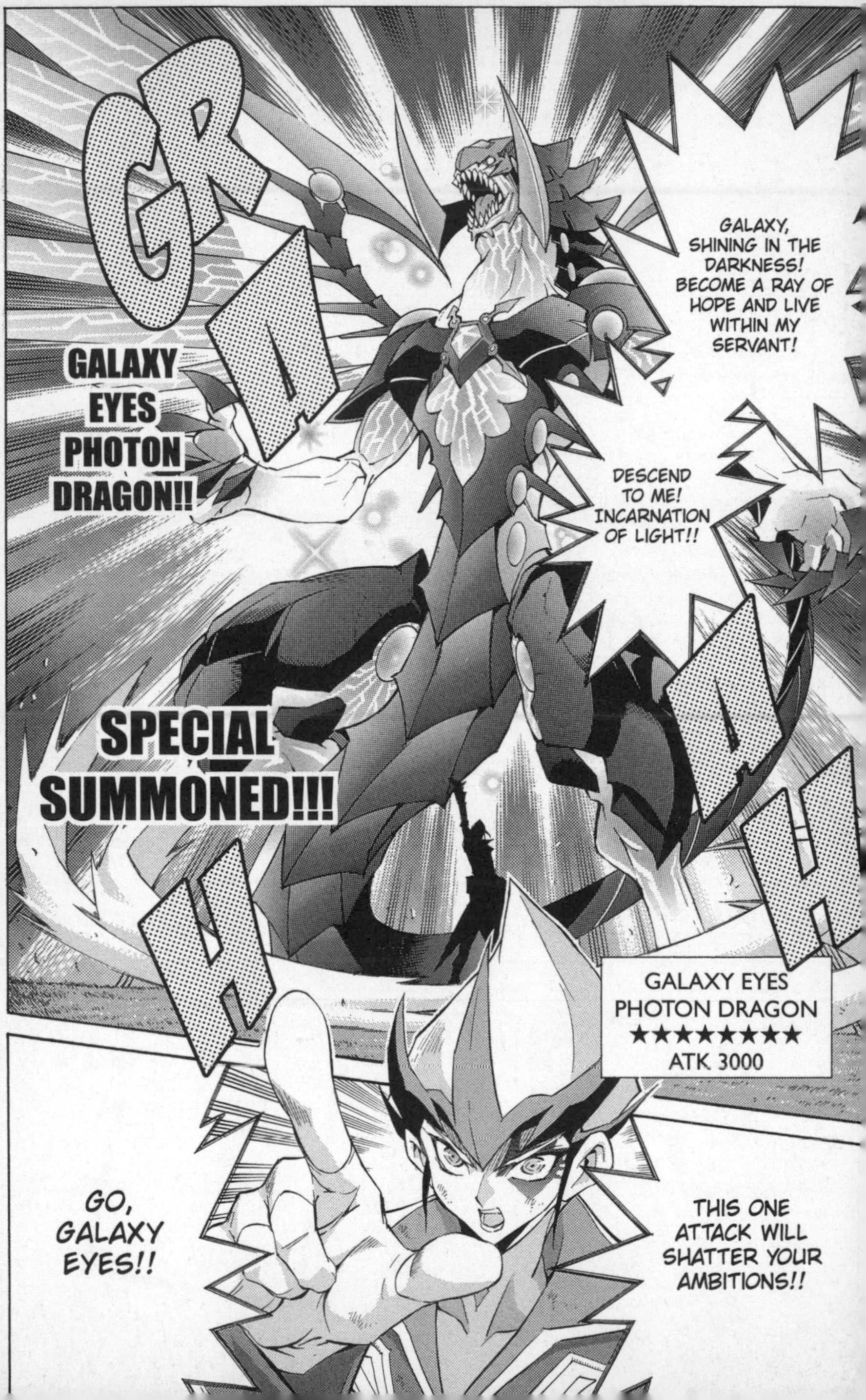
GALAXY, SHINING IN THE DARKNESS! BECOME A RAY OF HOPE AND LIVE WITHIN MY SERVANT!
DESCEND TO ME! INCARNATION OF LIGHT!!
GALAXY EYES PHOTON DRAGON!!
SPECIAL SUMMONED!!!
GALAXY EYES PHOTON DRAGON ★★★★★★★★ ATK 3000
THIS ONE ATTACK WILL SHATTER YOUR AMBITIONS!!
GO, GALAXY EYES!!

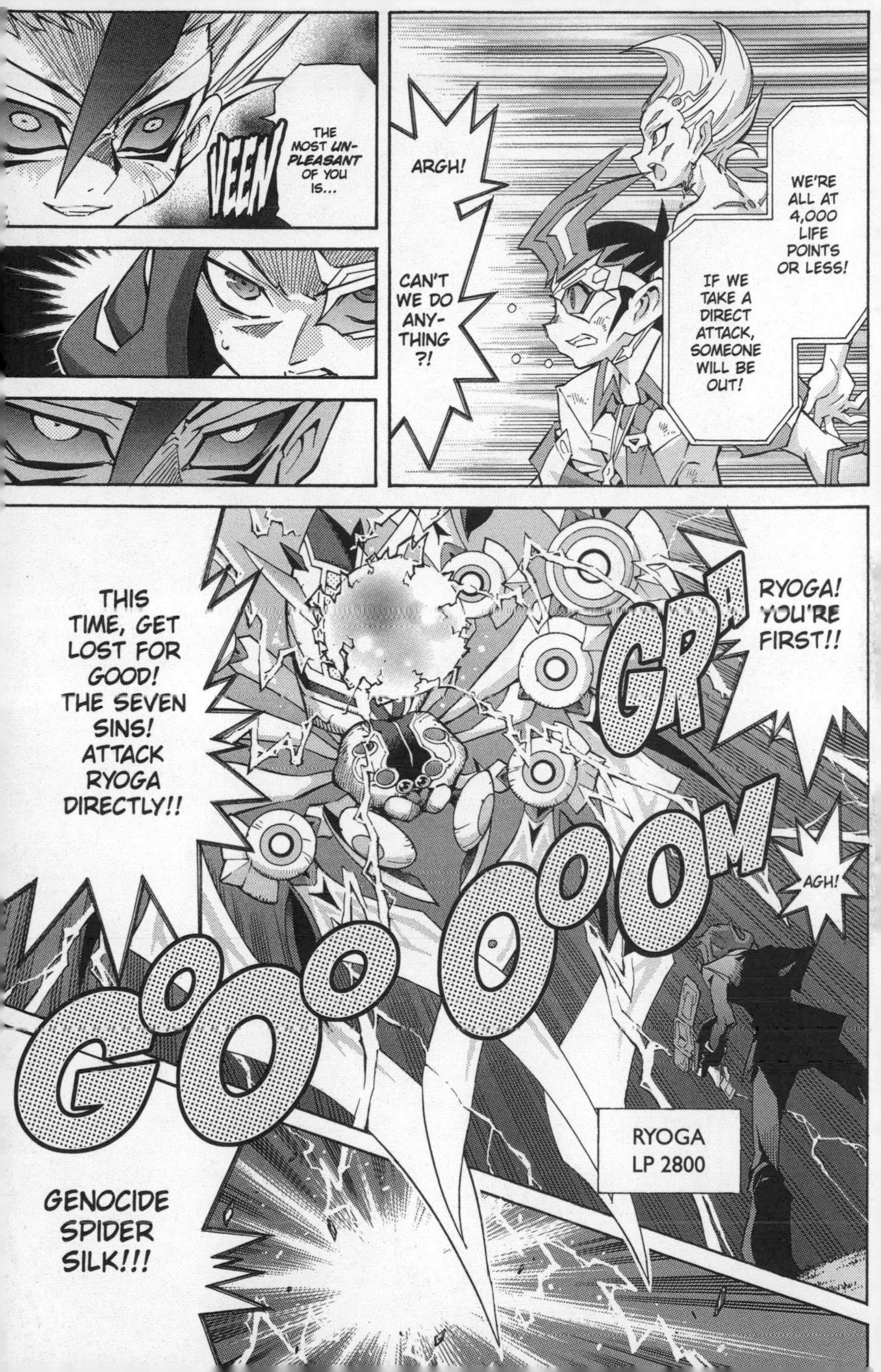
WE'RE ALL AT 4,000 LIFE POINTS OR LESS!
ARGH!
IF WE TAKE A DIRECT ATTACK, SOMEONE WILL BE OUT!
CAN'T WE DO ANY-THING?!
THE MOST UN-PLEASANT OF YOU IS...
VEEN
RYOGA! YOU'RE FIRST!!
GRA
THIS TIME, GET LOST FOR GOOD! THE SEVEN SINS! ATTACK RYOGA DIRECTLY!!
AGH!
GOOOOOOM
RYOGA LP 2800
GENOCIDE SPIDER SILK!!!

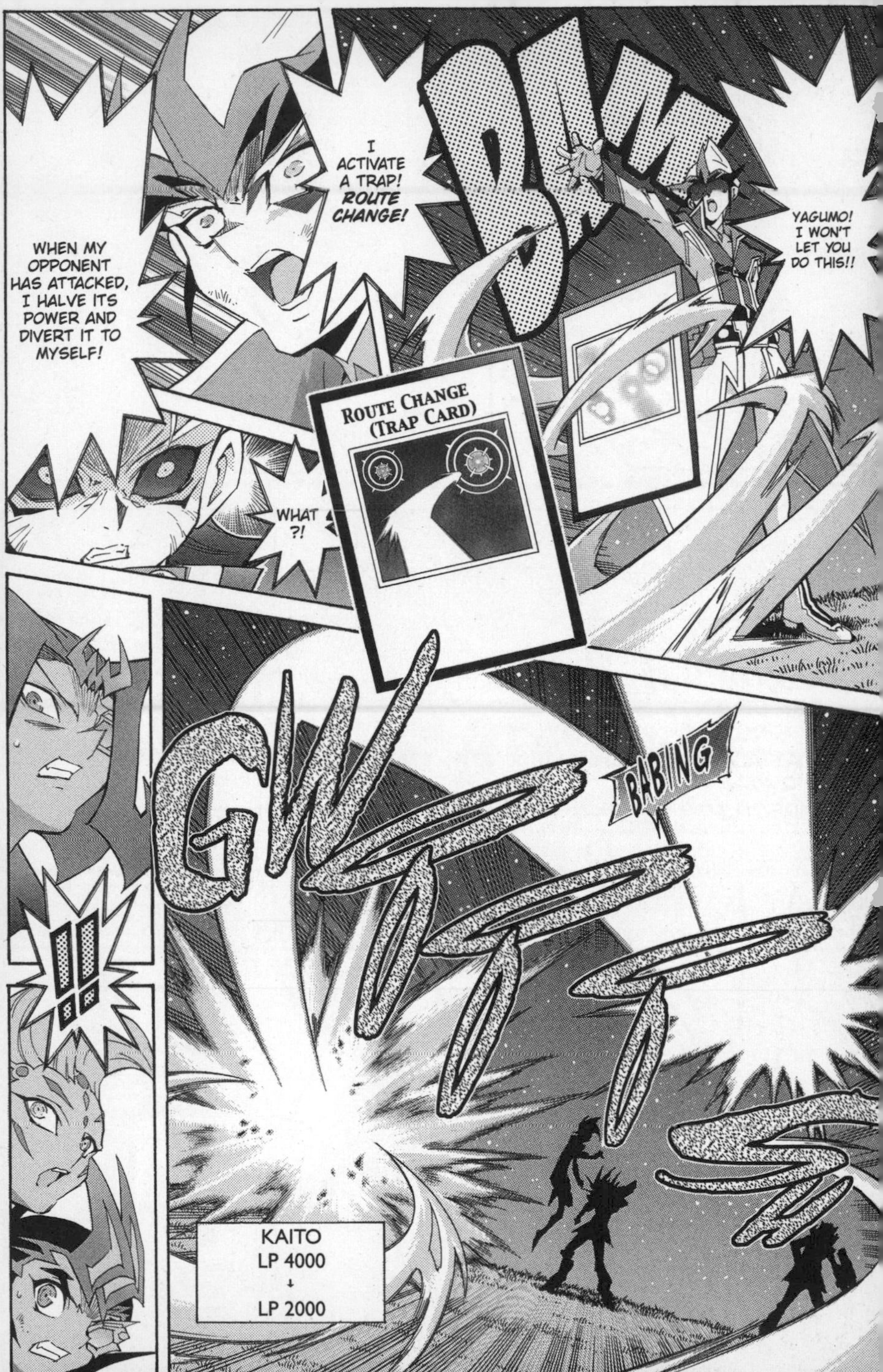
YAGUMO! I WON'T LET YOU DO THIS!!
I ACTIVATE A TRAP! ROUTE CHANGE!
WHEN MY OPPONENT HAS ATTACKED, I HALVE ITS POWER AND DIVERT IT TO MYSELF!
ROUTE CHANGE (TRAP CARD)
WHAT ?!
BABING
KAITO LP 4000 ↓ LP 2000
!!

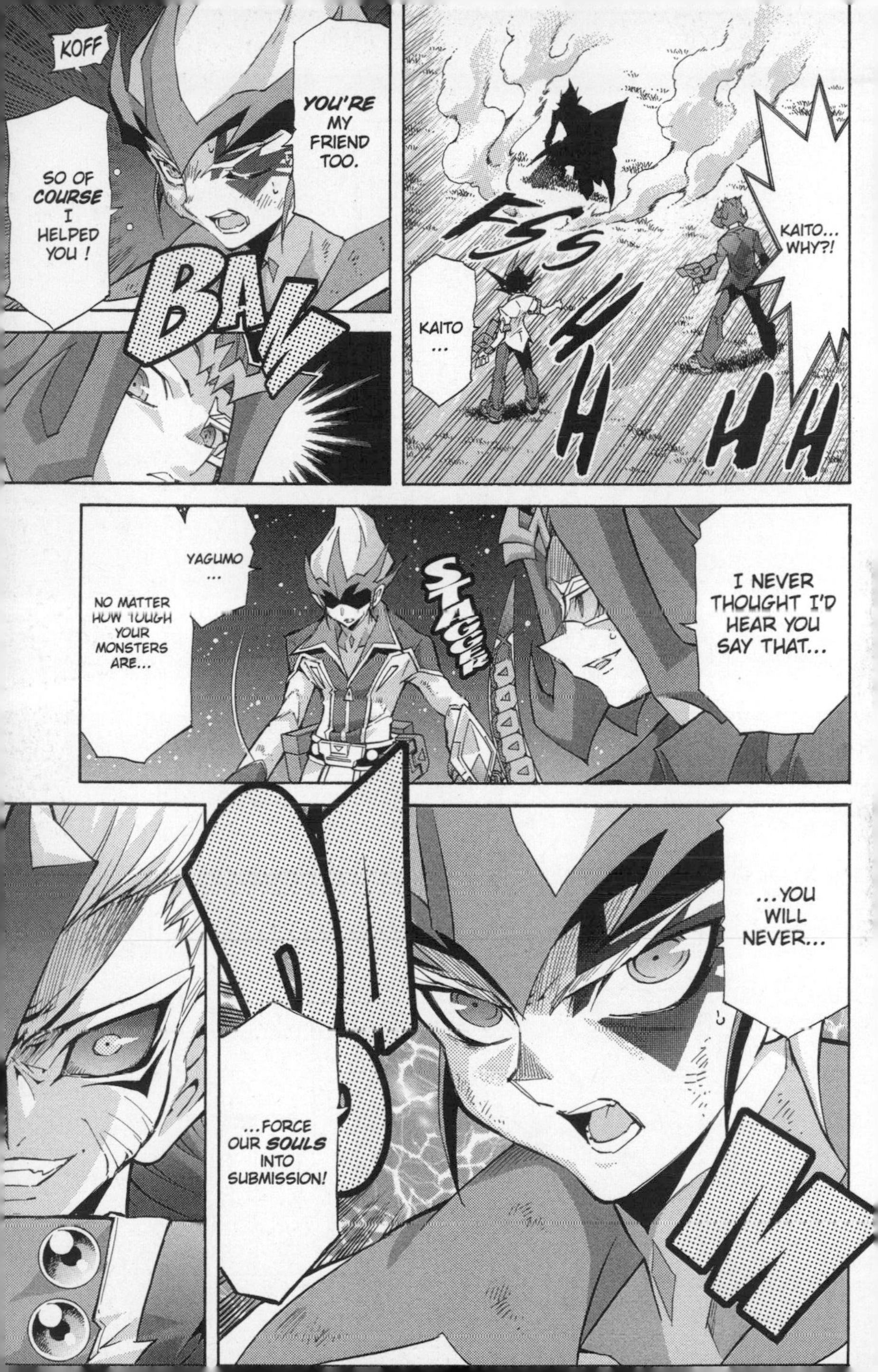
KAITO... WHY?!
KAITO ...
KOFF
YOU'RE MY FRIEND TOO.
SO OF COURSE I HELPED YOU!
I NEVER THOUGHT I'D HEAR YOU SAY THAT...
STAGGER
YAGUMO ...
NO MATTER HOW TOUGH YOUR MONSTERS ARE...
...YOU WILL NEVER...
...FORCE OUR SOULS INTO SUBMISSION!

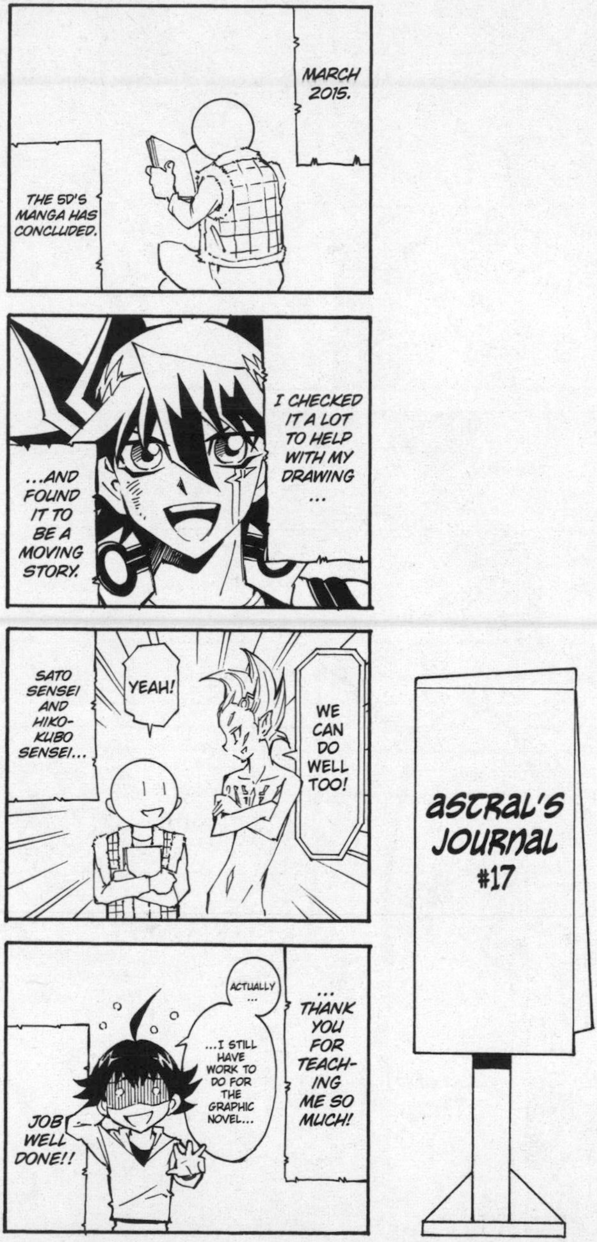
astral's journal #17
MARCH 2015.
THE 5D'S MANGA HAS CONCLUDED.
I CHECKED IT A LOT TO HELP WITH MY DRAWING ...
...AND FOUND IT TO BE A MOVING STORY.
WE CAN DO WELL TOO!
YEAH!
SATO SENSEI AND HIKO-KUBO SENSEI...
...THANK YOU FOR TEACH-ING ME SO MUCH!
ACTUALLY ...
...I STILL HAVE WORK TO DO FOR THE GRAPHIC NOVEL...
JOB WELL DONE!!

Rank 46: A Bond Between Us!!

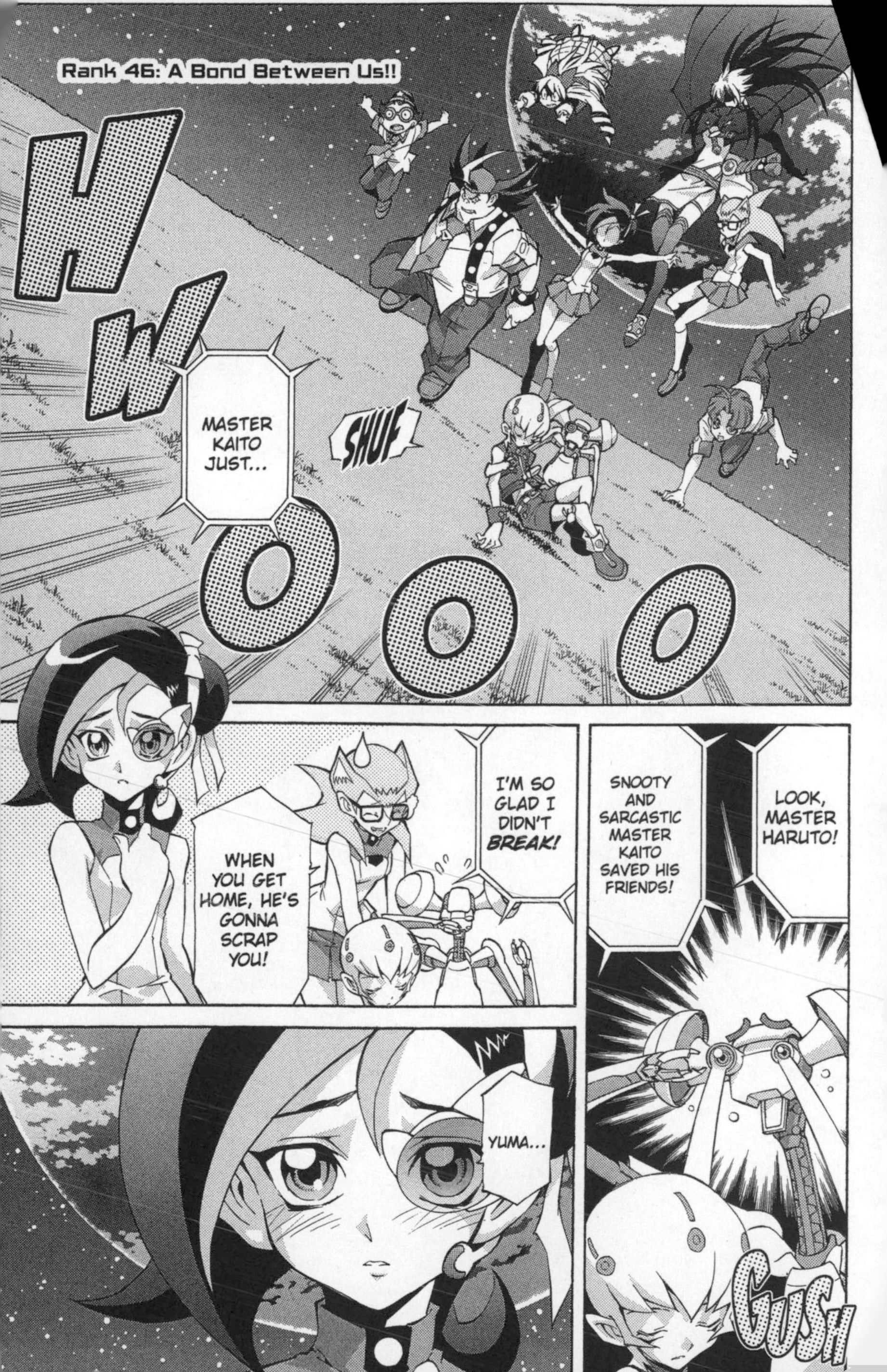
HWOOO
MASTER KAITO JUST...
SHUF
LOOK, MASTER HARUTO!
SNOOTY AND SARCASTIC MASTER KAITO SAVED HIS FRIENDS!
GUSH
I'M SO GLAD I DIDN'T **BREAK!**
WHEN YOU GET HOME, HE'S GONNA SCRAP YOU!
YUMA...

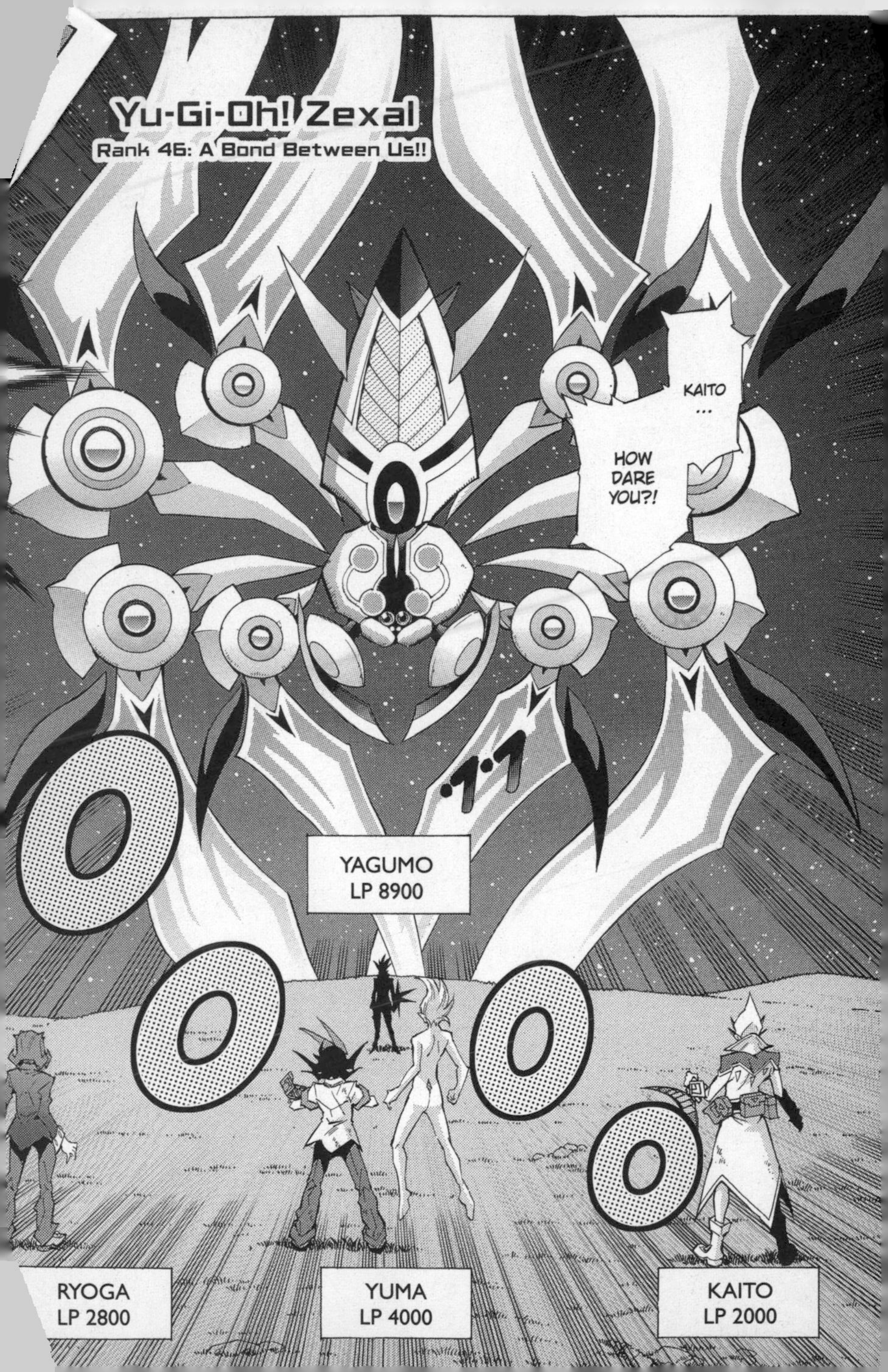
Yu-Gi-Oh! Zexal
Rank 46: A Bond Between Us!!
KAITO ...
HOW DARE YOU?!
YAGUMO LP 8900
KAITO LP 2000
YUMA LP 4000
RYOGA LP 2800

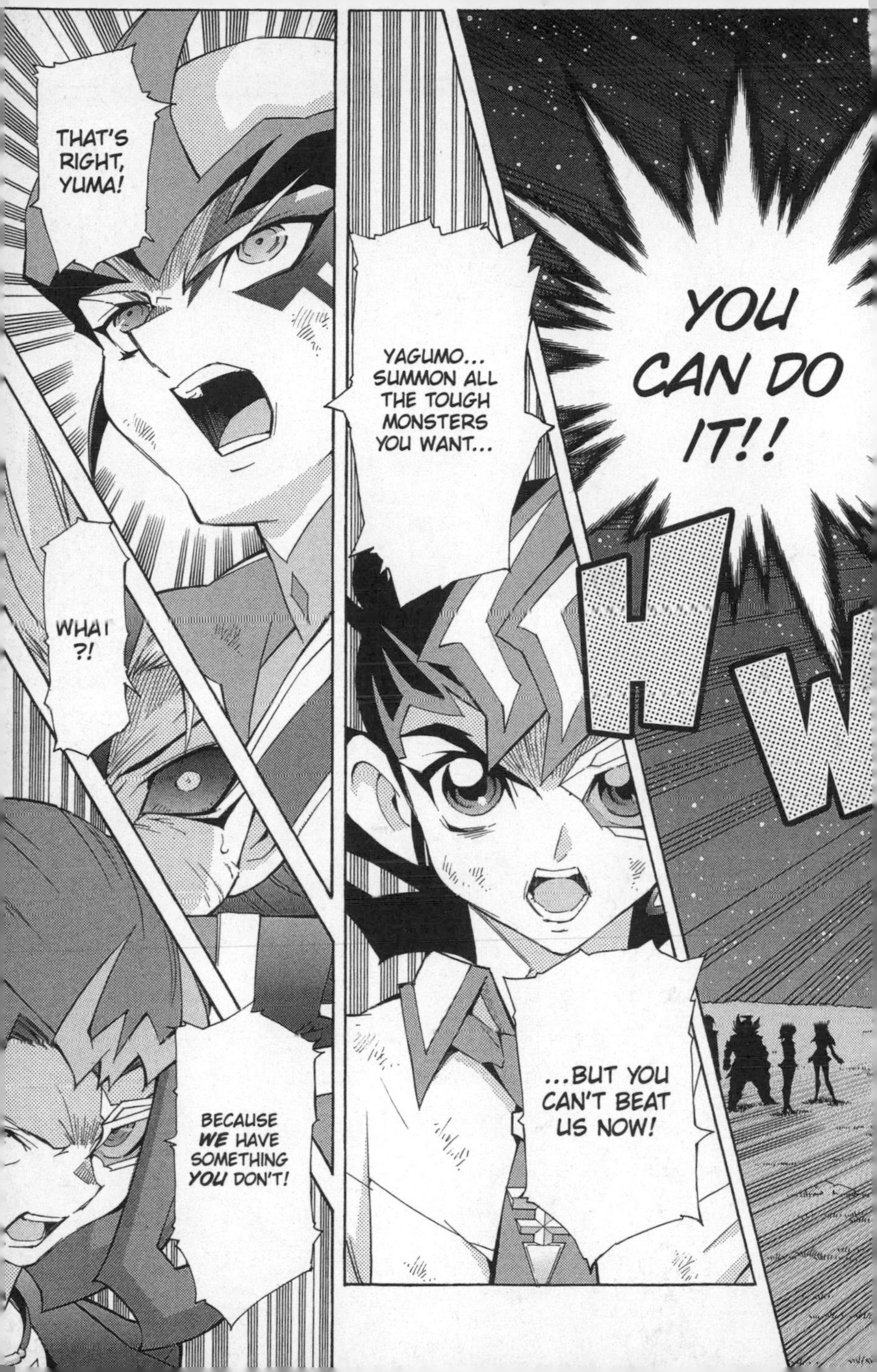
YOU CAN DO IT!!
HW
YAGUMO... SUMMON ALL THE TOUGH MONSTERS YOU WANT...
...BUT YOU CAN'T BEAT US NOW!
THAT'S RIGHT, YUMA!
WHAT?!
BECAUSE WE HAVE SOMETHING YOU DON'T!

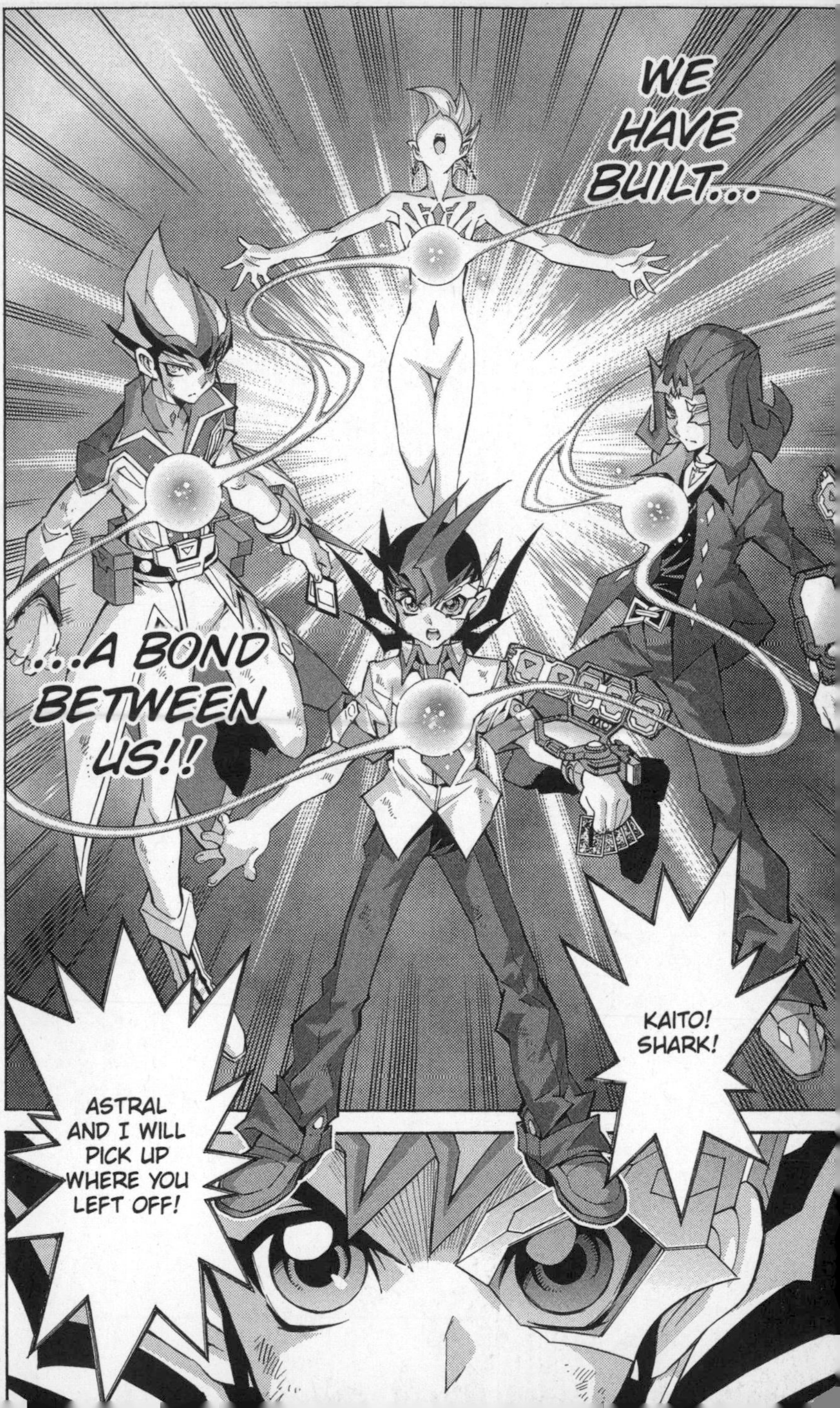
WE HAVE BUILT...
...A BOND BETWEEN US!!
KAITO! SHARK!
ASTRAL AND I WILL PICK UP WHERE YOU LEFT OFF!

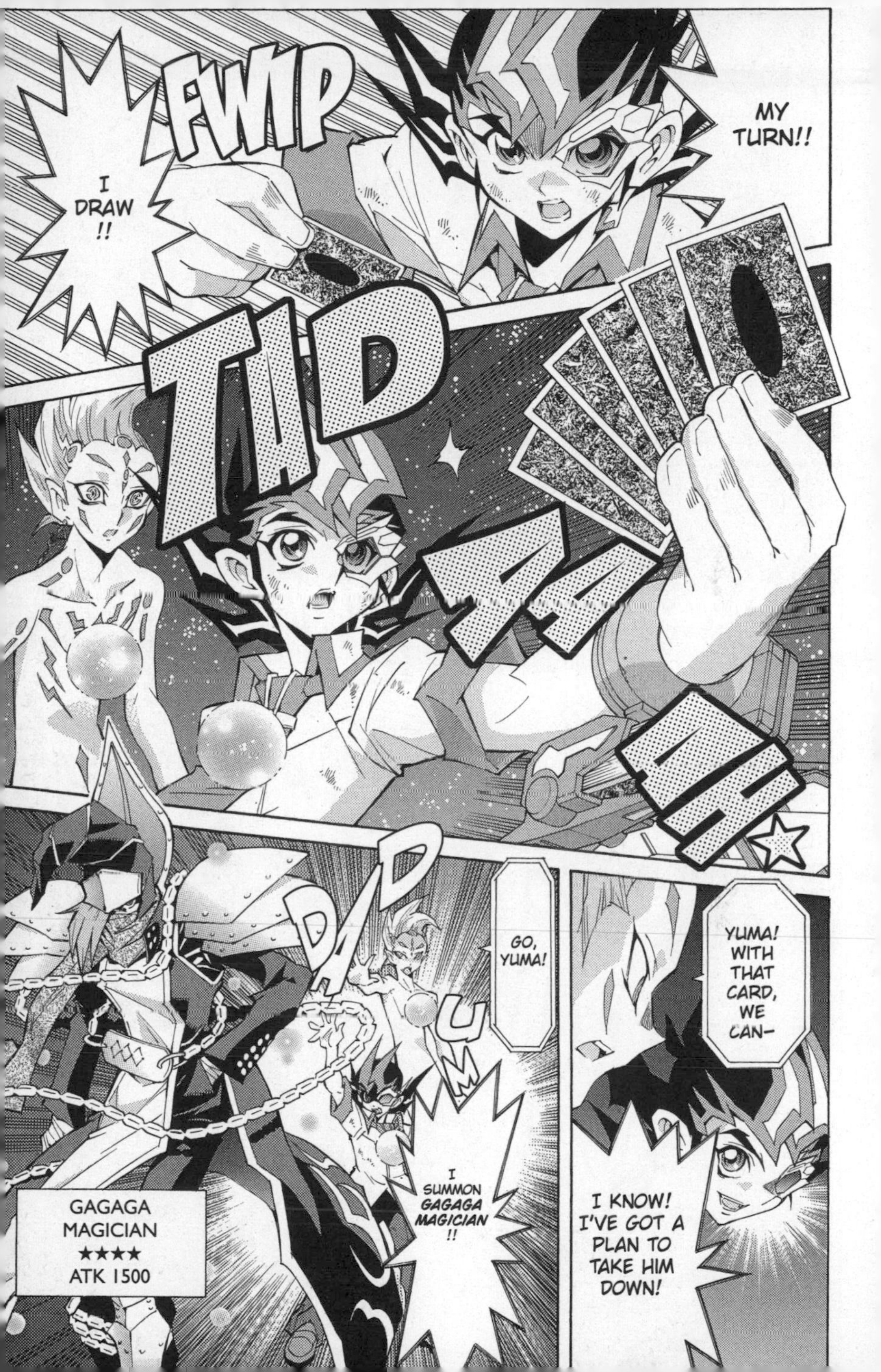
MY TURN!!
FWIP
I DRAW!!
TADAAA!!
YUMA! WITH THAT CARD, WE CAN—
I KNOW! I'VE GOT A PLAN TO TAKE HIM DOWN!
GO, YUMA!
DADUMM
I SUMMON GAGAGA MAGICIAN!!
GAGAGA MAGICIAN ★★★★ ATK 1500

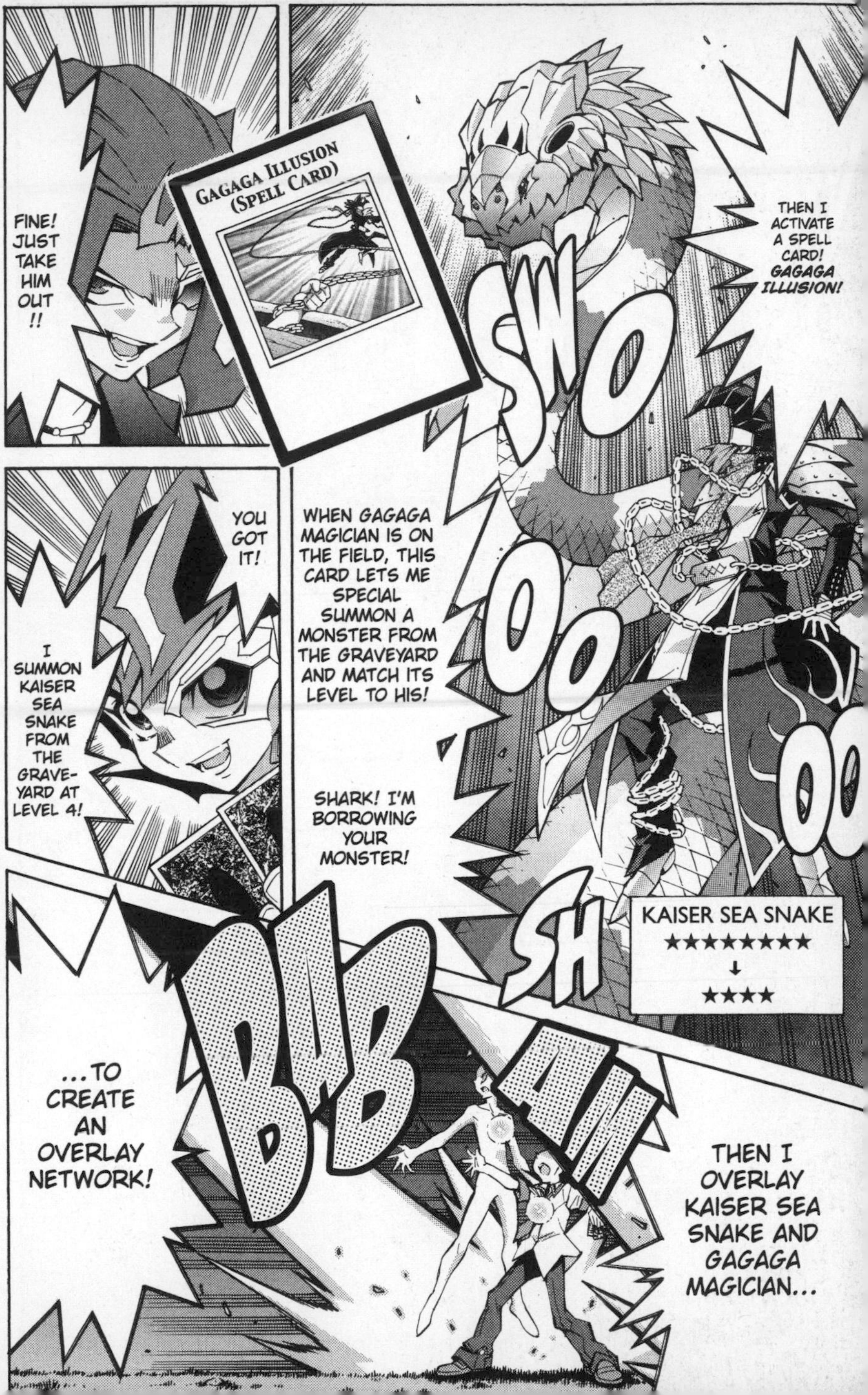
THEN I ACTIVATE A SPELL CARD! GAGAGA ILLUSION!
GAGAGA ILLUSION (SPELL CARD)
SWOOOO
SH
KAISER SEA SNAKE ★★★★★★★★ ↓ ★★★★
FINE! JUST TAKE HIM OUT!!
WHEN GAGAGA MAGICIAN IS ON THE FIELD, THIS CARD LETS ME SPECIAL SUMMON A MONSTER FROM THE GRAVEYARD AND MATCH ITS LEVEL TO HIS!
SHARK! I'M BORROWING YOUR MONSTER!
YOU GOT IT!
I SUMMON KAISER SEA SNAKE FROM THE GRAVEYARD AT LEVEL 4!
BABAM
THEN I OVERLAY KAISER SEA SNAKE AND GAGAGA MAGICIAN...
...TO CREATE AN OVERLAY NETWORK!

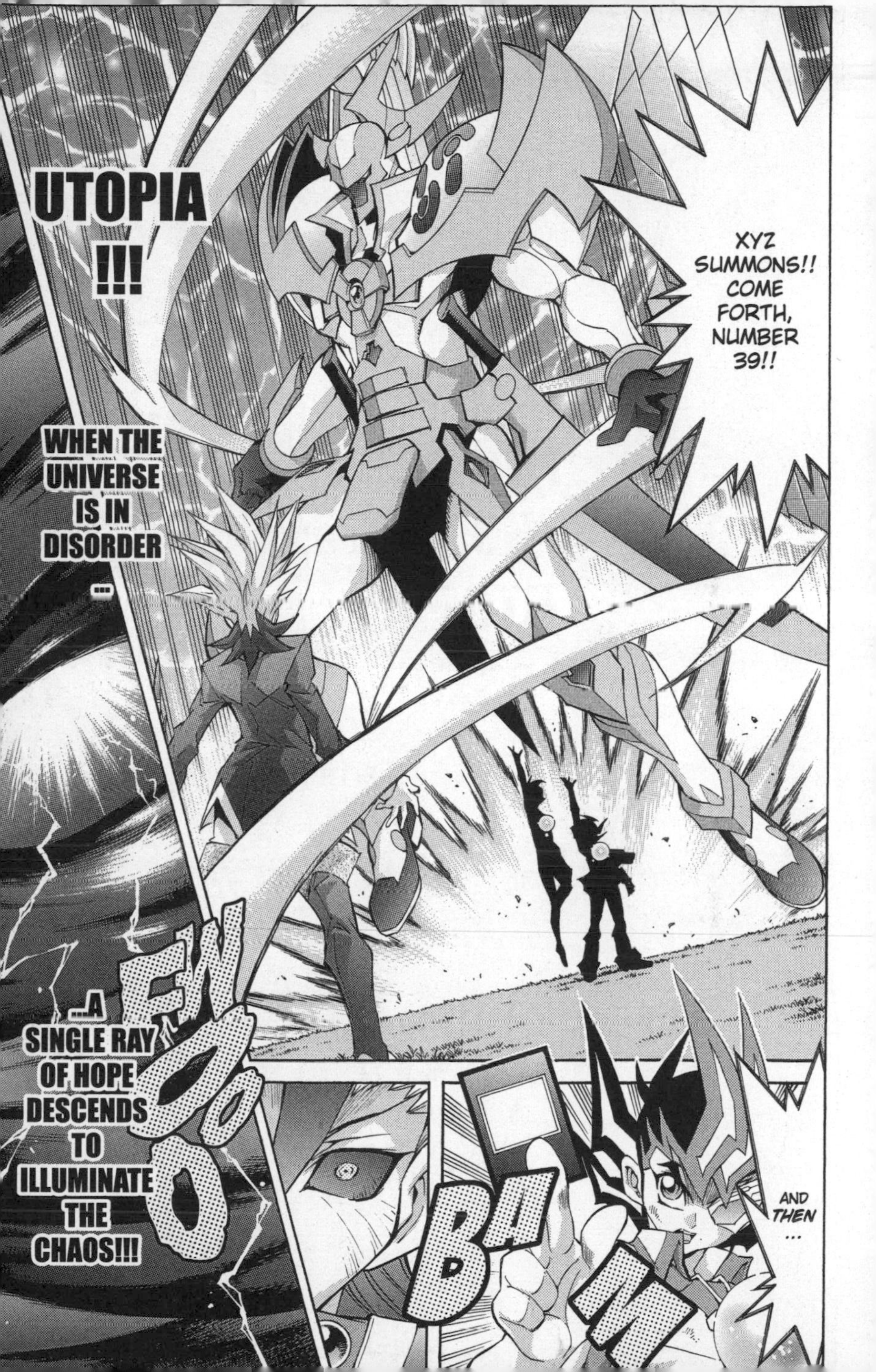
XYZ SUMMONS!! COME FORTH, NUMBER 39!!
UTOPIA!!!
WHEN THE UNIVERSE IS IN DISORDER...
...A SINGLE RAY OF HOPE DESCENDS TO ILLUMINATE THE CHAOS!!!
FWOOO
AND THEN...
BAM

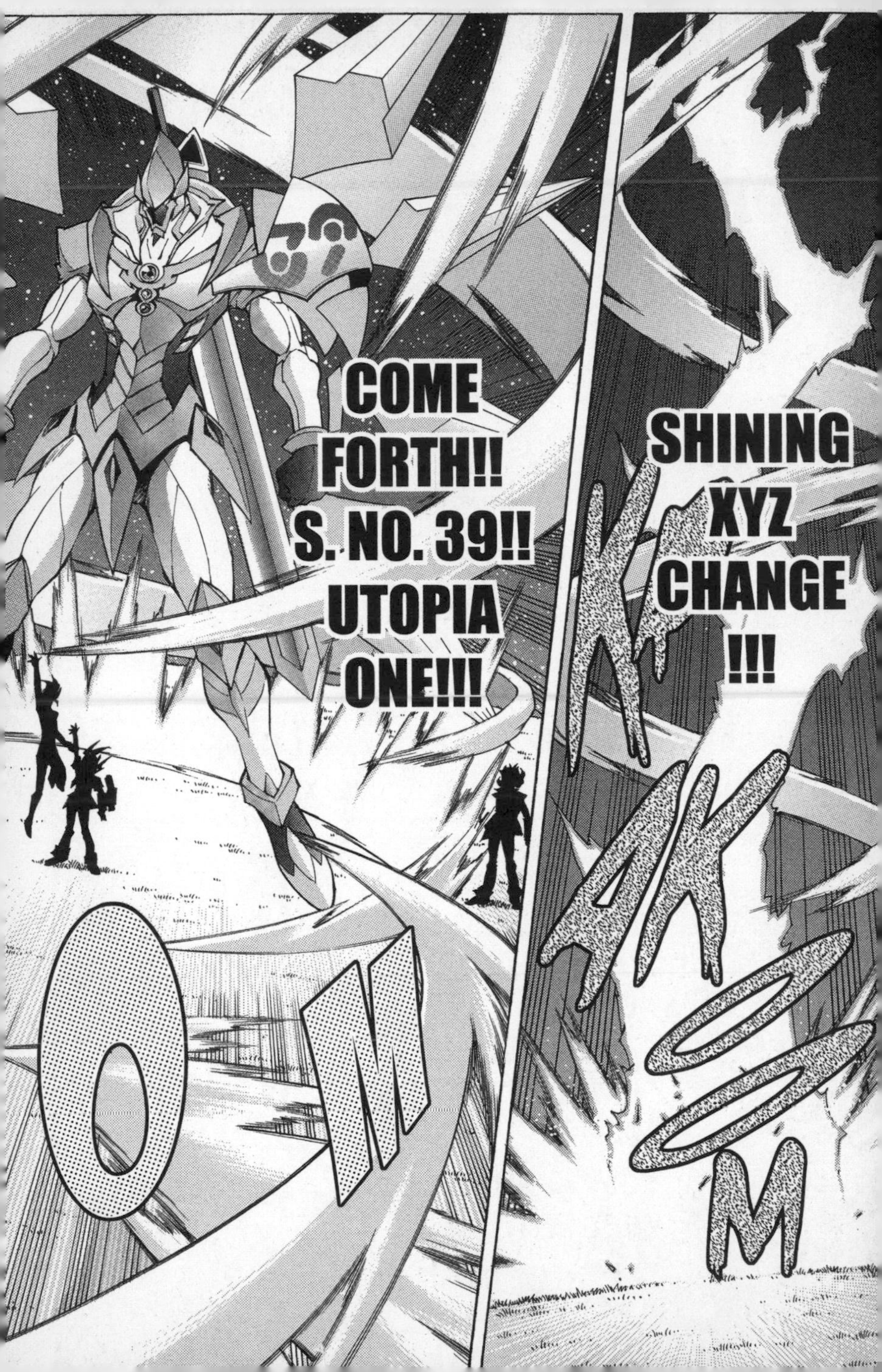
SHINING XYZ CHANGE!!!
KAKOOM
COME FORTH!! S. NO. 39!! UTOPIA ONE!!!
OM

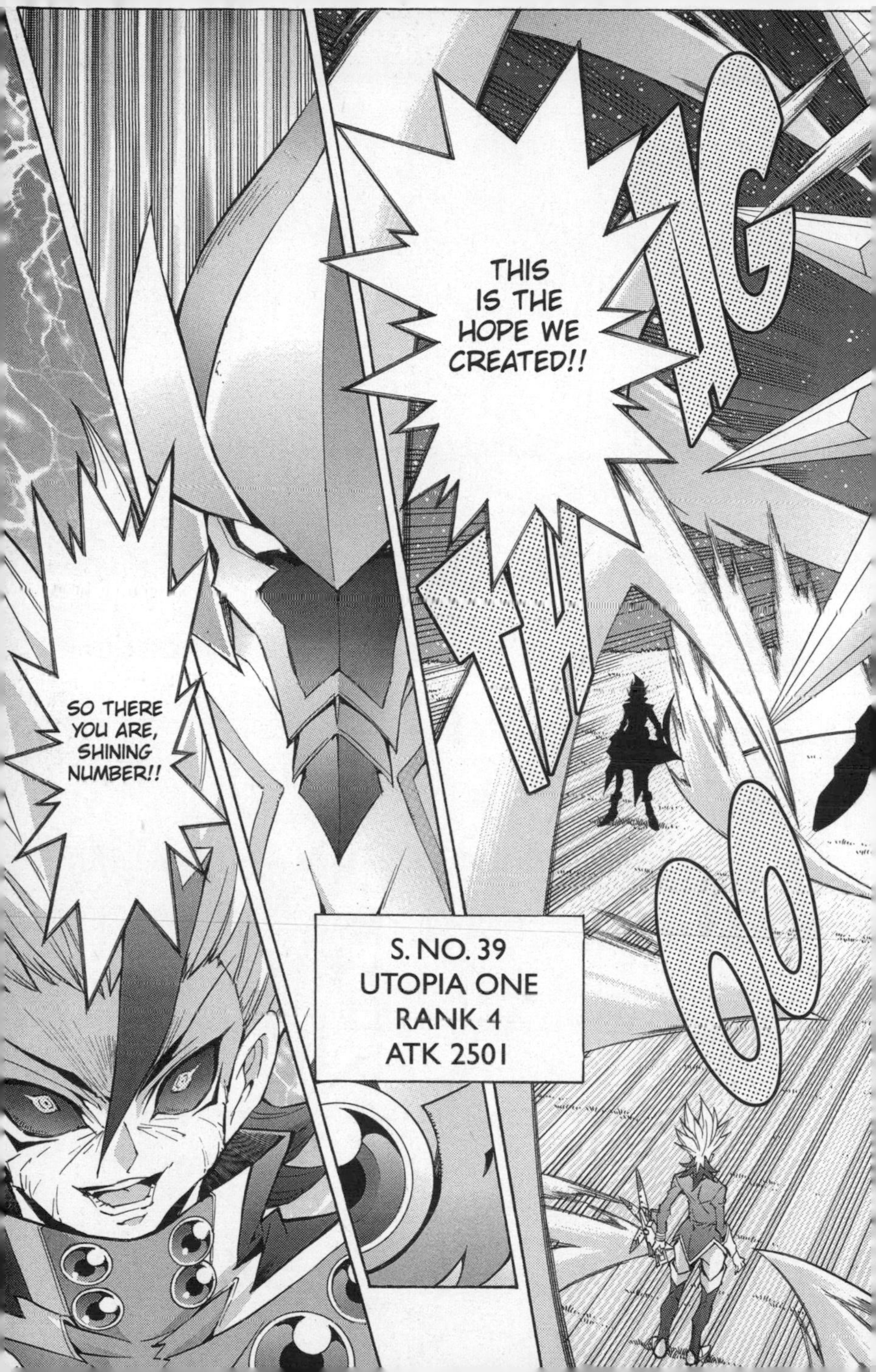
THIS IS THE HOPE WE CREATED!!
S. NO. 39 UTOPIA ONE RANK 4 ATK 2501
SO THERE YOU ARE, SHINING NUMBER!!

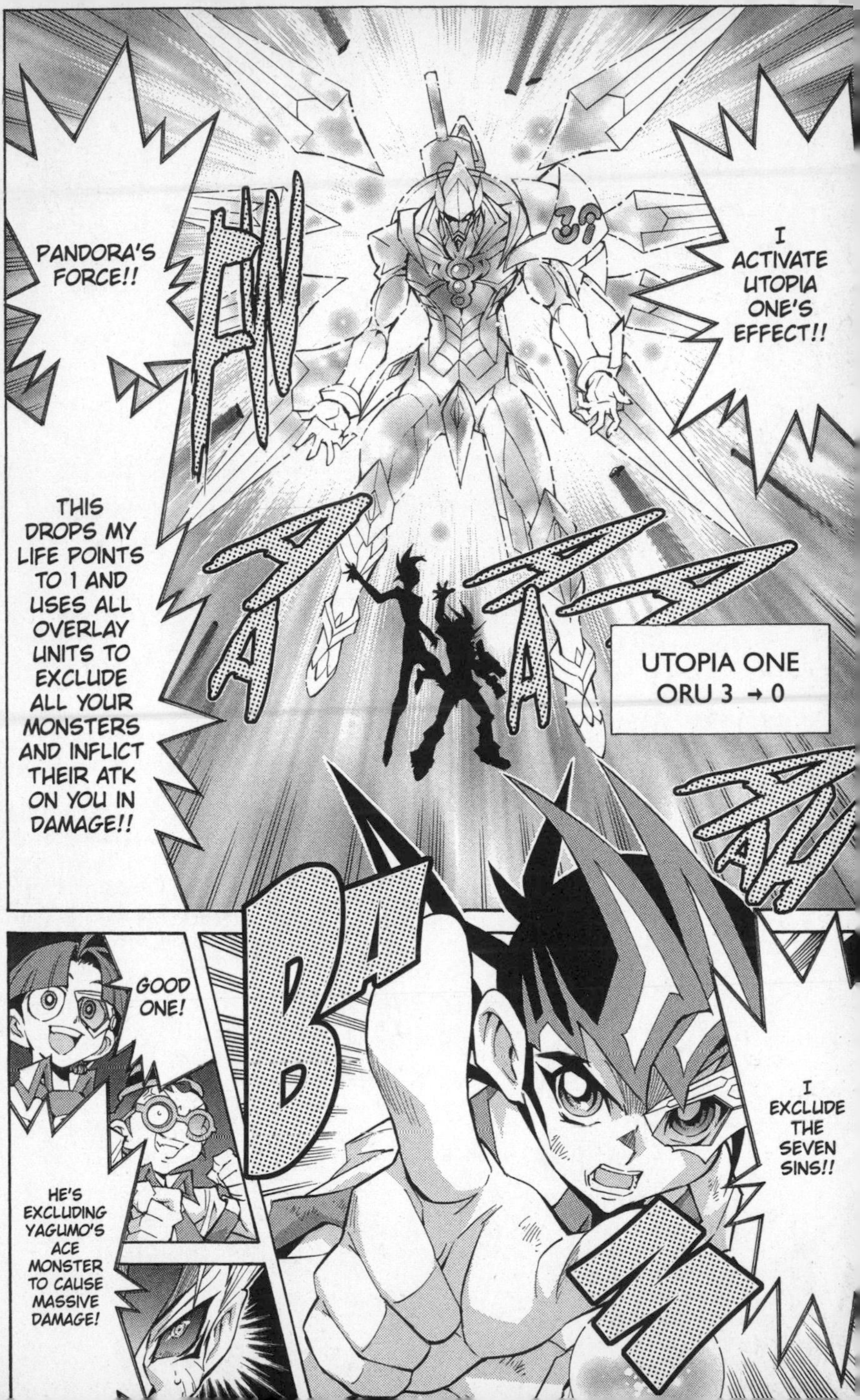
I ACTIVATE UTOPIA ONE'S EFFECT!!
PANDORA'S FORCE!!
FWN
UTOPIA ONE ORU 3 → 0
THIS DROPS MY LIFE POINTS TO 1 AND USES ALL OVERLAY UNITS TO EXCLUDE ALL YOUR MONSTERS AND INFLICT THEIR ATK ON YOU IN DAMAGE!!
I EXCLUDE THE SEVEN SINS!!
BA
GOOD ONE!
HE'S EXCLUDING YAGUMO'S ACE MONSTER TO CAUSE MASSIVE DAMAGE!

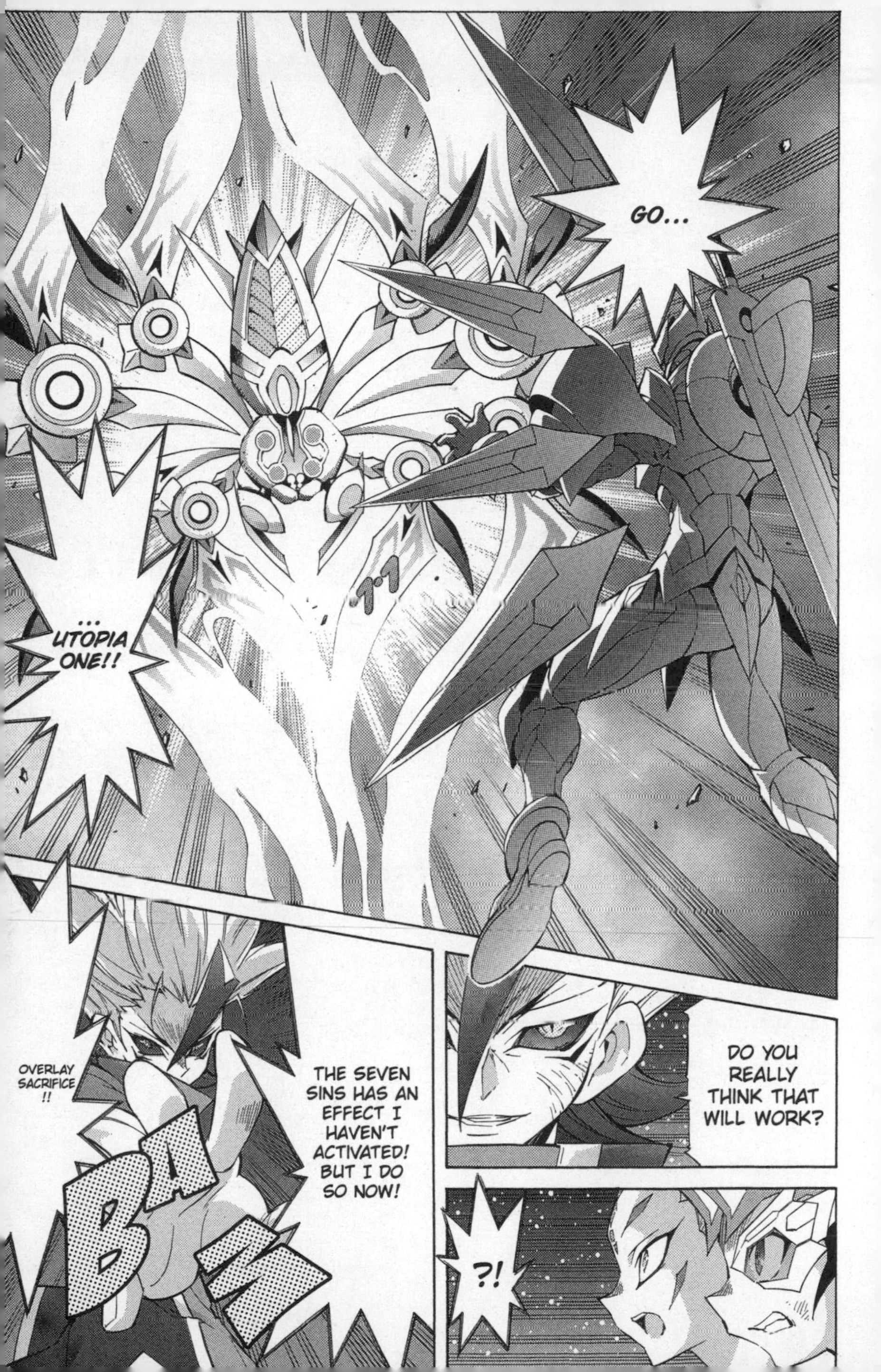
GO...
...UTOPIA ONE!!
DO YOU REALLY THINK THAT WILL WORK?
?!
THE SEVEN SINS HAS AN EFFECT I HAVEN'T ACTIVATED! BUT I DO SO NOW!
OVERLAY SACRIFICE!!

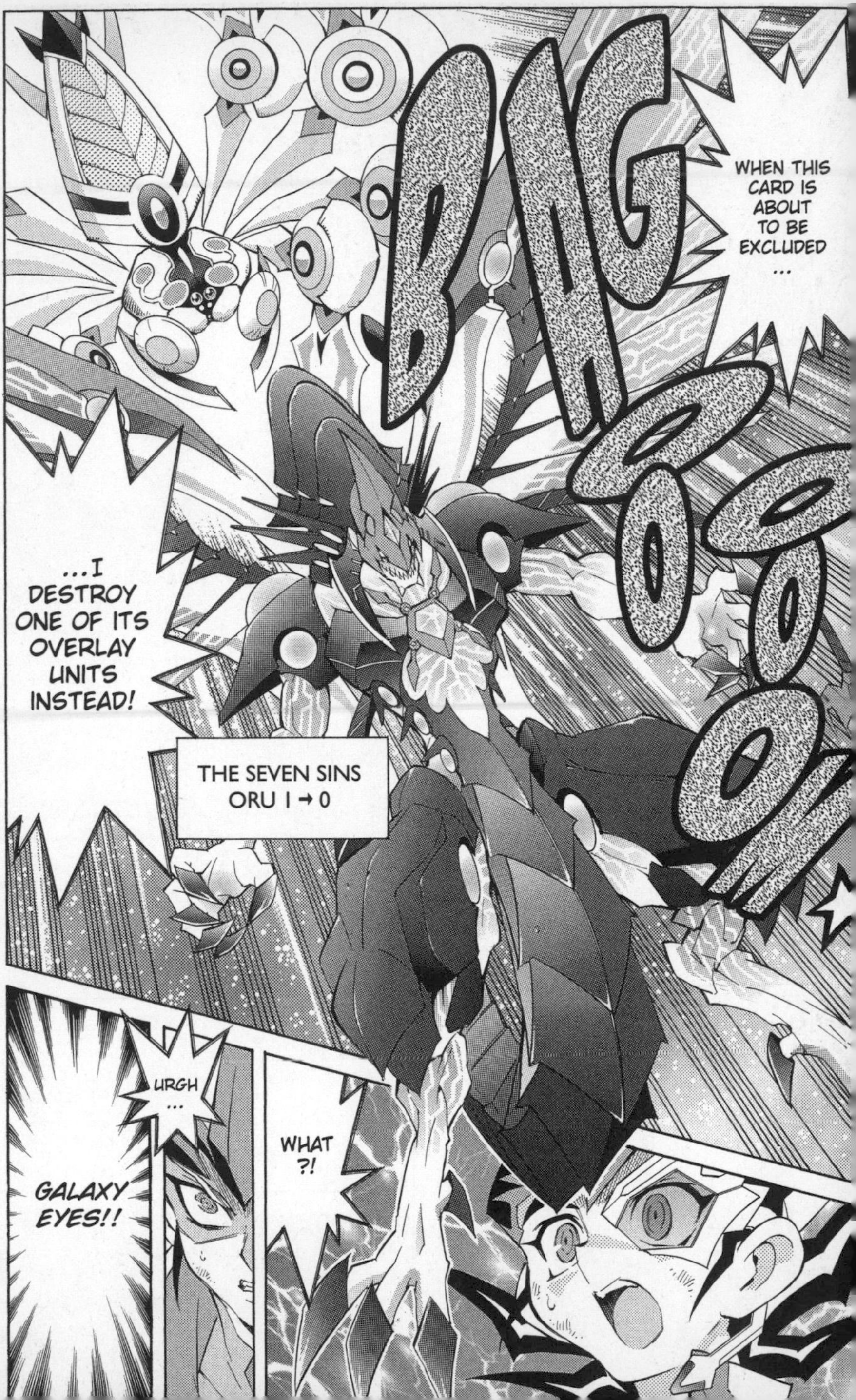
WHEN THIS CARD IS ABOUT TO BE EXCLUDED ...
BAGOOOOM
...I DESTROY ONE OF ITS OVERLAY UNITS INSTEAD!
THE SEVEN SINS ORU 1 → 0
WHAT ?!
URGH ...
GALAXY EYES!!

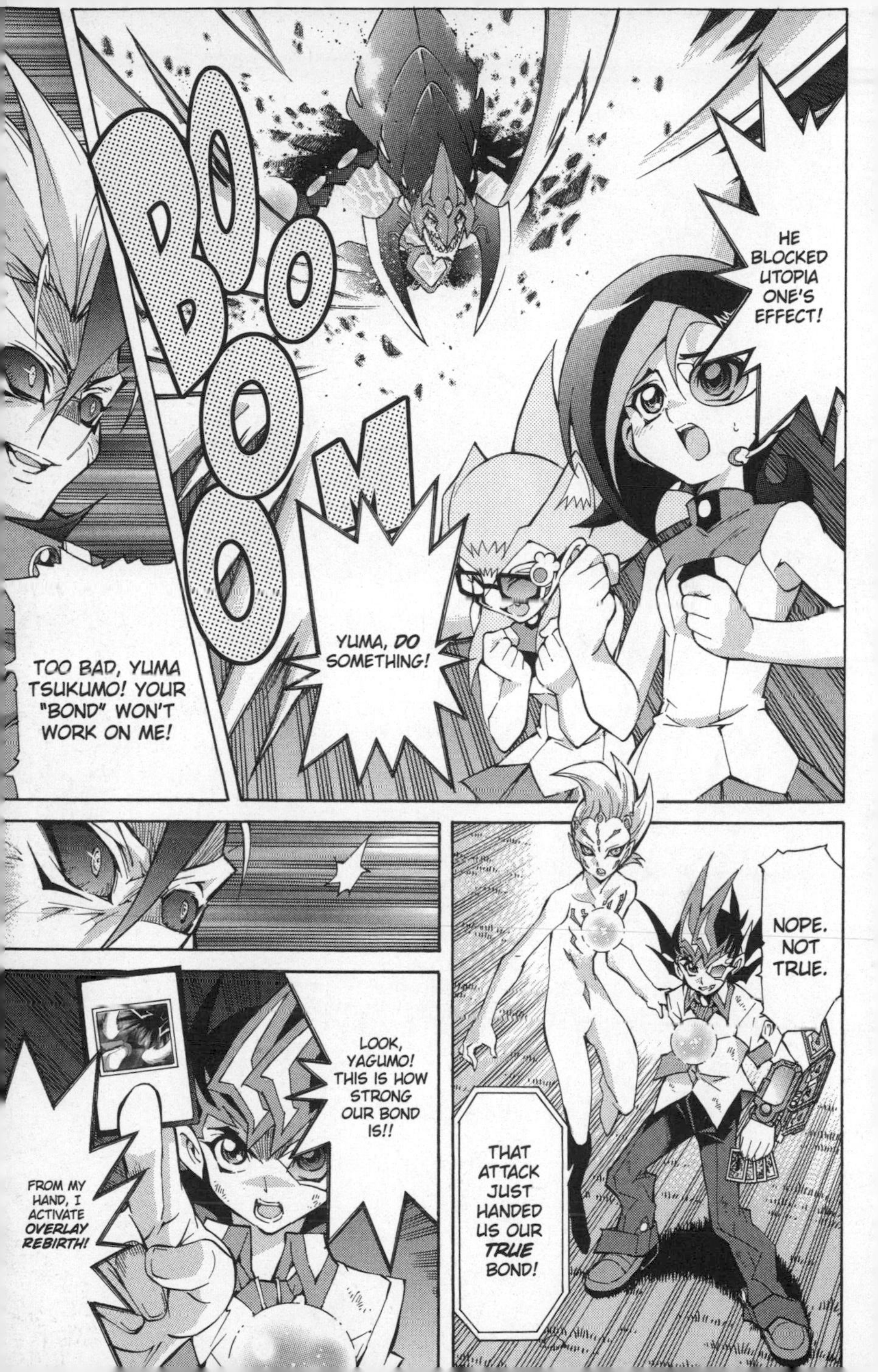
HE BLOCKED UTOPIA ONE'S EFFECT!
YUMA, *DO* SOMETHING!
BOOOOOM
TOO BAD, YUMA TSUKUMO! YOUR "BOND" WON'T WORK ON ME!
NOPE. NOT TRUE.
THAT ATTACK JUST HANDED US OUR *TRUE* BOND!
LOOK, YAGUMO! THIS IS HOW STRONG OUR BOND IS!!
FROM MY HAND, I ACTIVATE *OVERLAY REBIRTH!*

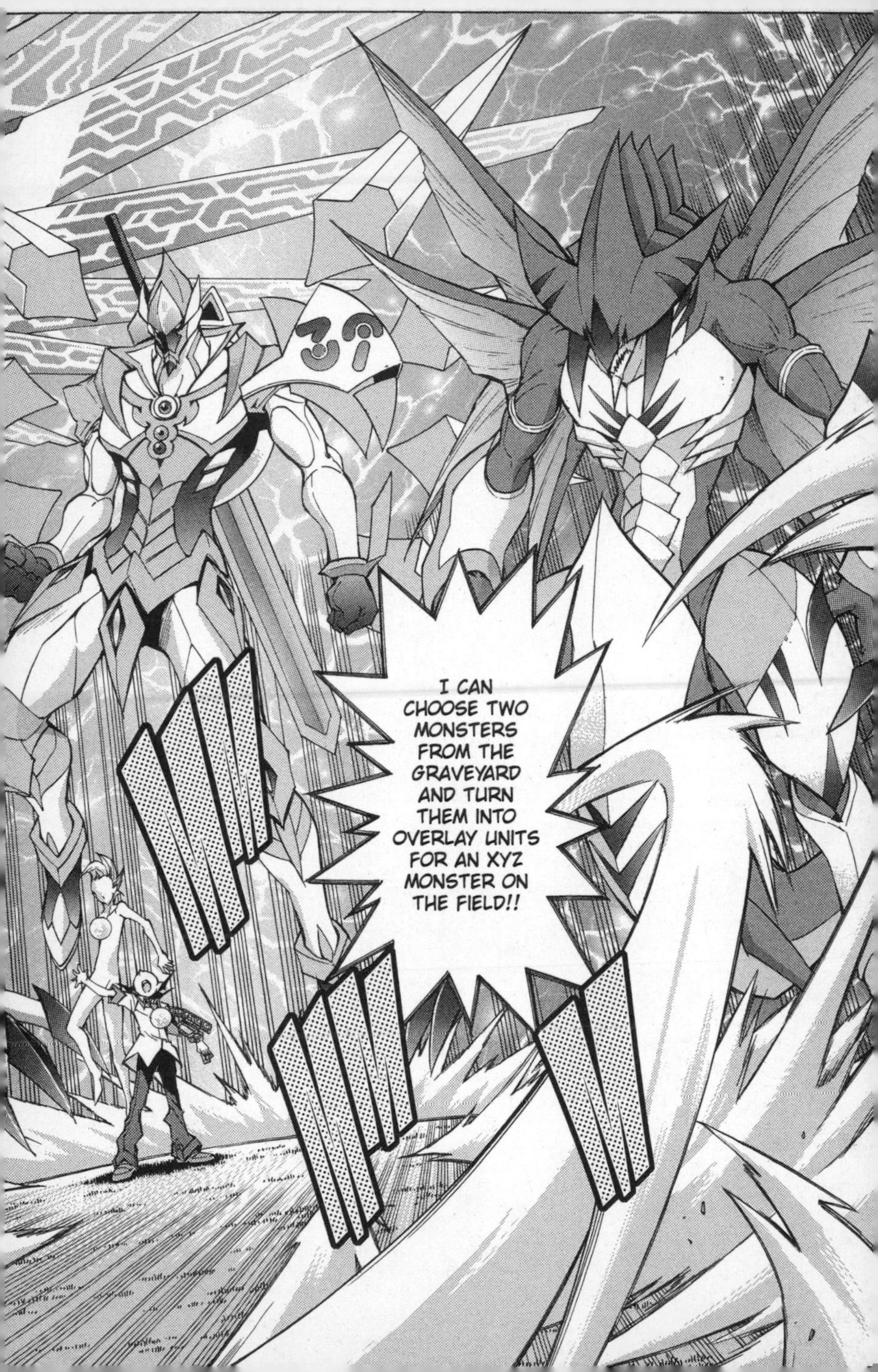
I CAN CHOOSE TWO MONSTERS FROM THE GRAVEYARD AND TURN THEM INTO OVERLAY UNITS FOR AN XYZ MONSTER ON THE FIELD!!

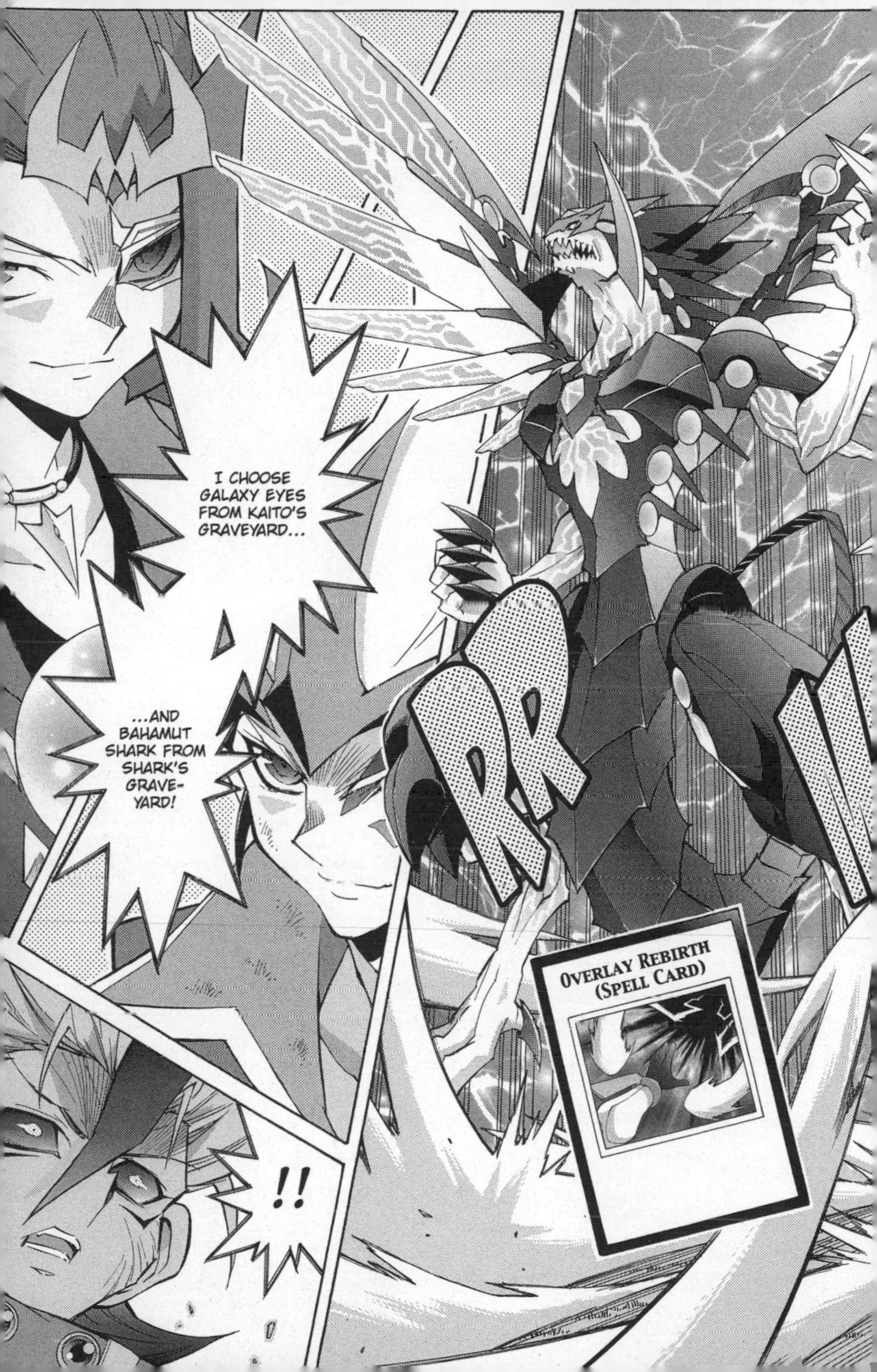
I CHOOSE GALAXY EYES FROM KAITO'S GRAVEYARD...
...AND BAHAMUT SHARK FROM SHARK'S GRAVE-YARD!
RR
OVERLAY REBIRTH (SPELL CARD)
!!

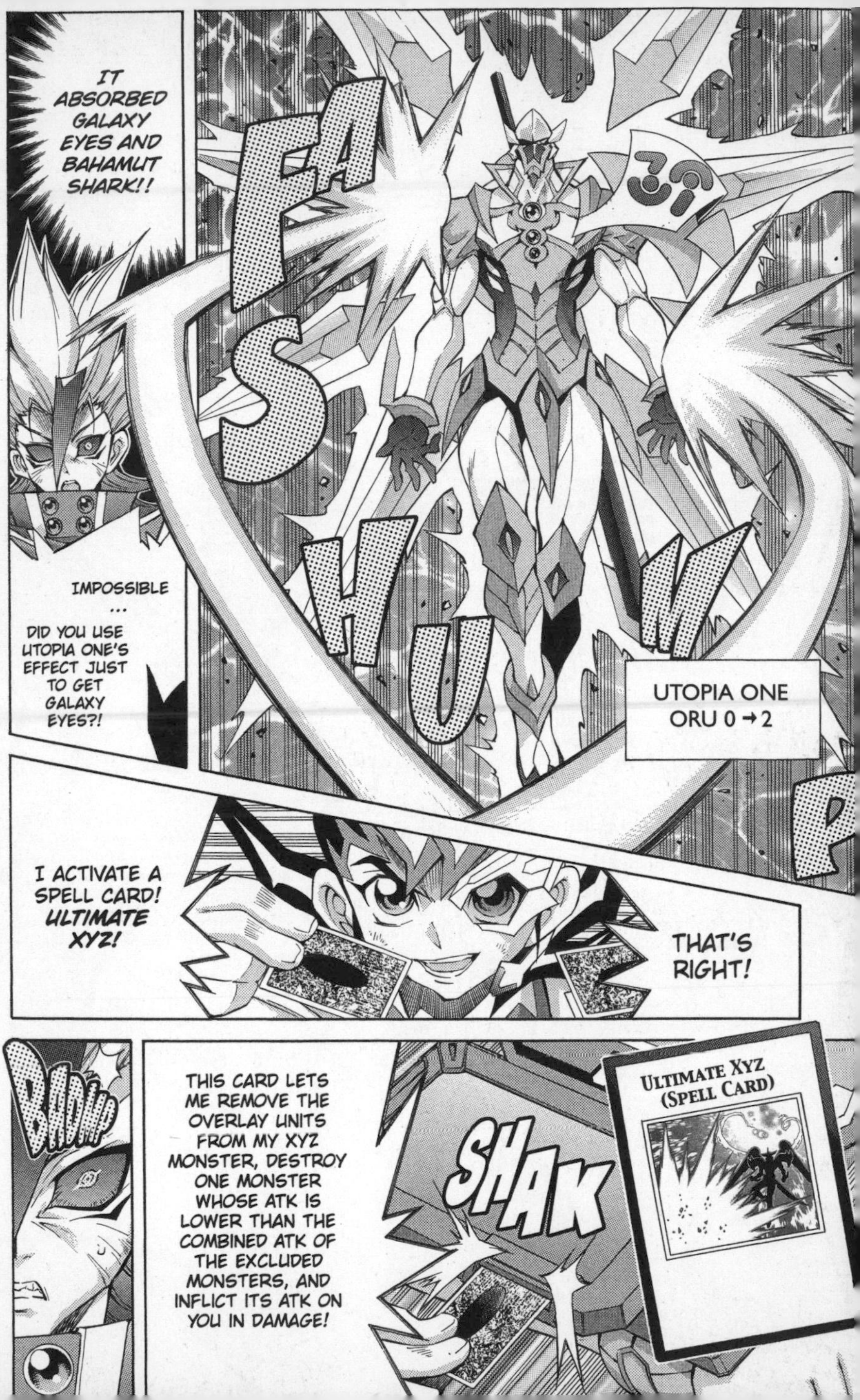
FASHUN
UTOPIA ONE ORU 0 → 2
IT ABSORBED GALAXY EYES AND BAHAMUT SHARK!!
IMPOSSIBLE...
DID YOU USE UTOPIA ONE'S EFFECT JUST TO GET GALAXY EYES?!
THAT'S RIGHT!
I ACTIVATE A SPELL CARD! ULTIMATE XYZ!
ULTIMATE XYZ (SPELL CARD)
SHAK
THIS CARD LETS ME REMOVE THE OVERLAY UNITS FROM MY XYZ MONSTER, DESTROY ONE MONSTER WHOSE ATK IS LOWER THAN THE COMBINED ATK OF THE EXCLUDED MONSTERS, AND INFLICT ITS ATK ON YOU IN DAMAGE!

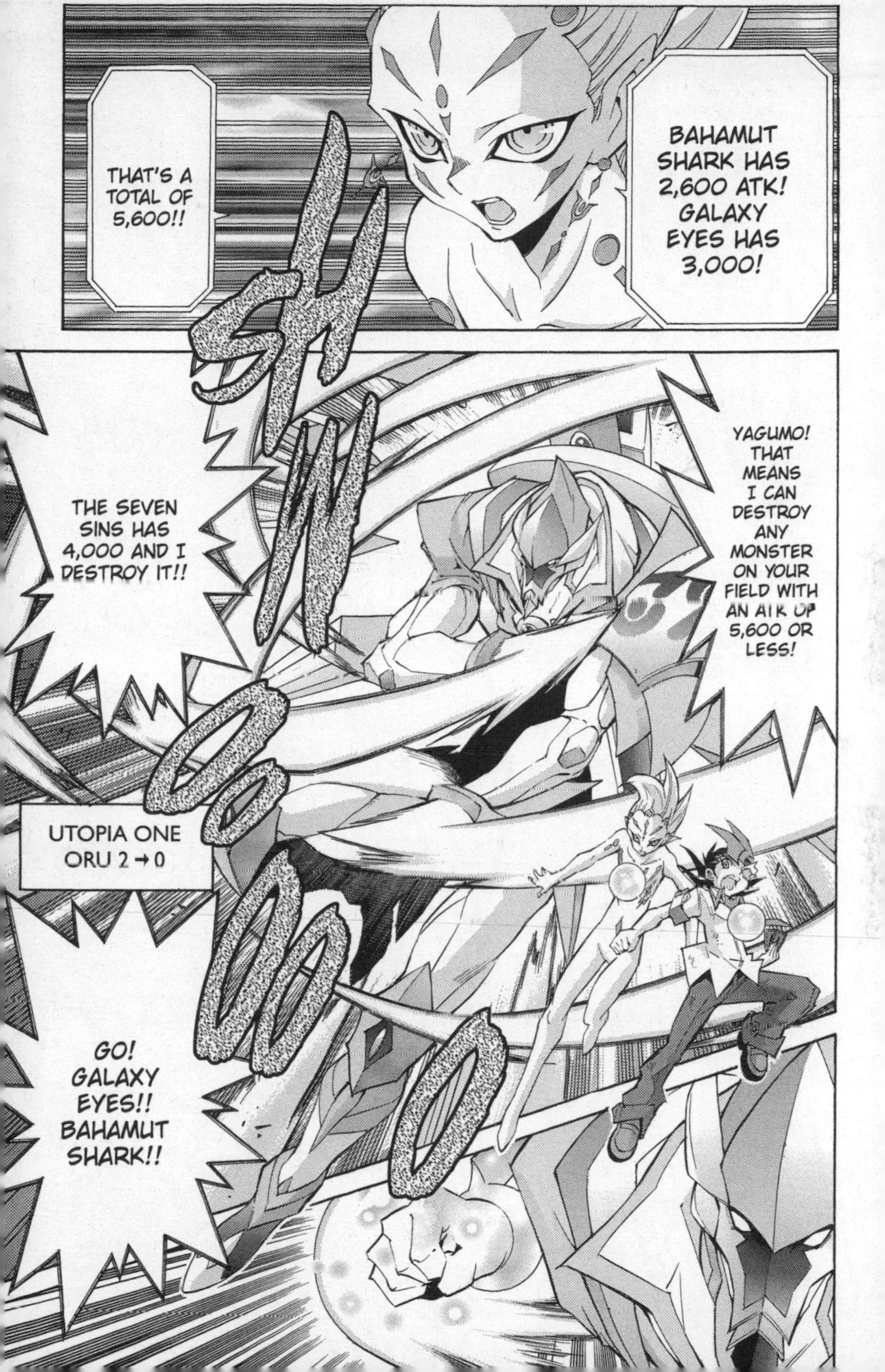
BAHAMUT SHARK HAS 2,600 ATK! GALAXY EYES HAS 3,000!
THAT'S A TOTAL OF 5,600!!
SHWOOOOOO
YAGUMO! THAT MEANS I CAN DESTROY ANY MONSTER ON YOUR FIELD WITH AN ATK OF 5,600 OR LESS!
THE SEVEN SINS HAS 4,000 AND I DESTROY IT!!
UTOPIA ONE ORU 2 → 0
GO! GALAXY EYES!! BAHAMUT SHARK!!

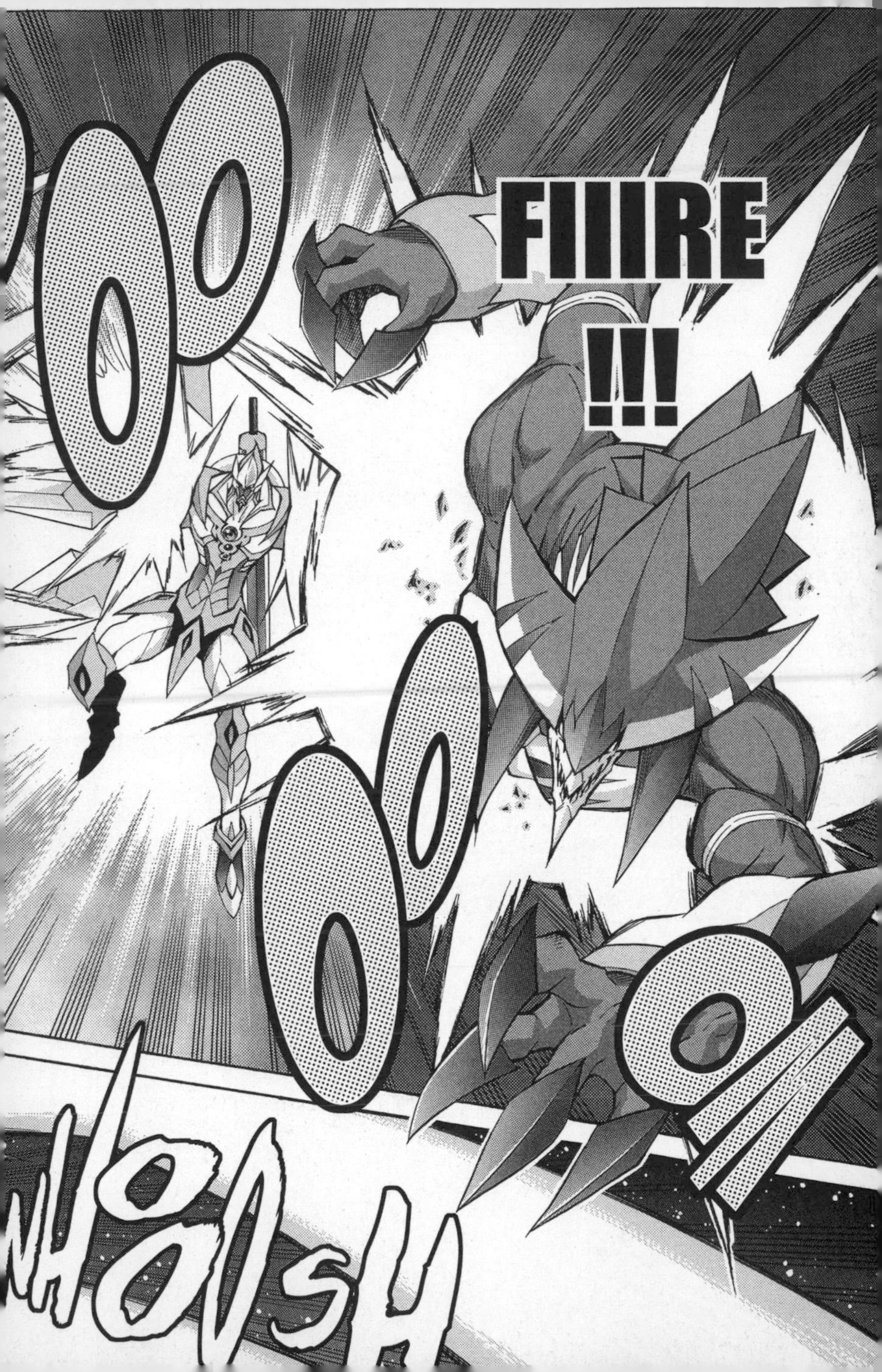
FIIIRE
!!!
WHOOSH

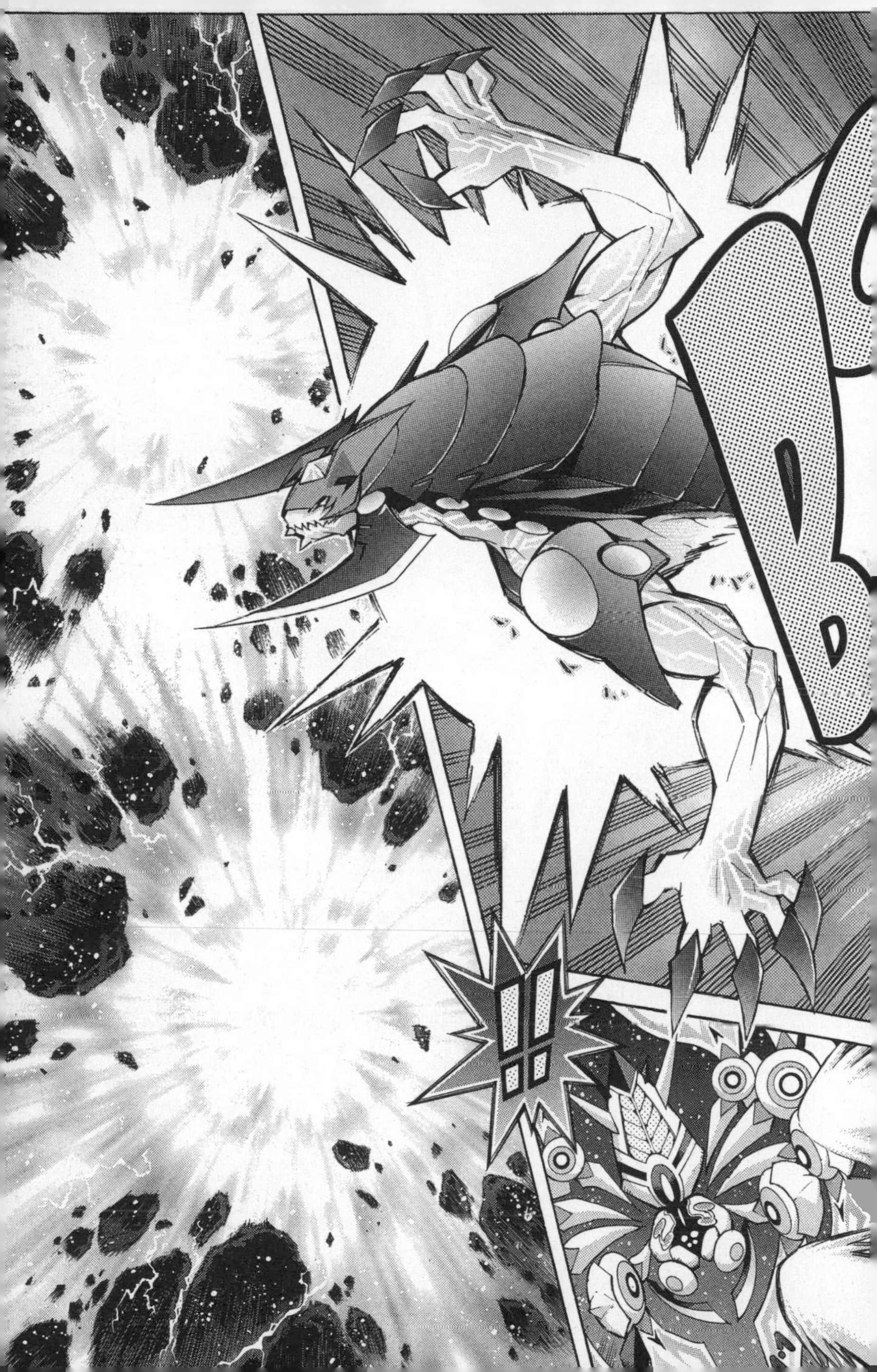
!!

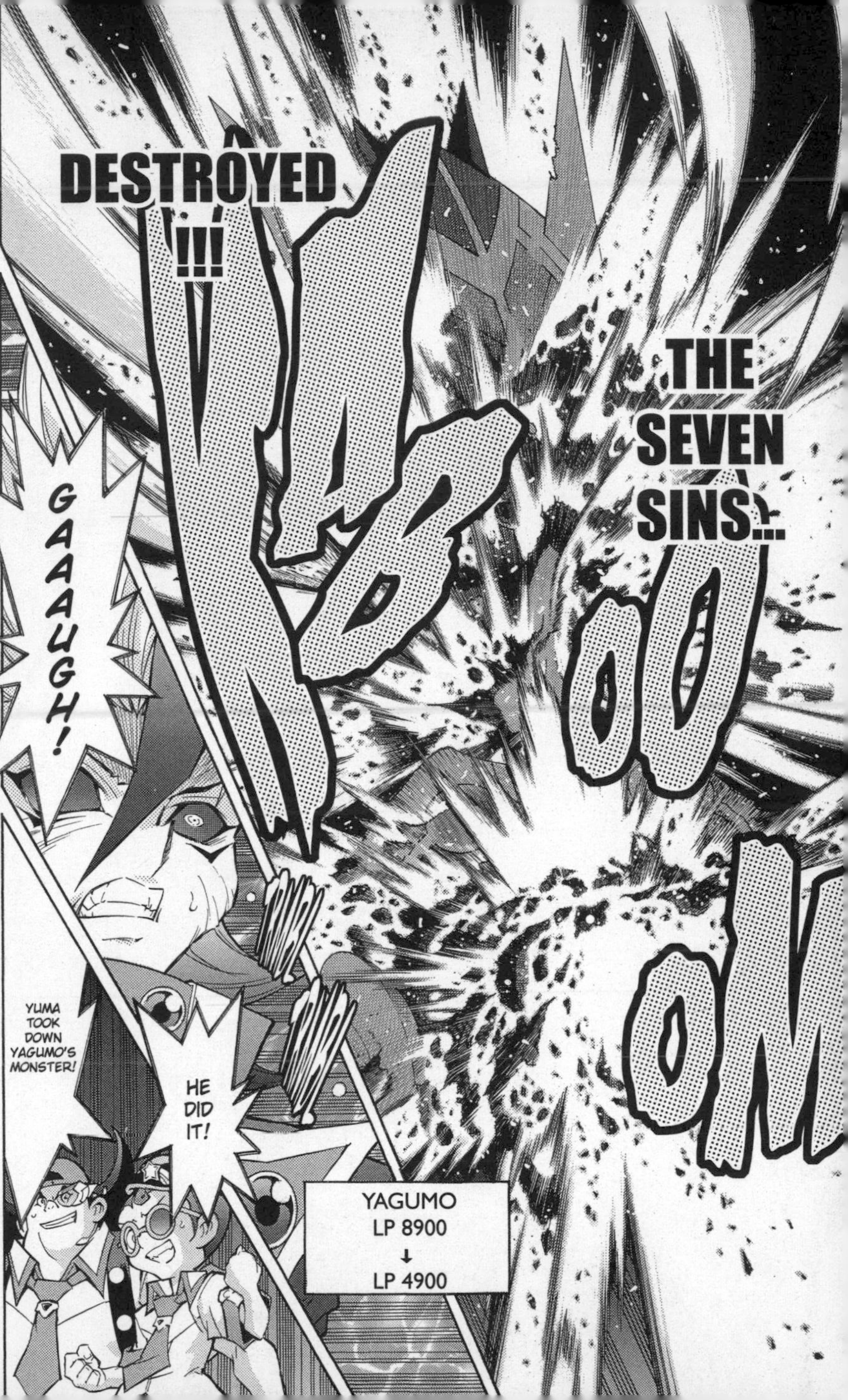
THE SEVEN SINS...
DESTROYED !!!
GAAAAUGH!
HE DID IT!
YUMA TOOK DOWN YAGUMO'S MONSTER!
YAGUMO LP 8900 ↓ LP 4900

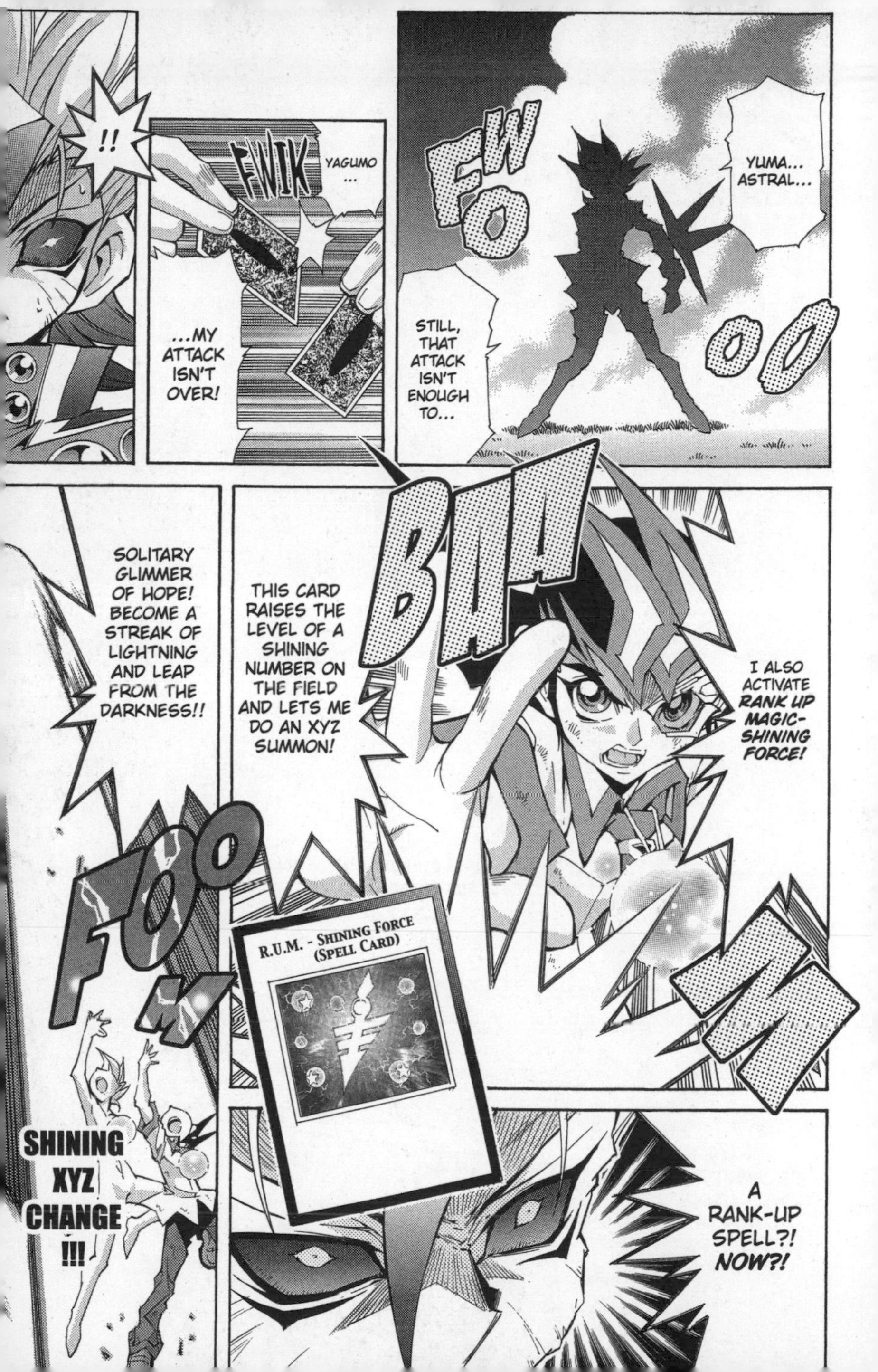
YUMA... ASTRAL...
STILL, THAT ATTACK ISN'T ENOUGH TO...
FWIK
YAGUMO ...
...MY ATTACK ISN'T OVER!
!!
BAM
I ALSO ACTIVATE *RANK UP MAGIC-SHINING FORCE!*
THIS CARD RAISES THE LEVEL OF A SHINING NUMBER ON THE FIELD AND LETS ME DO AN XYZ SUMMON!
R.U.M. - SHINING FORCE (SPELL CARD)
SOLITARY GLIMMER OF HOPE! BECOME A STREAK OF LIGHTNING AND LEAP FROM THE DARKNESS!!
A RANK-UP SPELL?! *NOW?!*
SHINING XYZ CHANGE!!!

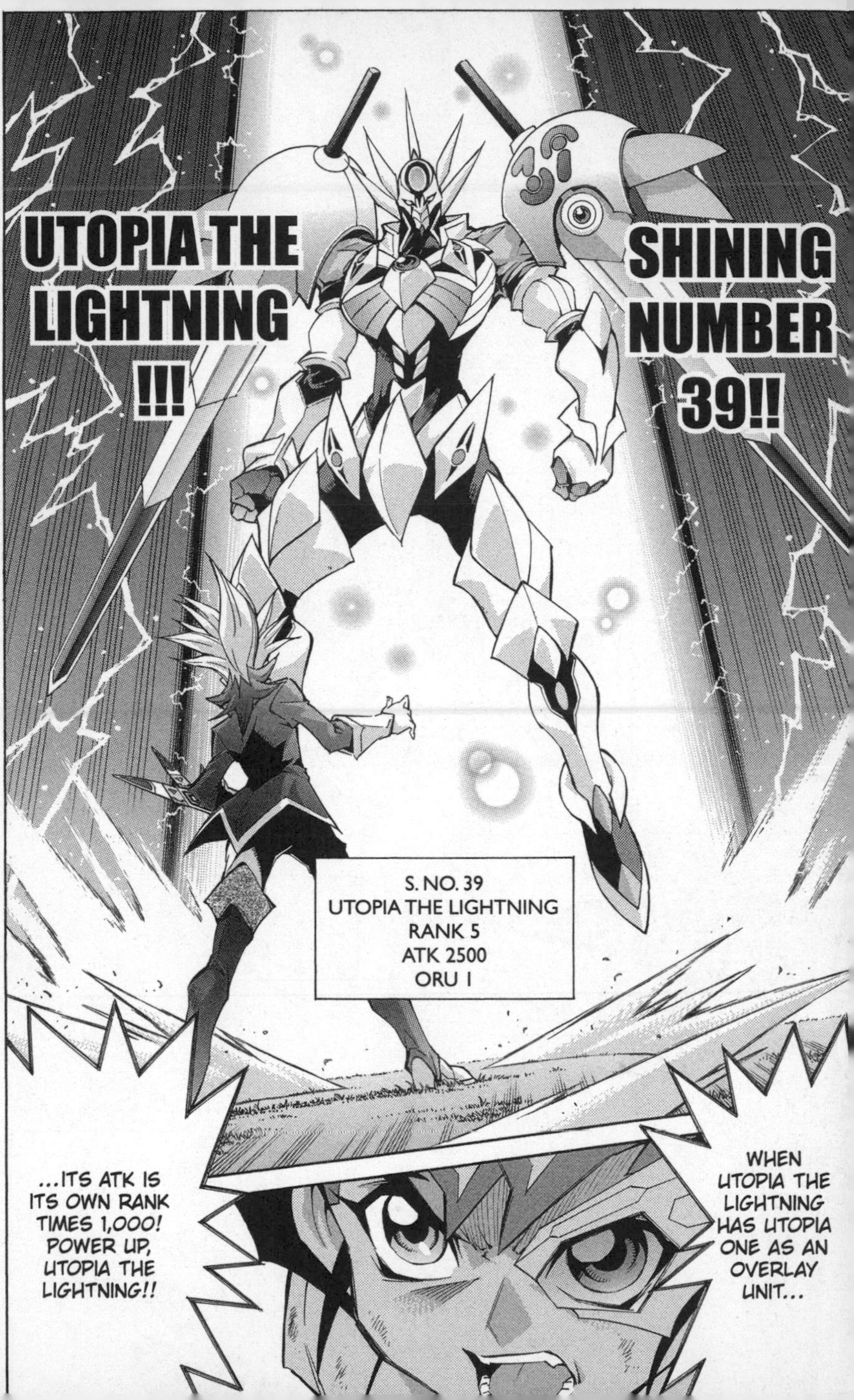
SHINING NUMBER 39!!
UTOPIA THE LIGHTNING!!!
S. NO. 39
UTOPIA THE LIGHTNING
RANK 5
ATK 2500
ORU 1
WHEN UTOPIA THE LIGHTNING HAS UTOPIA ONE AS AN OVERLAY UNIT...
...ITS ATK IS ITS OWN RANK TIMES 1,000! POWER UP, UTOPIA THE LIGHTNING!!

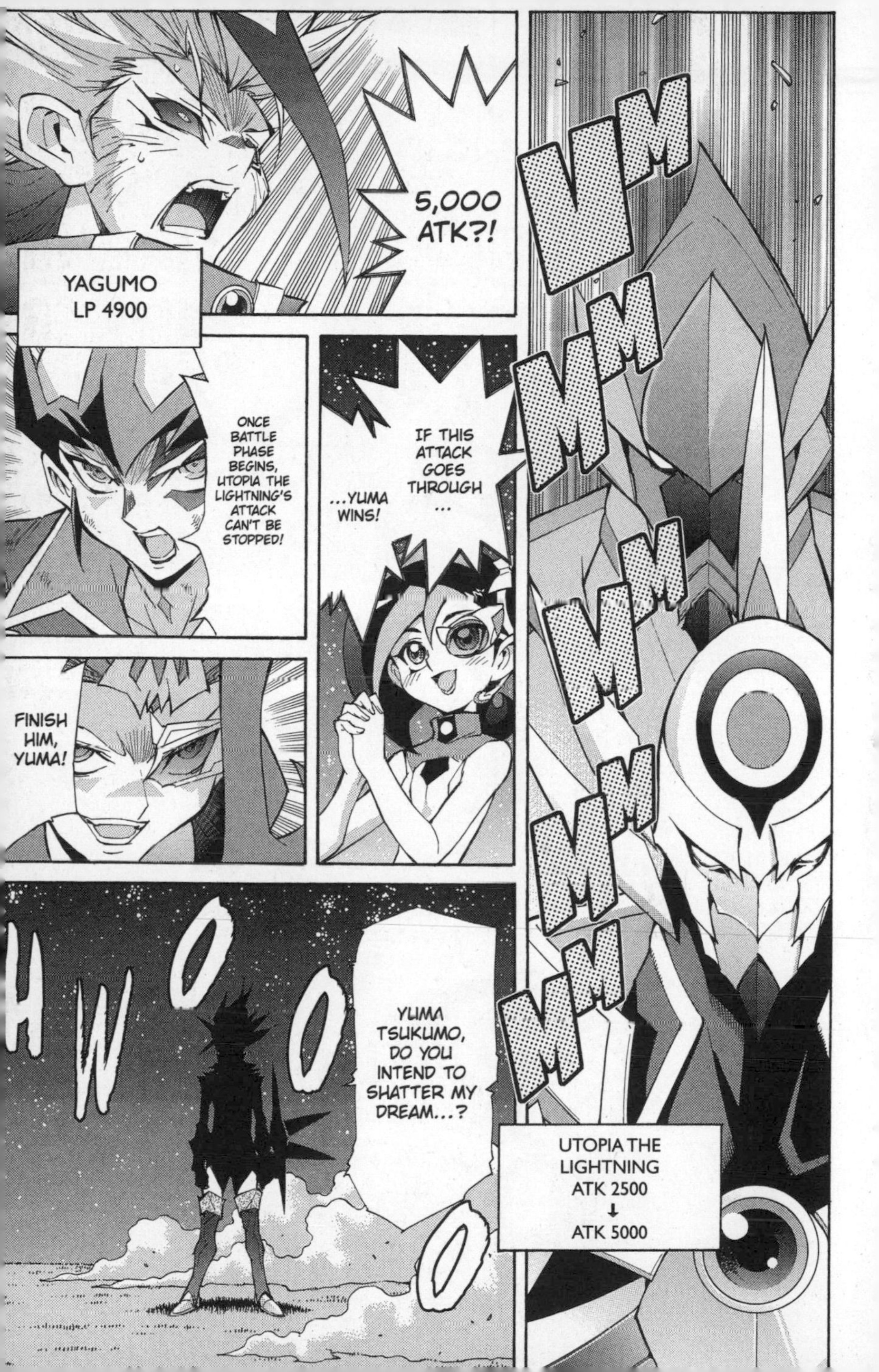
MMMMMMMMMMMMMMM
UTOPIA THE LIGHTNING
ATK 2500
↓
ATK 5000
5,000 ATK?!
YAGUMO
LP 4900
IF THIS ATTACK GOES THROUGH...
...YUMA WINS!
ONCE BATTLE PHASE BEGINS, UTOPIA THE LIGHTNING'S ATTACK CAN'T BE STOPPED!
FINISH HIM, YUMA!
YUMA TSUKUMO, DO YOU INTEND TO SHATTER MY DREAM...?
HWOOOO

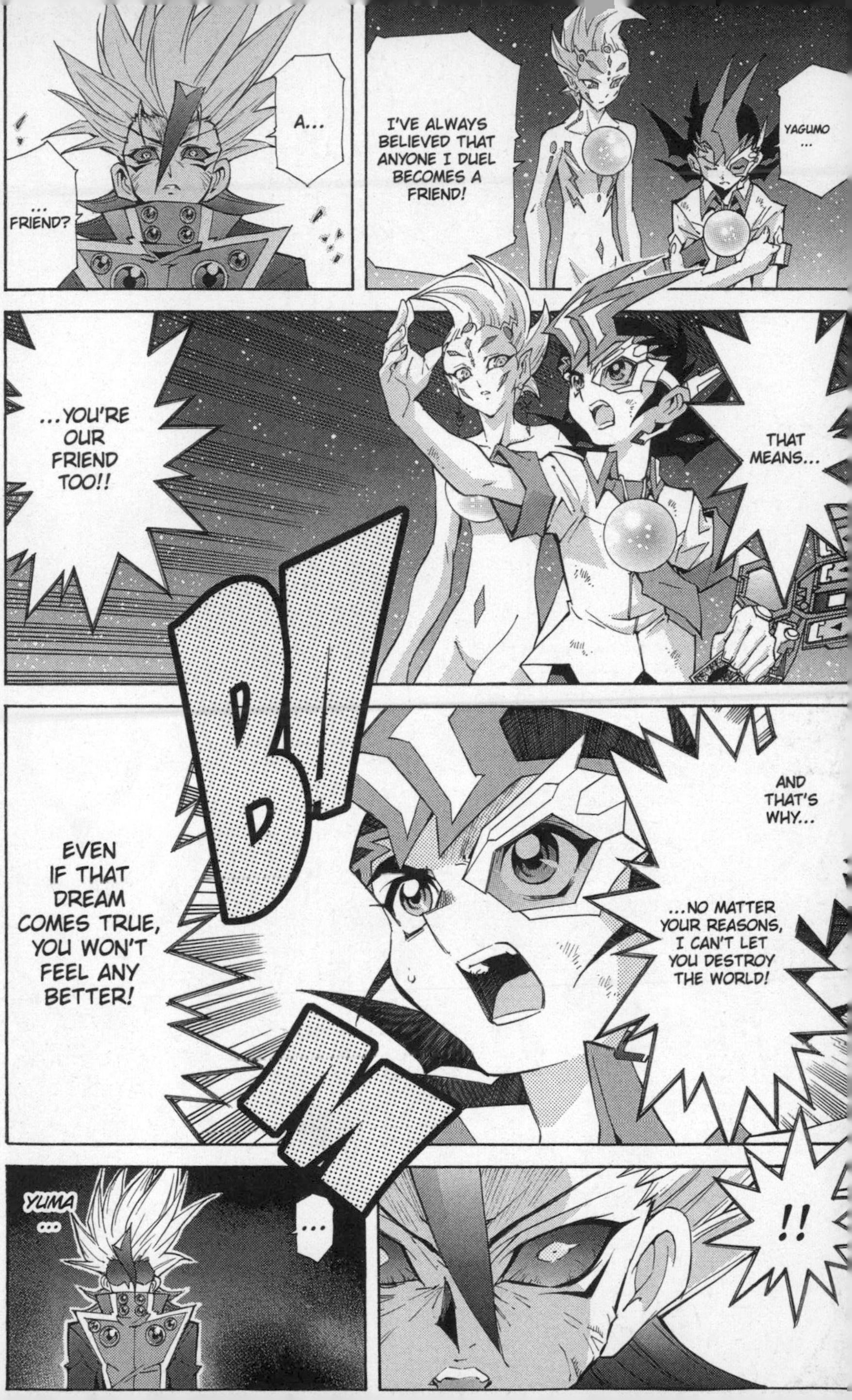
YAGUMO ...
I'VE ALWAYS BELIEVED THAT ANYONE I DUEL BECOMES A FRIEND!
A...
... FRIEND?
THAT MEANS...
...YOU'RE OUR FRIEND TOO!!
AND THAT'S WHY...
...NO MATTER YOUR REASONS, I CAN'T LET YOU DESTROY THE WORLD!
EVEN IF THAT DREAM COMES TRUE, YOU WON'T FEEL ANY BETTER!
!!
...
YUMA ...

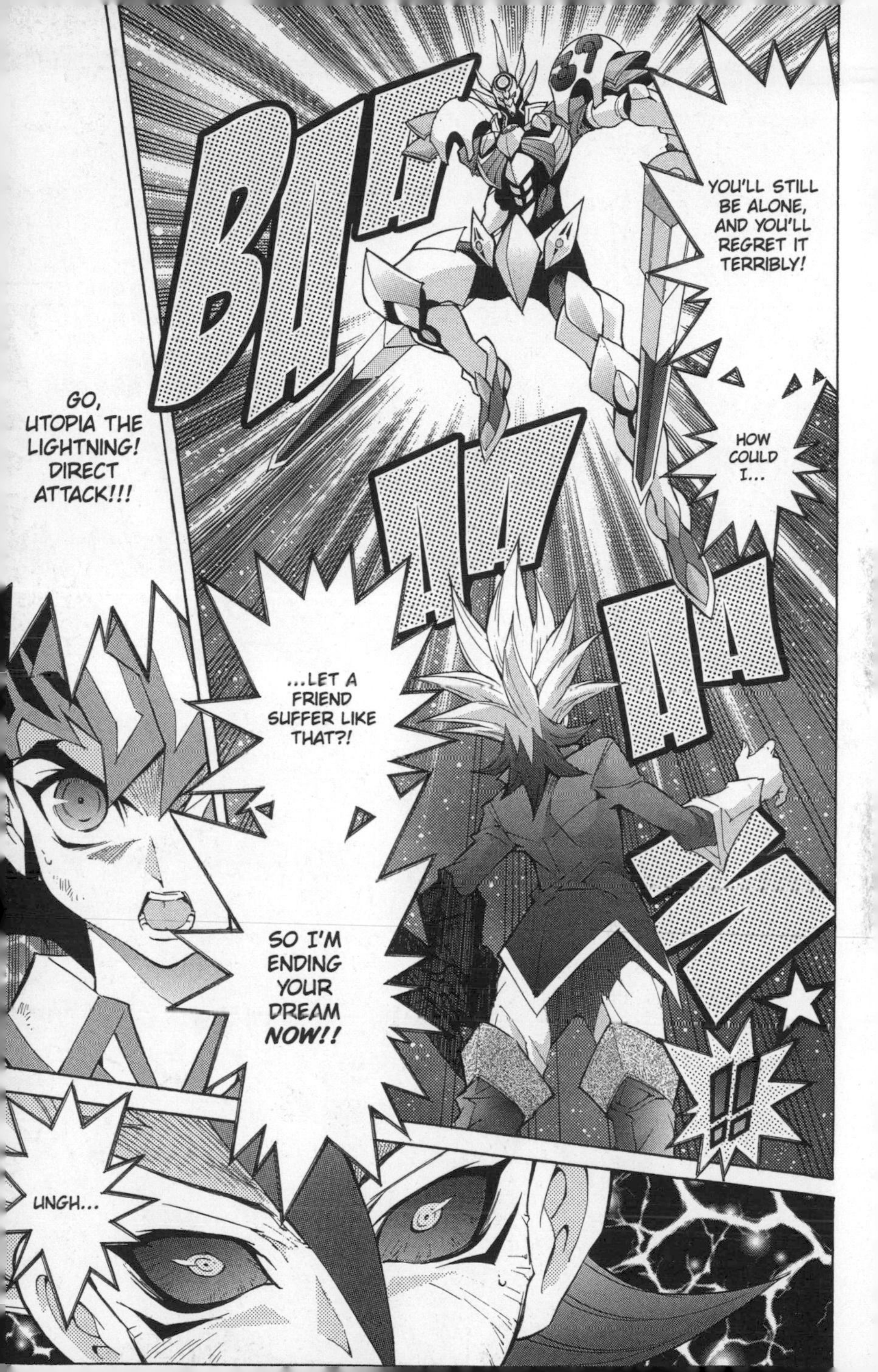
YOU'LL STILL BE ALONE, AND YOU'LL REGRET IT TERRIBLY!
HOW COULD I...
...LET A FRIEND SUFFER LIKE THAT?!
SO I'M ENDING YOUR DREAM *NOW!!*
GO, UTOPIA THE LIGHTNING! DIRECT ATTACK!!!
!!
UNGH...

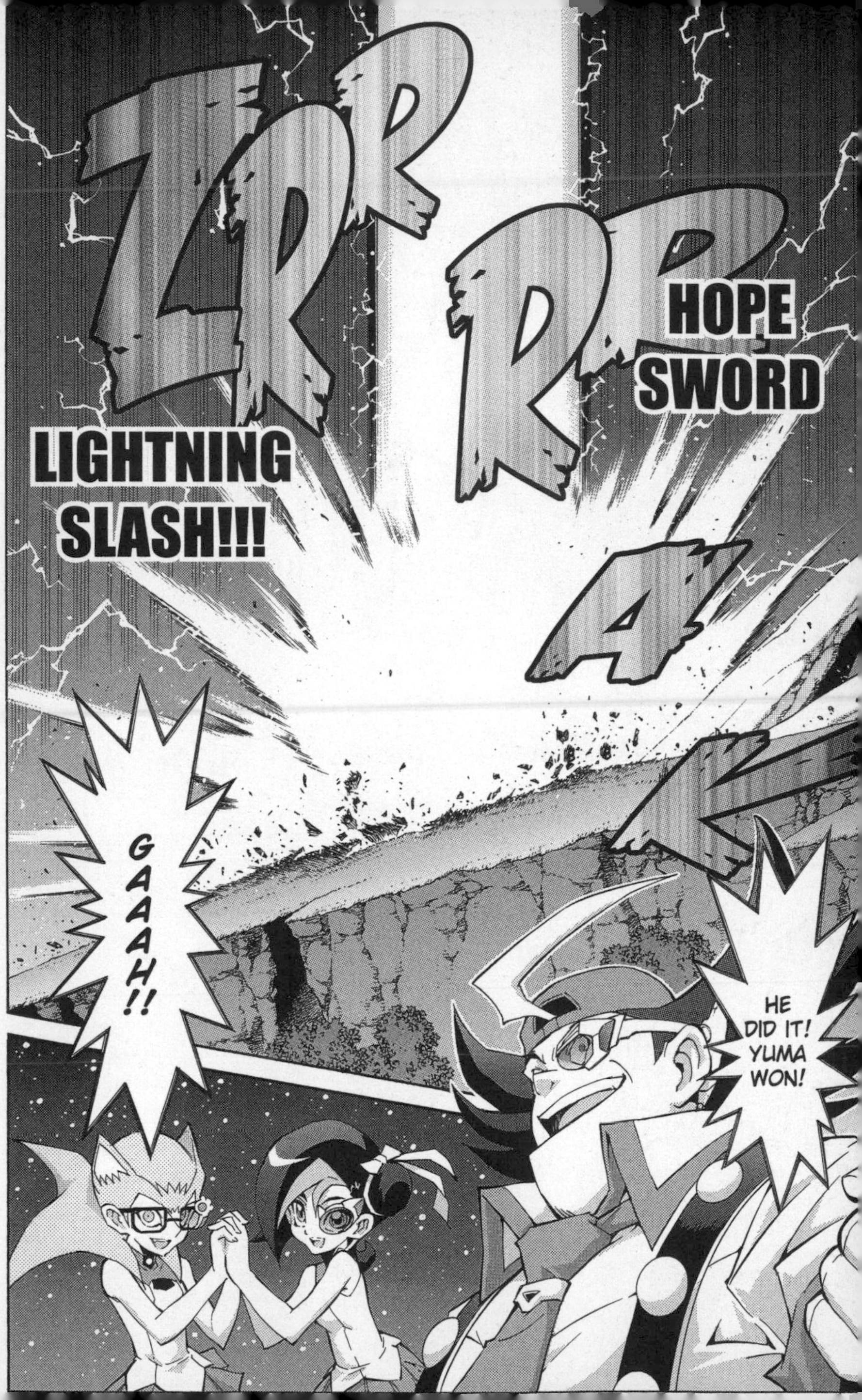
HOPE SWORD
LIGHTNING SLASH!!!
GAAAAH!!
HE DID IT! YUMA WON!

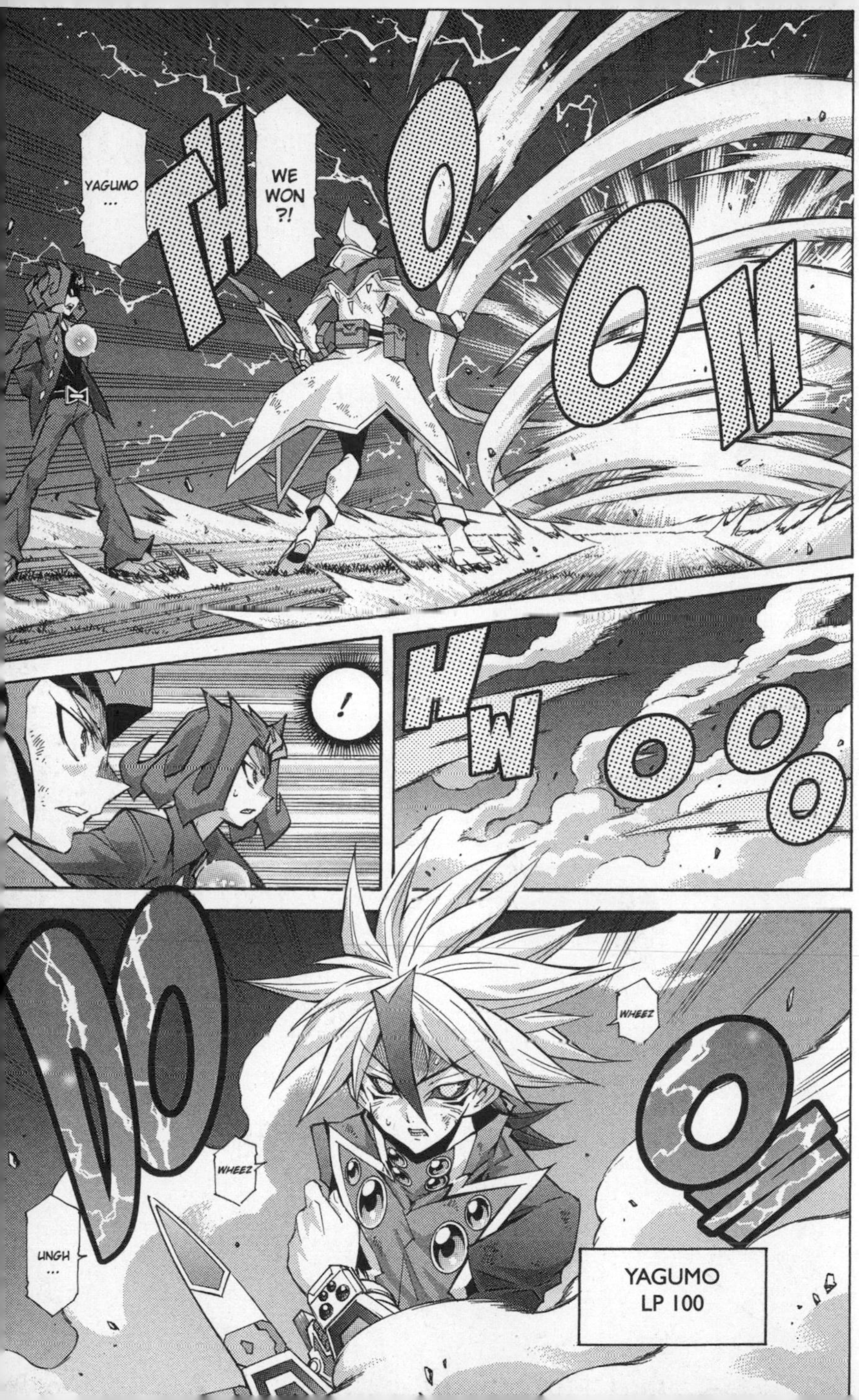
THOOM
WE WON ?!
YAGUMO ...
HWOOO
!
WHEEZ
DOO
WHEEZ
UNGH ...
YAGUMO LP 100

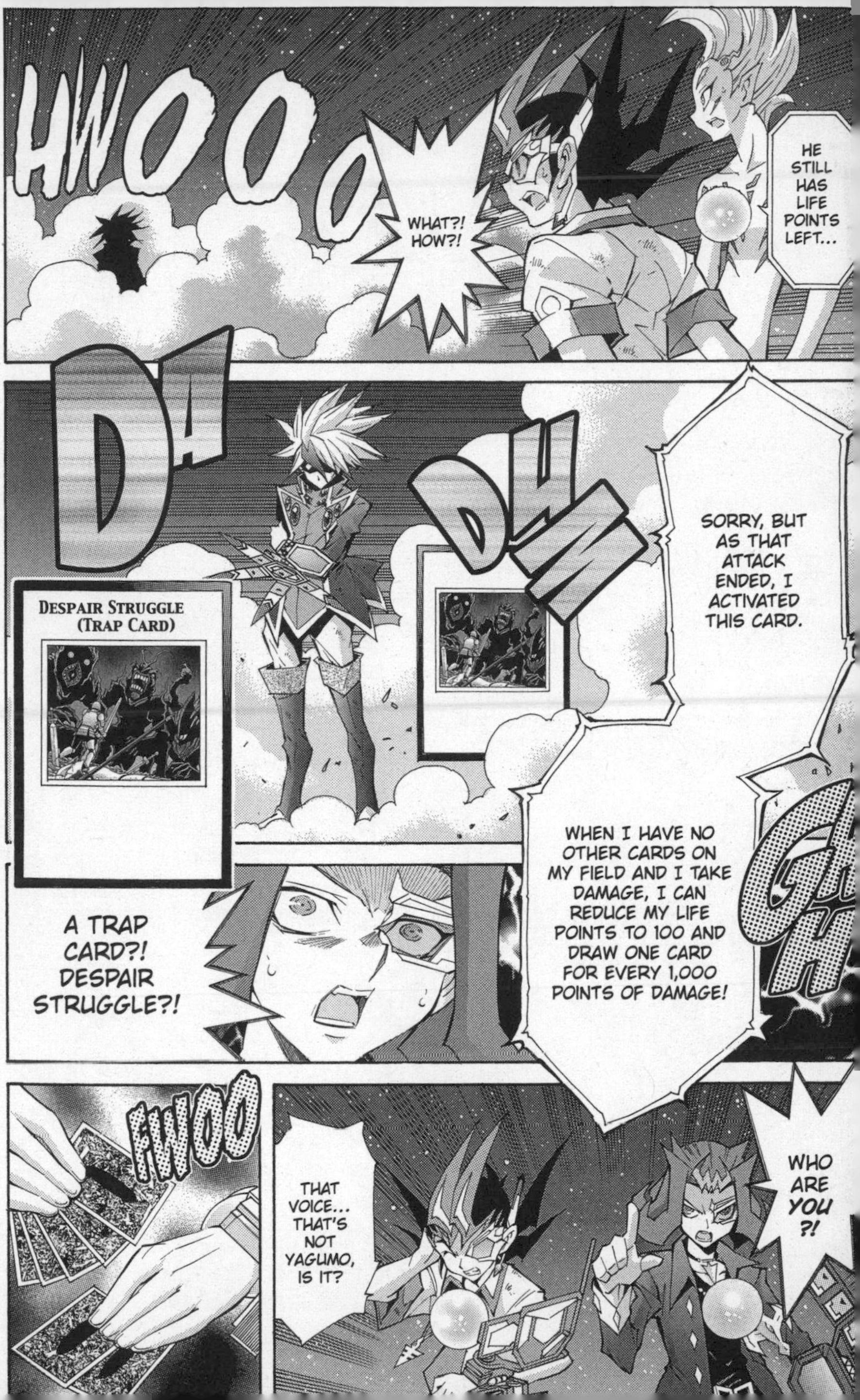
HE STILL HAS LIFE POINTS LEFT...
WHAT?! HOW?!
HWOOO
SORRY, BUT AS THAT ATTACK ENDED, I ACTIVATED THIS CARD.
DUM
DA
DESPAIR STRUGGLE (TRAP CARD)
GAH
WHEN I HAVE NO OTHER CARDS ON MY FIELD AND I TAKE DAMAGE, I CAN REDUCE MY LIFE POINTS TO 100 AND DRAW ONE CARD FOR EVERY 1,000 POINTS OF DAMAGE!
A TRAP CARD?! DESPAIR STRUGGLE?!
WHO ARE *YOU* ?!
THAT VOICE... THAT'S NOT YAGUMO, IS IT?
FWOO

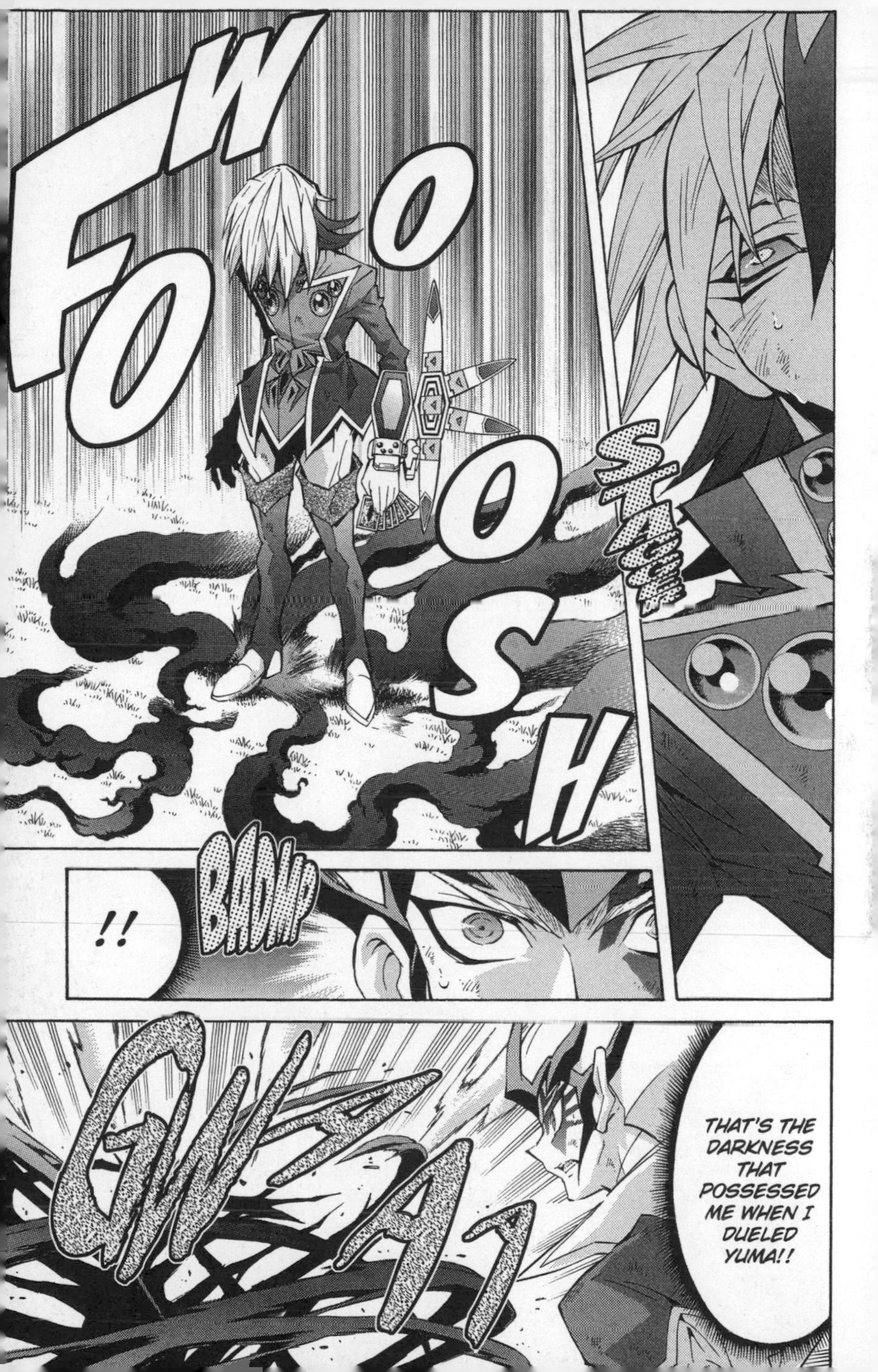
FWOOOSH
!!
BADMP
THAT'S THE DARKNESS THAT POSSESSED ME WHEN I DUELED YUMA!!

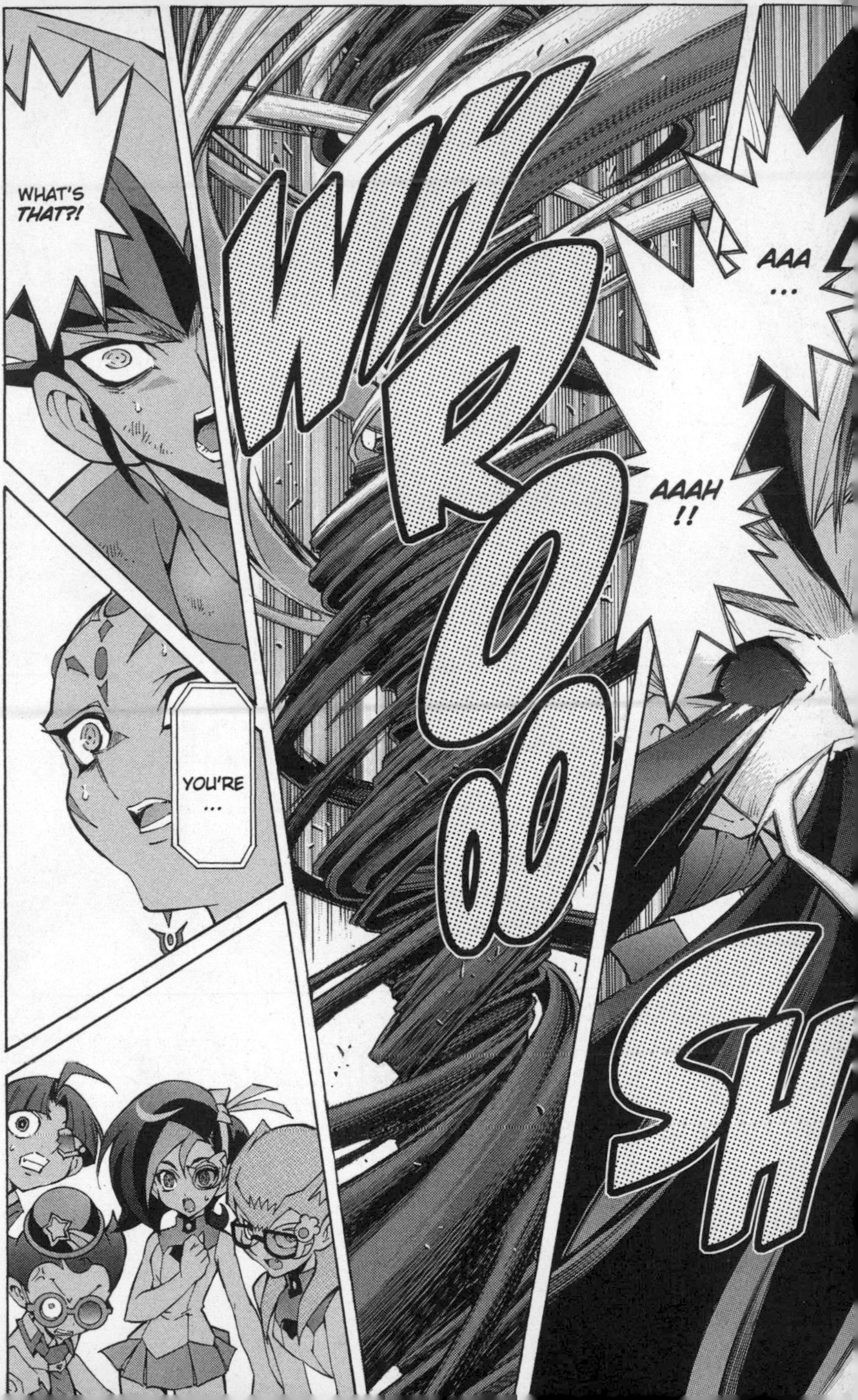
AAA ...
AAAH !!
WHOOOO
SH
WHAT'S *THAT?!*
YOU'RE ...

Series composition for the *ZEXAL* anime
The author of the *ZEXAL* manga

SHIN YOSHIDA SPEAKS:

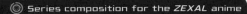

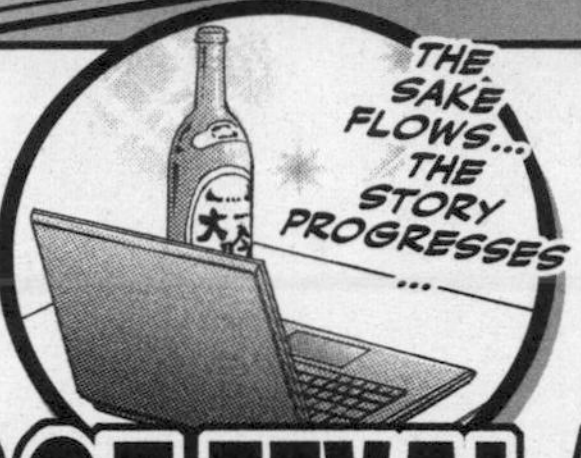
THE SAKE FLOWS... THE STORY PROGRESSES...

BEHIND THE SCENES OF ZEXAL 4

*** THE SHADOW AND E'RAH INCIDENTS**

Shadow sure did torment Yuma, Kaito and Ryoga! I was actually going to have him leave right after he set that trap for Kaito and Ryoga, but Miyoshi Sensei started grumbling—"He's going to die right away?! After I worked so hard to design him?!"—so I hastily gave him more page time.

Then there's E'Rah, the last boss. At first, she wasn't in the works at all and Yagumo was going to be the last boss, but Miyoshi Sensei started grumbling again—"I'm sorta tired of drawing Yagumo..."—so I hastily came up with E'Rah.

I told myself that I would do it so Miyoshi Sensei would enjoy drawing and that even if it wasn't what I originally had in mind, I could make it work! I thought of E'Rah as godlike, but then she ended up with a considerable bosom...

I bet you just wanted to draw that, Miyoshi Sensei!
KRASH (overturning the desk)

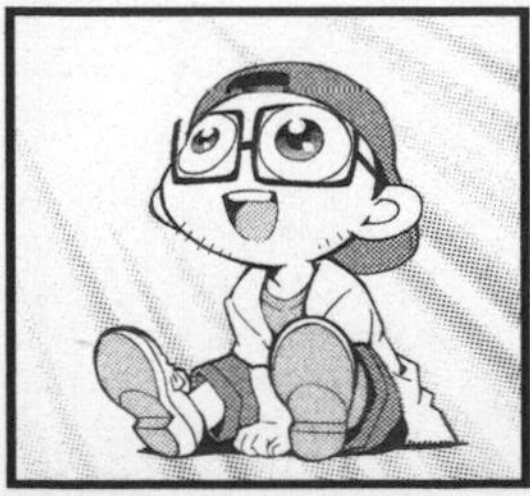

A Message from Miyoshi Sensei!

Ha ha ha! Yeah, we've been through a lot! And the Shadow incident has become legend! Hm? E'Rah? Huh? Her chest? I have no idea what you're talking about! (lol) *SMACK!* (catching the desk) *GLINT!*

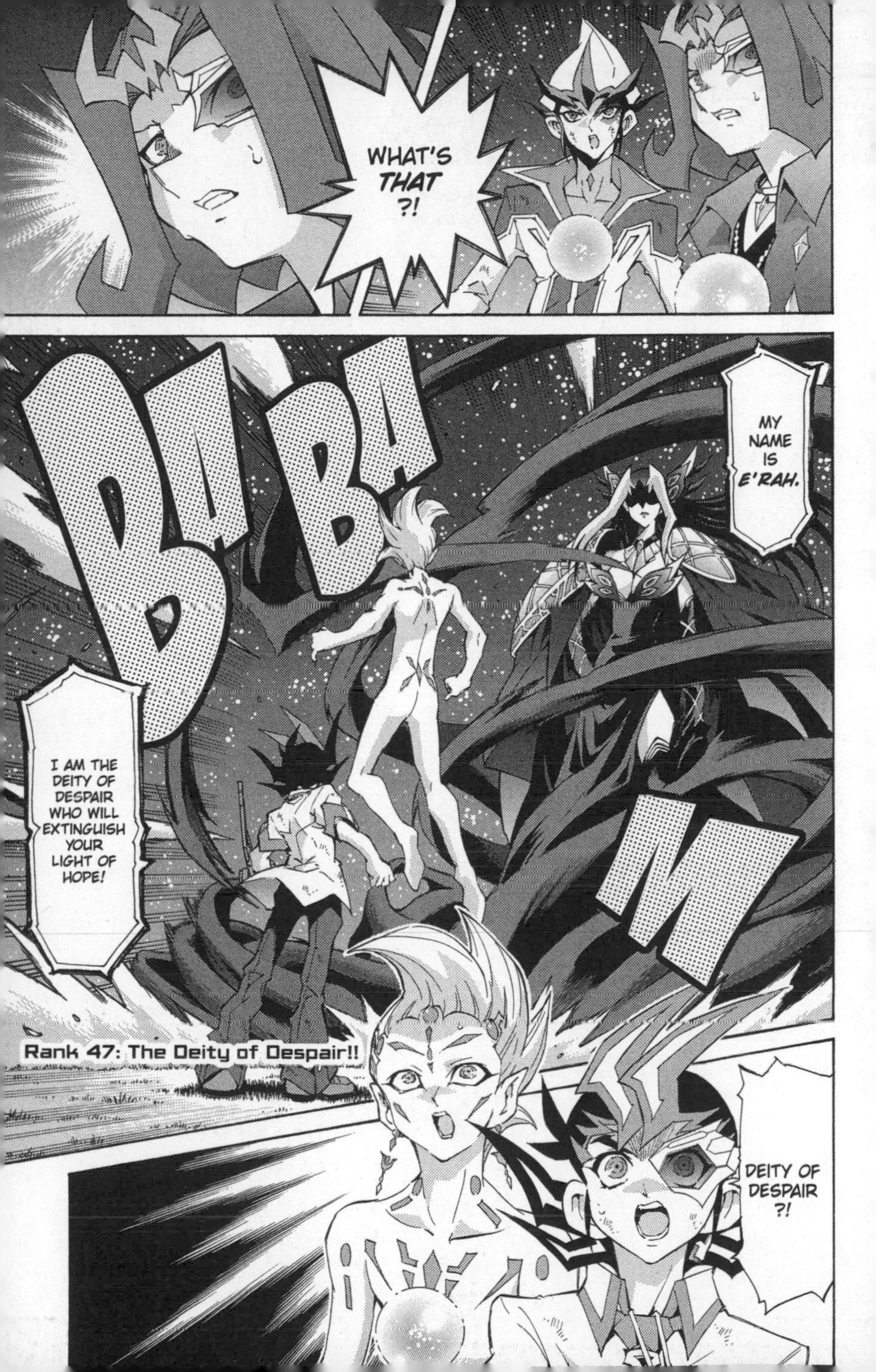
WHAT'S THAT ?!
MY NAME IS E'RAH.
BABA
M
I AM THE DEITY OF DESPAIR WHO WILL EXTINGUISH YOUR LIGHT OF HOPE!
Rank 47: The Deity of Despair!!
DEITY OF DESPAIR ?!

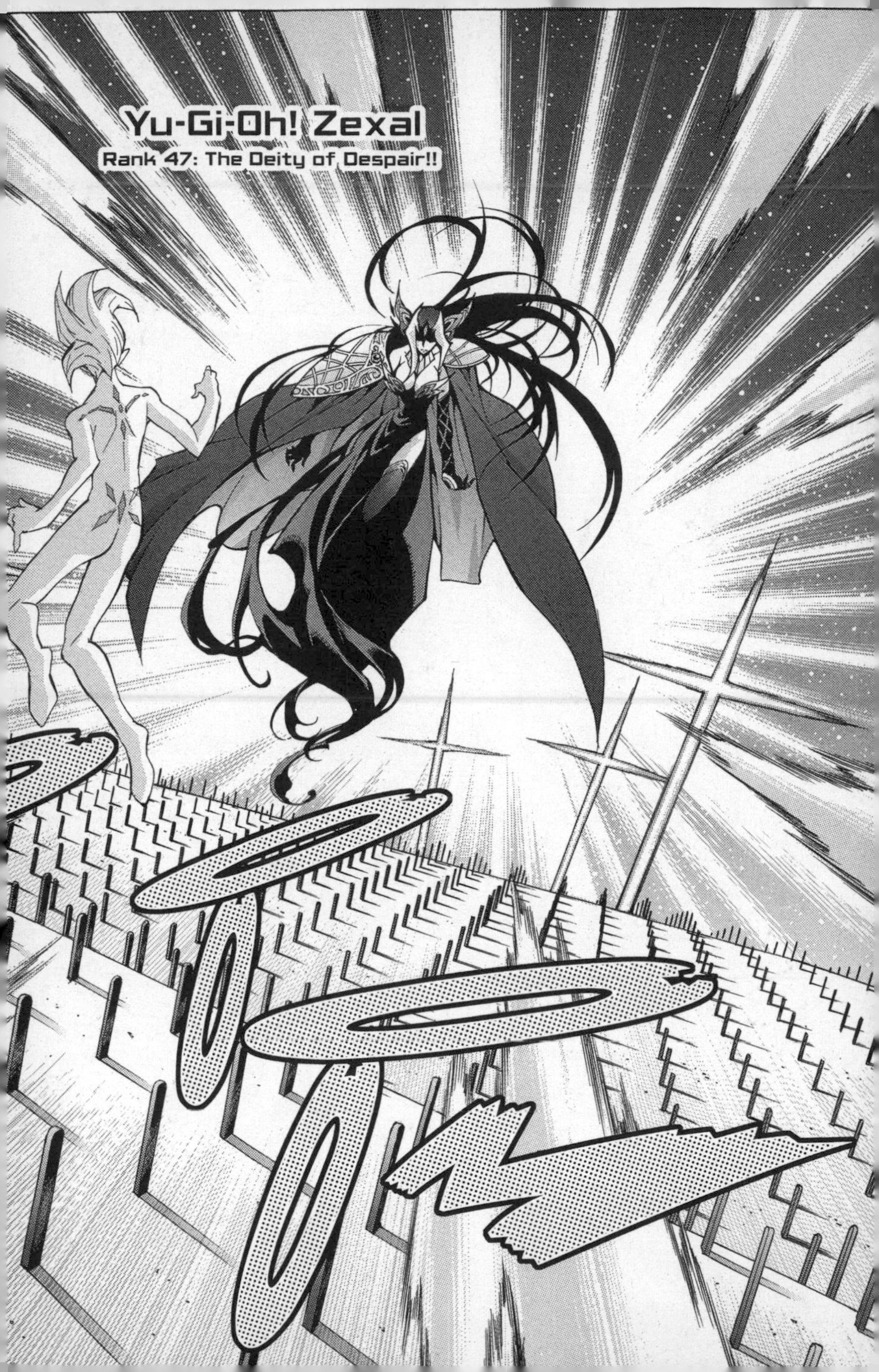
Yu-Gi-Oh! Zexal
Rank 47: The Deity of Despair!!

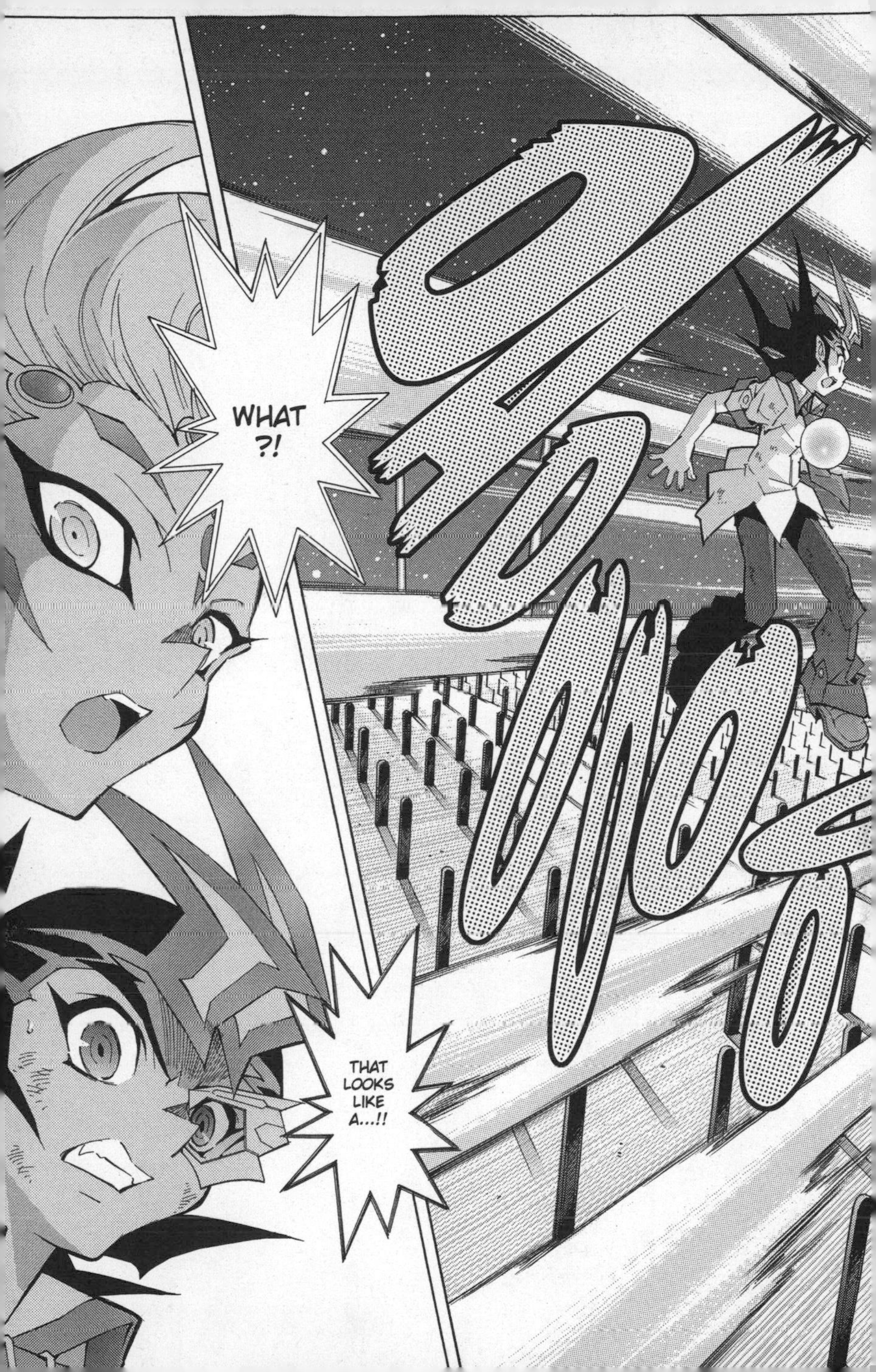
WHAT ?!
THAT LOOKS LIKE A...!!

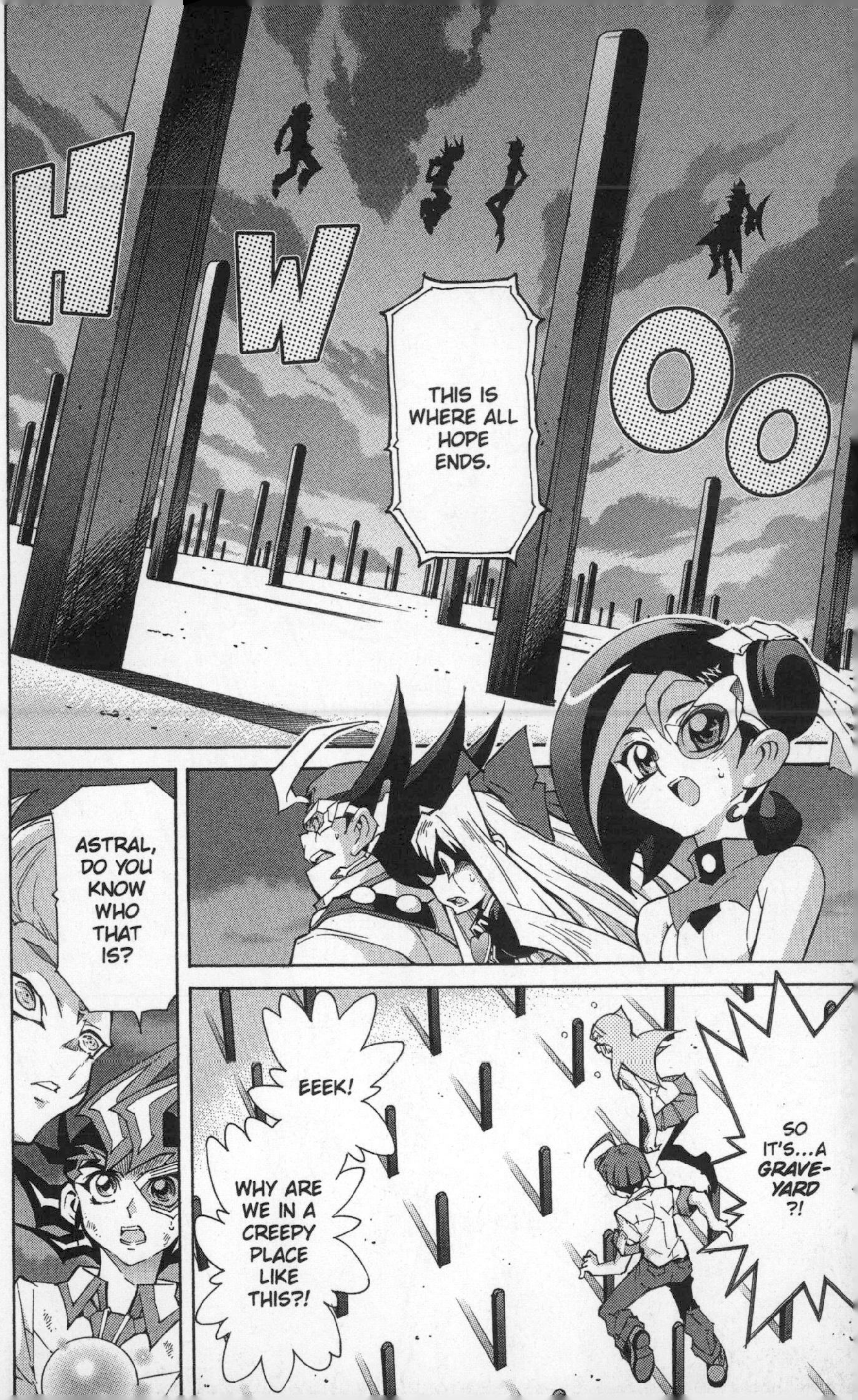
HWOO
THIS IS WHERE ALL HOPE ENDS.
SO IT'S...A GRAVEYARD?!
EEEK!
WHY ARE WE IN A CREEPY PLACE LIKE THIS?!
ASTRAL, DO YOU KNOW WHO THAT IS?

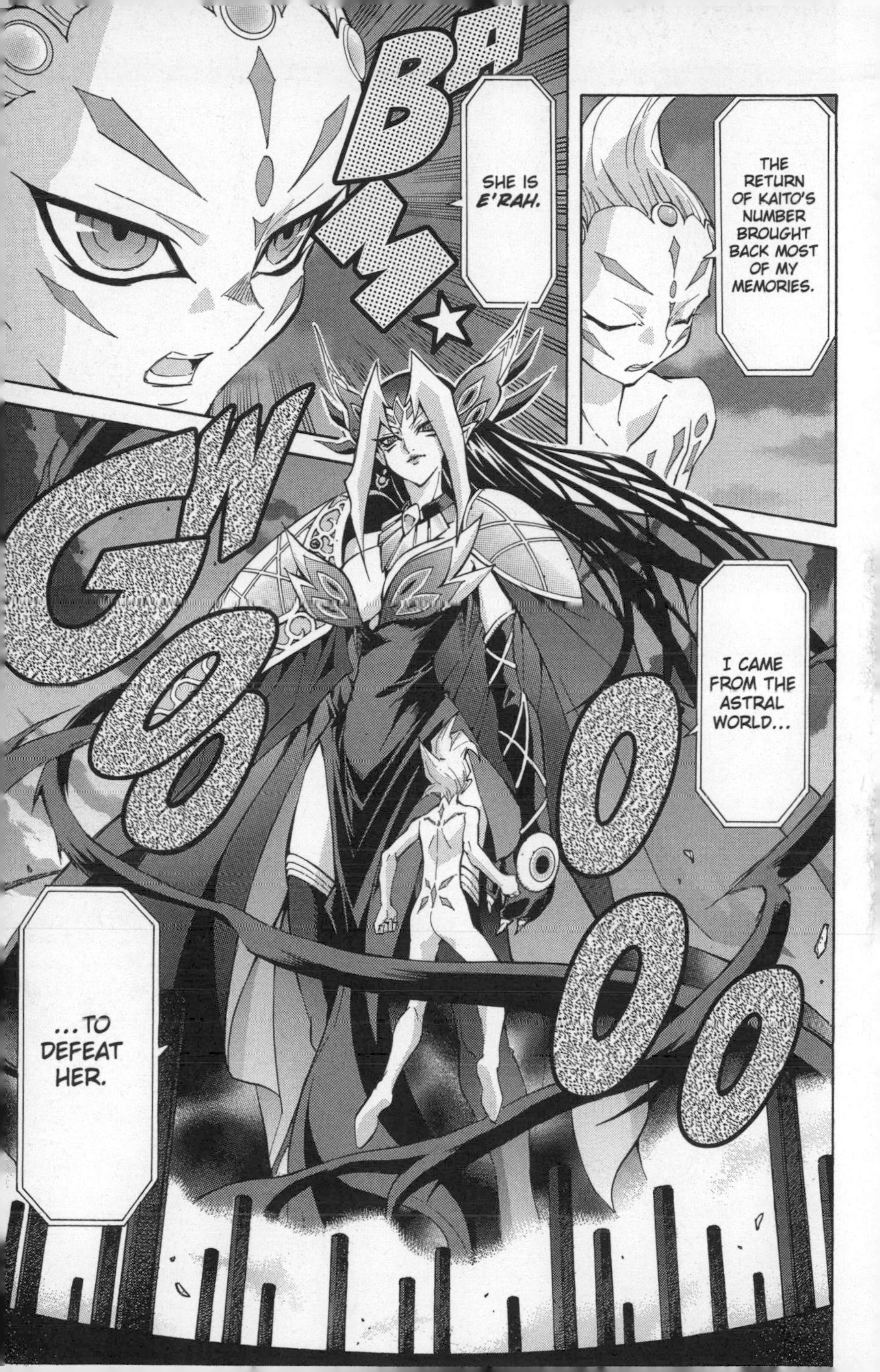
THE RETURN OF KAITO'S NUMBER BROUGHT BACK MOST OF MY MEMORIES.
BAM★
SHE IS *E'RAH.*
I CAME FROM THE ASTRAL WORLD...
GWOOOO
...TO DEFEAT HER.

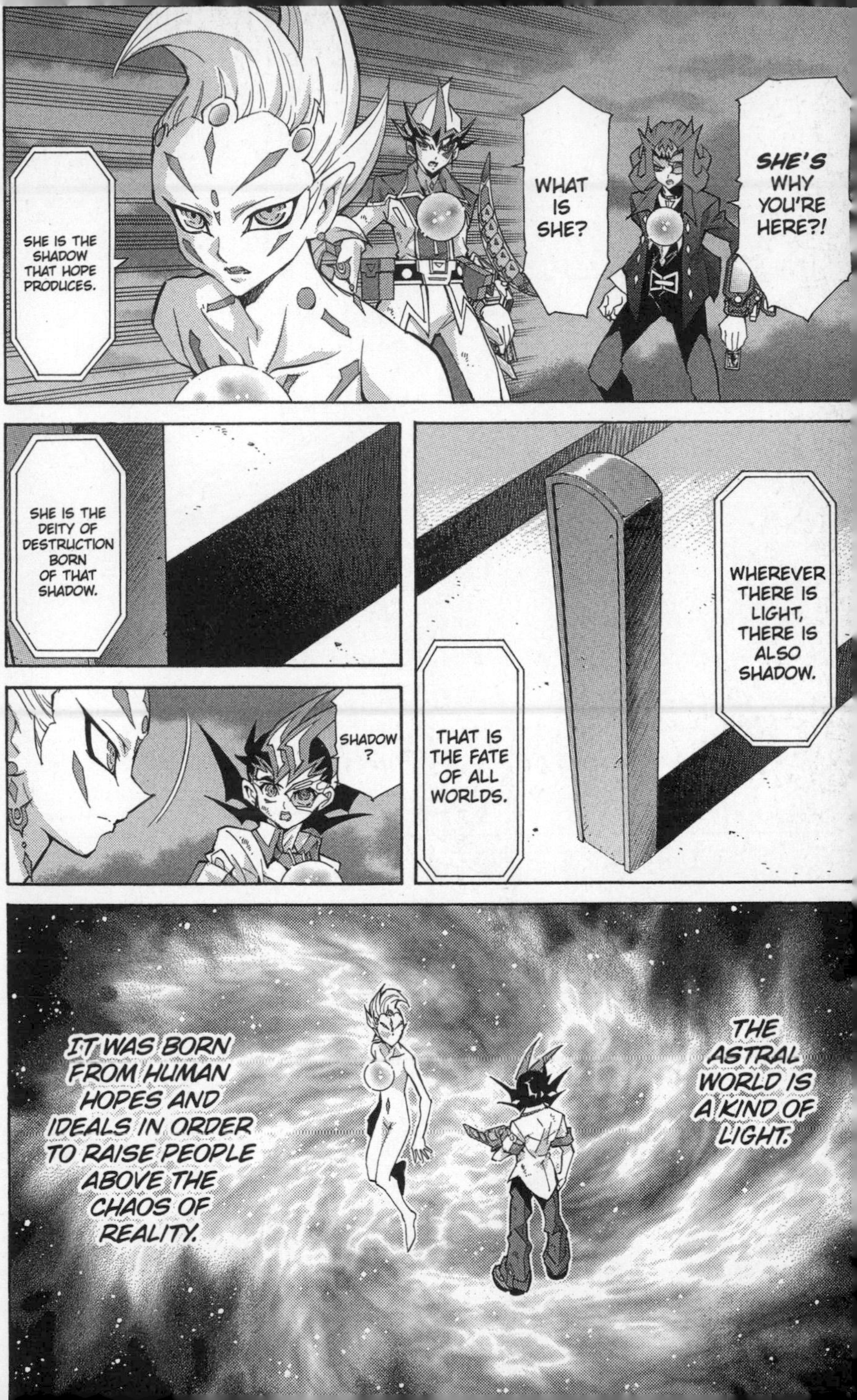
SHE'S WHY YOU'RE HERE?!
WHAT IS SHE?
SHE IS THE SHADOW THAT HOPE PRODUCES.
WHEREVER THERE IS LIGHT, THERE IS ALSO SHADOW.
THAT IS THE FATE OF ALL WORLDS.
SHE IS THE DEITY OF DESTRUCTION BORN OF THAT SHADOW.
SHADOW?
THE ASTRAL WORLD IS A KIND OF LIGHT.
IT WAS BORN FROM HUMAN HOPES AND IDEALS IN ORDER TO RAISE PEOPLE ABOVE THE CHAOS OF REALITY.

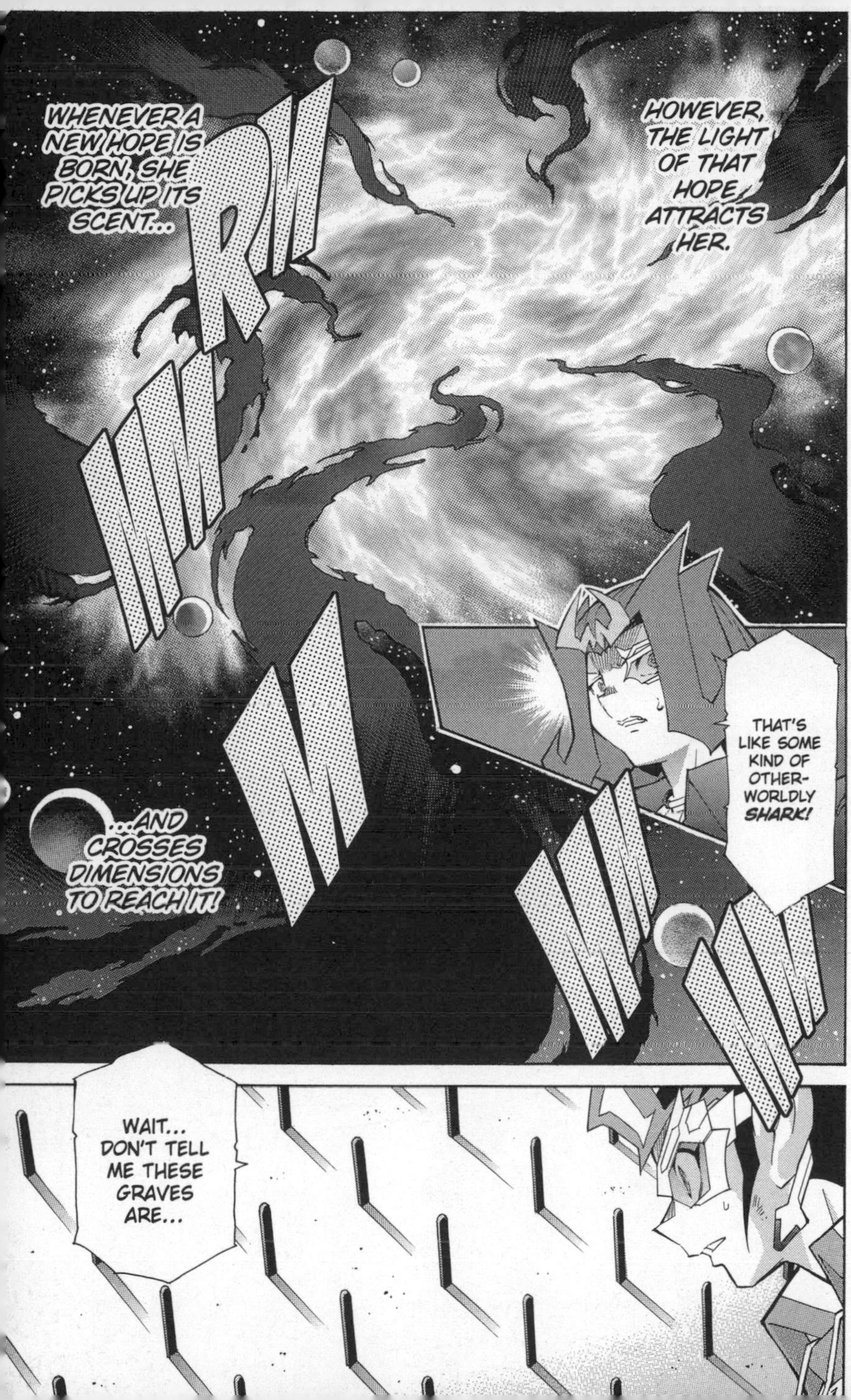
HOWEVER, THE LIGHT OF THAT HOPE ATTRACTS HER.
WHENEVER A NEW HOPE IS BORN, SHE PICKS UP ITS SCENT...
...AND CROSSES DIMENSIONS TO REACH IT!
THAT'S LIKE SOME KIND OF OTHER-WORLDLY SHARK!
WAIT... DON'T TELL ME THESE GRAVES ARE...

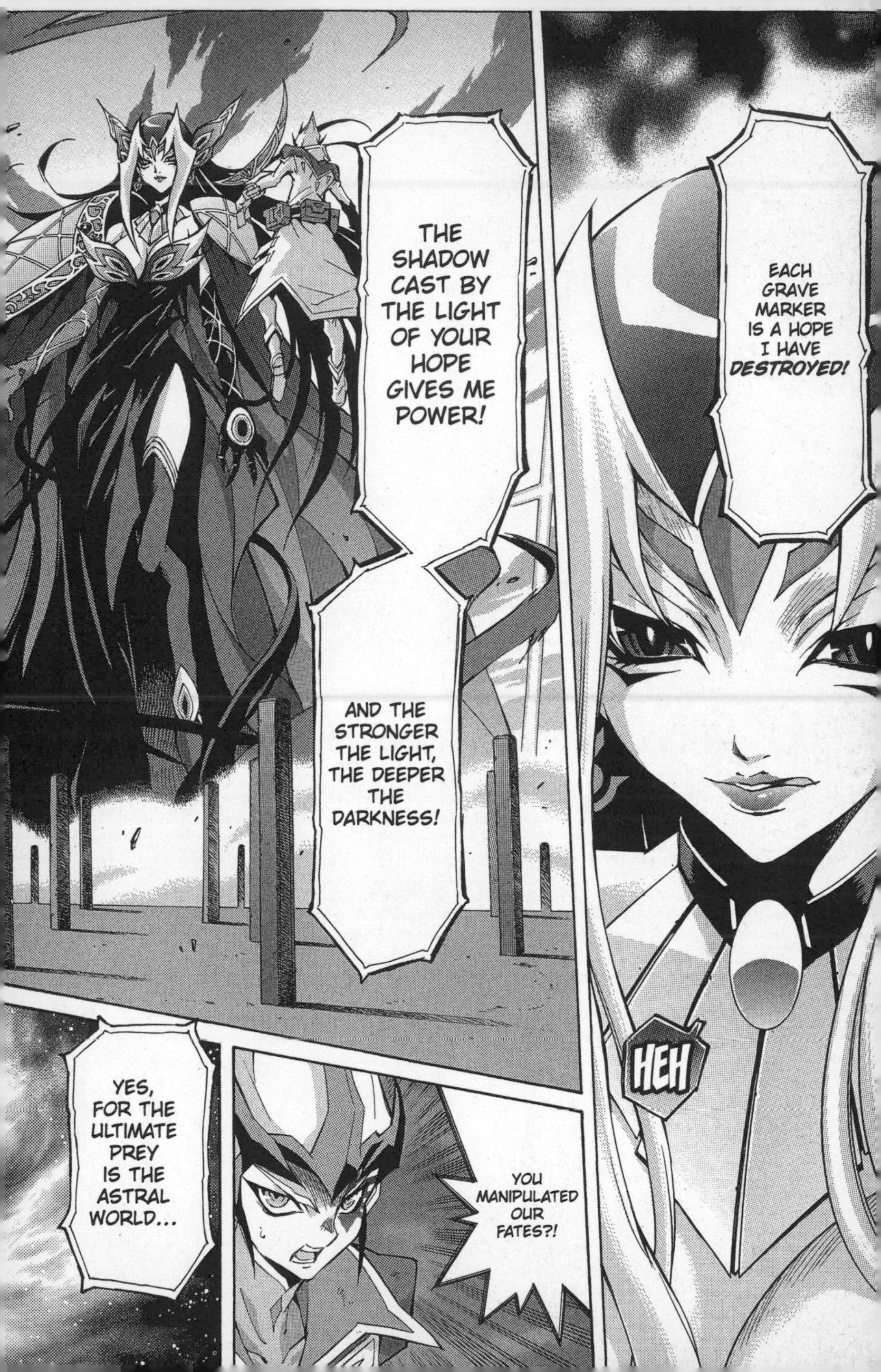
EACH GRAVE MARKER IS A HOPE I HAVE *DESTROYED!*
HEH
THE SHADOW CAST BY THE LIGHT OF YOUR HOPE GIVES ME POWER!
AND THE STRONGER THE LIGHT, THE DEEPER THE DARKNESS!
YOU MANIPULATED OUR FATES?!
YES, FOR THE ULTIMATE PREY IS THE ASTRAL WORLD...

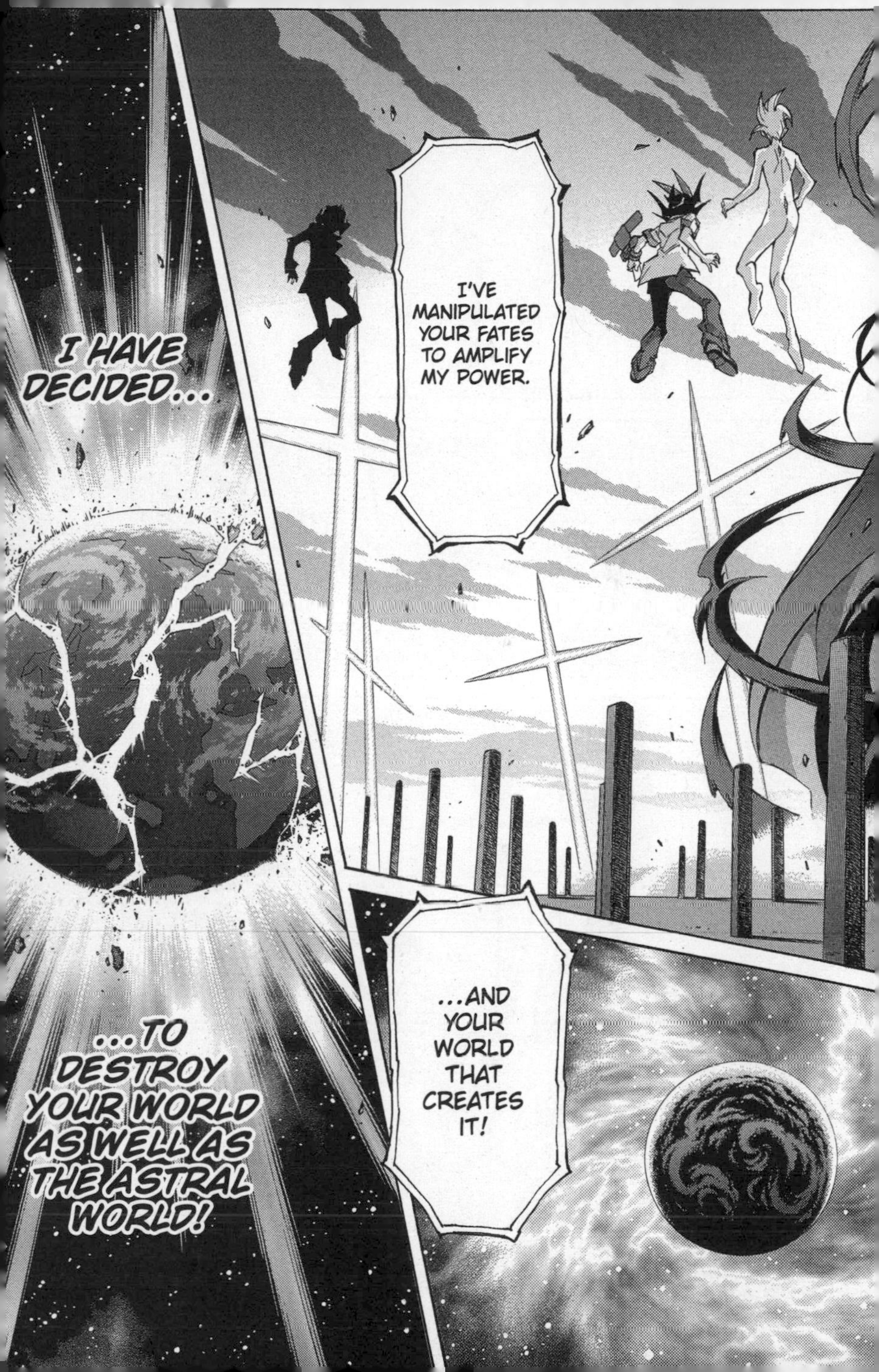
I'VE MANIPULATED YOUR FATES TO AMPLIFY MY POWER.
...AND YOUR WORLD THAT CREATES IT!
I HAVE DECIDED...
...TO DESTROY YOUR WORLD AS WELL AS THE ASTRAL WORLD!

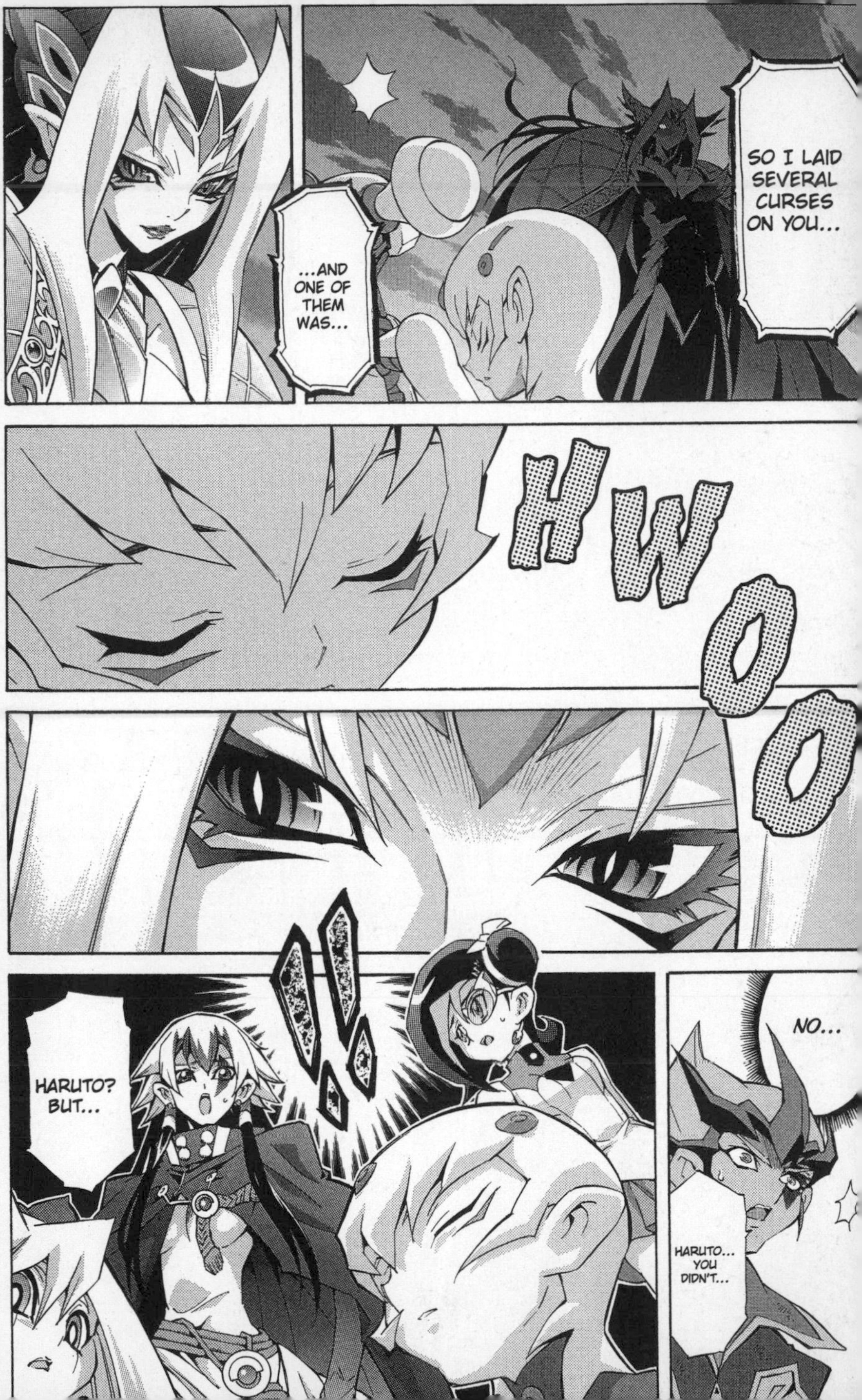
SO I LAID SEVERAL CURSES ON YOU...
...AND ONE OF THEM WAS...
HWOOO
NO...
HARUTO... YOU DIDN'T...
HARUTO? BUT...

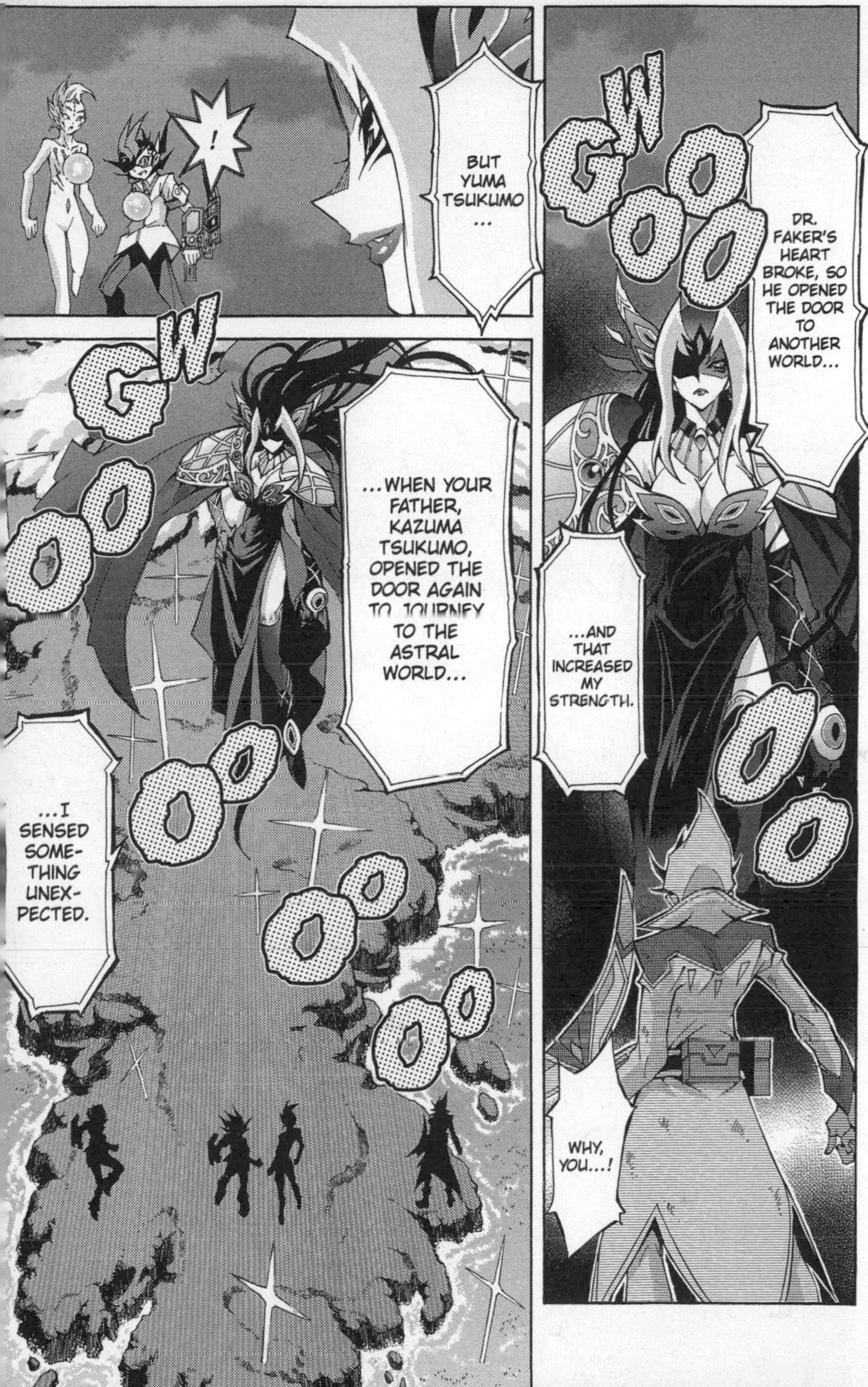
GWOOOO
DR. FAKER'S HEART BROKE, SO HE OPENED THE DOOR TO ANOTHER WORLD...
...AND THAT INCREASED MY STRENGTH.
OOO
WHY, YOU...!
BUT YUMA TSUKUMO...
!
...WHEN YOUR FATHER, KAZUMA TSUKUMO, OPENED THE DOOR AGAIN TO JOURNEY TO THE ASTRAL WORLD...
GWOOOOOOOOOO
...I SENSED SOME-THING UNEX-PECTED.

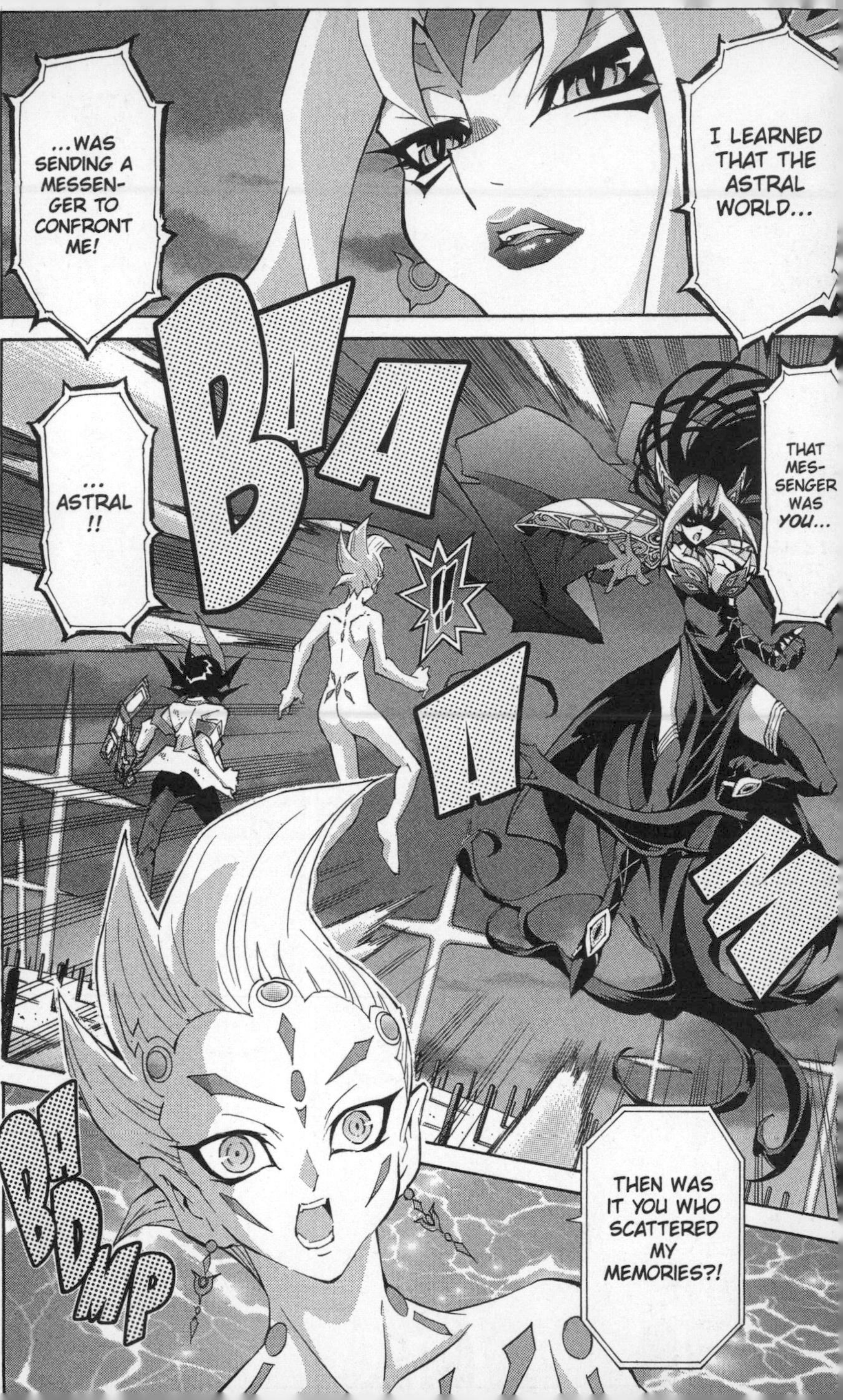
I LEARNED THAT THE ASTRAL WORLD...
...WAS SENDING A MESSENGER TO CONFRONT ME!
THAT MESSENGER WAS *YOU*...
BAAM
!!
...ASTRAL!!
THEN WAS IT YOU WHO SCATTERED MY MEMORIES?!
BA-BUMP

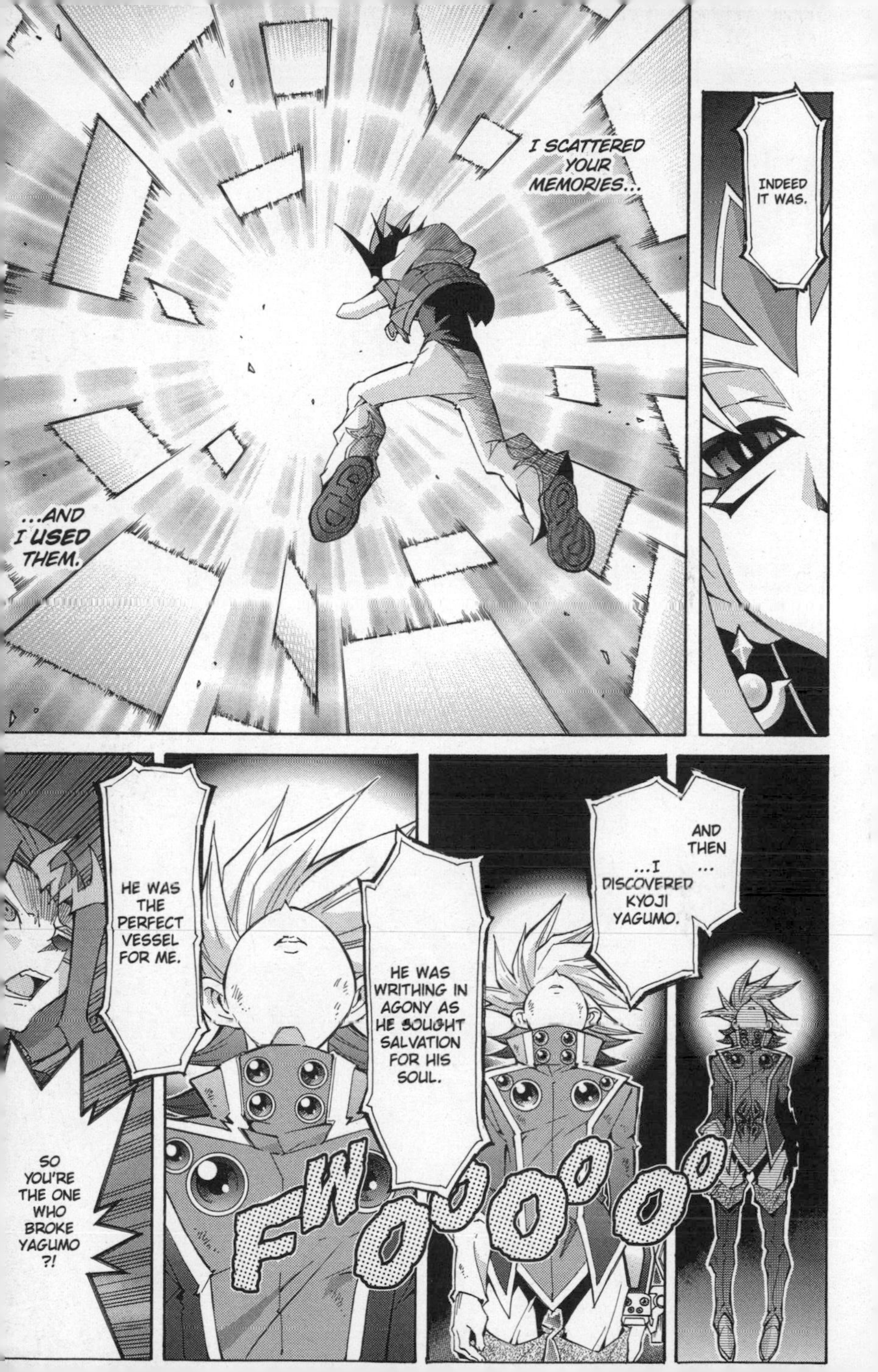
INDEED IT WAS.
I SCATTERED YOUR MEMORIES...
...AND I USED THEM.
AND THEN ...
...I DISCOVERED KYOJI YAGUMO.
HE WAS WRITHING IN AGONY AS HE SOUGHT SALVATION FOR HIS SOUL.
HE WAS THE PERFECT VESSEL FOR ME.
FWOOOOOOO
SO YOU'RE THE ONE WHO BROKE YAGUMO ?!

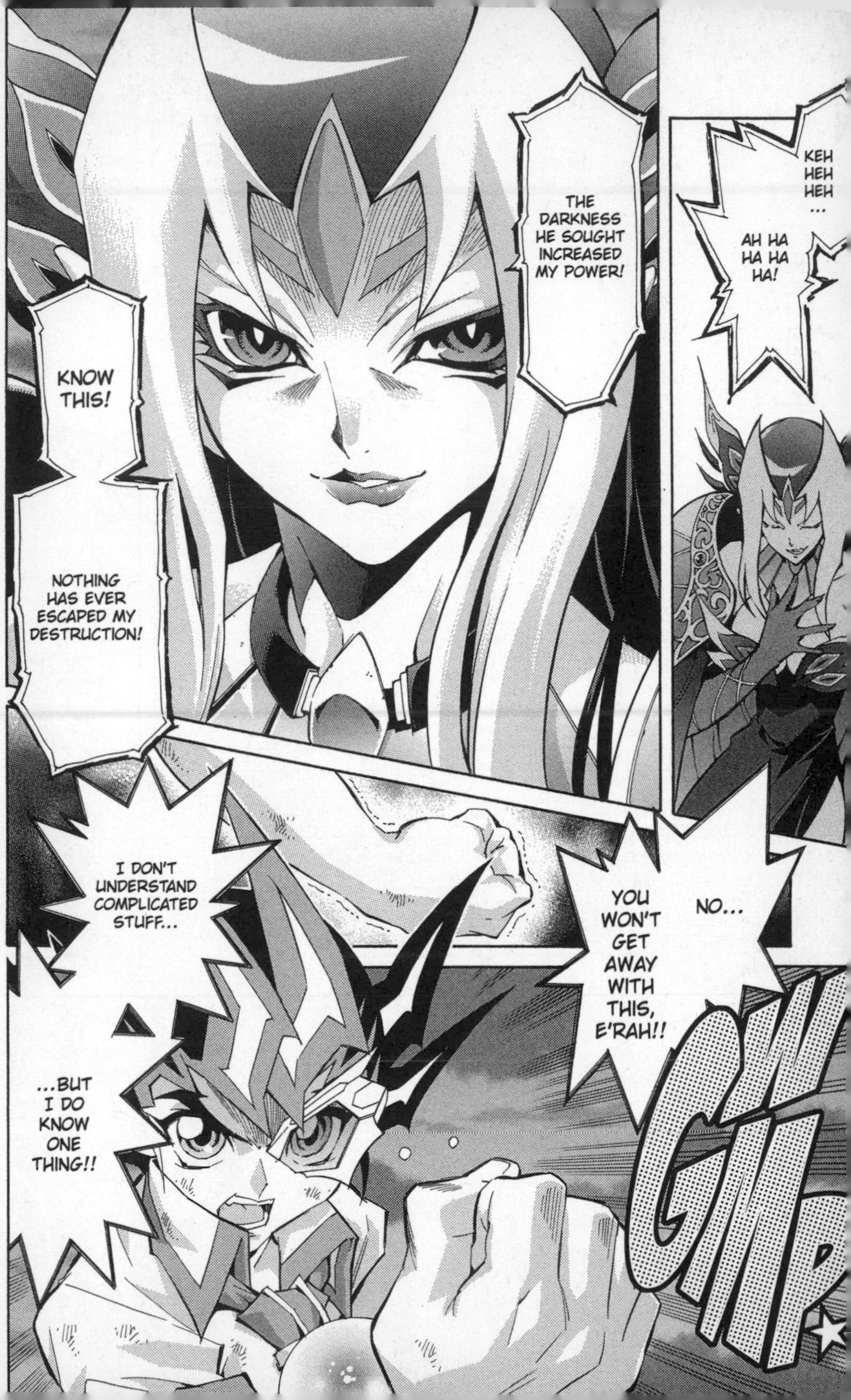
KEH HEH HEH...
AH HA HA HA HA!
THE DARKNESS HE SOUGHT INCREASED MY POWER!
KNOW THIS!
NOTHING HAS EVER ESCAPED MY DESTRUCTION!
NO...
YOU WON'T GET AWAY WITH THIS, E'RAH!!
I DON'T UNDERSTAND COMPLICATED STUFF...
...BUT I DO KNOW ONE THING!!

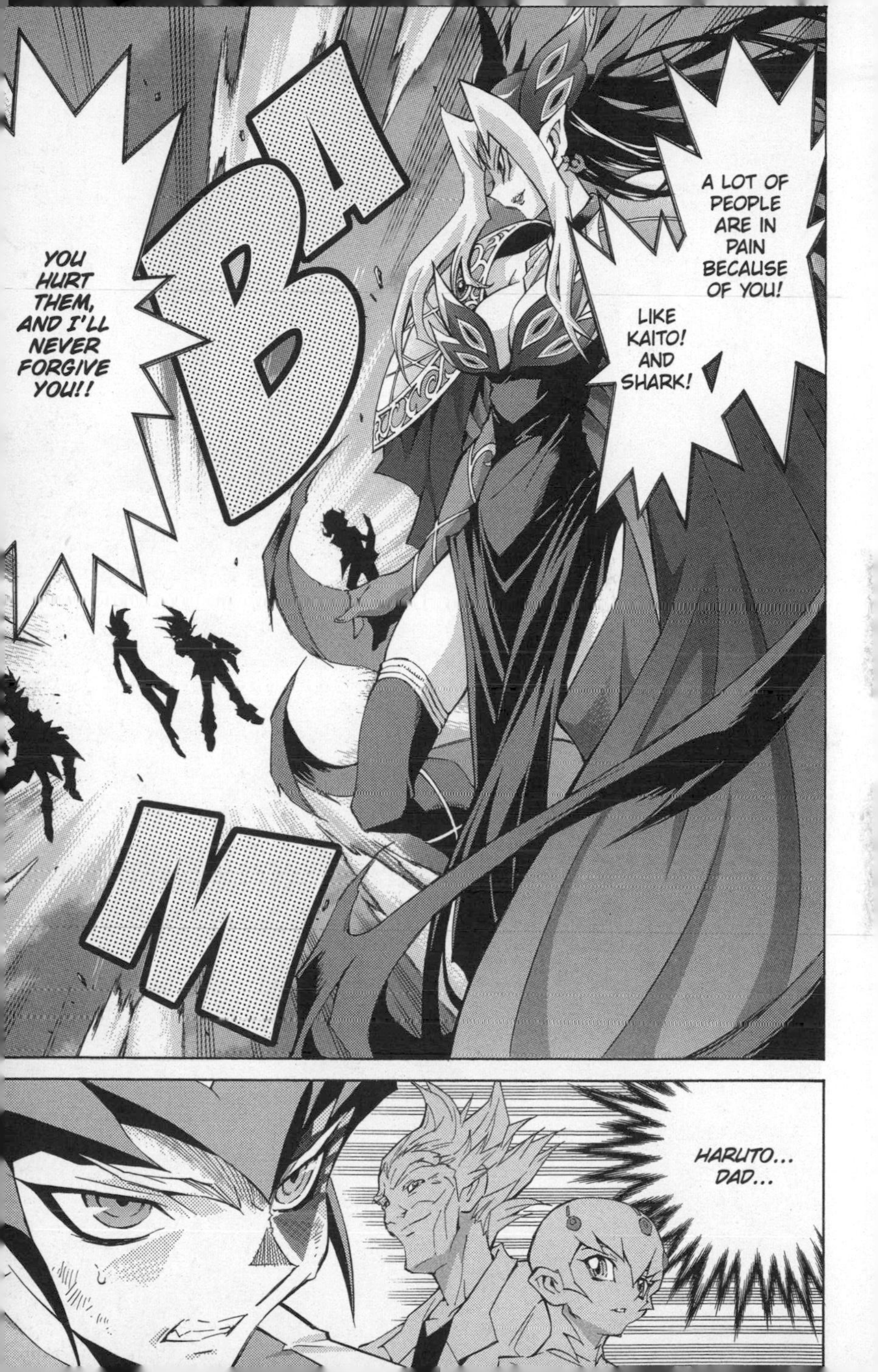
A LOT OF PEOPLE ARE IN PAIN BECAUSE OF YOU!
LIKE KAITO! AND SHARK!
BAM
YOU HURT THEM, AND I'LL NEVER FORGIVE YOU!!
HARUTO... DAD...

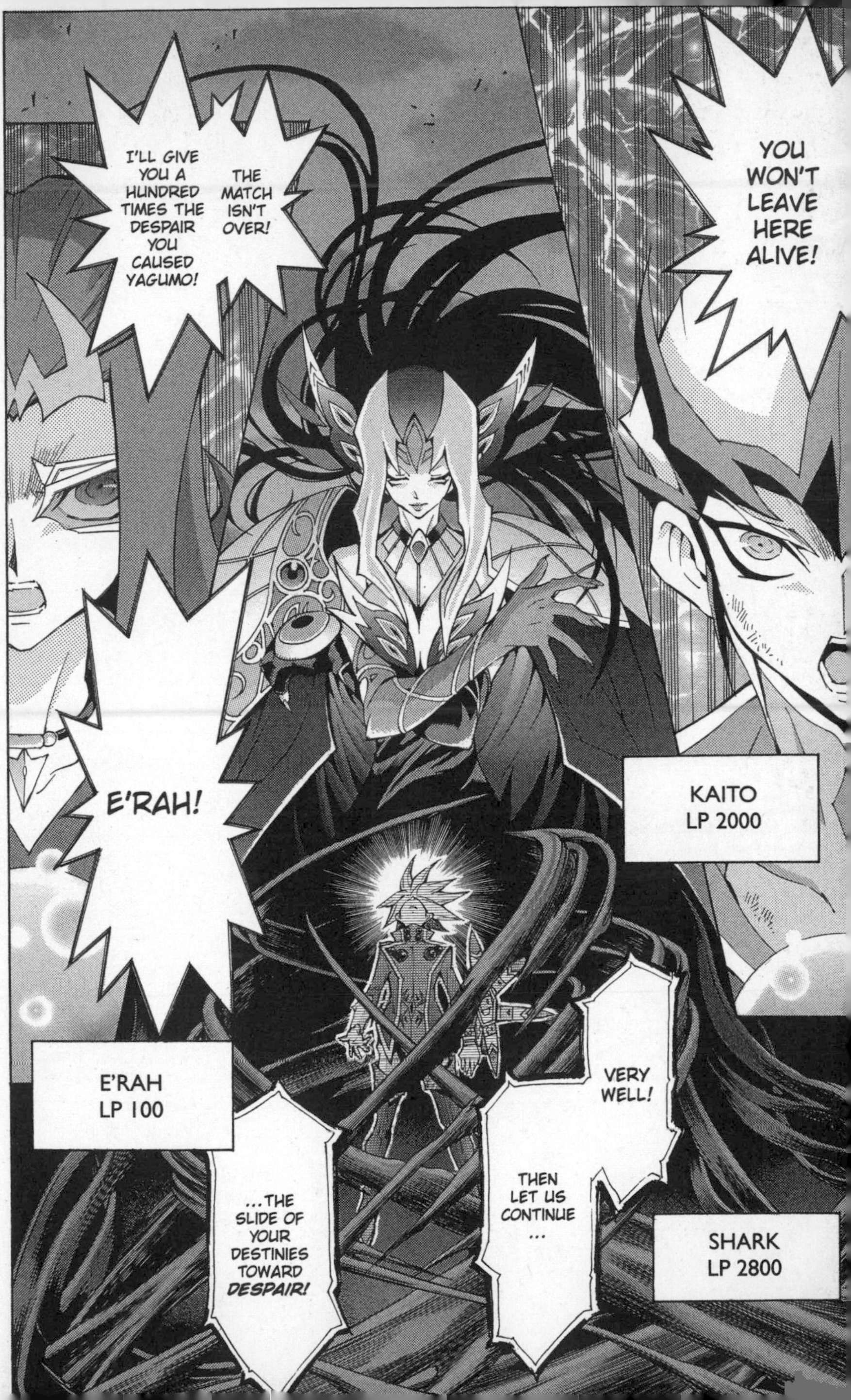
YOU WON'T LEAVE HERE ALIVE!
THE MATCH ISN'T OVER!
I'LL GIVE YOU A HUNDRED TIMES THE DESPAIR YOU CAUSED YAGUMO!
KAITO LP 2000
E'RAH!
SHARK LP 2800
VERY WELL!
THEN LET US CONTINUE ...
...THE SLIDE OF YOUR DESTINIES TOWARD *DESPAIR!*
E'RAH LP 100

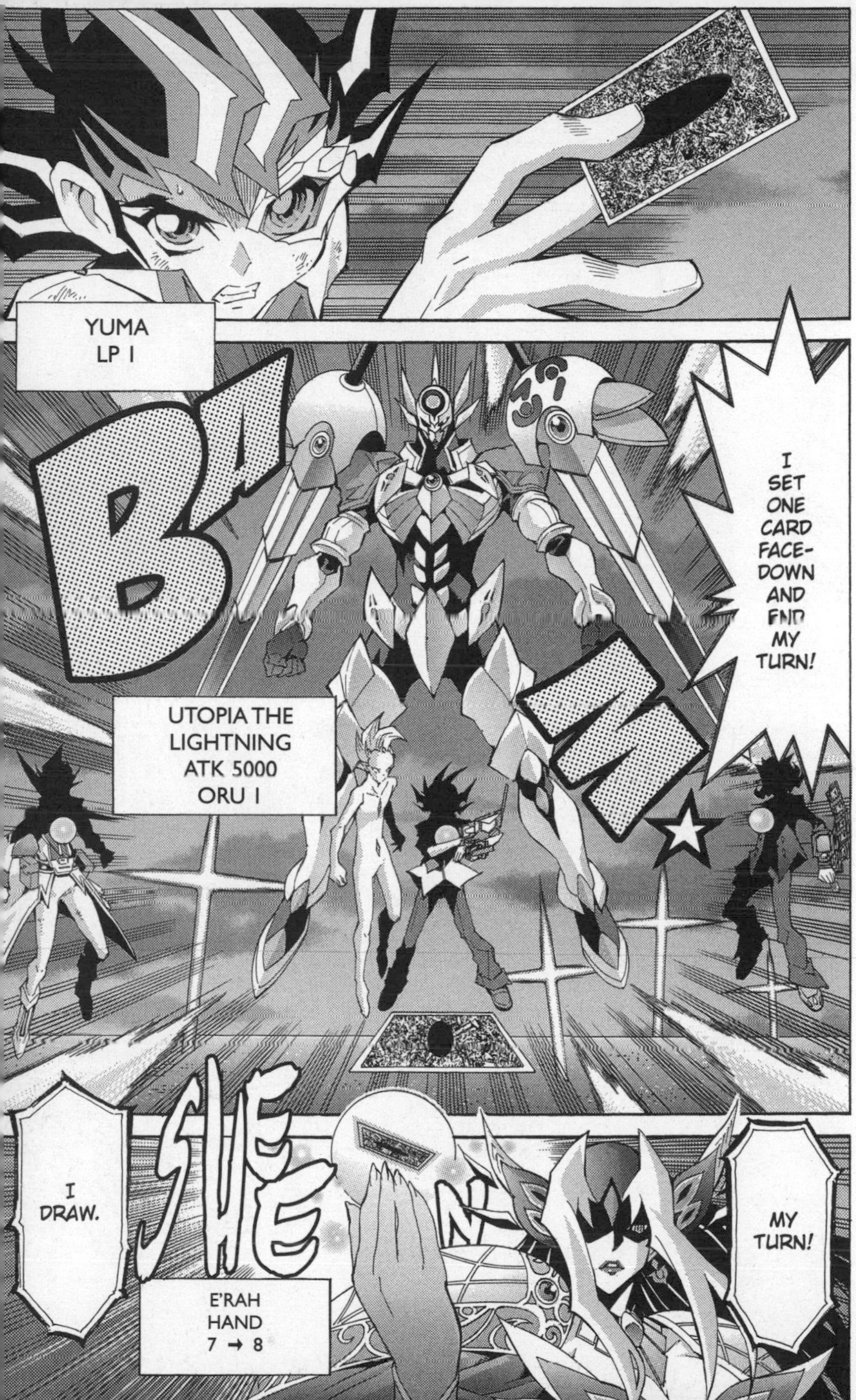
YUMA LP 1
I SET ONE CARD FACE-DOWN AND END MY TURN!
UTOPIA THE LIGHTNING ATK 5000 ORU 1
MY TURN!
I DRAW.
E'RAH HAND 7 → 8

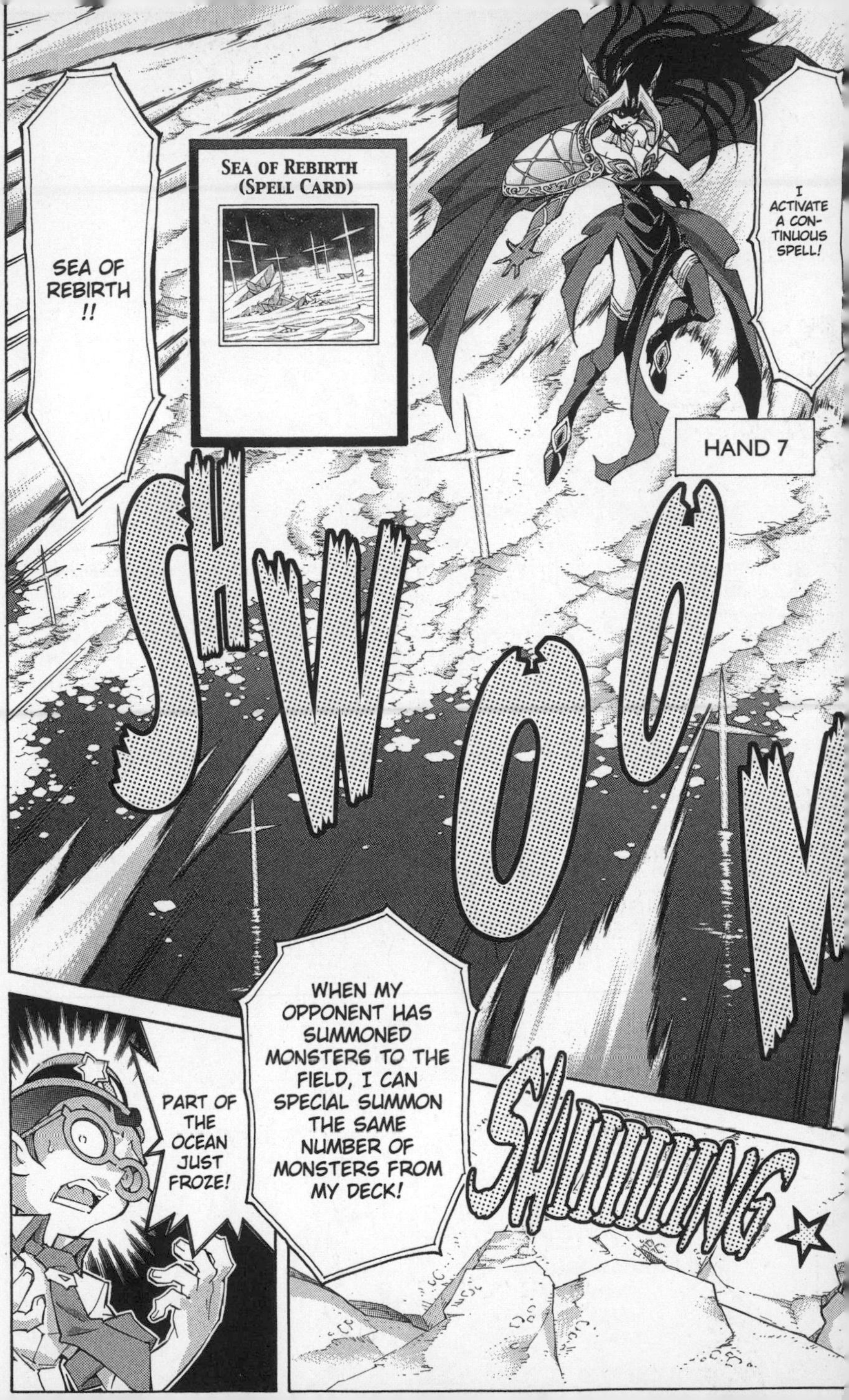
I ACTIVATE A CON-TINUOUS SPELL!
SEA OF REBIRTH (SPELL CARD)
SEA OF REBIRTH!!
HAND 7
SHWOOM
SHIIIIING
WHEN MY OPPONENT HAS SUMMONED MONSTERS TO THE FIELD, I CAN SPECIAL SUMMON THE SAME NUMBER OF MONSTERS FROM MY DECK!
PART OF THE OCEAN JUST FROZE!

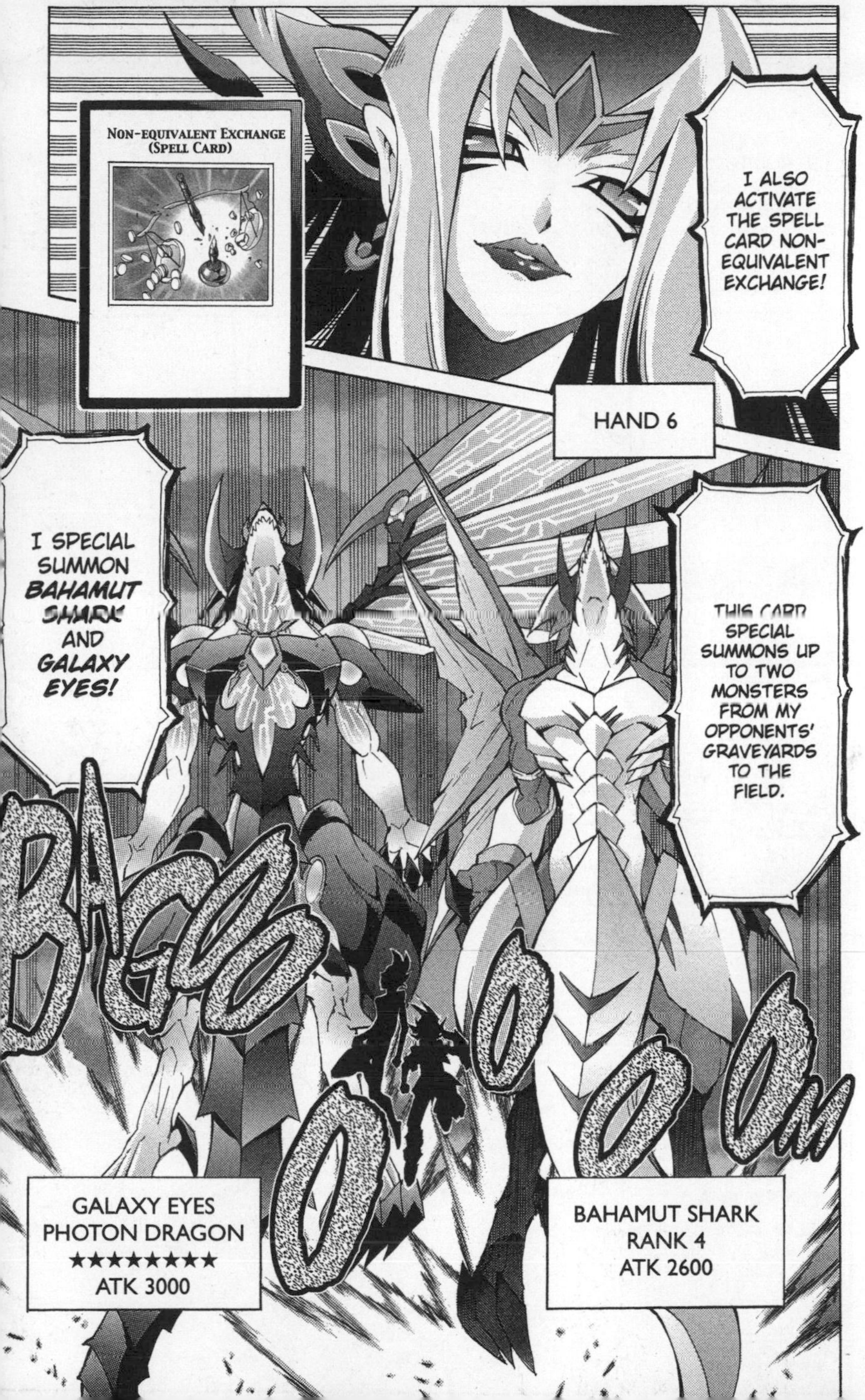
I ALSO ACTIVATE THE SPELL CARD NON-EQUIVALENT EXCHANGE!
NON-EQUIVALENT EXCHANGE
(SPELL CARD)
HAND 6
THIS CARD SPECIAL SUMMONS UP TO TWO MONSTERS FROM MY OPPONENTS' GRAVEYARDS TO THE FIELD.
I SPECIAL SUMMON *BAHAMUT SHARK* AND *GALAXY EYES!*
BAGOOOOOM
BAHAMUT SHARK
RANK 4
ATK 2600
GALAXY EYES
PHOTON DRAGON
★★★★★★★★
ATK 3000

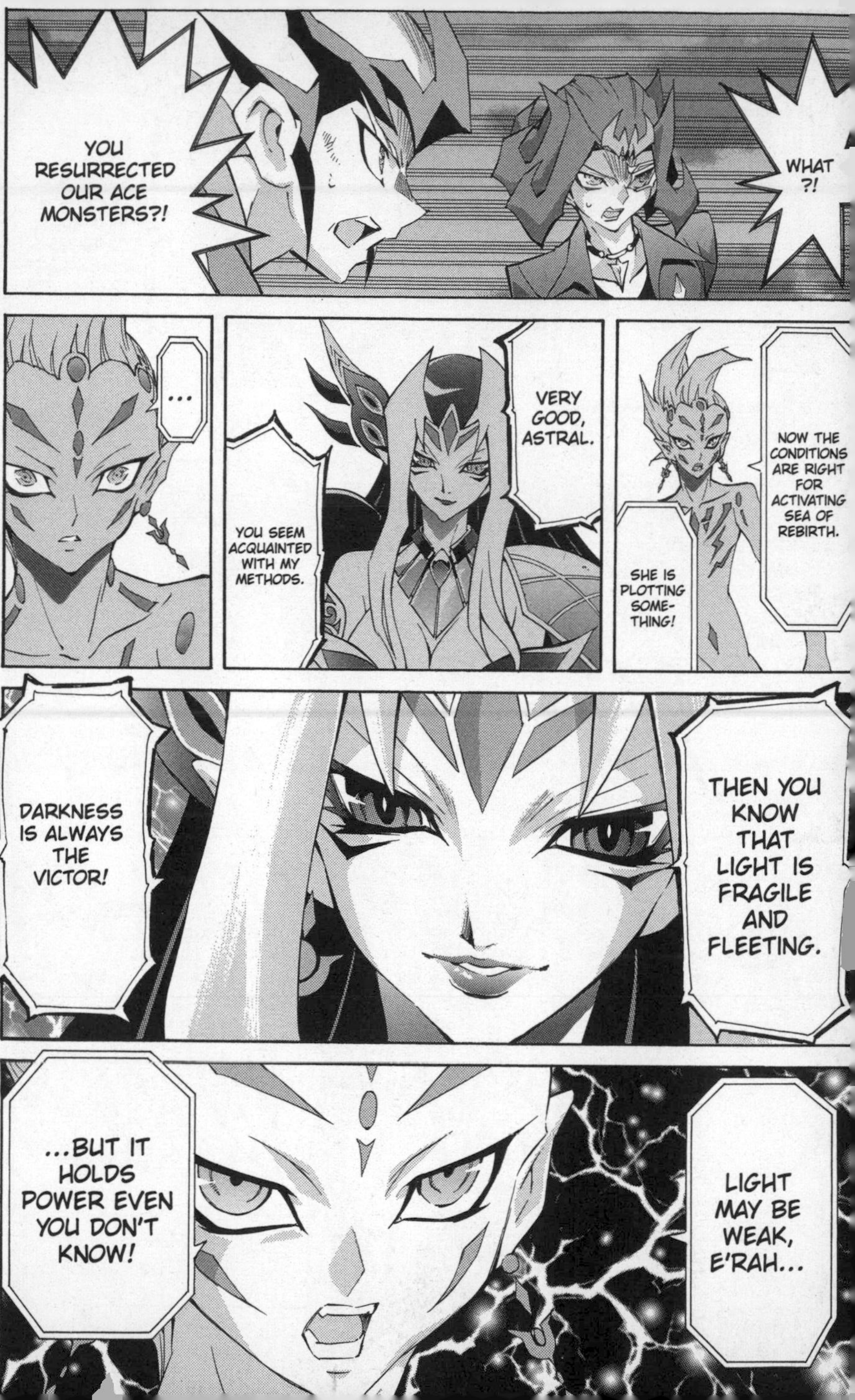
WHAT ?!
YOU RESURRECTED OUR ACE MONSTERS?!
NOW THE CONDITIONS ARE RIGHT FOR ACTIVATING SEA OF REBIRTH.
SHE IS PLOTTING SOME-THING!
VERY GOOD, ASTRAL.
YOU SEEM ACQUAINTED WITH MY METHODS.
...
THEN YOU KNOW THAT LIGHT IS FRAGILE AND FLEETING.
DARKNESS IS ALWAYS THE VICTOR!
LIGHT MAY BE WEAK, E'RAH...
...BUT IT HOLDS POWER EVEN YOU DON'T KNOW!

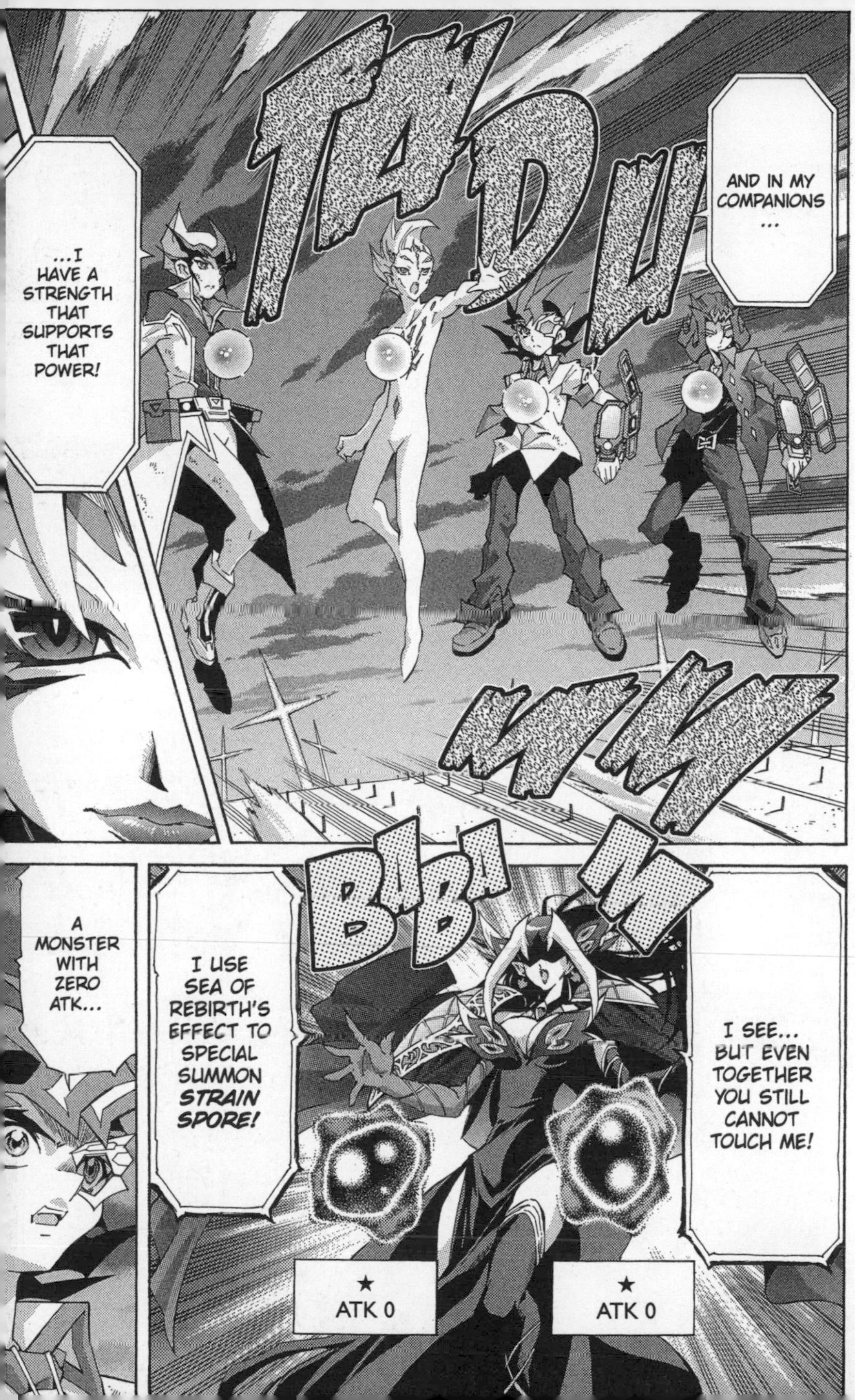
AND IN MY COMPANIONS...
...I HAVE A STRENGTH THAT SUPPORTS THAT POWER!
BABAM
I SEE... BUT EVEN TOGETHER YOU STILL CANNOT TOUCH ME!
I USE SEA OF REBIRTH'S EFFECT TO SPECIAL SUMMON STRAIN SPORE!
★ ATK 0
★ ATK 0
A MONSTER WITH ZERO ATK...

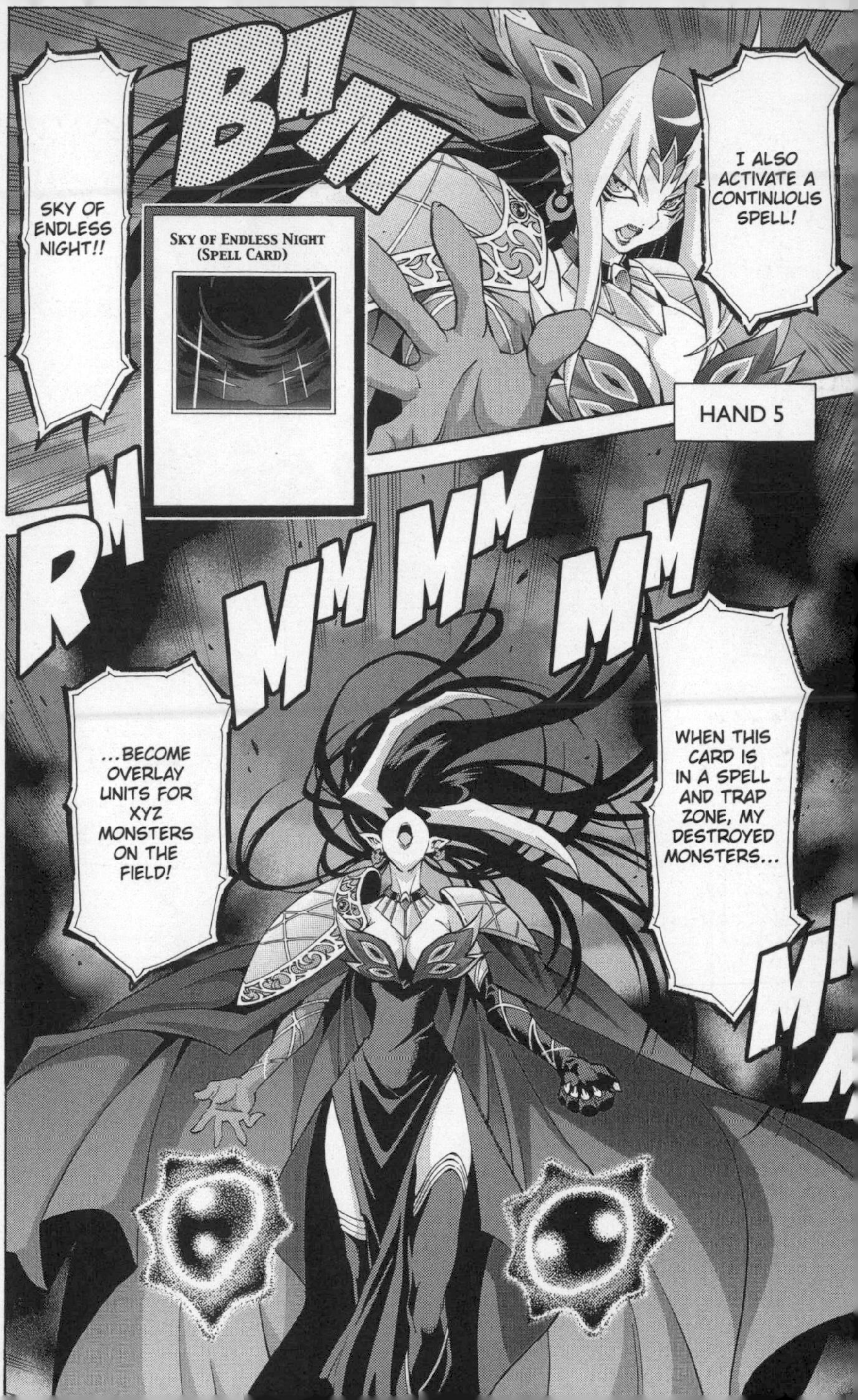
I ALSO ACTIVATE A CONTINUOUS SPELL!
HAND 5
BAM
SKY OF ENDLESS NIGHT!!
Sky of Endless Night (Spell Card)
RMMMMMMMMMM
WHEN THIS CARD IS IN A SPELL AND TRAP ZONE, MY DESTROYED MONSTERS...
...BECOME OVERLAY UNITS FOR XYZ MONSTERS ON THE FIELD!

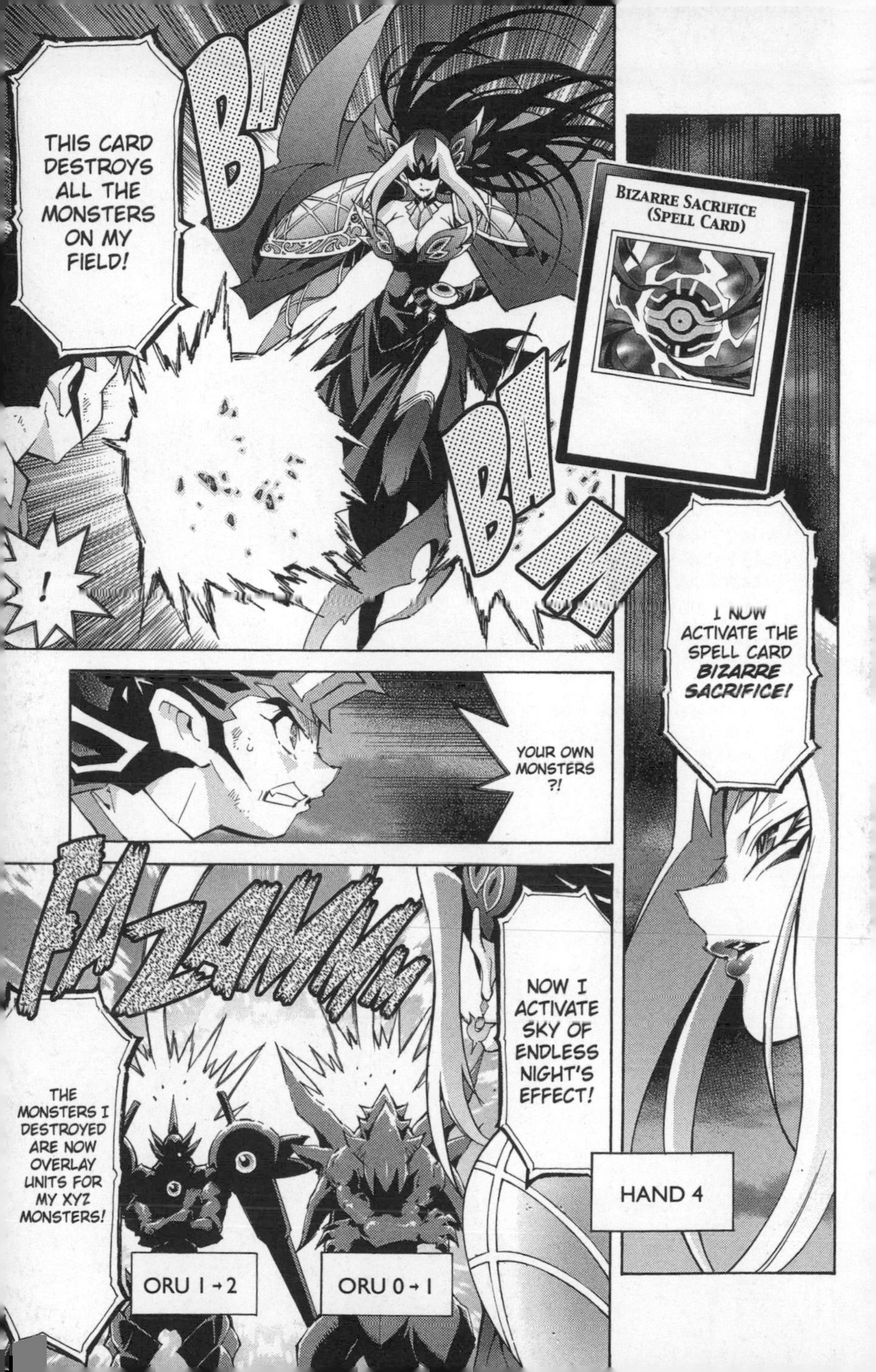

I NOW ACTIVATE THE SPELL CARD *BIZARRE SACRIFICE!*
HAND 4
BIZARRE SACRIFICE (SPELL CARD)
THIS CARD DESTROYS ALL THE MONSTERS ON MY FIELD!
BA BAM
!
YOUR OWN MONSTERS ?!
FAZAMMM
NOW I ACTIVATE SKY OF ENDLESS NIGHT'S EFFECT!
THE MONSTERS I DESTROYED ARE NOW OVERLAY UNITS FOR MY XYZ MONSTERS!
ORU 0→1
ORU 1→2

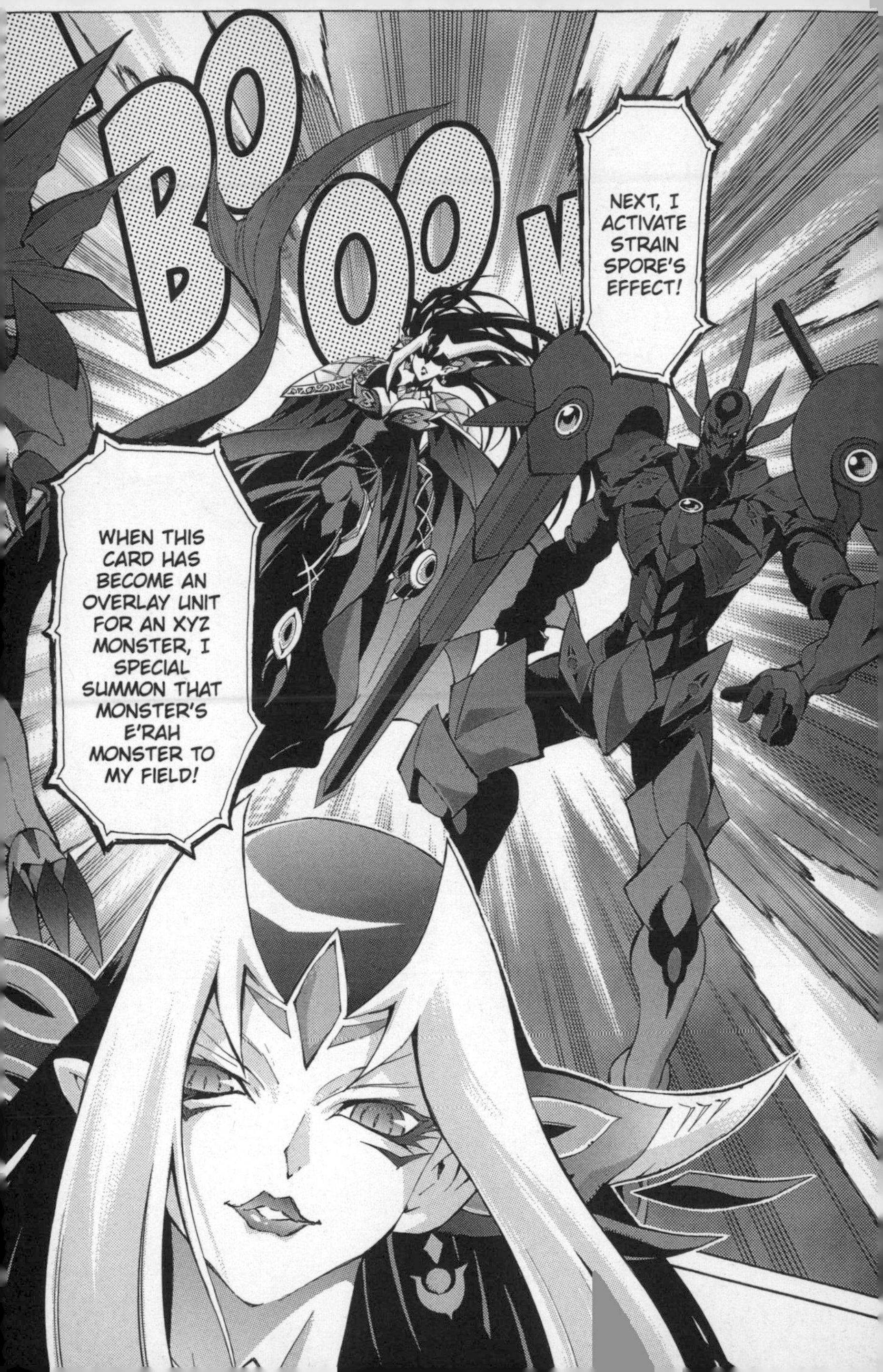
NEXT, I ACTIVATE STRAIN SPORE'S EFFECT!
BOOOM
WHEN THIS CARD HAS BECOME AN OVERLAY UNIT FOR AN XYZ MONSTER, I SPECIAL SUMMON THAT MONSTER'S E'RAH MONSTER TO MY FIELD!

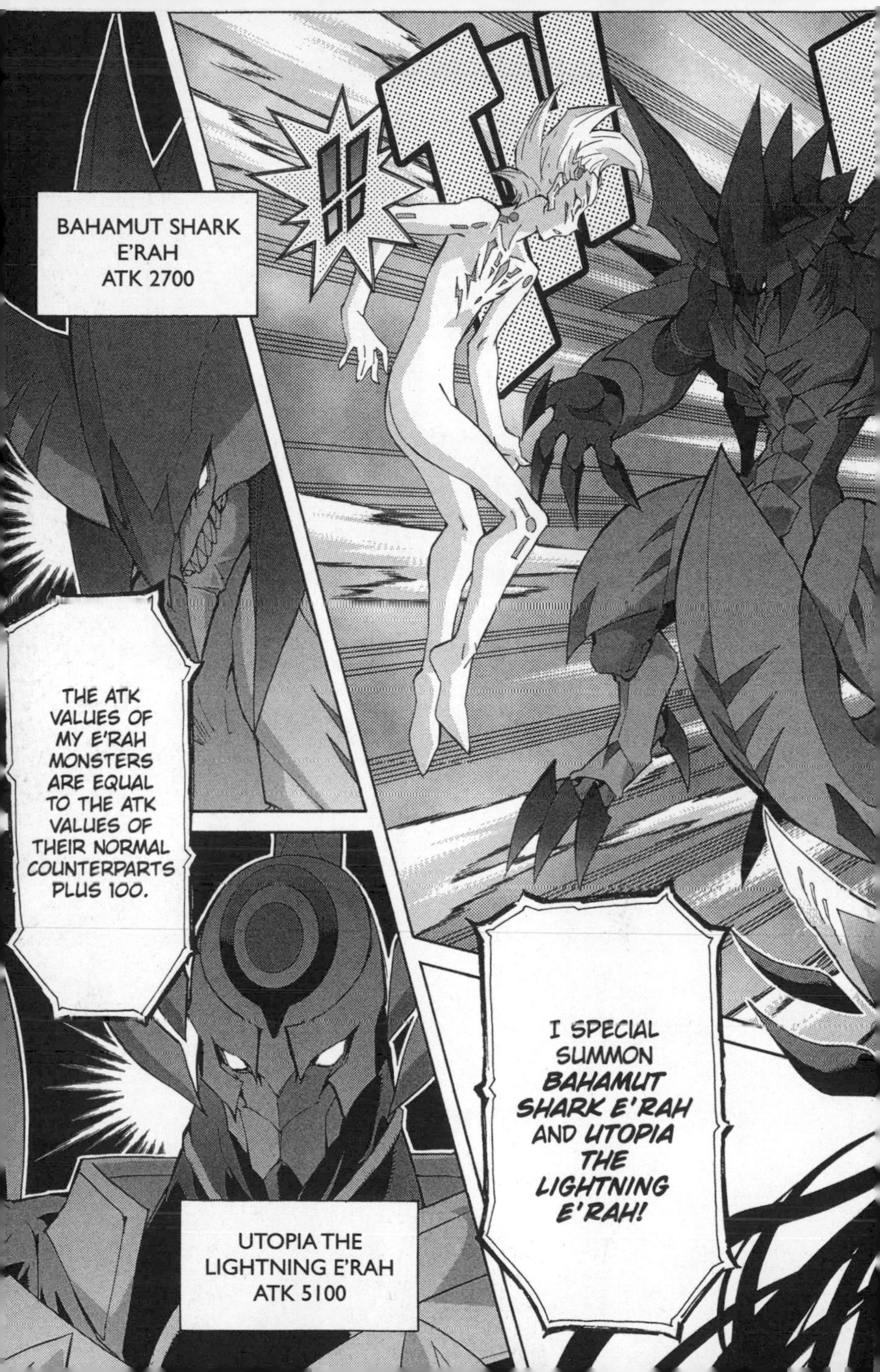
!!
I SPECIAL SUMMON BAHAMUT SHARK E'RAH AND UTOPIA THE LIGHTNING E'RAH!
BAHAMUT SHARK E'RAH ATK 2700
THE ATK VALUES OF MY E'RAH MONSTERS ARE EQUAL TO THE ATK VALUES OF THEIR NORMAL COUNTERPARTS PLUS 100.
UTOPIA THE LIGHTNING E'RAH ATK 5100

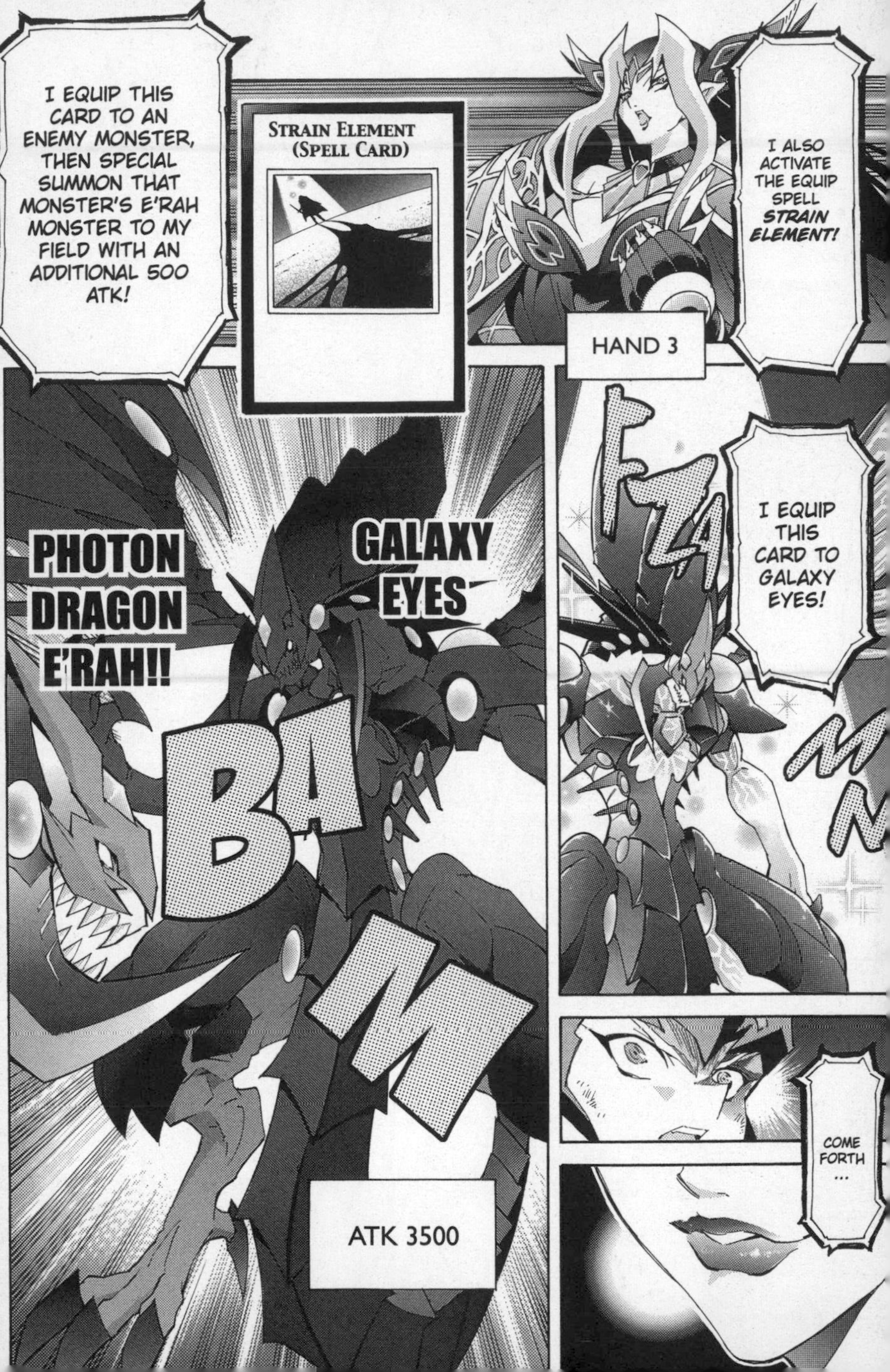
I ALSO ACTIVATE THE EQUIP SPELL STRAIN ELEMENT!
HAND 3
Strain Element (Spell Card)
I EQUIP THIS CARD TO AN ENEMY MONSTER, THEN SPECIAL SUMMON THAT MONSTER'S E'RAH MONSTER TO MY FIELD WITH AN ADDITIONAL 500 ATK!
FZA
I EQUIP THIS CARD TO GALAXY EYES!
COME FORTH ...
GALAXY EYES
PHOTON DRAGON E'RAH!!
BAM
ATK 3500

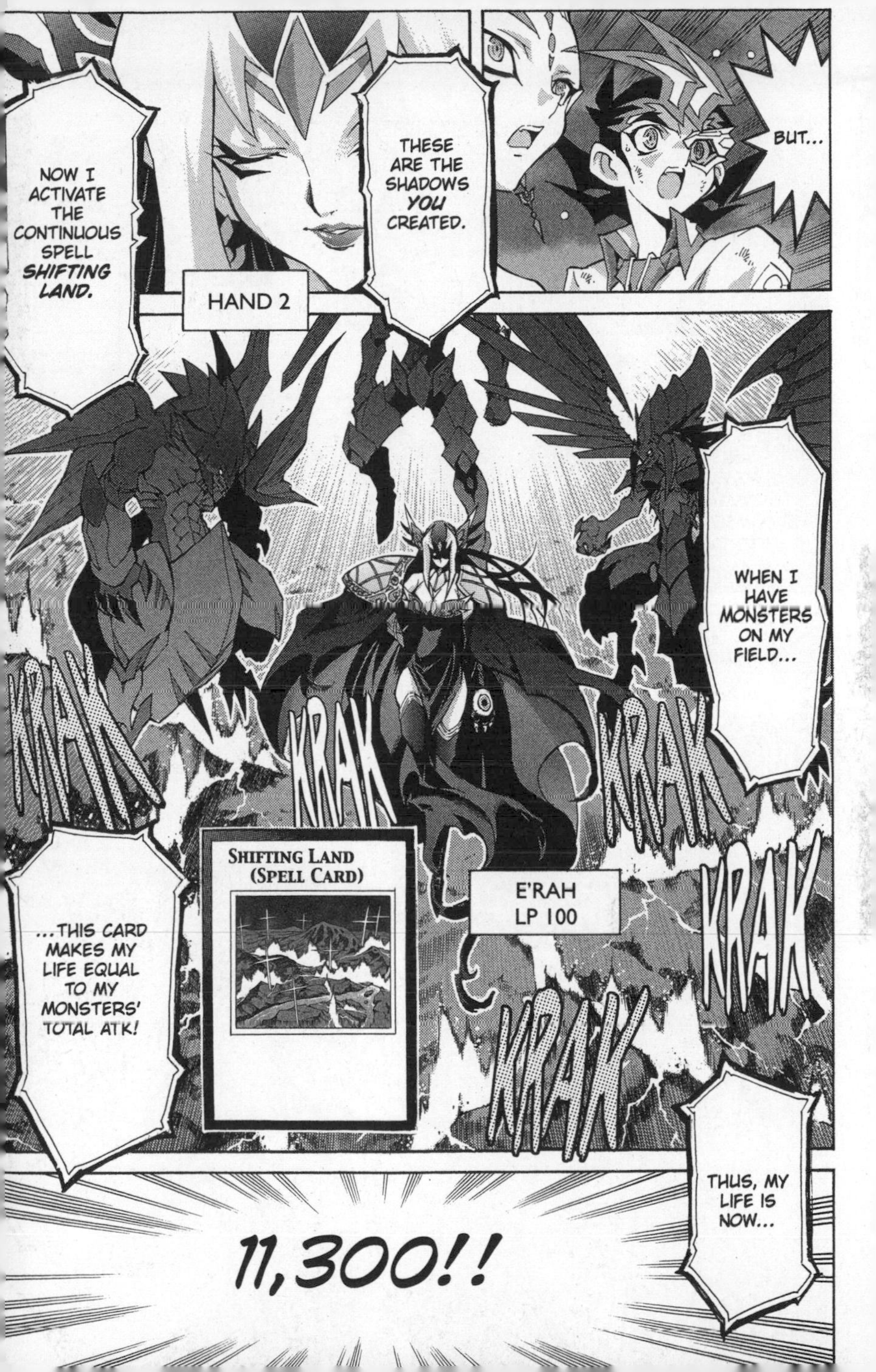
BUT...
THESE ARE THE SHADOWS *YOU* CREATED.
NOW I ACTIVATE THE CONTINUOUS SPELL ***SHIFTING LAND.***
HAND 2
WHEN I HAVE MONSTERS ON MY FIELD...
KRAK
KRAK
KRAK
KRAK
E'RAH
LP 100
...THIS CARD MAKES MY LIFE EQUAL TO MY MONSTERS' TOTAL ATK!
SHIFTING LAND (SPELL CARD)
KRAK
THUS, MY LIFE IS NOW...
11,300!!

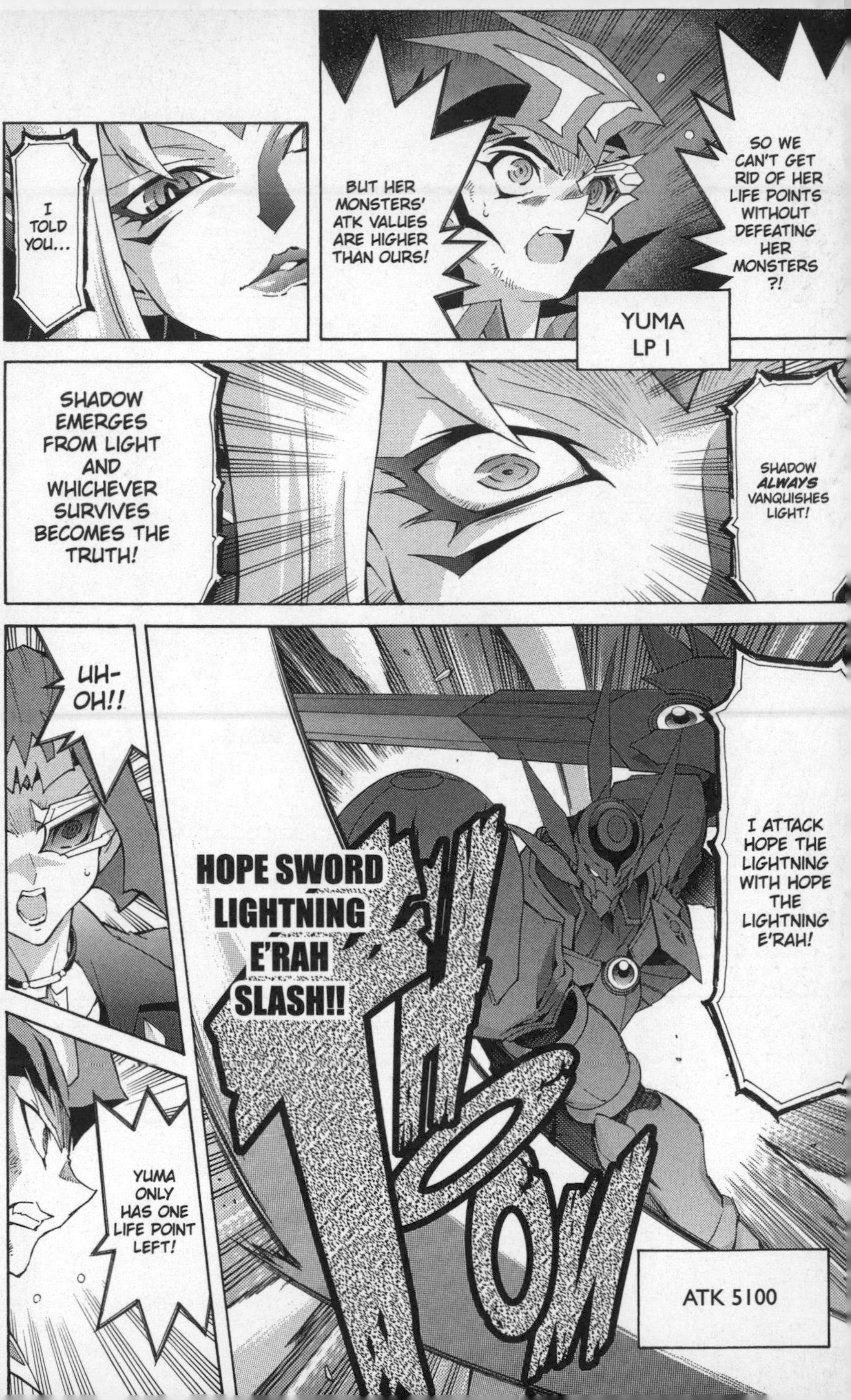
SO WE CAN'T GET RID OF HER LIFE POINTS WITHOUT DEFEATING HER MONSTERS ?!
BUT HER MONSTERS' ATK VALUES ARE HIGHER THAN OURS!
YUMA
LP 1
I TOLD YOU...
SHADOW *ALWAYS* VANQUISHES LIGHT!
SHADOW EMERGES FROM LIGHT AND WHICHEVER SURVIVES BECOMES THE TRUTH!
I ATTACK HOPE THE LIGHTNING WITH HOPE THE LIGHTNING E'RAH!
HOPE SWORD LIGHTNING E'RAH SLASH!!
ATK 5100
UH-OH!!
YUMA ONLY HAS ONE LIFE POINT LEFT!

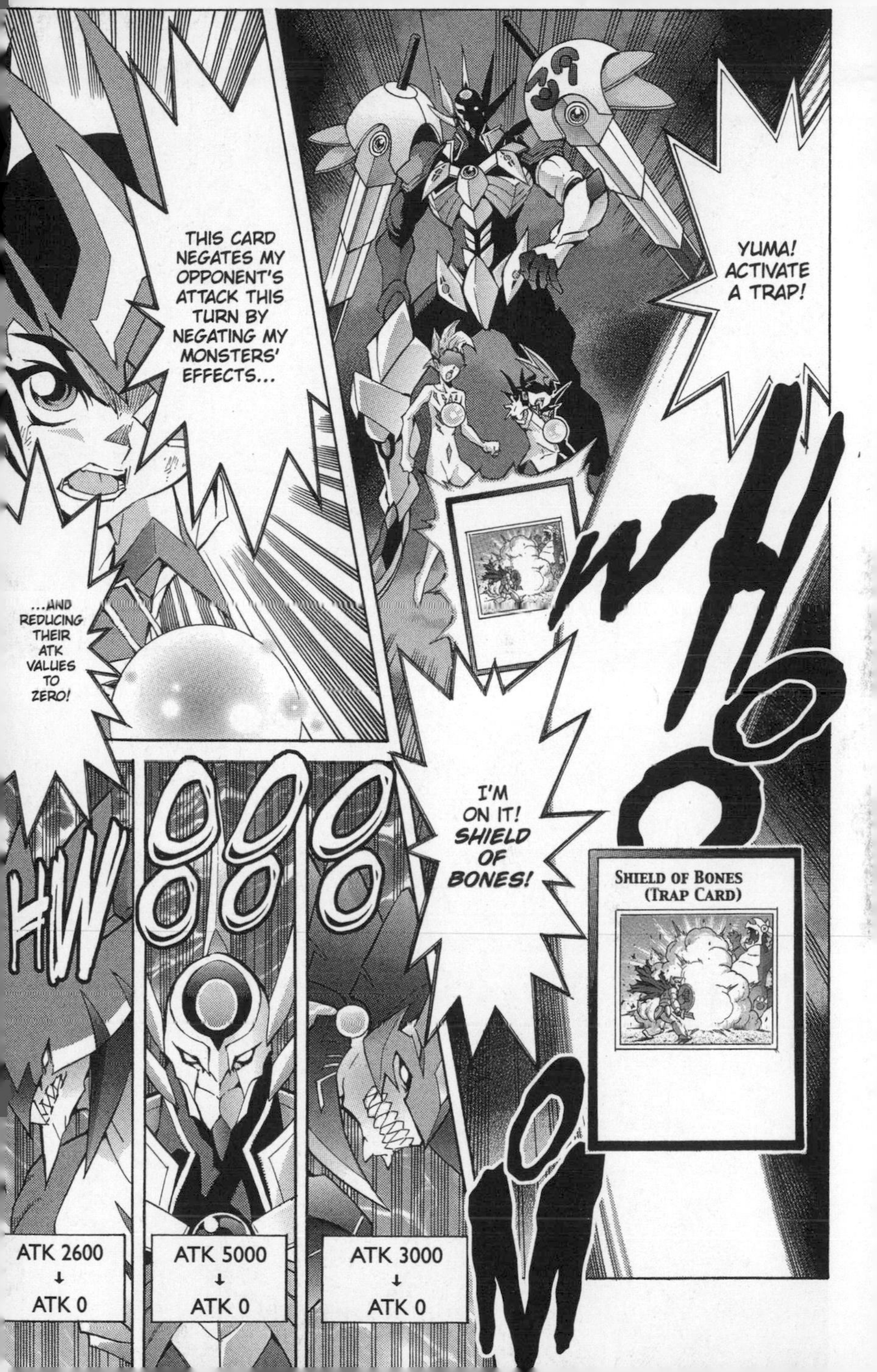

YUMA! ACTIVATE A TRAP!
I'M ON IT! SHIELD OF BONES!
SHIELD OF BONES (TRAP CARD)
WHOOOM
THIS CARD NEGATES MY OPPONENT'S ATTACK THIS TURN BY NEGATING MY MONSTERS' EFFECTS...
...AND REDUCING THEIR ATK VALUES TO ZERO!
HWOOO
ATK 3000 ↓ ATK 0
ATK 5000 ↓ ATK 0
ATK 2600 ↓ ATK 0

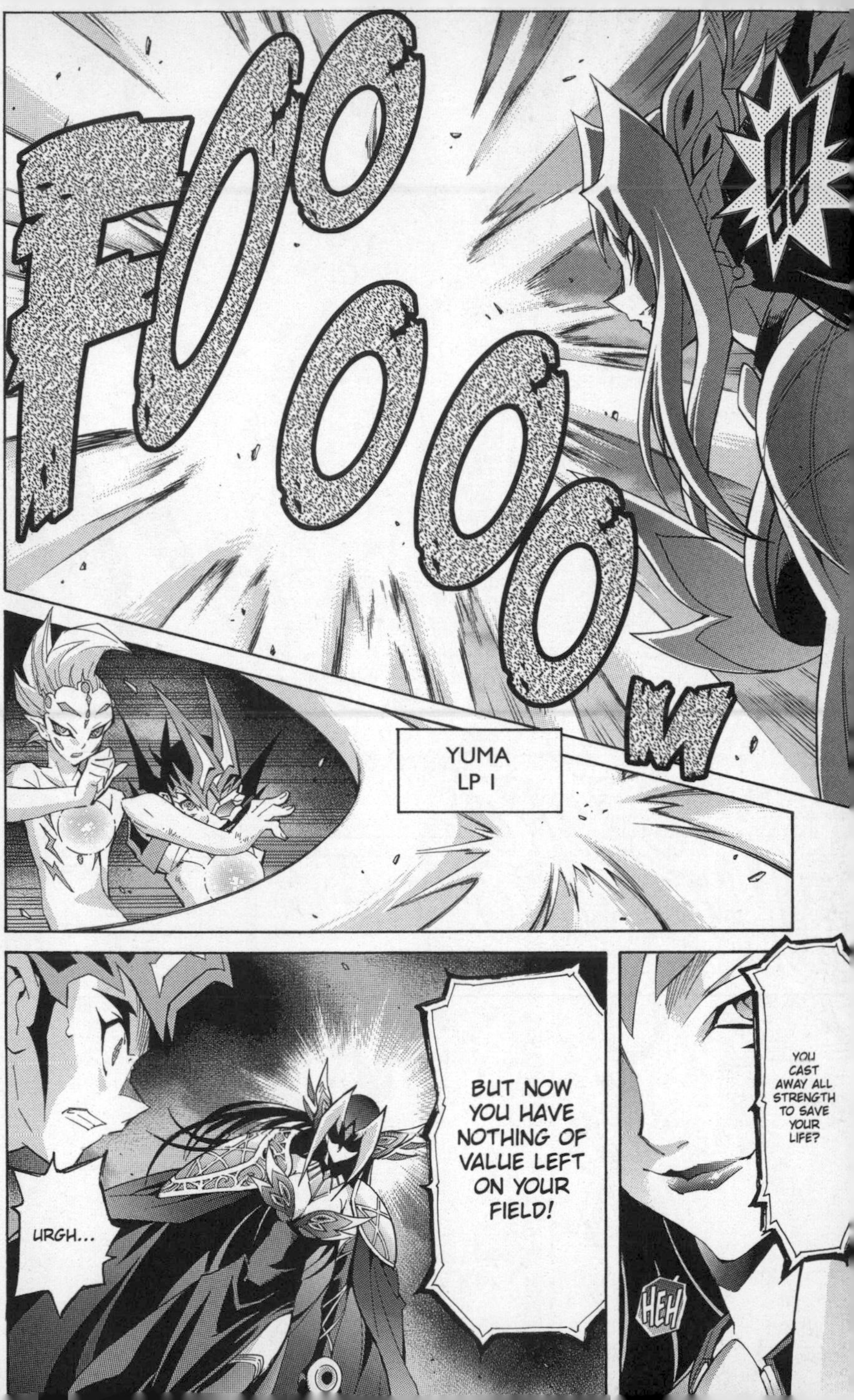
!!
FOOOOOM
YUMA
LP 1
YOU CAST AWAY ALL STRENGTH TO SAVE YOUR LIFE?
HEH
BUT NOW YOU HAVE NOTHING OF VALUE LEFT ON YOUR FIELD!
URGH...

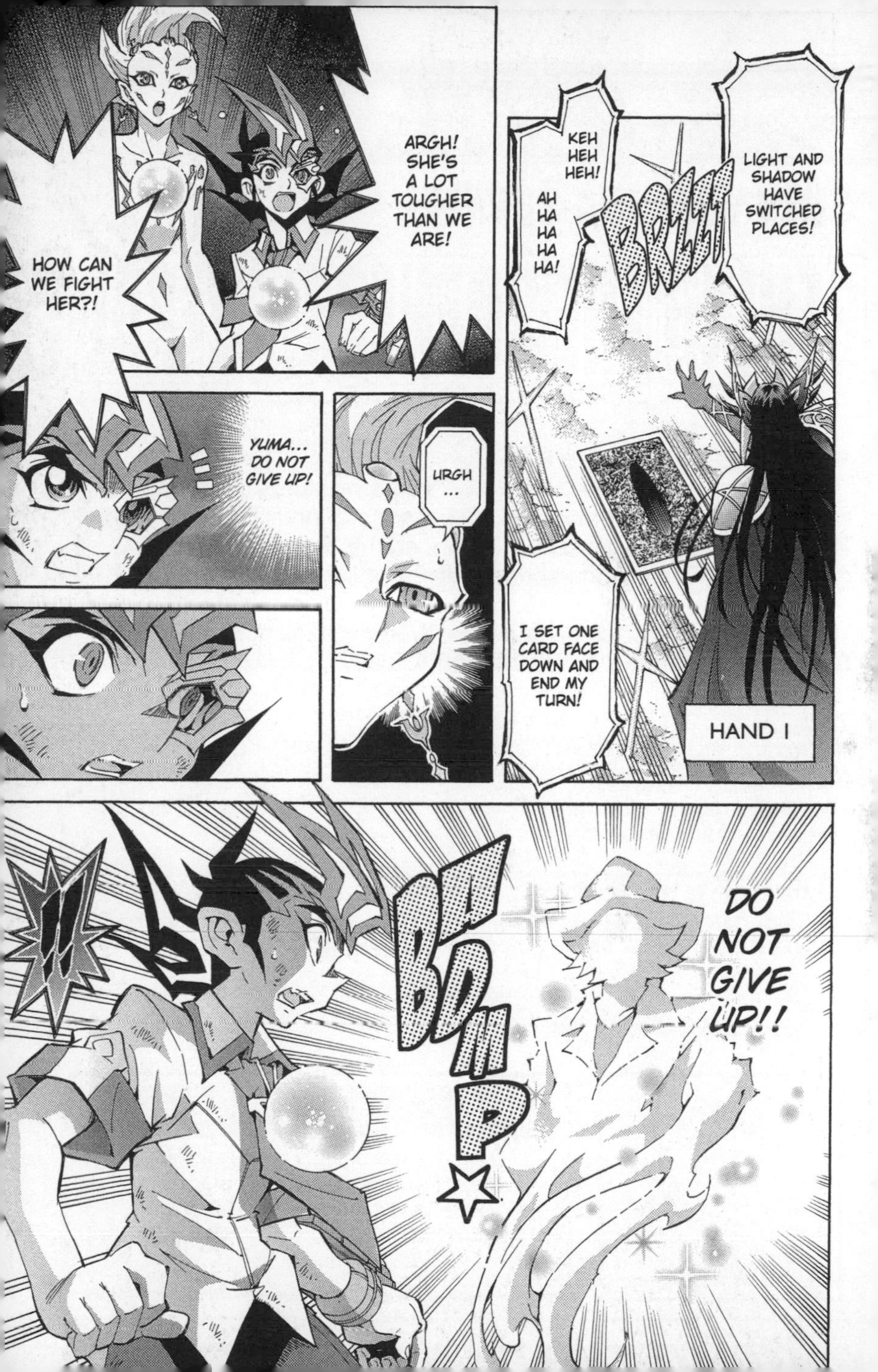
LIGHT AND SHADOW HAVE SWITCHED PLACES!
KEH HEH HEH!
AH HA HA HA HA!
BRZZT
I SET ONE CARD FACE DOWN AND END MY TURN!
HAND 1
ARGH! SHE'S A LOT TOUGHER THAN WE ARE!
HOW CAN WE FIGHT HER?!
URGH...
YUMA... DO NOT GIVE UP!
DO NOT GIVE UP!!
!!

Series composition for the *ZEXAL* anime

The author of the *ZEXAL* manga

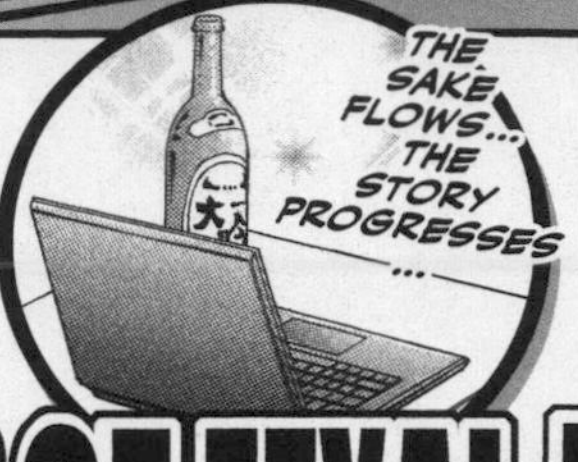
THE SAKE FLOWS... THE STORY PROGRESSES...

SHIN YOSHIDA SPEAKS:

BEHIND THE SCENES OF ZEXAL 5

*** THE DUEL AGAINST E'RAH**

Most of the duels in the *Yu-Gi-Oh!* anime were designed by Hikokubo-san, the writer of the *5D's* manga. Since Hikokubo-san had already begun the *5D's* series, I planned the duels in the *ZEXAL* manga myself to give the series a different flare.

However, I asked Uchida-san from Wedge Holdings to handle the E'Rah battle. A duel with effects from Galaxy Eyes, Utopia and the other monsters all mixed together was too tough for me... (^_^)

Watching the early anime, I noticed how, when Kaiba uses a spell card to boost his attack power, Yugi mutters over how Kaiba really knows the game. I thought, "Duels sure were simple back then!" It made me realize how long I'd been involved with this!

Uchida-san is a true card expert! To make the final duel exciting, he thinks of cards that would never have occurred to me. Enjoy Miyoshi Sensei's superlative art as you read the climax of *Yu-Gi-Oh! ZEXAL*!

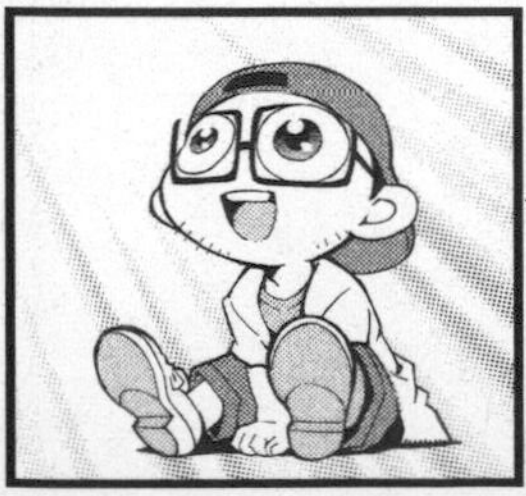

A Message from Miyoshi Sensei!

Yoshida Sensei's duels have unique themes and they're a blizzard of fun names and effects, and Uchida-san always puts together amazing duels with lightning speed. I respect both of those guys!

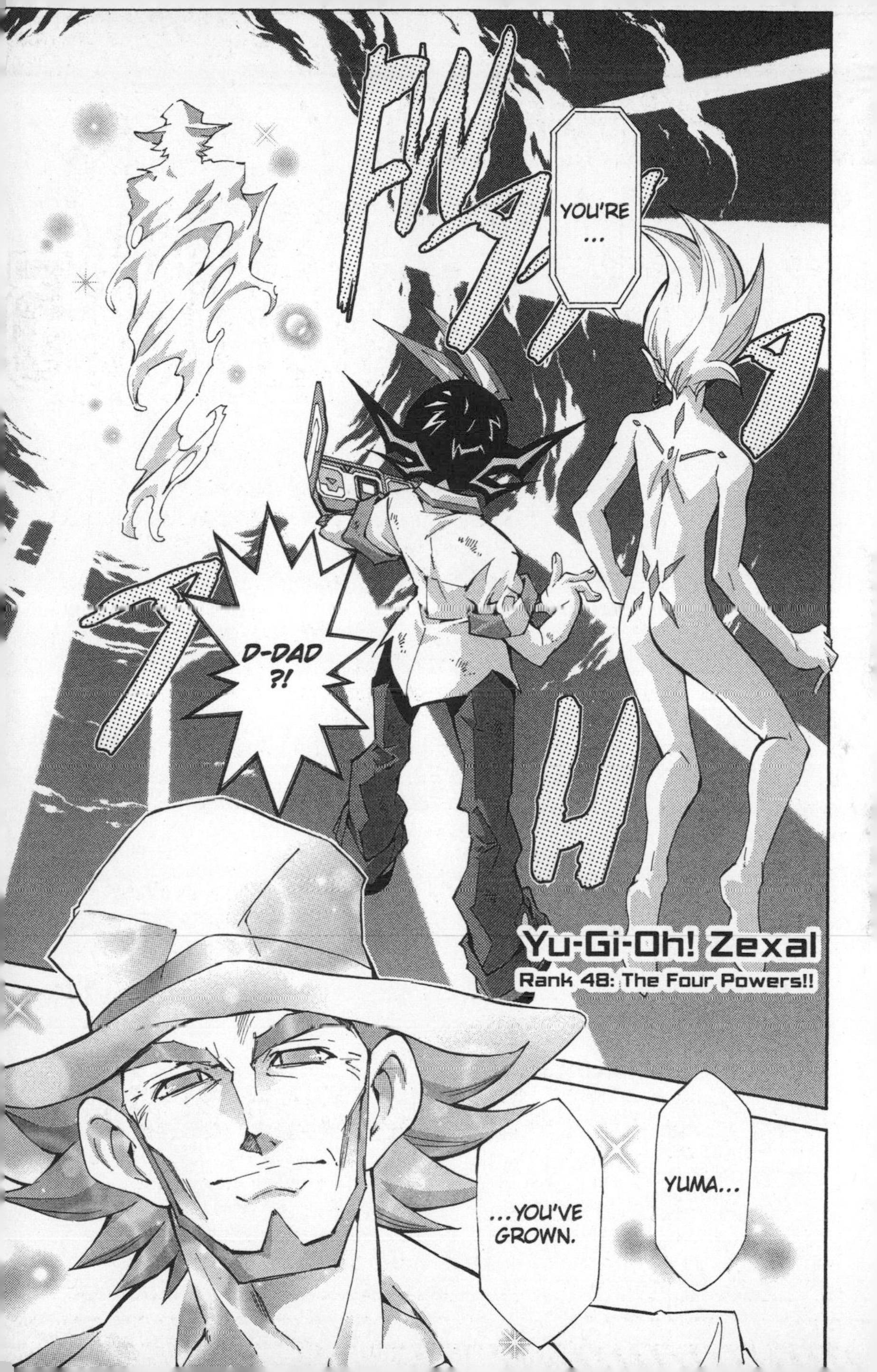
YOU'RE ...
D-DAD ?!
Yu-Gi-Oh! Zexal
Rank 48: The Four Powers!!
YUMA...
...YOU'VE GROWN.

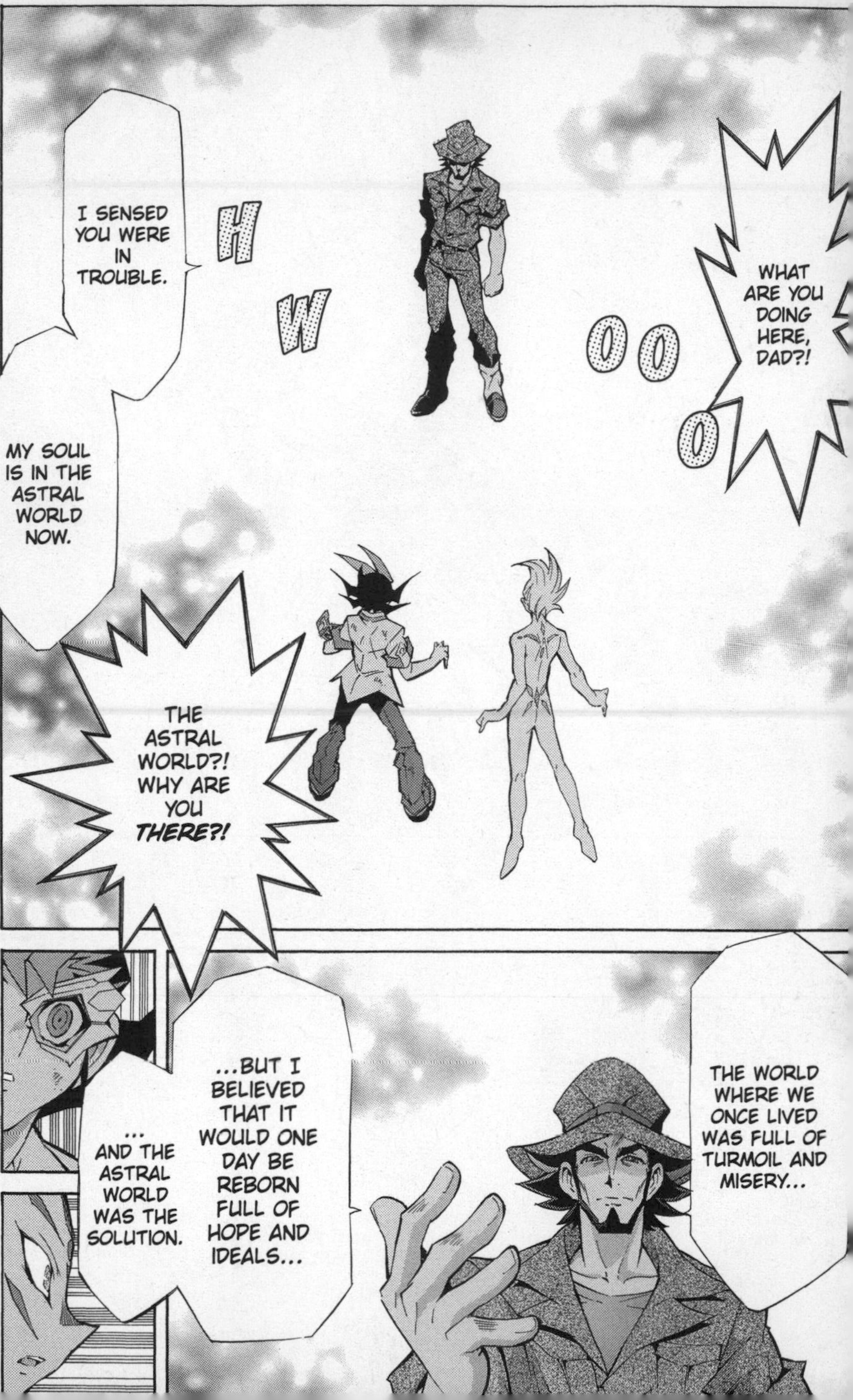
WHAT ARE YOU DOING HERE, DAD?!
WHOOO
I SENSED YOU WERE IN TROUBLE.
MY SOUL IS IN THE ASTRAL WORLD NOW.
THE ASTRAL WORLD?! WHY ARE YOU *THERE?!*
THE WORLD WHERE WE ONCE LIVED WAS FULL OF TURMOIL AND MISERY...
...BUT I BELIEVED THAT IT WOULD ONE DAY BE REBORN FULL OF HOPE AND IDEALS...
... AND THE ASTRAL WORLD WAS THE SOLUTION.

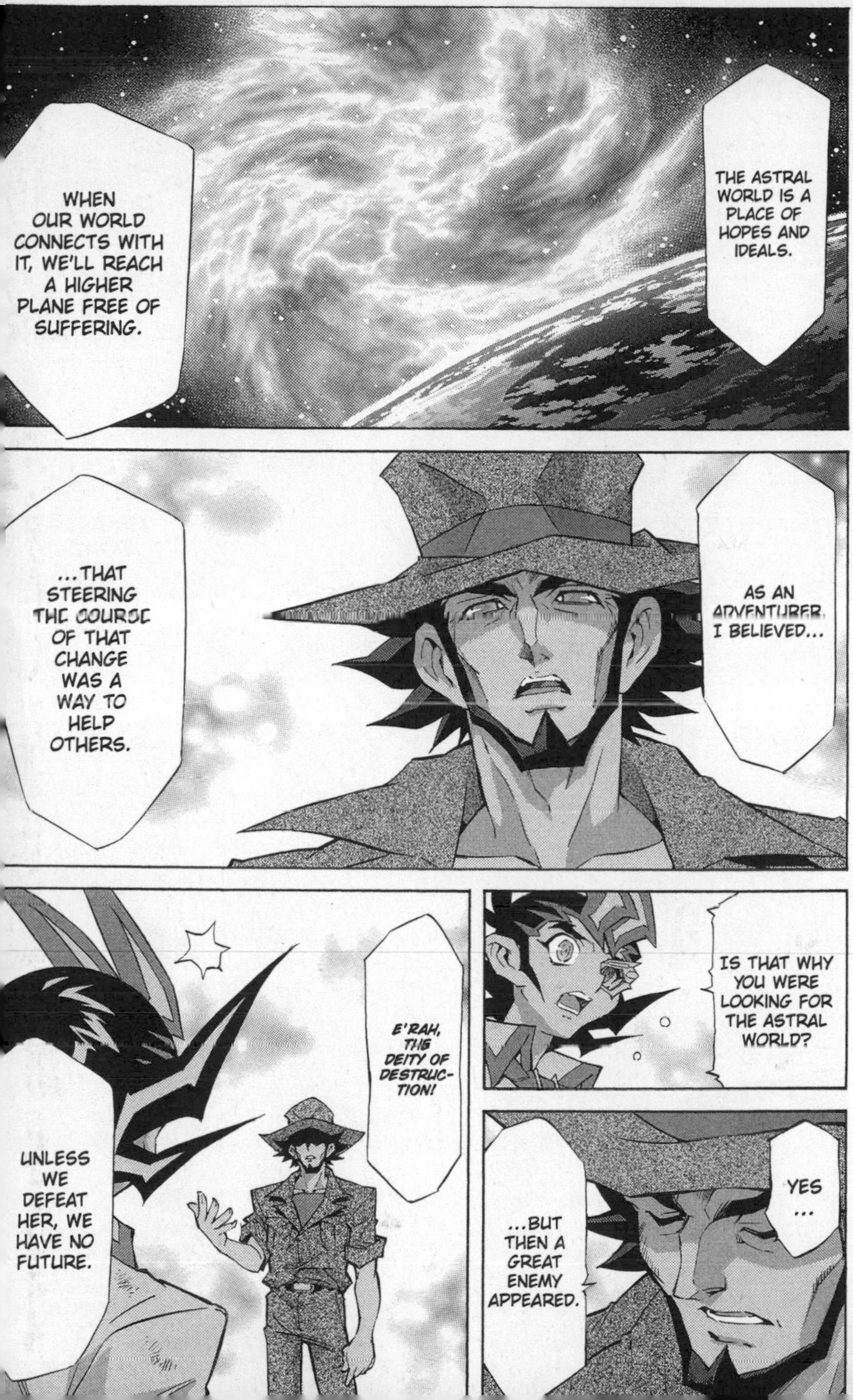
THE ASTRAL WORLD IS A PLACE OF HOPES AND IDEALS.
WHEN OUR WORLD CONNECTS WITH IT, WE'LL REACH A HIGHER PLANE FREE OF SUFFERING.
AS AN ADVENTURER, I BELIEVED...
...THAT STEERING THE COURSE OF THAT CHANGE WAS A WAY TO HELP OTHERS.
IS THAT WHY YOU WERE LOOKING FOR THE ASTRAL WORLD?
YES...
...BUT THEN A GREAT ENEMY APPEARED.
E'RAH, THE DEITY OF DESTRUCTION!
UNLESS WE DEFEAT HER, WE HAVE NO FUTURE.

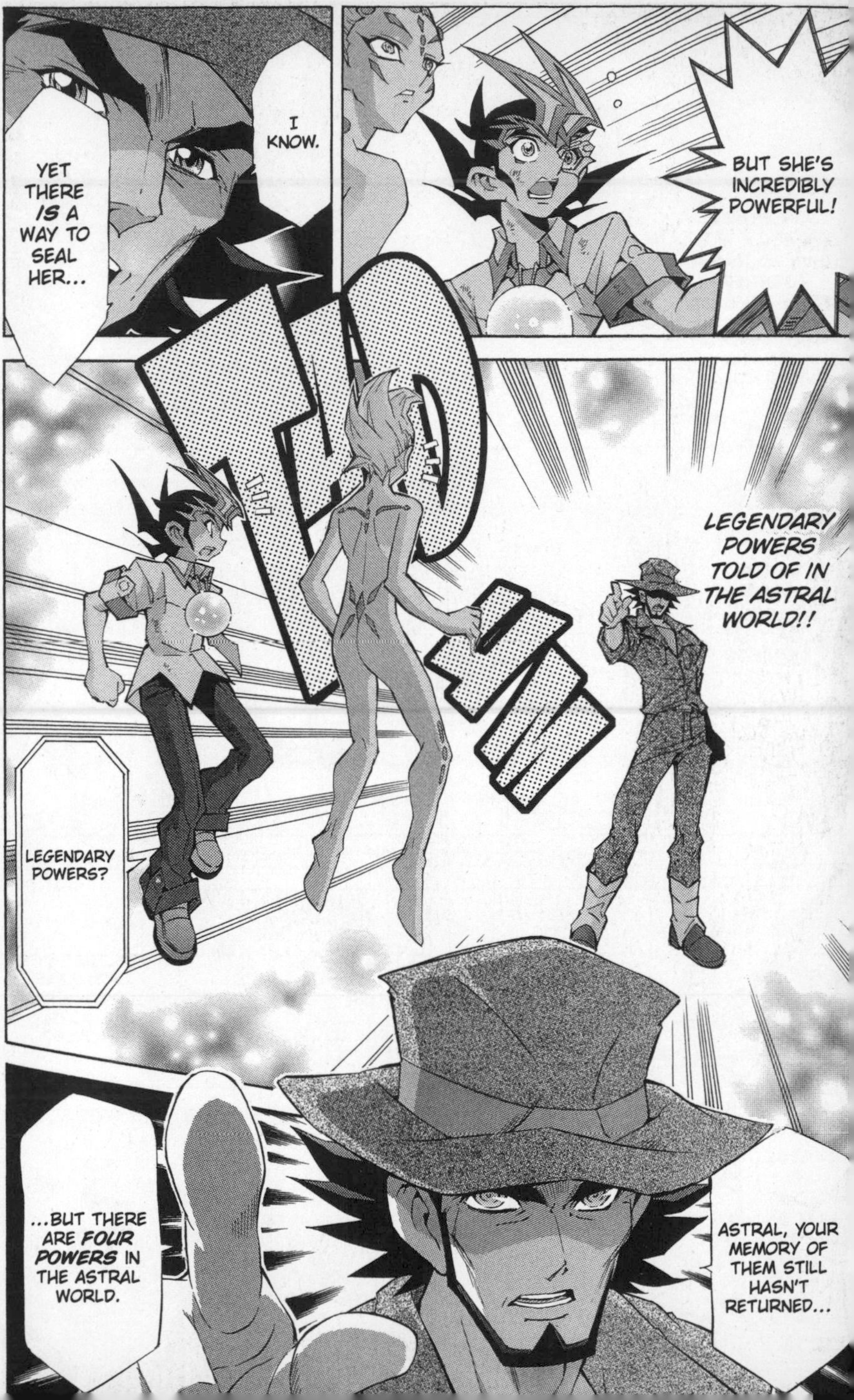
BUT SHE'S INCREDIBLY POWERFUL!
I KNOW.
YET THERE *IS* A WAY TO SEAL HER...
LEGENDARY POWERS TOLD OF IN THE ASTRAL WORLD!!
LEGENDARY POWERS?
ASTRAL, YOUR MEMORY OF THEM STILL HASN'T RETURNED...
...BUT THERE ARE *FOUR POWERS* IN THE ASTRAL WORLD.

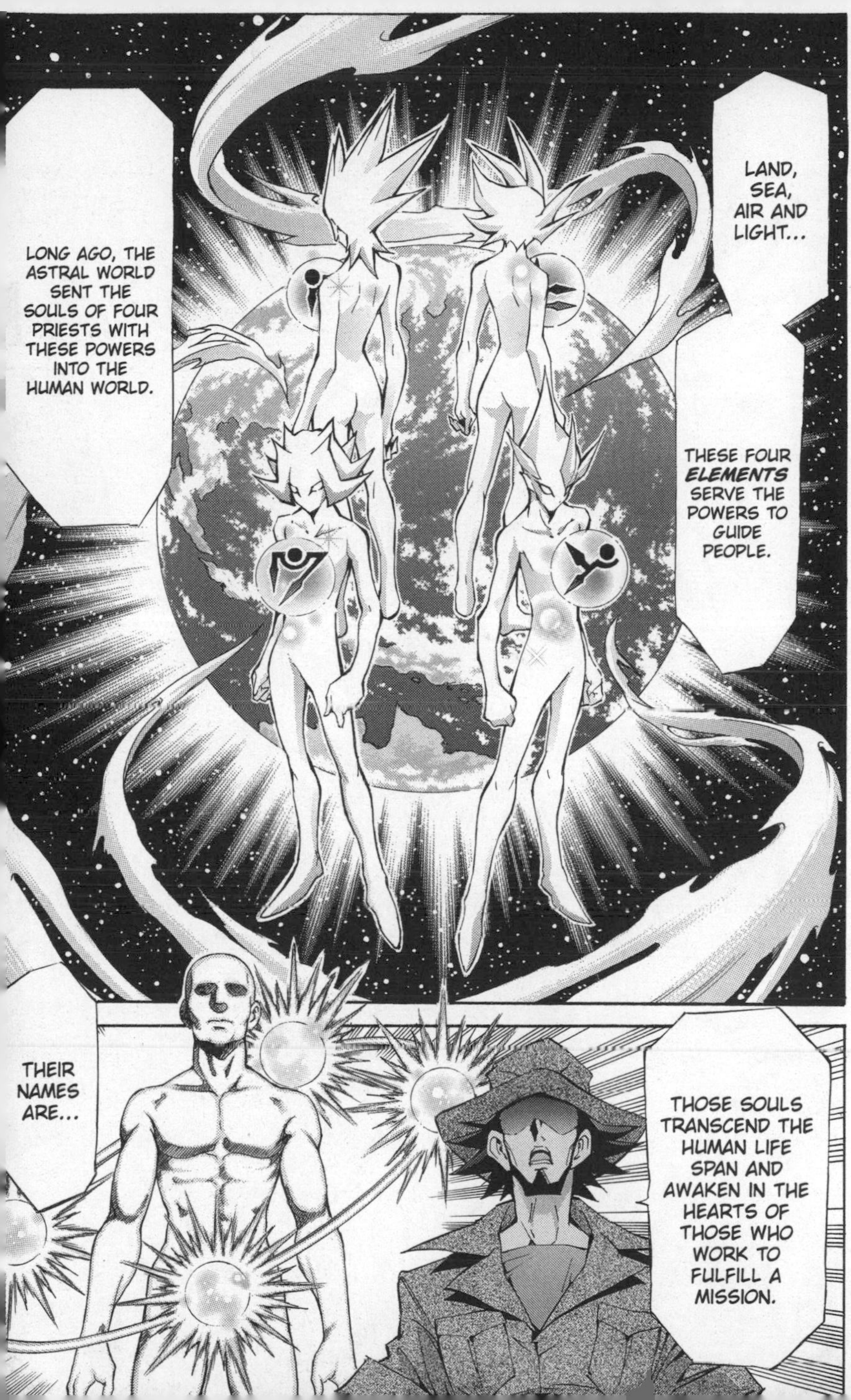
LAND, SEA, AIR AND LIGHT...
LONG AGO, THE ASTRAL WORLD SENT THE SOULS OF FOUR PRIESTS WITH THESE POWERS INTO THE HUMAN WORLD.
THESE FOUR *ELEMENTS* SERVE THE POWERS TO GUIDE PEOPLE.
THOSE SOULS TRANSCEND THE HUMAN LIFE SPAN AND AWAKEN IN THE HEARTS OF THOSE WHO WORK TO FULFILL A MISSION.
THEIR NAMES ARE...

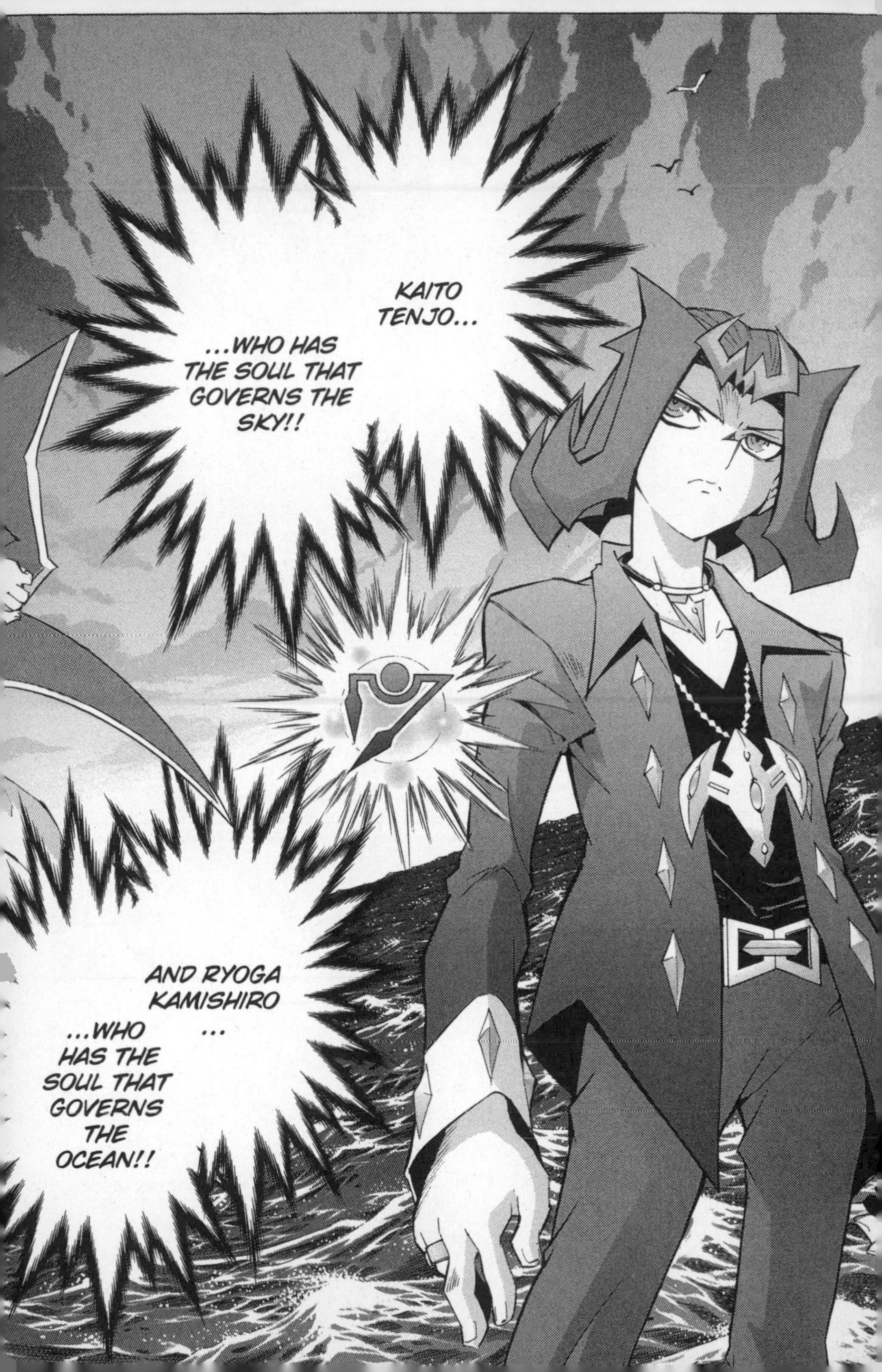
KAITO TENJO...
...WHO HAS THE SOUL THAT GOVERNS THE SKY!!
AND RYOGA KAMISHIRO ...
...WHO HAS THE SOUL THAT GOVERNS THE OCEAN!!

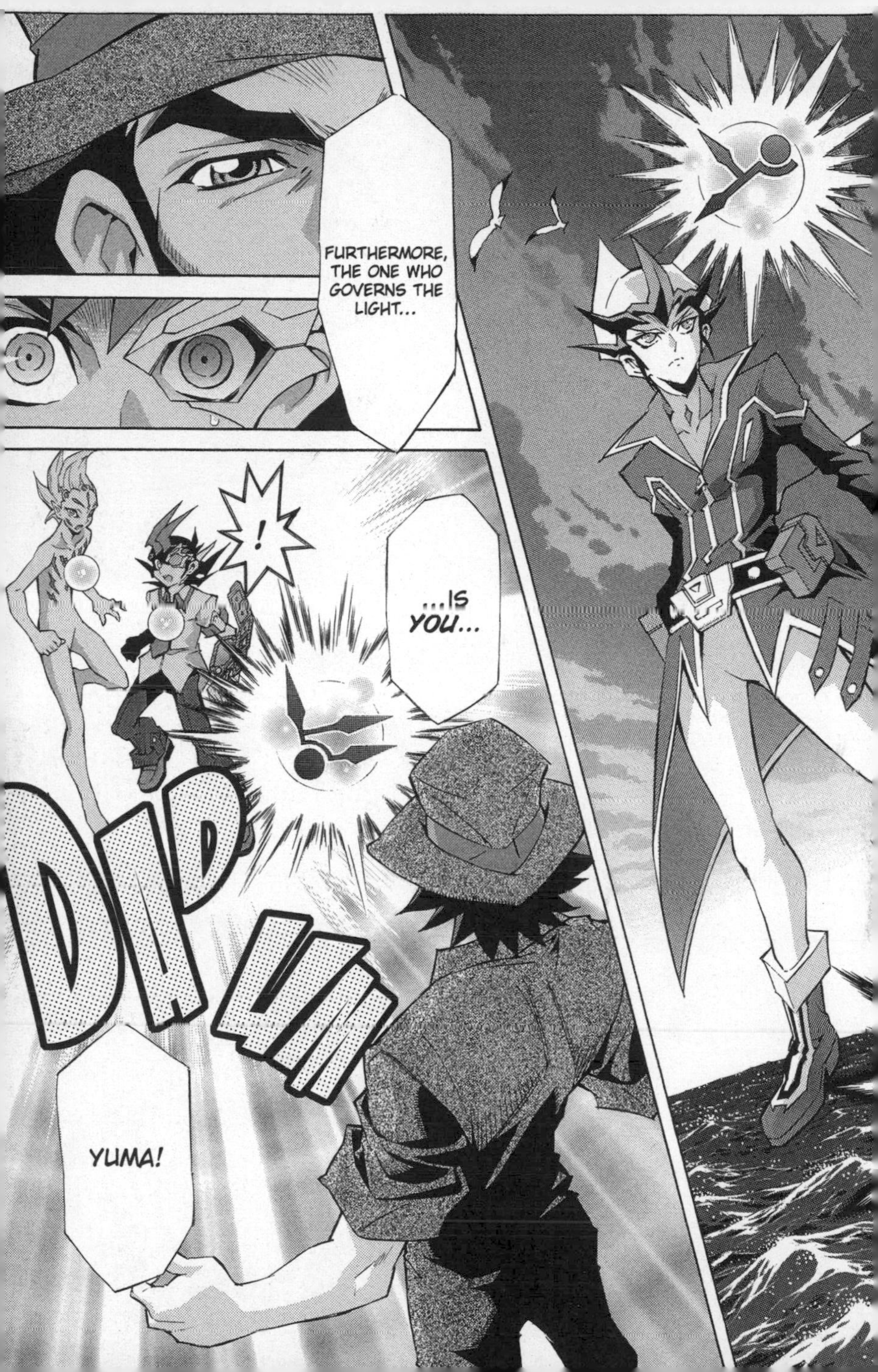
FURTHERMORE, THE ONE WHO GOVERNS THE LIGHT...
...IS YOU...
!
YUMA!

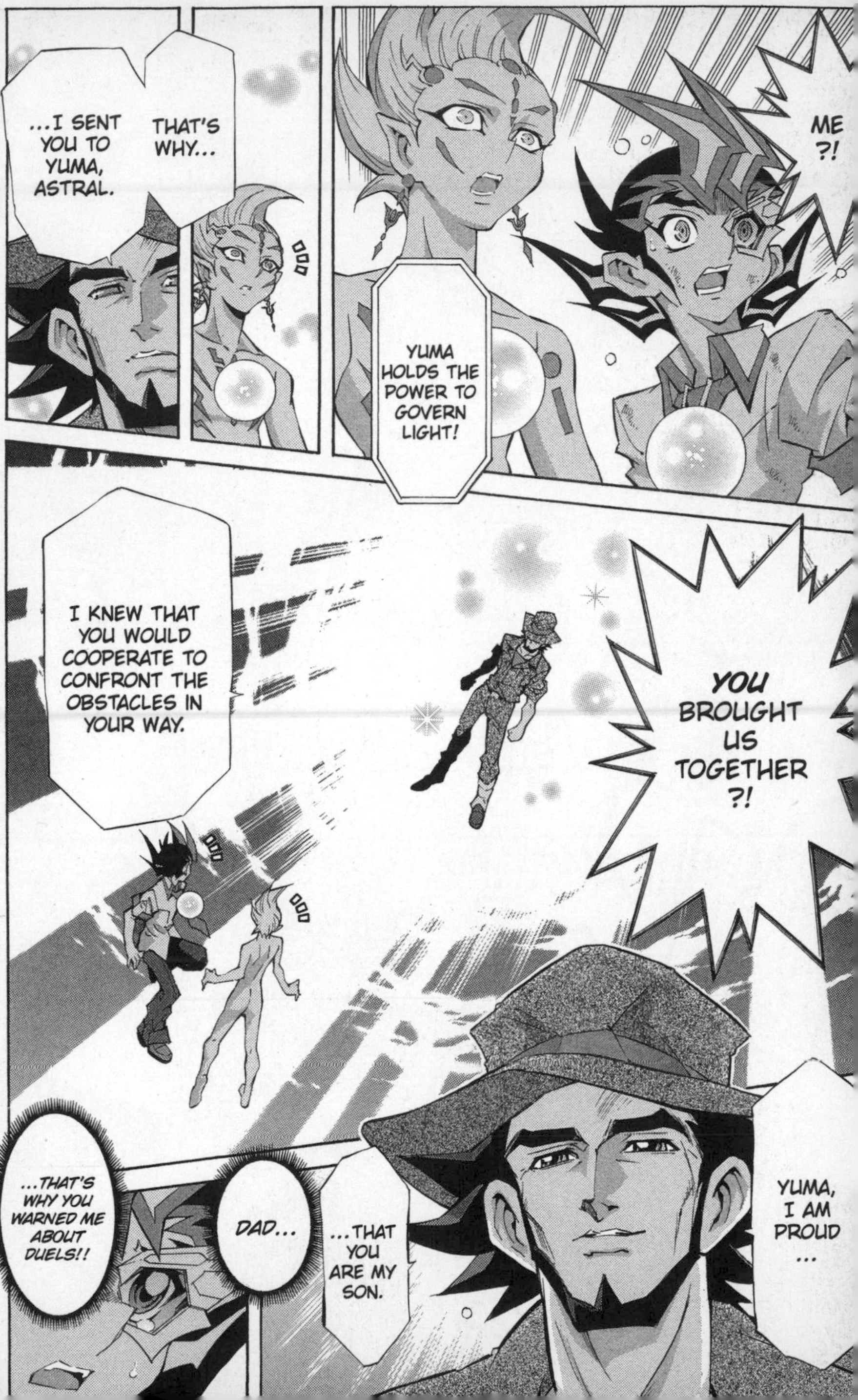
ME ?!
YUMA HOLDS THE POWER TO GOVERN LIGHT!
THAT'S WHY...
...I SENT YOU TO YUMA, ASTRAL.
YOU BROUGHT US TOGETHER ?!
I KNEW THAT YOU WOULD COOPERATE TO CONFRONT THE OBSTACLES IN YOUR WAY.
YUMA, I AM PROUD ...
...THAT YOU ARE MY SON.
DAD...
...THAT'S WHY YOU WARNED ME ABOUT DUELS!!

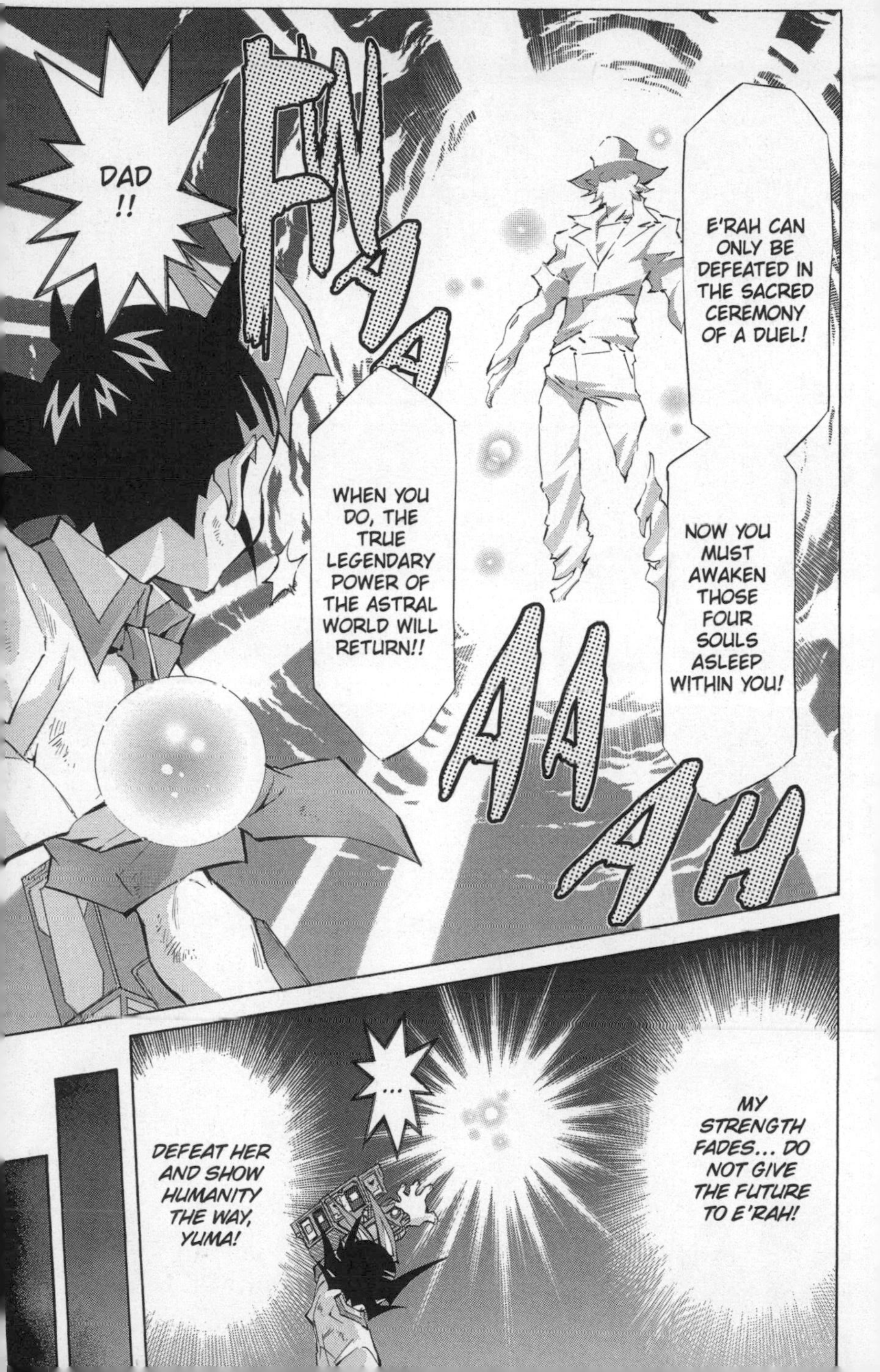
E'RAH CAN ONLY BE DEFEATED IN THE SACRED CEREMONY OF A DUEL!
NOW YOU MUST AWAKEN THOSE FOUR SOULS ASLEEP WITHIN YOU!
WHEN YOU DO, THE TRUE LEGENDARY POWER OF THE ASTRAL WORLD WILL RETURN!!
DAD !!
MY STRENGTH FADES... DO NOT GIVE THE FUTURE TO E'RAH!
...
DEFEAT HER AND SHOW HUMANITY THE WAY, YUMA!

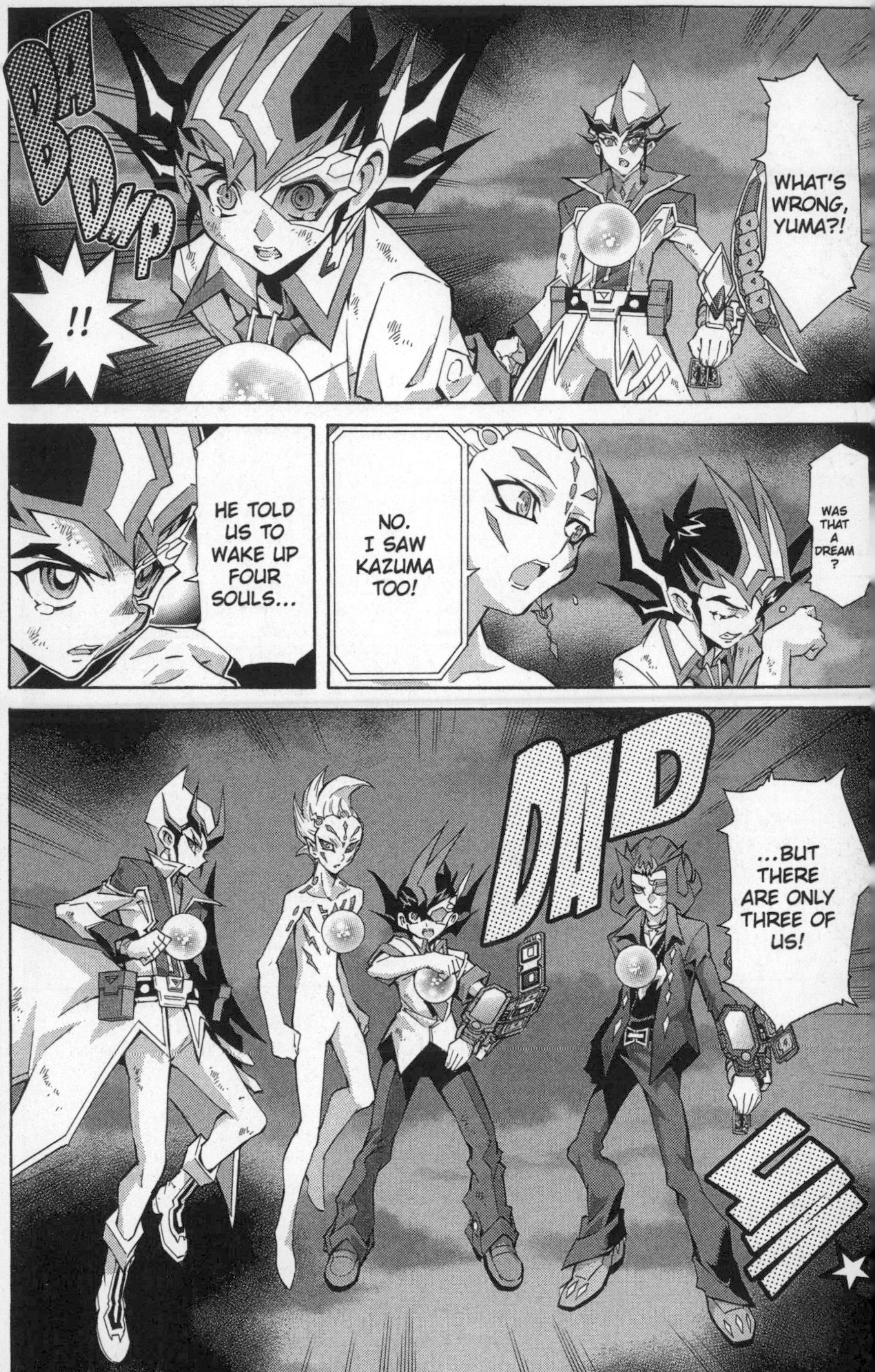
WHAT'S WRONG, YUMA?!
BADUMP
!!
WAS THAT A DREAM?
NO. I SAW KAZUMA TOO!
HE TOLD US TO WAKE UP FOUR SOULS...
...BUT THERE ARE ONLY THREE OF US!
DAP

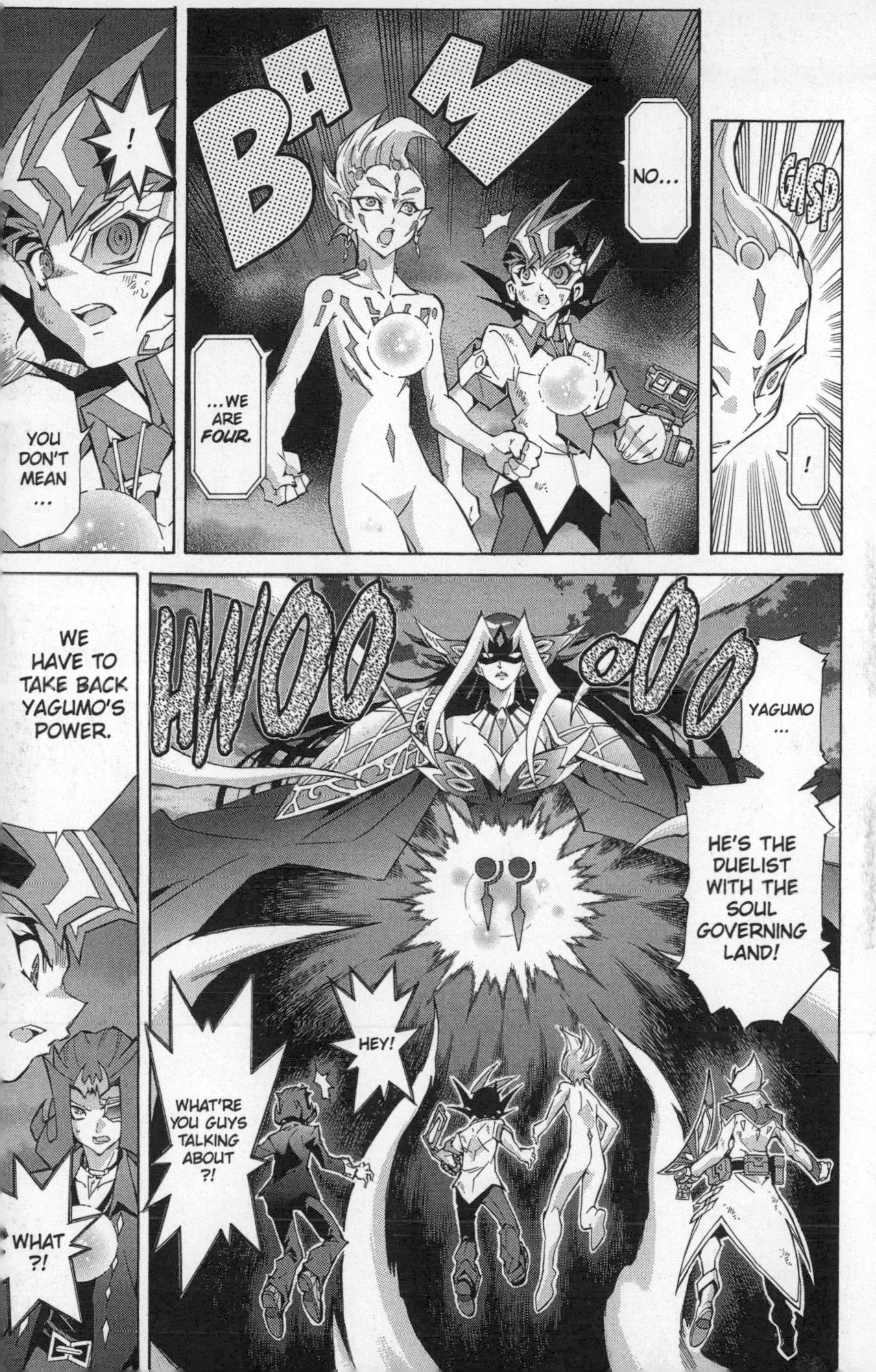
GASP
!
BAM
NO...
...WE ARE FOUR.
!
YOU DON'T MEAN ...
YAGUMO ...
HWOO-OOO
HE'S THE DUELIST WITH THE SOUL GOVERNING LAND!
HEY!
WHAT'RE YOU GUYS TALKING ABOUT ?!
WE HAVE TO TAKE BACK YAGUMO'S POWER.
WHAT ?!

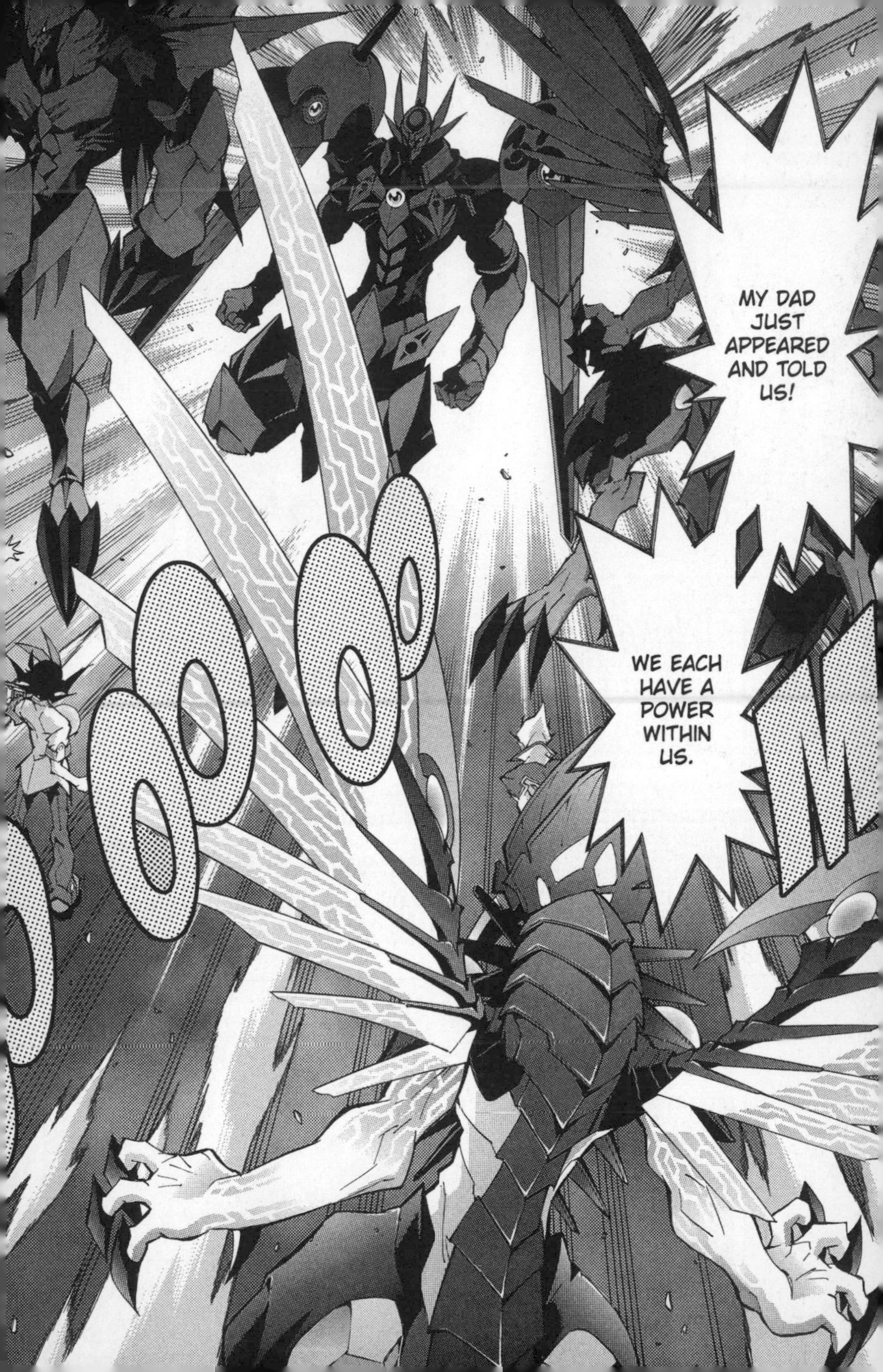
MY DAD JUST APPEARED AND TOLD US!
WE EACH HAVE A POWER WITHIN US.

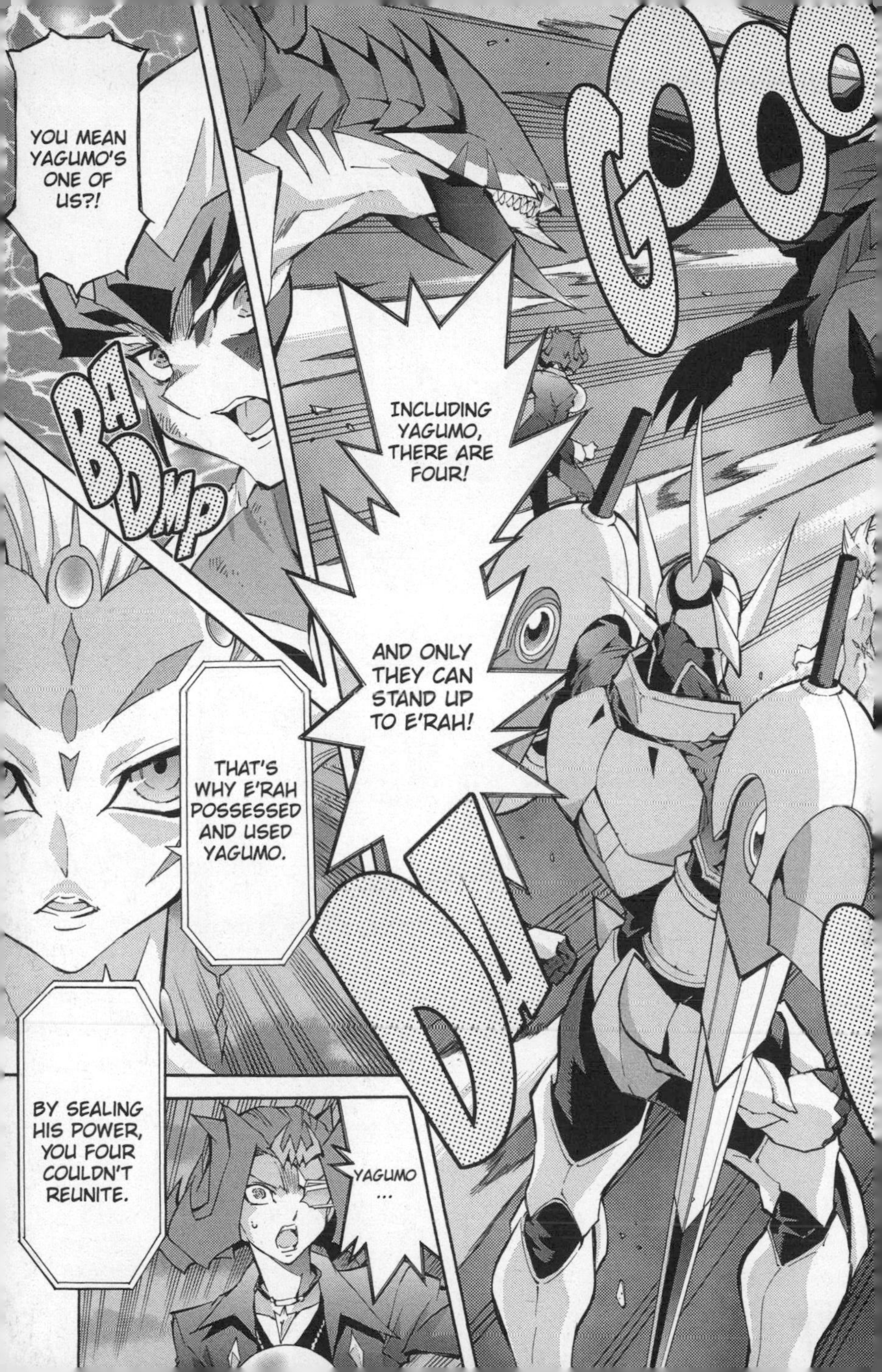
YOU MEAN YAGUMO'S ONE OF US?!
BA DUMP
GOOO
INCLUDING YAGUMO, THERE ARE FOUR!
AND ONLY THEY CAN STAND UP TO E'RAH!
THAT'S WHY E'RAH POSSESSED AND USED YAGUMO.
BY SEALING HIS POWER, YOU FOUR COULDN'T REUNITE.
YAGUMO ...

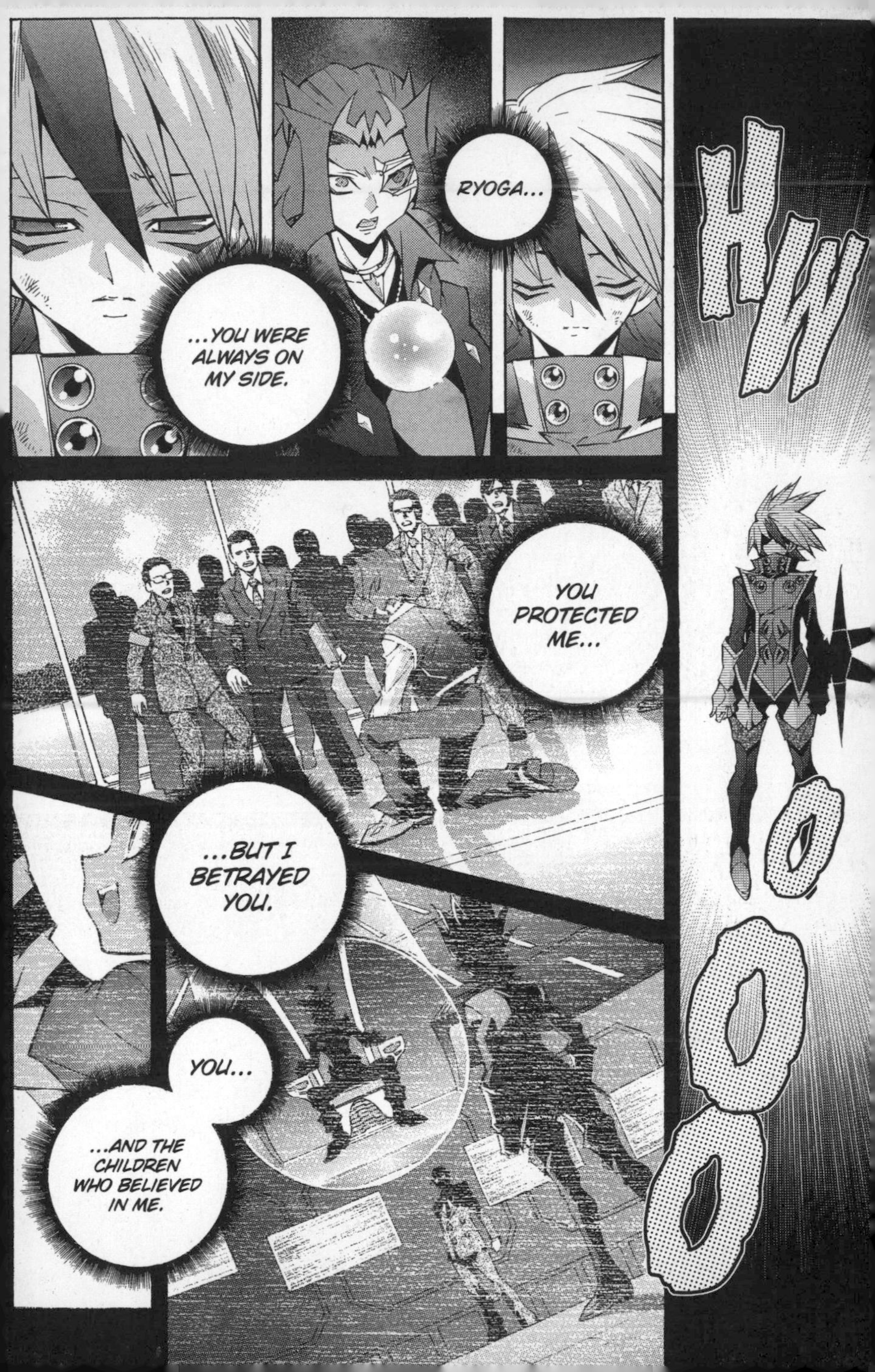
HWOOO
RYOGA...
...YOU WERE ALWAYS ON MY SIDE.
YOU PROTECTED ME...
...BUT I BETRAYED YOU.
YOU...
...AND THE CHILDREN WHO BELIEVED IN ME.

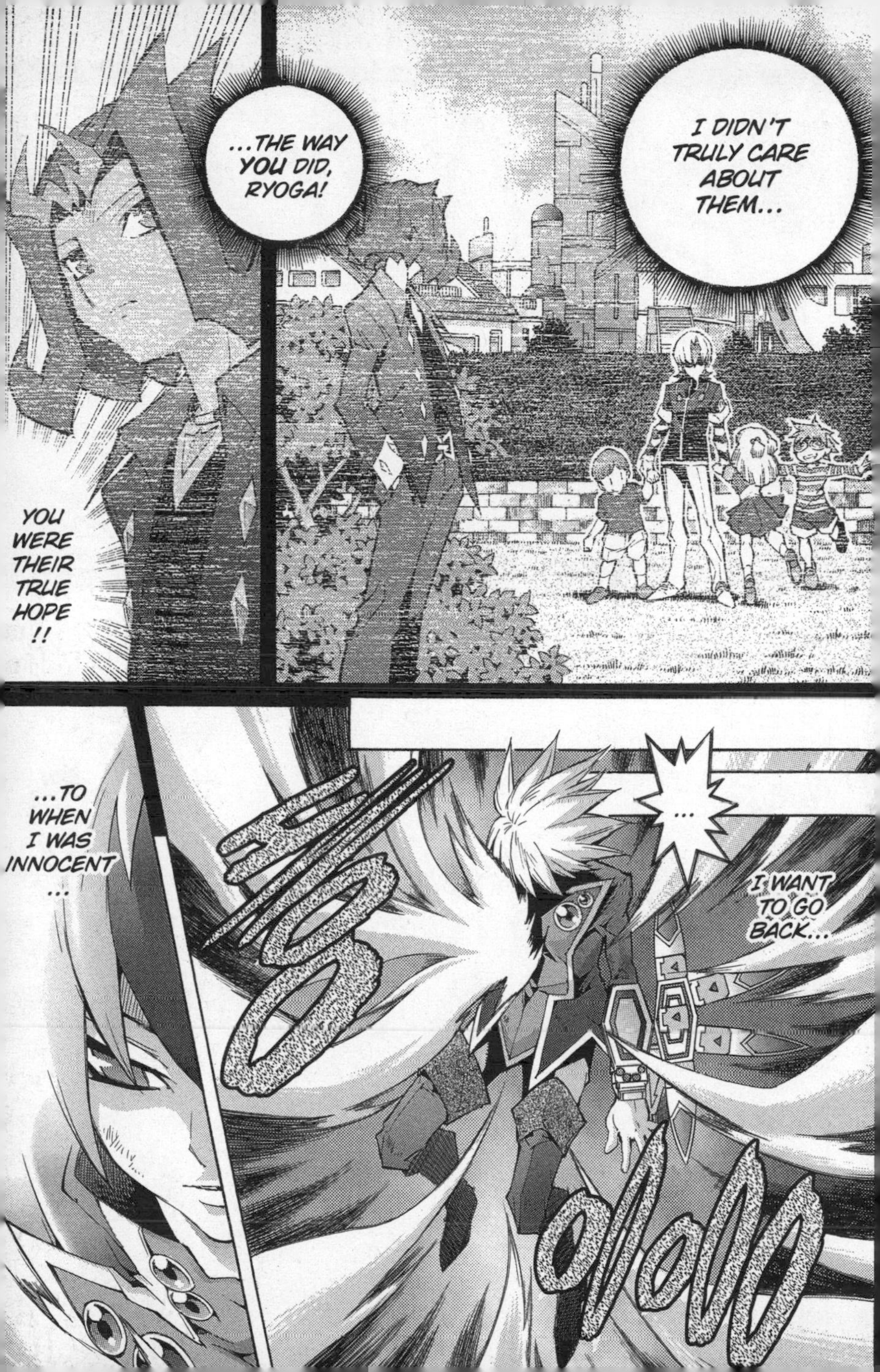
I DIDN'T TRULY CARE ABOUT THEM...
...THE WAY YOU DID, RYOGA!
YOU WERE THEIR TRUE HOPE!!
...
I WANT TO GO BACK...
...TO WHEN I WAS INNOCENT...

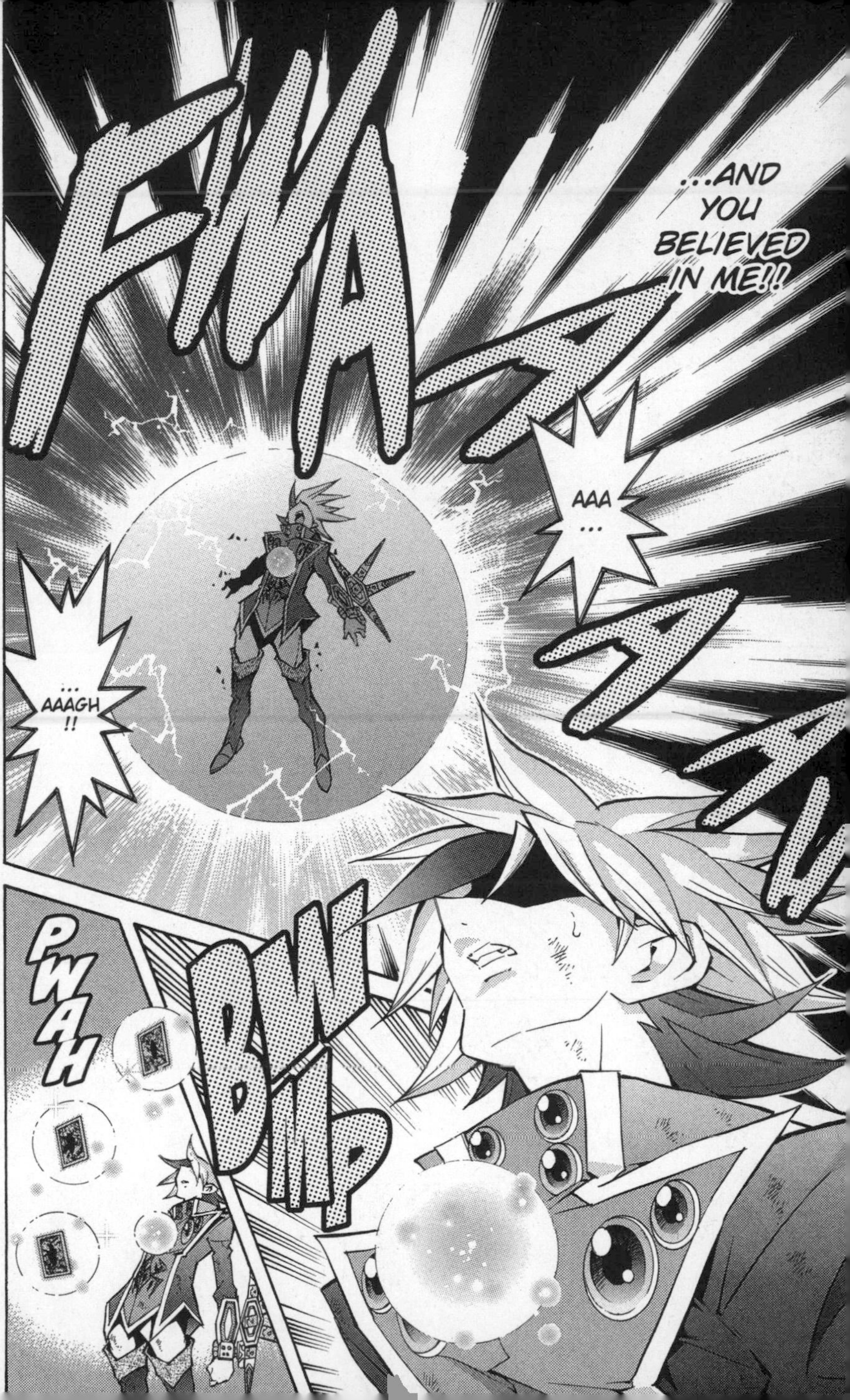
...AND YOU BELIEVED IN ME!!
AAA ...
...AAAGH !!
PWAH

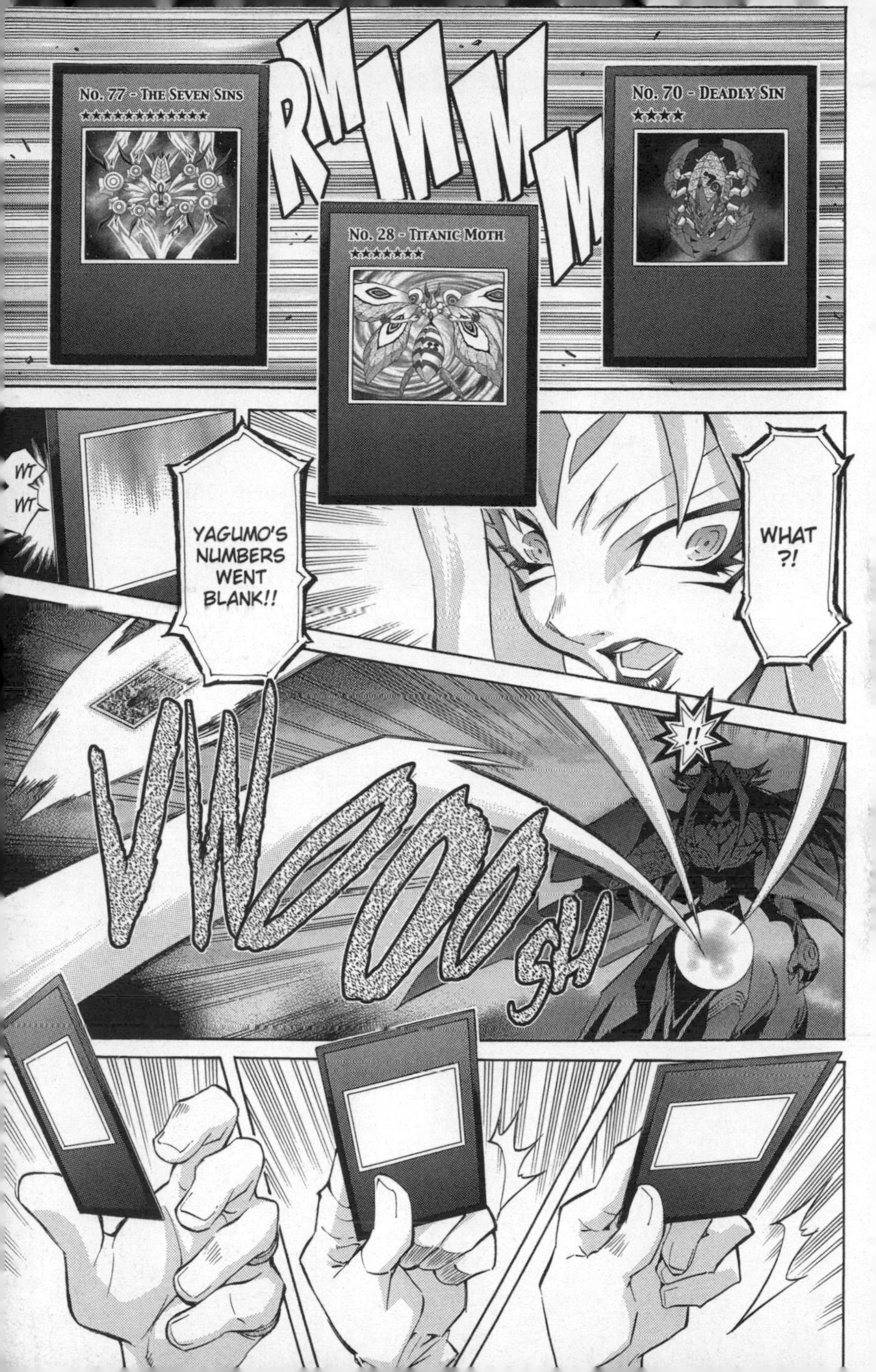
No. 70 - Deadly Sin
RMMMM
No. 28 - Titanic Moth
No. 77 - The Seven Sins
WHAT?!
!!
YAGUMO'S NUMBERS WENT BLANK!!
WT WT
VWOOOSH

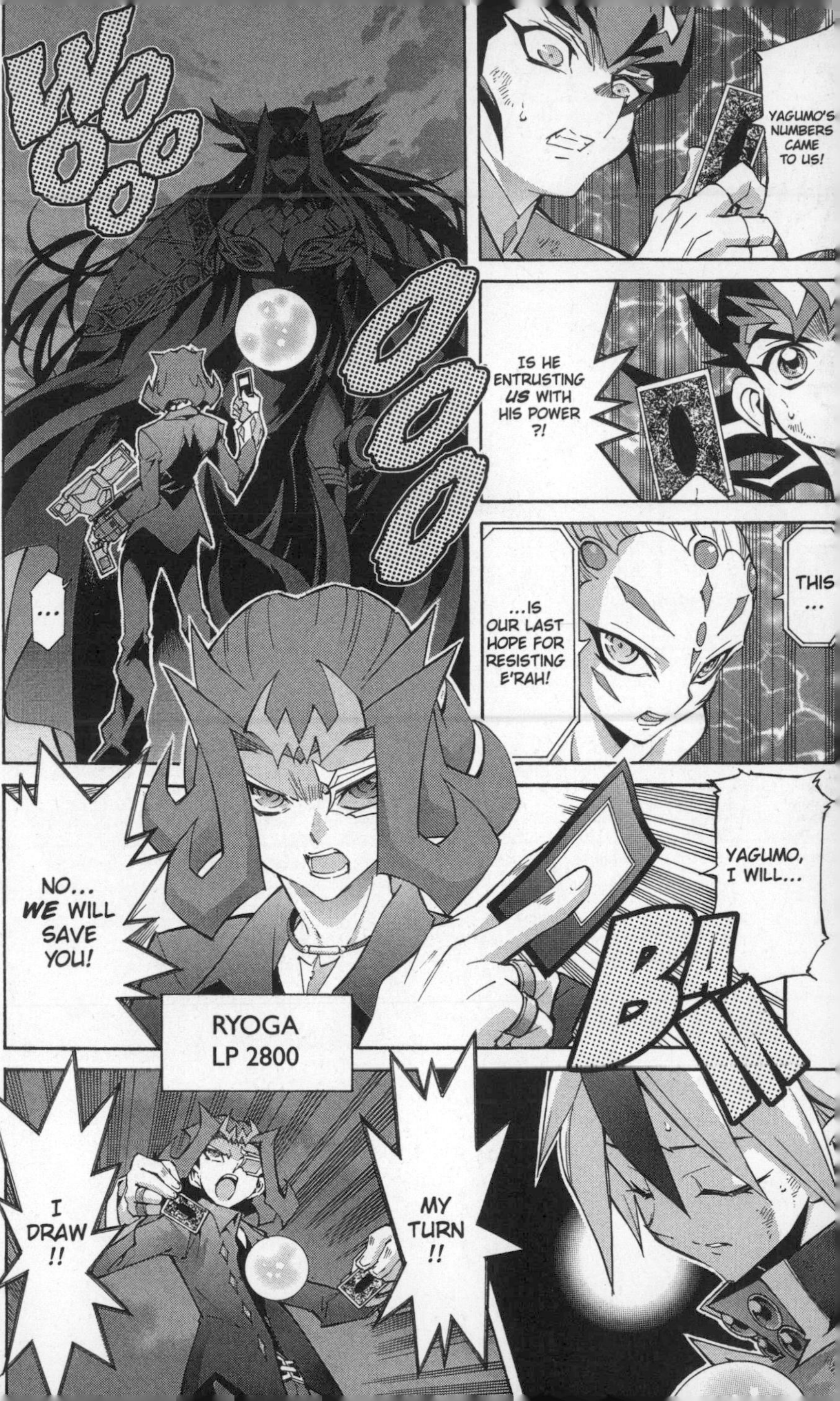
YAGUMO'S NUMBERS CAME TO US!
IS HE ENTRUSTING *US* WITH HIS POWER ?!
THIS ...
...IS OUR LAST HOPE FOR RESISTING E'RAH!
WOOOO
OOOO
...
YAGUMO, I WILL...
BAM
NO... *WE* WILL SAVE YOU!
RYOGA LP 2800
MY TURN !!
I DRAW !!

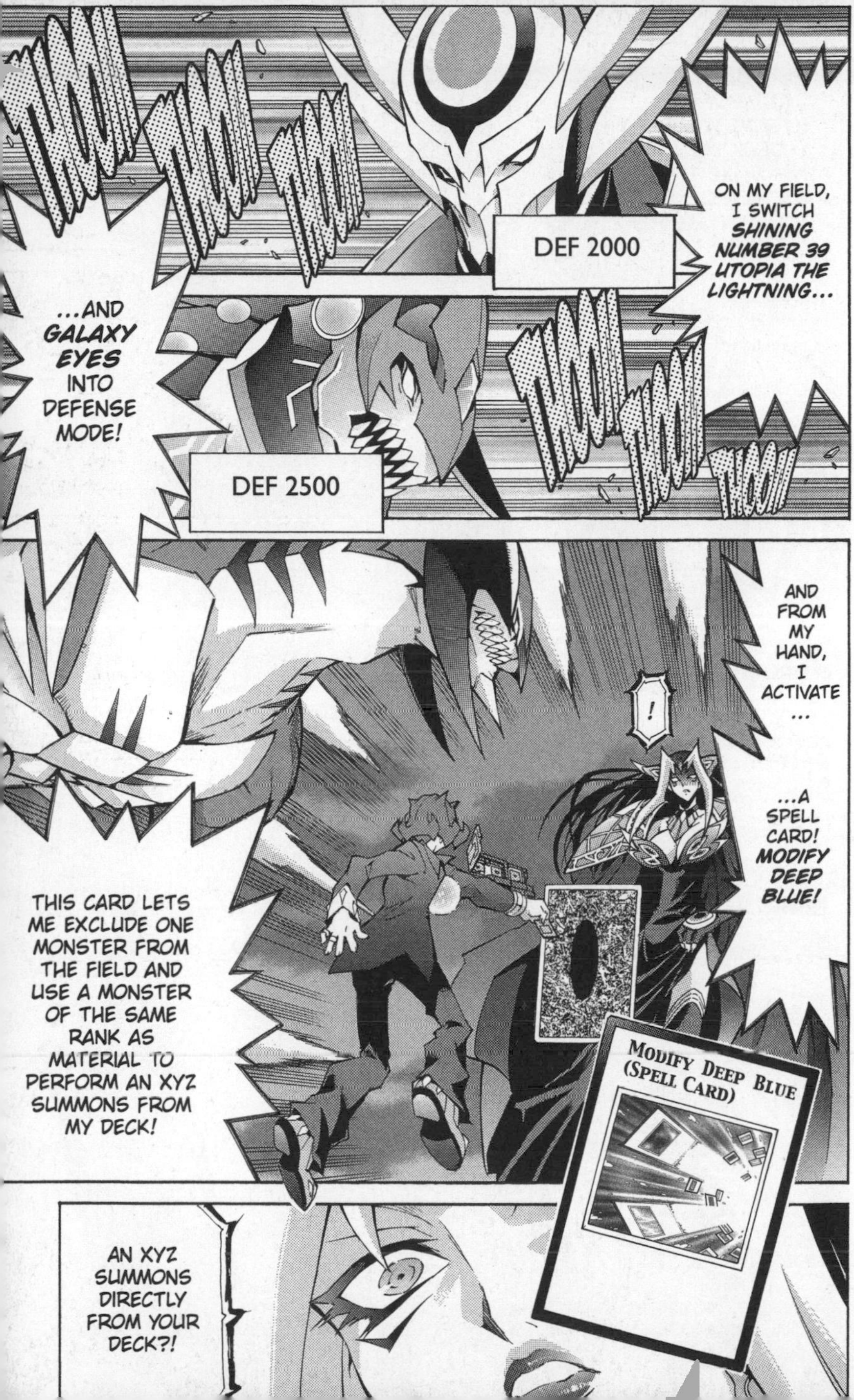
THOOM THOOM THOOM
ON MY FIELD, I SWITCH SHINING NUMBER 39 UTOPIA THE LIGHTNING...
DEF 2000
...AND GALAXY EYES INTO DEFENSE MODE!
THOOM THOOM THOOM
DEF 2500
AND FROM MY HAND, I ACTIVATE ...
!
...A SPELL CARD! MODIFY DEEP BLUE!
MODIFY DEEP BLUE (SPELL CARD)
THIS CARD LETS ME EXCLUDE ONE MONSTER FROM THE FIELD AND USE A MONSTER OF THE SAME RANK AS MATERIAL TO PERFORM AN XYZ SUMMONS FROM MY DECK!
AN XYZ SUMMONS DIRECTLY FROM YOUR DECK?!

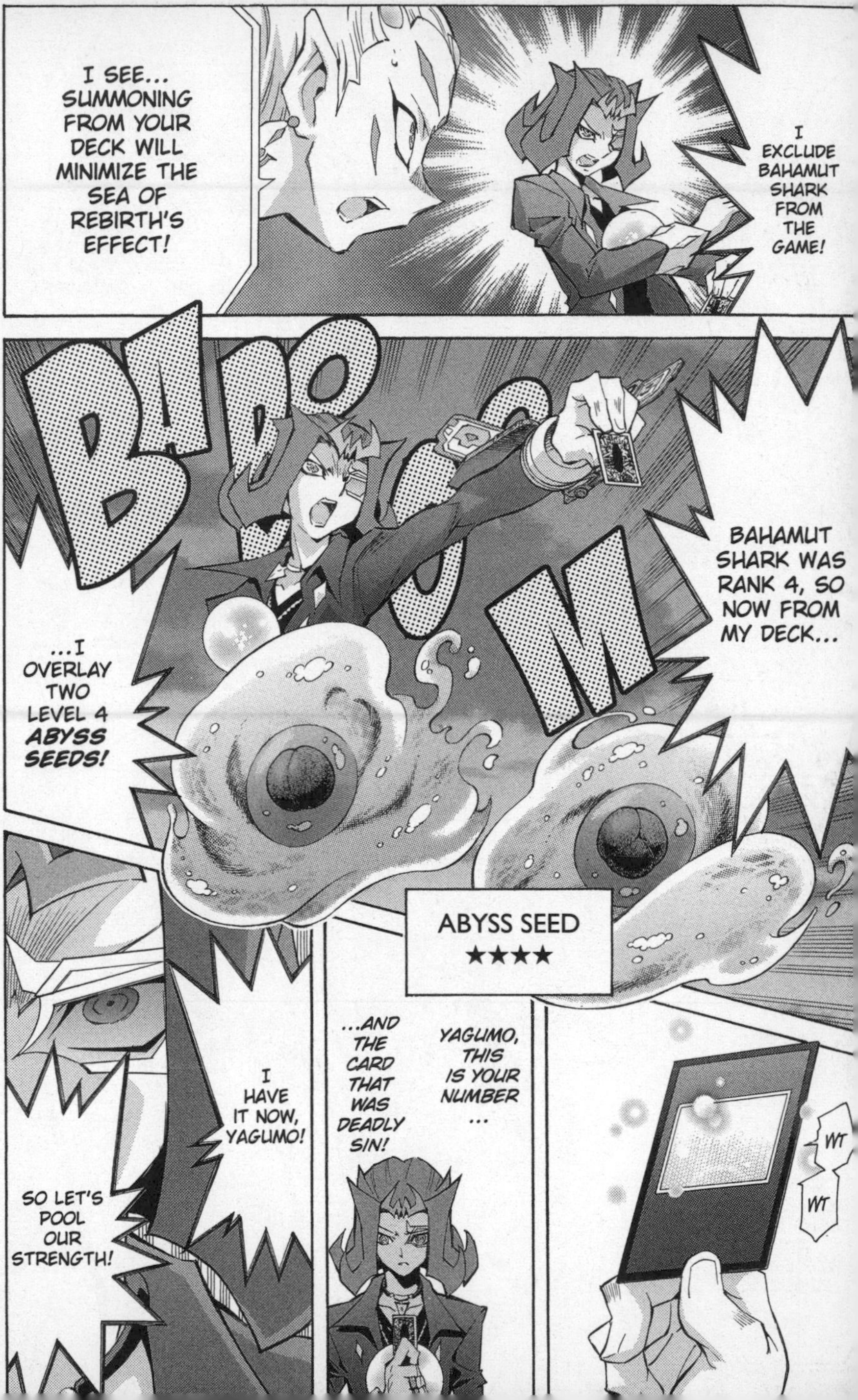
I EXCLUDE BAHAMUT SHARK FROM THE GAME!
I SEE... SUMMONING FROM YOUR DECK WILL MINIMIZE THE SEA OF REBIRTH'S EFFECT!
BADOOOM
BAHAMUT SHARK WAS RANK 4, SO NOW FROM MY DECK...
...I OVERLAY TWO LEVEL 4 *ABYSS SEEDS!*
ABYSS SEED
★★★★
WT
WT
YAGUMO, THIS IS YOUR NUMBER...
...AND THE CARD THAT WAS DEADLY SIN!
I HAVE IT NOW, YAGUMO!
SO LET'S POOL OUR STRENGTH!

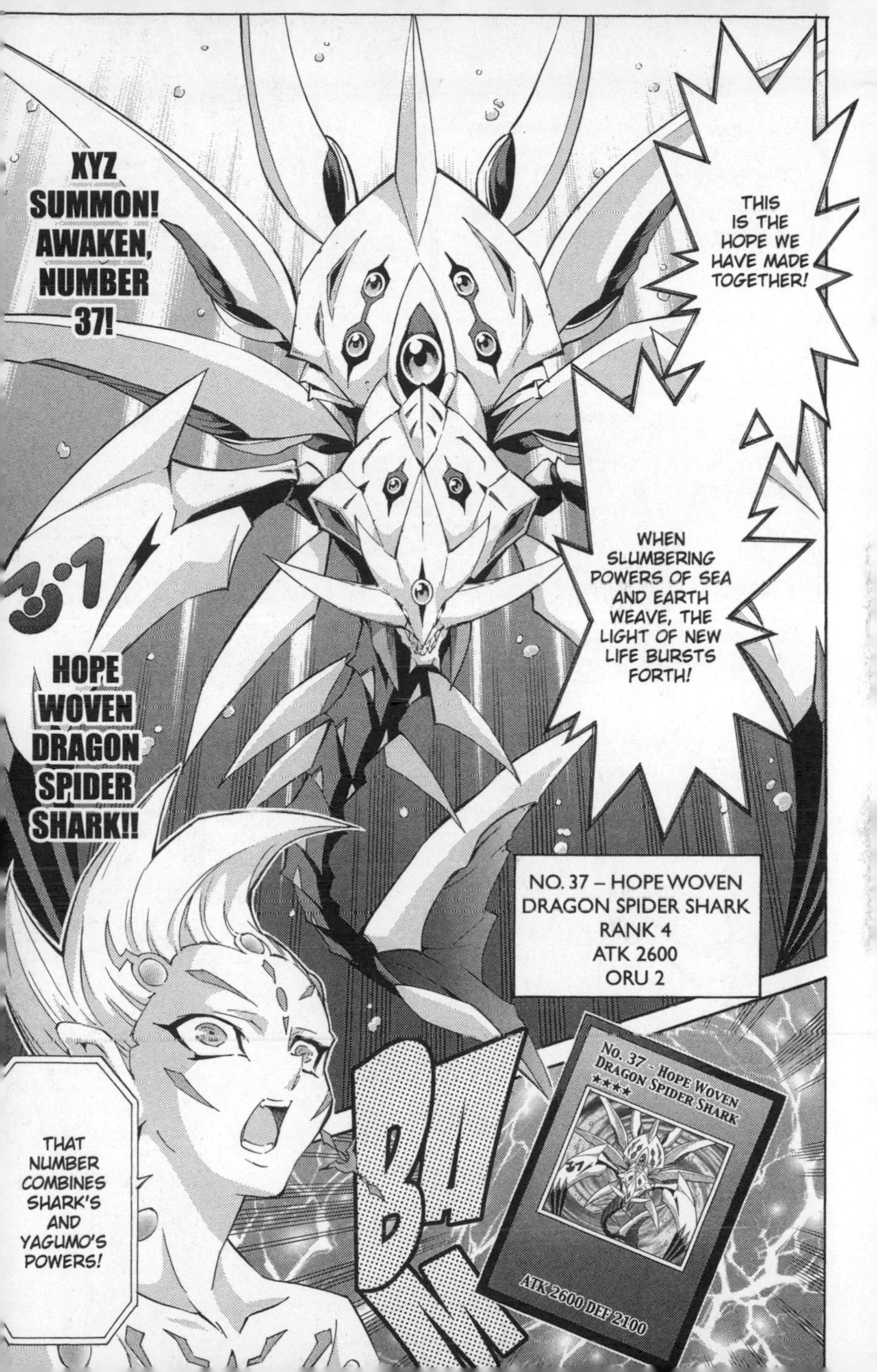

THIS IS THE HOPE WE HAVE MADE TOGETHER!
WHEN SLUMBERING POWERS OF SEA AND EARTH WEAVE, THE LIGHT OF NEW LIFE BURSTS FORTH!
XYZ SUMMON! AWAKEN, NUMBER 37!
HOPE WOVEN DRAGON SPIDER SHARK!!
NO. 37 – HOPE WOVEN DRAGON SPIDER SHARK
RANK 4
ATK 2600
ORU 2
No. 37 - Hope Woven Dragon Spider Shark
ATK 2600 DEF 2100
BAM
THAT NUMBER COMBINES SHARK'S AND YAGUMO'S POWERS!

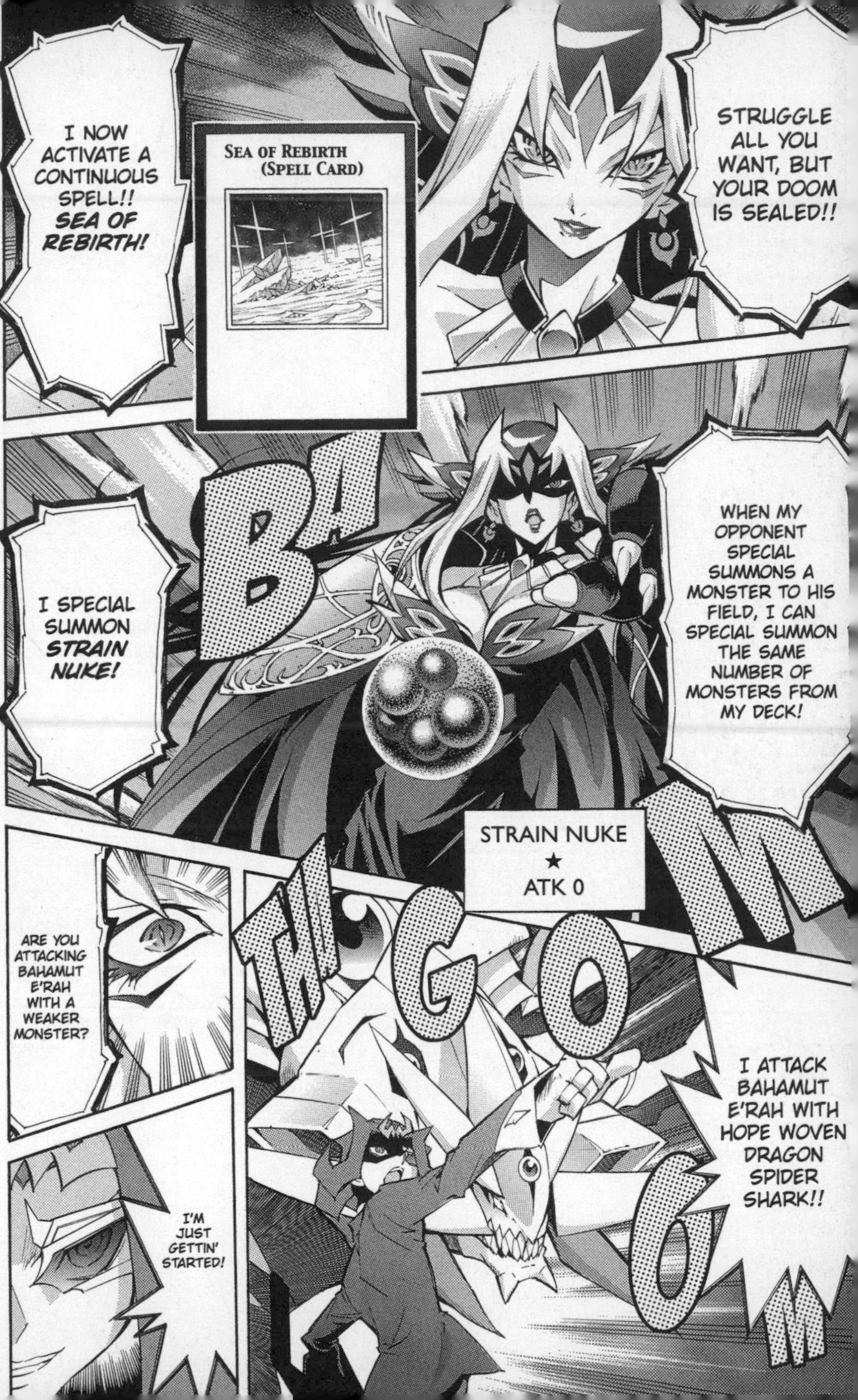
STRUGGLE ALL YOU WANT, BUT YOUR DOOM IS SEALED!!
I NOW ACTIVATE A CONTINUOUS SPELL!! SEA OF REBIRTH!
Sea of Rebirth
(Spell Card)
WHEN MY OPPONENT SPECIAL SUMMONS A MONSTER TO HIS FIELD, I CAN SPECIAL SUMMON THE SAME NUMBER OF MONSTERS FROM MY DECK!
BA
I SPECIAL SUMMON STRAIN NUKE!
STRAIN NUKE ★ ATK 0
I ATTACK BAHAMUT E'RAH WITH HOPE WOVEN DRAGON SPIDER SHARK!!
THGOOM
ARE YOU ATTACKING BAHAMUT E'RAH WITH A WEAKER MONSTER?
I'M JUST GETTIN' STARTED!

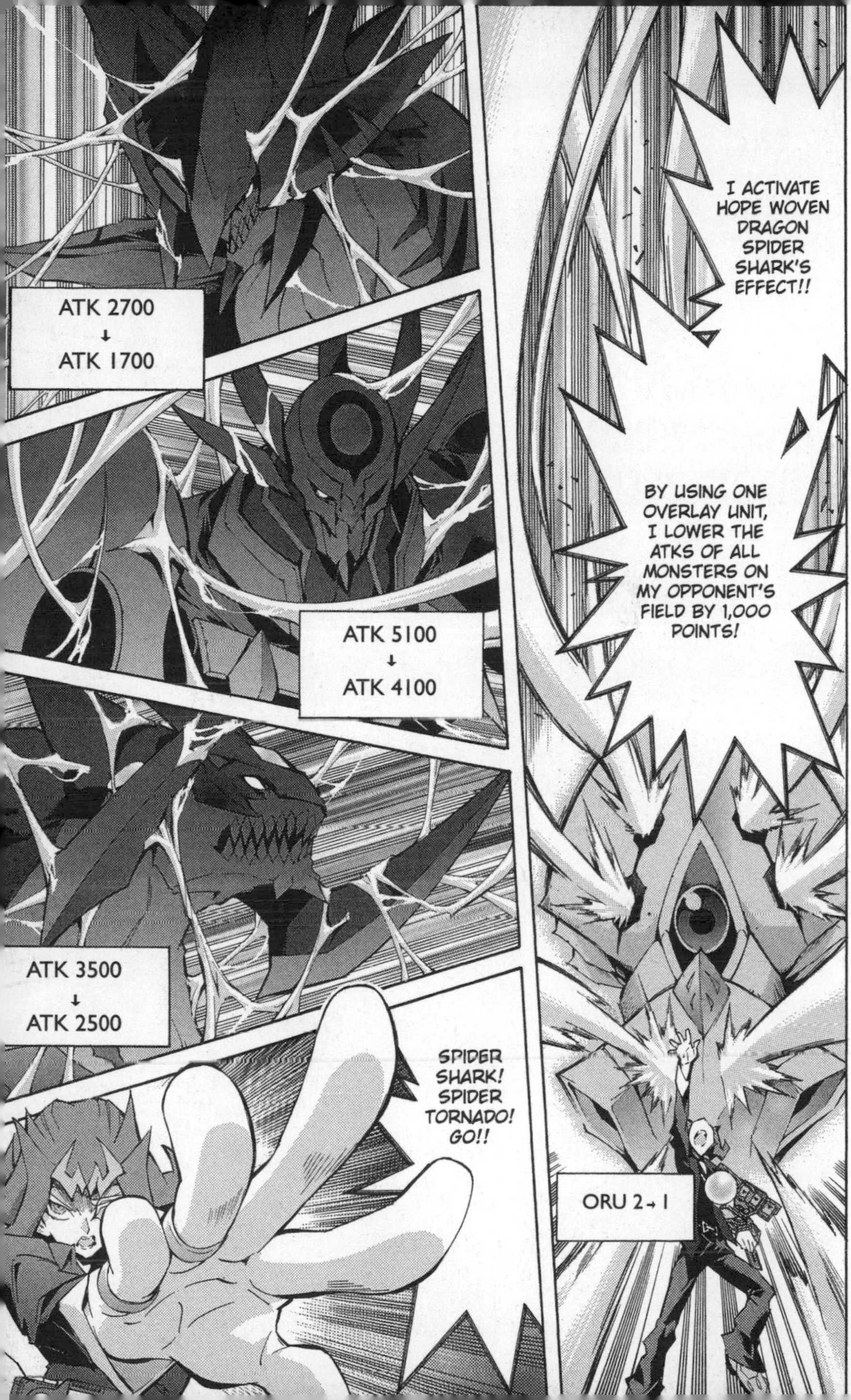
I ACTIVATE HOPE WOVEN DRAGON SPIDER SHARK'S EFFECT!!
BY USING ONE OVERLAY UNIT, I LOWER THE ATKS OF ALL MONSTERS ON MY OPPONENT'S FIELD BY 1,000 POINTS!
ORU 2→1
ATK 2700 ↓ ATK 1700
ATK 5100 ↓ ATK 4100
ATK 3500 ↓ ATK 2500
SPIDER SHARK! SPIDER TORNADO! GO!!

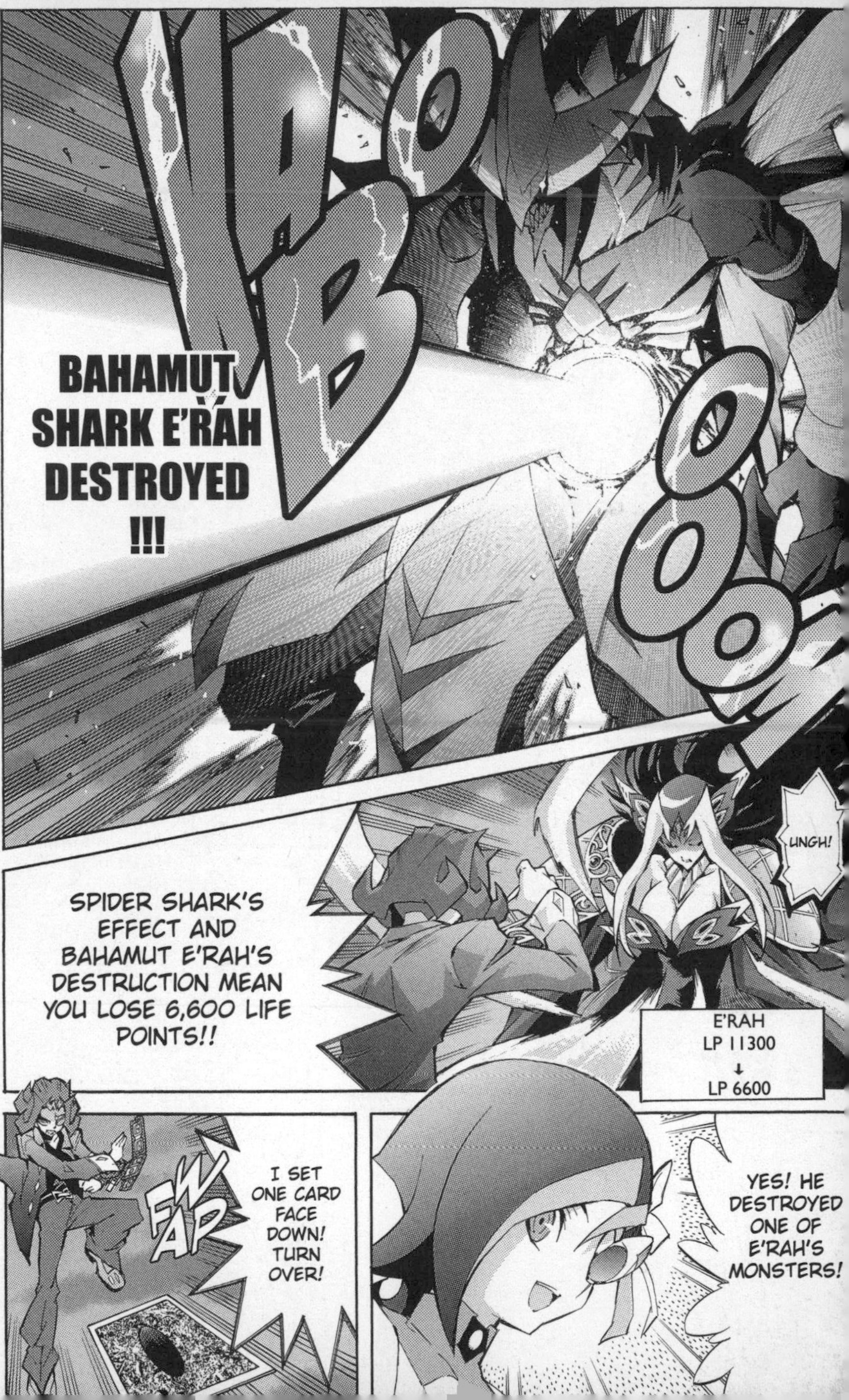
BAHAMUT SHARK E'RAH DESTROYED !!!
UNGH!
E'RAH LP 11300 ↓ LP 6600
SPIDER SHARK'S EFFECT AND BAHAMUT E'RAH'S DESTRUCTION MEAN YOU LOSE 6,600 LIFE POINTS!!
YES! HE DESTROYED ONE OF E'RAH'S MONSTERS!
I SET ONE CARD FACE DOWN! TURN OVER!
FWAP

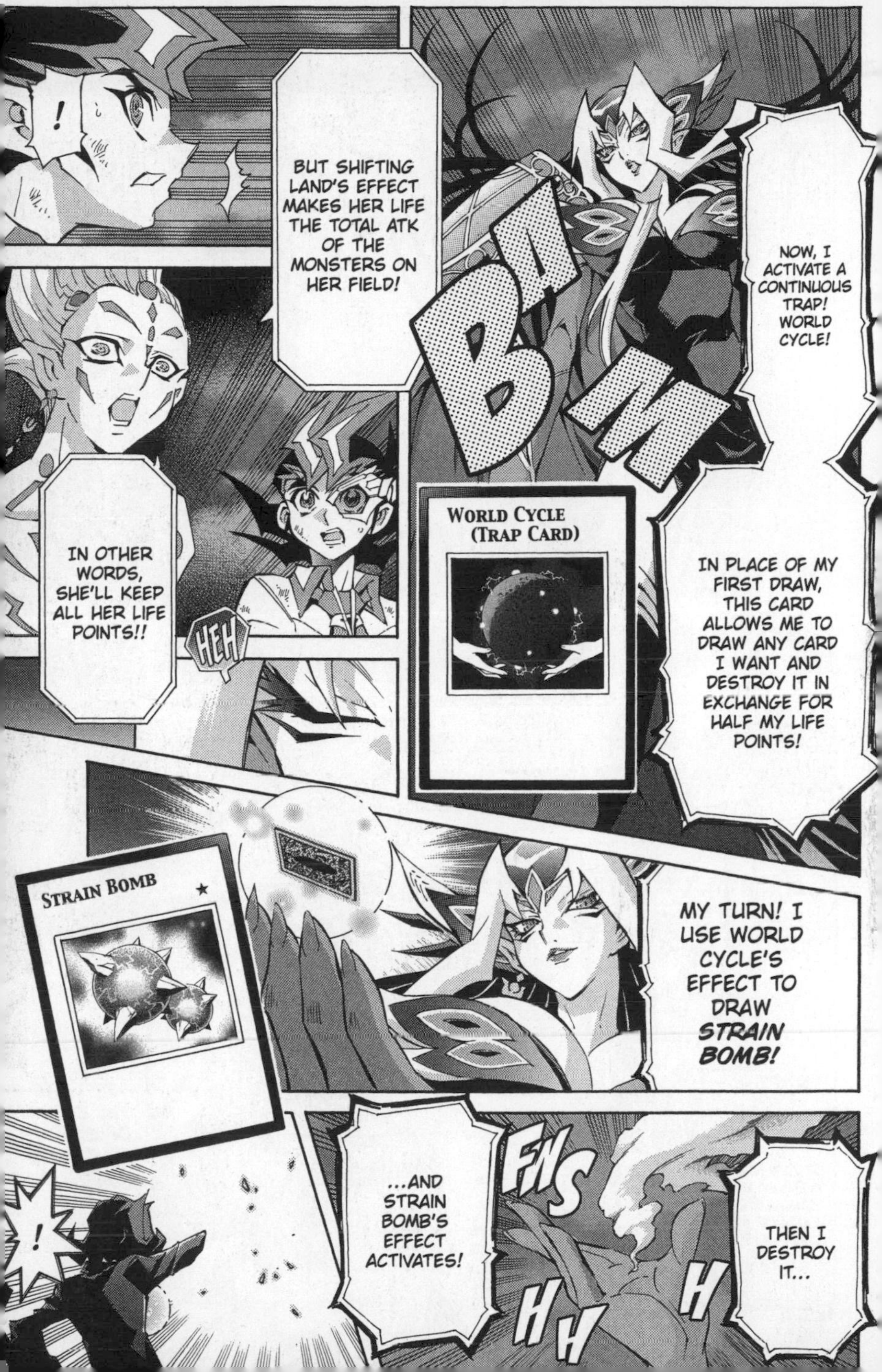
NOW, I ACTIVATE A CONTINUOUS TRAP! WORLD CYCLE!
BAM
WORLD CYCLE (TRAP CARD)
IN PLACE OF MY FIRST DRAW, THIS CARD ALLOWS ME TO DRAW ANY CARD I WANT AND DESTROY IT IN EXCHANGE FOR HALF MY LIFE POINTS!
!
BUT SHIFTING LAND'S EFFECT MAKES HER LIFE THE TOTAL ATK OF THE MONSTERS ON HER FIELD!
IN OTHER WORDS, SHE'LL KEEP ALL HER LIFE POINTS!!
HEH
MY TURN! I USE WORLD CYCLE'S EFFECT TO DRAW *STRAIN BOMB!*
STRAIN BOMB
THEN I DESTROY IT...
HHH
FNS
...AND STRAIN BOMB'S EFFECT ACTIVATES!
!

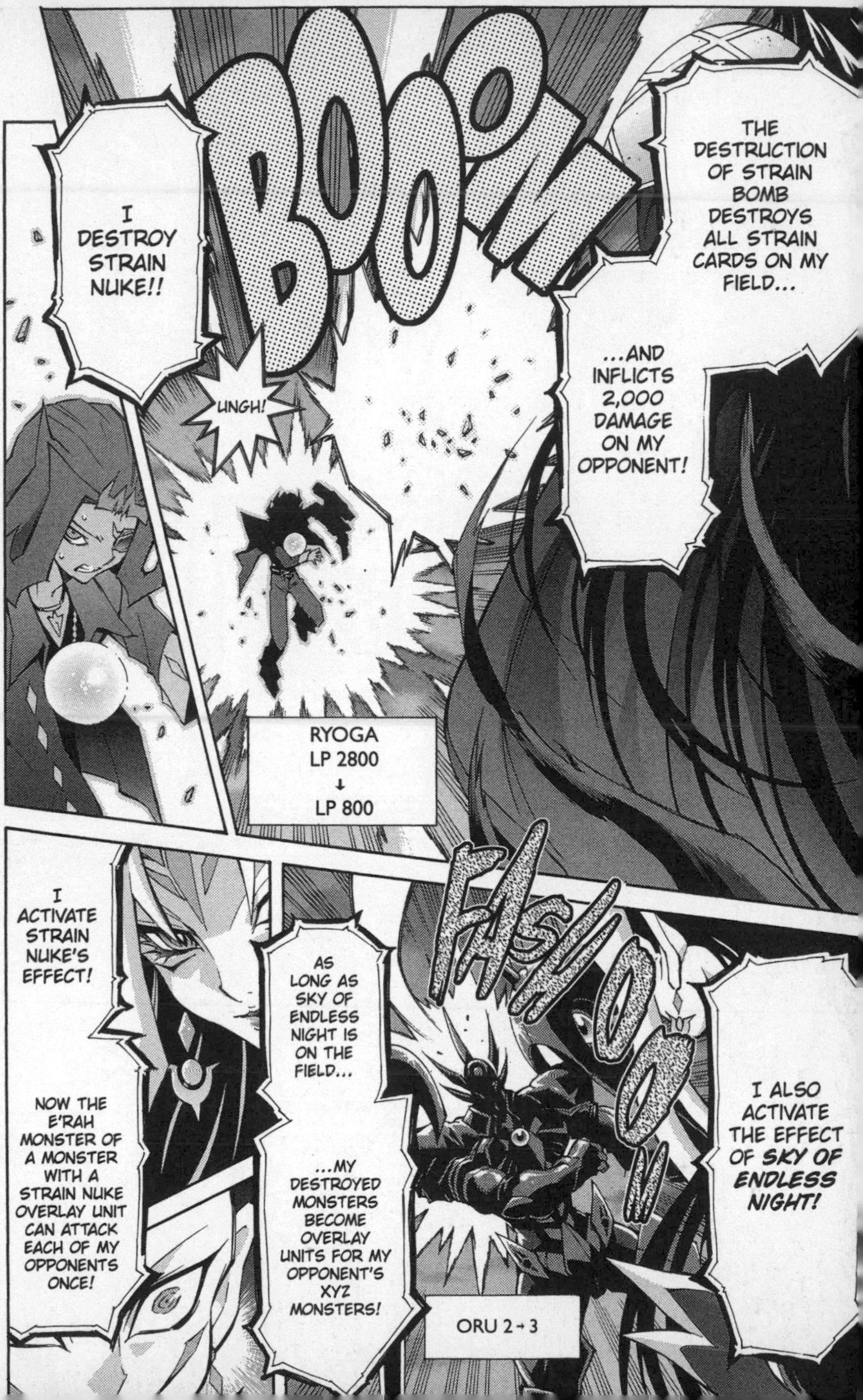
THE DESTRUCTION OF STRAIN BOMB DESTROYS ALL STRAIN CARDS ON MY FIELD...
BOOOM
I DESTROY STRAIN NUKE!!
...AND INFLICTS 2,000 DAMAGE ON MY OPPONENT!
UNGH!
RYOGA LP 2800 ↓ LP 800
I ALSO ACTIVATE THE EFFECT OF SKY OF ENDLESS NIGHT!
FSHOOOO
AS LONG AS SKY OF ENDLESS NIGHT IS ON THE FIELD...
...MY DESTROYED MONSTERS BECOME OVERLAY UNITS FOR MY OPPONENT'S XYZ MONSTERS!
ORU 2→3
I ACTIVATE STRAIN NUKE'S EFFECT!
NOW THE E'RAH MONSTER OF A MONSTER WITH A STRAIN NUKE OVERLAY UNIT CAN ATTACK EACH OF MY OPPONENTS ONCE!

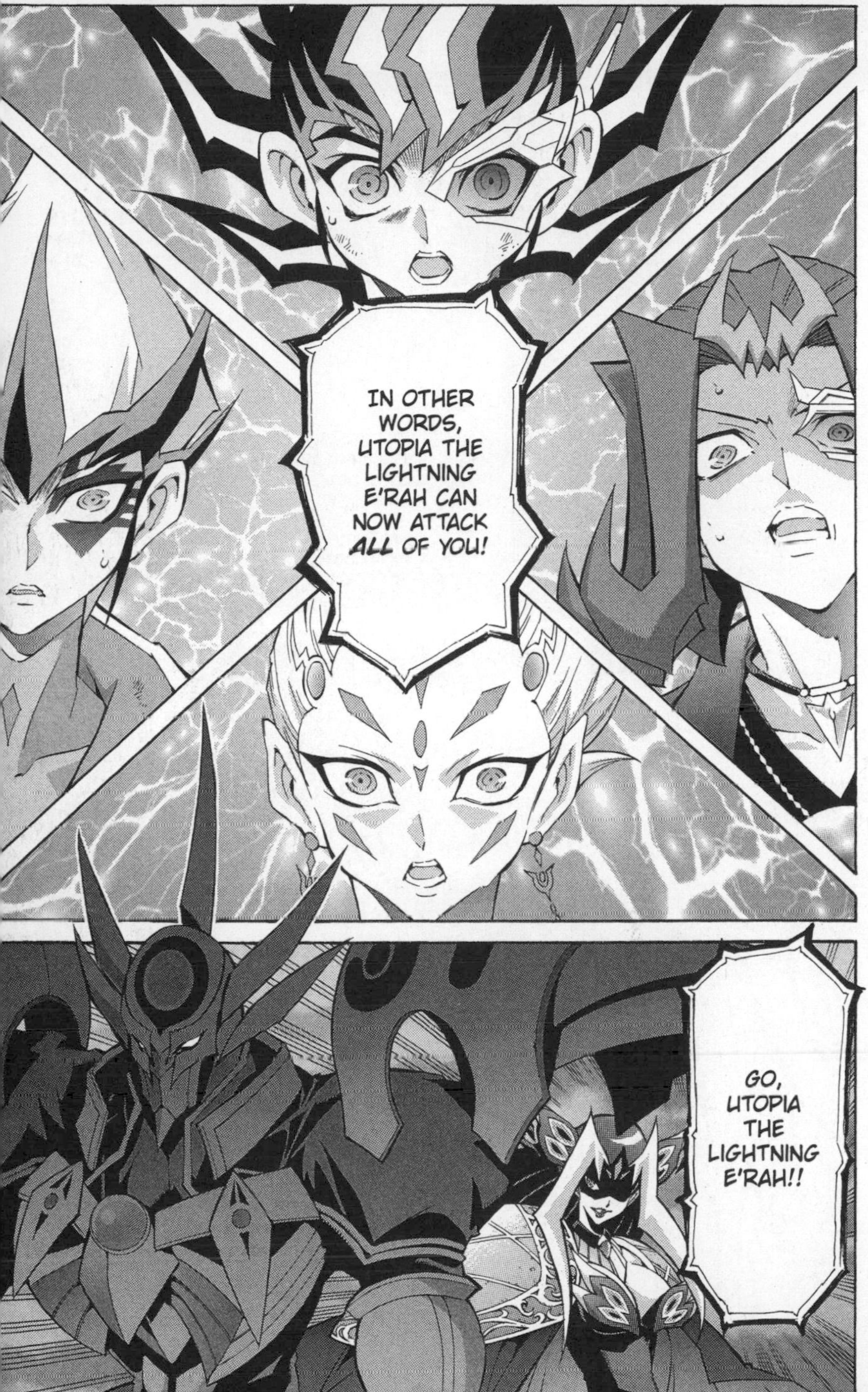
IN OTHER WORDS, UTOPIA THE LIGHTNING E'RAH CAN NOW ATTACK ALL OF YOU!
GO, UTOPIA THE LIGHTNING E'RAH!!

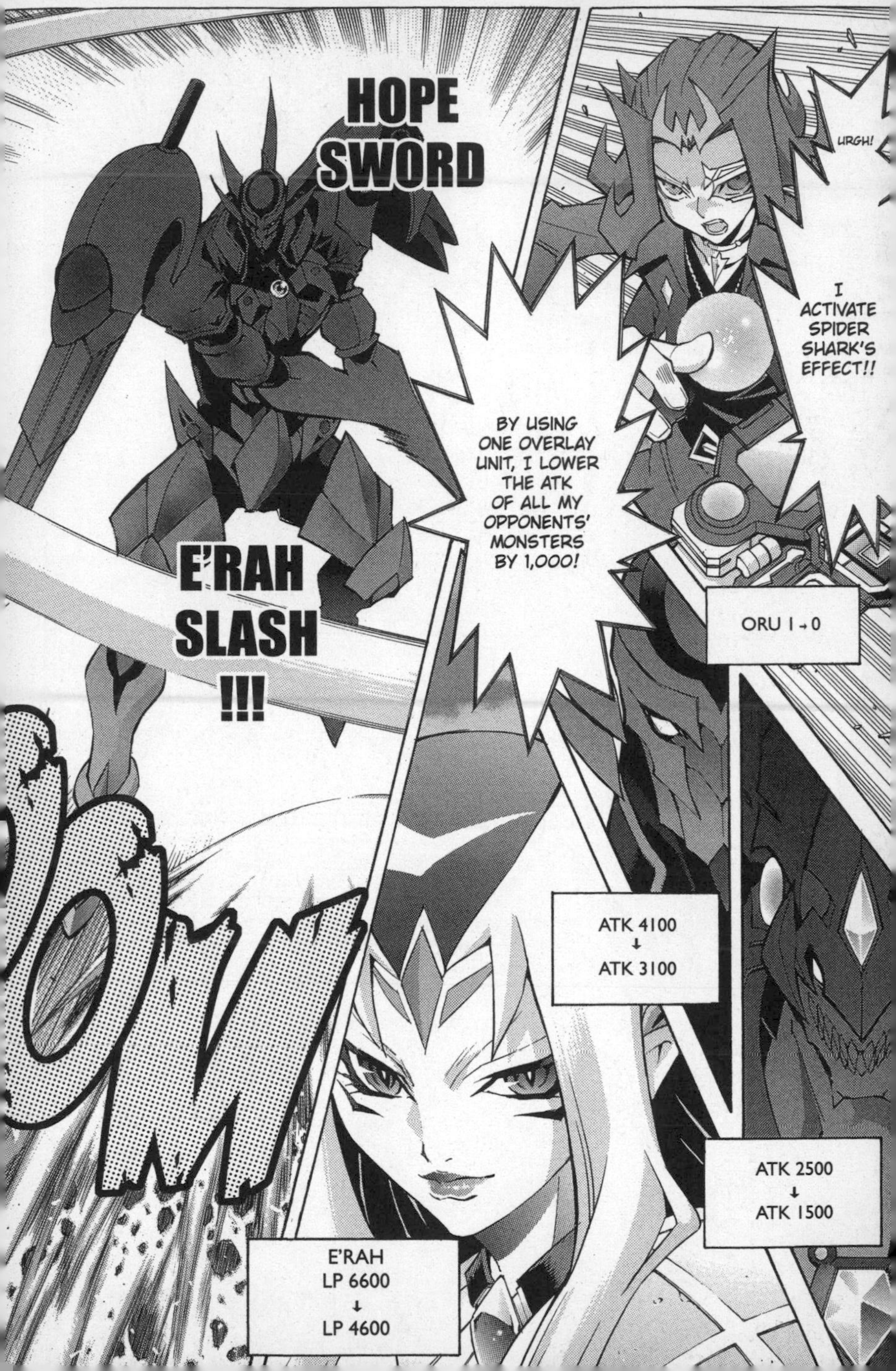

URGH!
I ACTIVATE SPIDER SHARK'S EFFECT!!
BY USING ONE OVERLAY UNIT, I LOWER THE ATK OF ALL MY OPPONENTS' MONSTERS BY 1,000!
ORU 1 → 0
HOPE SWORD
E'RAH SLASH !!!
ATK 2500 ↓ ATK 1500
ATK 4100 ↓ ATK 3100
E'RAH LP 6600 ↓ LP 4600

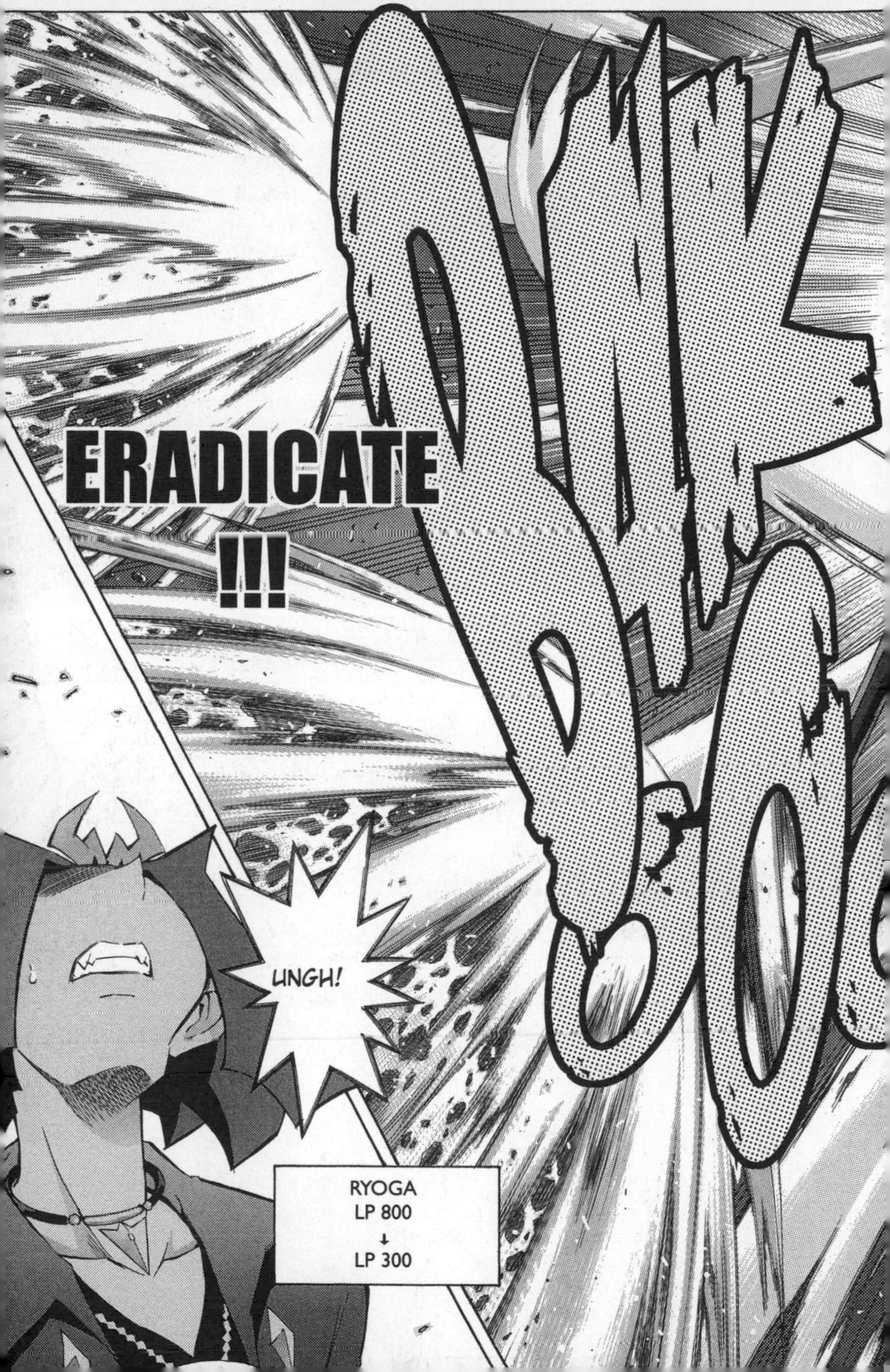
ERADICATE
!!!
UNGH!
RYOGA
LP 800
↓
LP 300

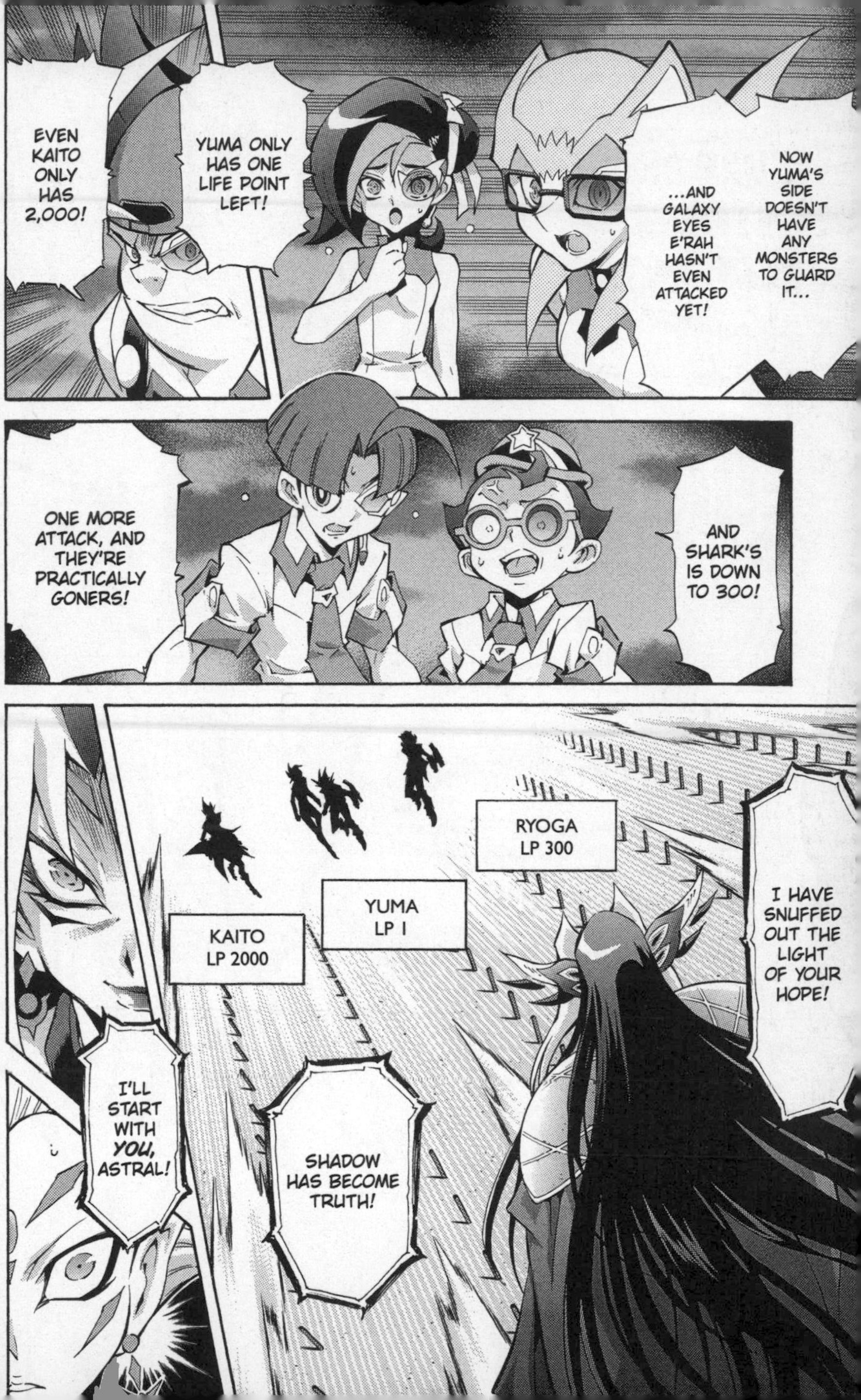
NOW YUMA'S SIDE DOESN'T HAVE ANY MONSTERS TO GUARD IT...
...AND GALAXY EYES E'RAH HASN'T EVEN ATTACKED YET!
YUMA ONLY HAS ONE LIFE POINT LEFT!
EVEN KAITO ONLY HAS 2,000!
AND SHARK'S IS DOWN TO 300!
ONE MORE ATTACK, AND THEY'RE PRACTICALLY GONERS!
I HAVE SNUFFED OUT THE LIGHT OF YOUR HOPE!
RYOGA LP 300
YUMA LP 1
KAITO LP 2000
SHADOW HAS BECOME TRUTH!
I'LL START WITH *YOU*, ASTRAL!

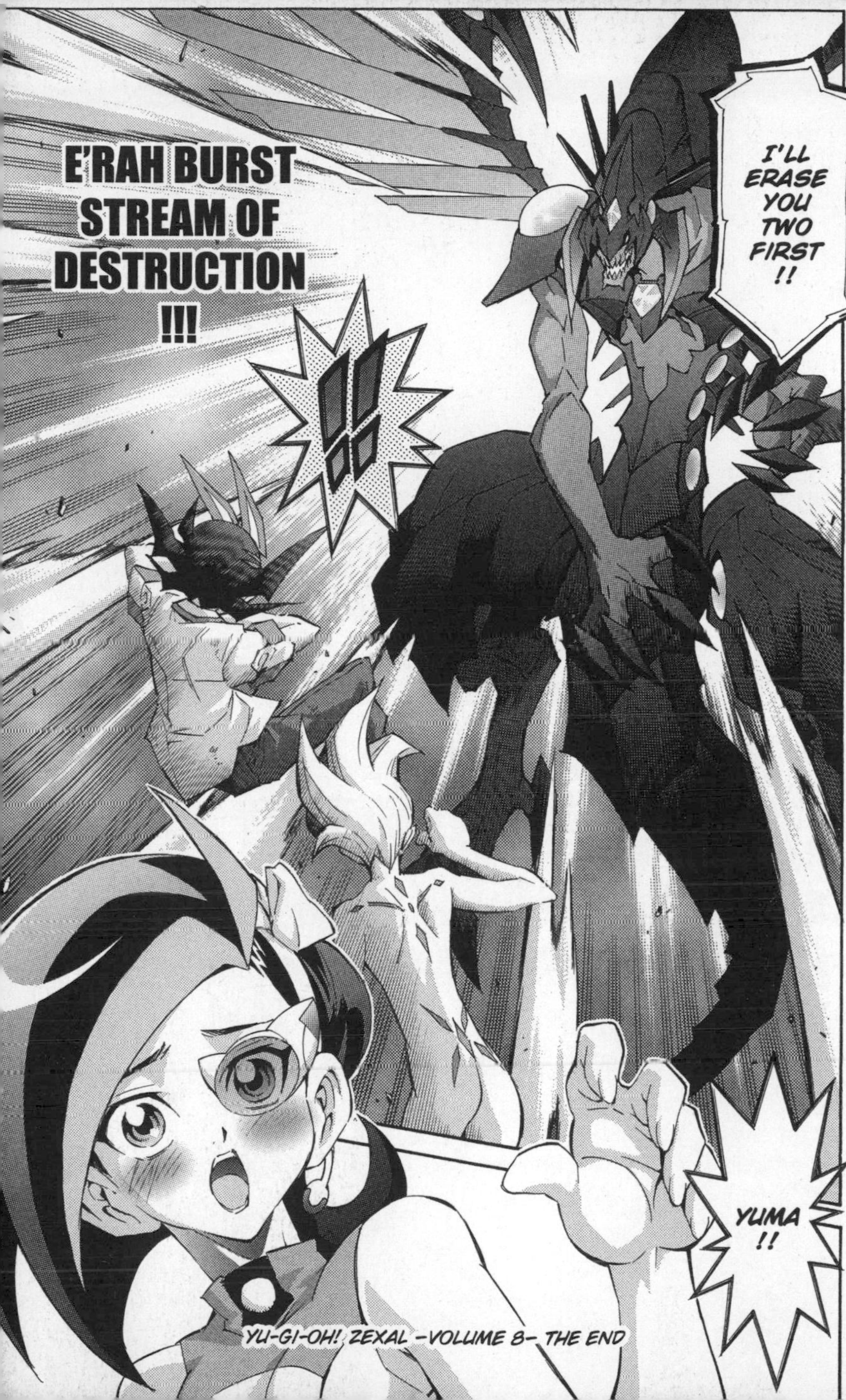
I'LL ERASE YOU TWO FIRST!!
E'RAH BURST STREAM OF DESTRUCTION!!!
!!
YUMA!!
YU-GI-OH! ZEXAL -VOLUME 8- THE END

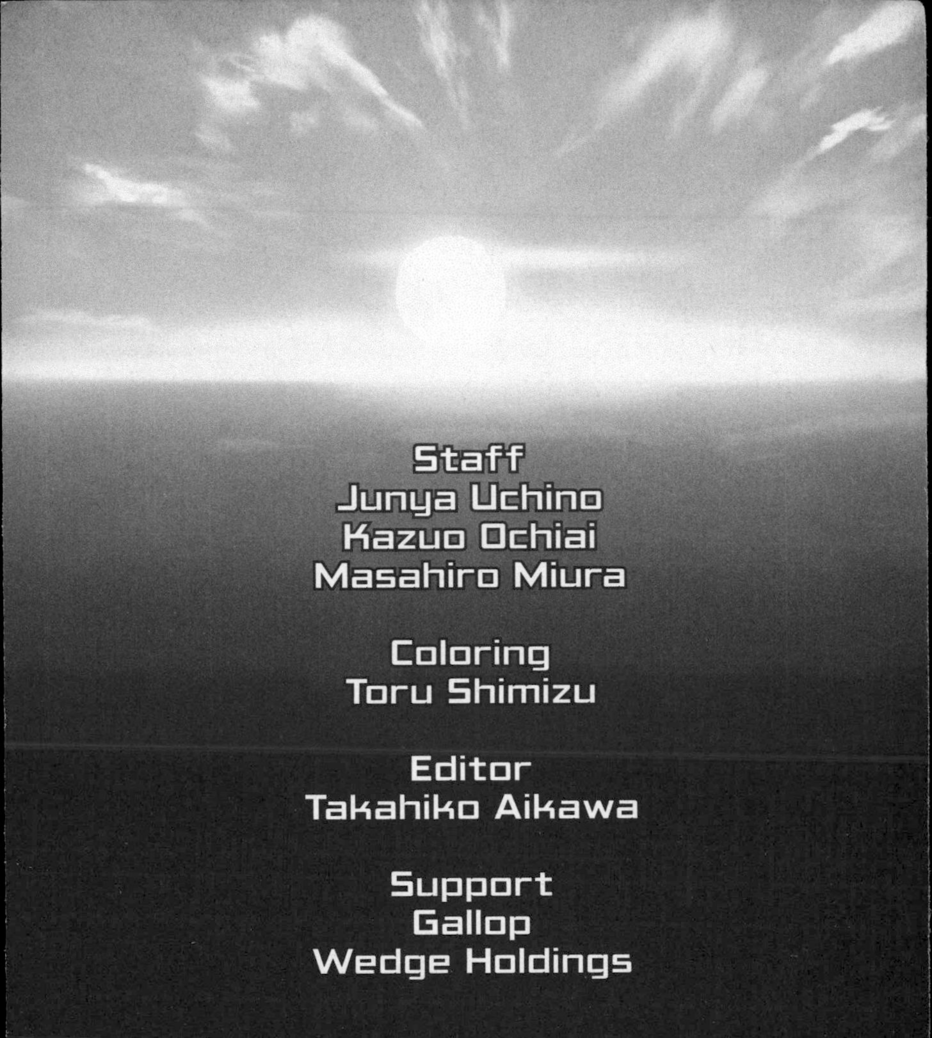

Staff
Junya Uchino
Kazuo Ochiai
Masahiro Miura

Coloring
Toru Shimizu

Editor
Takahiko Aikawa

Support
Gallop
Wedge Holdings

Hikaru no GO

Story by YUMI HOTTA
Art by TAKESHI OBATA

The breakthrough series by Takeshi Obata, the artist of *Death Note!*

Hikaru Shindo is like any sixth-grader in Japan: a pretty normal schoolboy with a penchant for antics. One day, he finds an old bloodstained Go board in his grandfather's attic. Trapped inside the Go board is Fujiwara-no-Sai, the ghost of an ancient Go master. In one fateful moment, Sai becomes a part of Hikaru's consciousness and together, through thick and thin, they make an unstoppable Go-playing team.

Will they be able to defeat Go players who have dedicated their lives to the game? And will Sai achieve the "Divine Move" so he'll finally be able to rest in peace? Find out in this *Shonen Jump* classic!

YOU ARE READING IN THE WRONG DIRECTION!!

Whoops!
Guess what?
You're starting at the wrong end of the comic!

...It's true! In keeping with the original Japanese format, *Yu-Gi-Oh! ZEXAL* is meant to be read from right to left, starting in the upper-right corner.

Unlike English, which is read from left to right, Japanese is read from right to left, meaning that action, sound effects and word-balloon order are completely reversed... something which can make readers unfamiliar with Japanese feel pretty backwards themselves. For this reason, manga or Japanese comics published in the U.S. in English have sometimes been published "flopped"—that is, printed in exact reverse order, as though seen from the other side of a mirror.

By flopping pages, U.S. publishers can avoid confusing readers, but the compromise is not without its downside. For one thing, a character in a flopped manga series who once wore in the original Japanese version a T-shirt emblazoned with "M A Y" (as in "the merry month of") now wears one which reads "Y A M"! Additionally, many manga creators in Japan are themselves unhappy with the process, as some feel the mirror-imaging of their art alters their original intentions.

We are proud to bring you Shin Yoshida and Naohito Miyoshi's *Yu-Gi-Oh! ZEXAL* in the original unflopped format. For now, though, turn to the other side of the book and let the duel begin...!

—Editor